NORTH BRITTANY & CHANNEL ISLANDS

CRUISING COMPANION

ENGLISH

N

kilometres
nautical miles

0   40
0   20

ATLANTIC
OCEAN

Ile Vierge

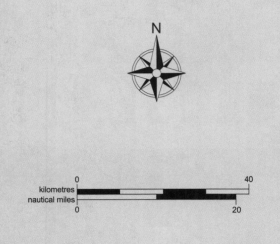

Ile de
Batz

Roscoff

Trég
Ile Grand

Trébeurden
Locquémeau

Pontusval

Moguériec

Primel

Locqui

Le Four

L'Abervrac'h

Penzé R

Morlaix R

Le Stiff

L'Aberbenoît

FINISTERE

Morlaix

Portsall

Créac'h

Ushant   Chenal
du Four

L'Aberildut

Brest

I. de
Molène

Le Conquet

Kéréon

Pte de St
Mathieu

B R I T

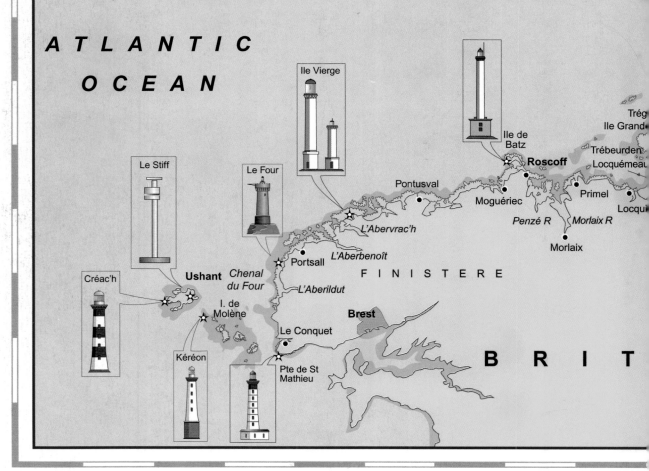

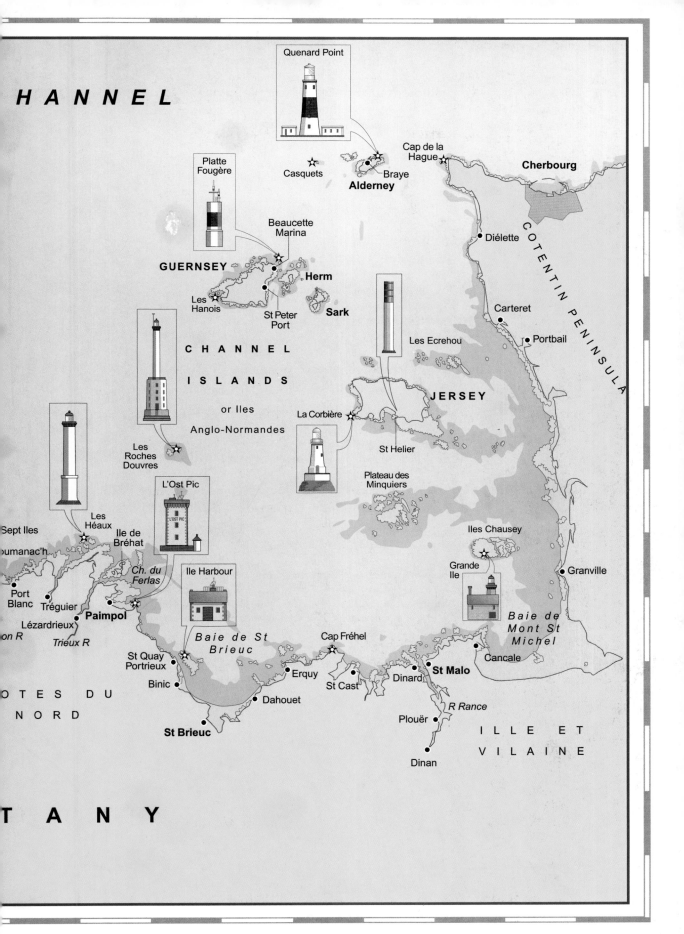

HANNEL

Quenard Point

Casquets ☆

Cap de la Hague

Braye
Alderney

Cherbourg

COTENTIN PENINSULA

Diélette

Carteret

Portbail

Platte Fougère

Beaucette Marina

GUERNSEY

Herm

Les Hanois

St Peter Port

Sark

Les Ecrehou

JERSEY

C H A N N E L

I S L A N D S

or Iles Anglo-Normandes

La Corbière

St Helier

Plateau des Minquiers

Les Roches Douvres ☆

L'Ost Pic

L'OST PIC

Iles Chausey

Grande Ile ☆

Granville

Ile Harbour

Baie de Mont St Michel

Sept Iles ☆

Les Héaux

Ile de Bréhat

Ch. du Ferlas

oumanac'h

Port Blanc

Tréguier

Paimpol

Lézardrieux

Baie de St Brieuc

Cap Fréhel ☆

Cancale

on R

Trieux R

St Quay Portrieux ☆

Erquy

St Cast

Dinard

St Malo

Binic

Dahouet

R Rance

OTES   DU

N O R D

St Brieuc

Plouër

I L L E   E T

V I L A I N E

Dinan

T A N Y

Cover picture: Ploumanac'h

Photographs by Peter Cumberlidge

Charts: Tony Garrett, Jamie Russell,
Garold West & Edward Lee-Elliott

Art direction: Chris Stevens & Brett Lewis

Cover design: Slatter Anderson

Cruising Companion series editor: Mike Balmforth
Consultant editor: Edward Lee-Elliott

Colour reproduction: Patrick Roach

Published by Nautical Data Ltd,
The Book Barn, Westbourne, Hampshire, PO10 8RS

First Edition of this Cruising Companion volume 2001
revised from the first edition of North Brittany and Channel Islands Cruising,
originally published 1991 by Yachting Monthly

ISBN 0-333-904524

IMPORTANT NOTE

This Companion is intended as an aid to navigation only. The information contained within should not solely
be relied on for navigational use, rather it should be used in conjunction with official hydrographic data.
Whilst every care has been taken in compiling the information contained in this Companion, the publishers,
author, editors and their agents accept no responsibility for any errors or omissions, or for any accidents
or mishaps which may arise from its use.

Neither the publisher nor the author can accept responsibility for errors, omissions or alterations in this book.
They will be grateful for any information from readers to assist in the update and accuracy of the publication.

Readers are advised at all times to refer to official charts, publications and notices. The charts
contained in this book are sketch plans and are not to be used for navigation.
Some details are omitted for the sake of clarity and the scales have been chosen to allow best
coverage in relation to page size.

Printed in Italy by Milanostampa

Typeset by Chris Stevens

YACHTING
MONTHLY

NORTH BRITTANY & CHANNEL ISLANDS

CRUISING COMPANION

Passages, ports and harbours from the
Alderney Race to the Chenal du Four

PETER CUMBERLIDGE
NAUTICAL DATA LIMITED

CONTENTS

St Peter Port, Guernsey

■ **Chapter 1**

PASSAGES TO THE CHANNEL ISLANDS
AND NORTH BRITTANY

■ **Chapter 2**

THE CHANNEL ISLANDS

■ **Chapter 3**

PASSAGES BETWEEN NORTH BRITTANY
AND THE CHANNEL ISLANDS

Le Grand Jardin lighthouse off St Malo

PREFACE

This new edition of North Brittany and Channel Islands Cruising Companion follows on from the first edition of Yachting Monthly's North Brittany and Channel Islands Cruising. The new volume has been completely updated with the latest navigational changes, marina developments and as many new or restyled restaurants as I've been able to sample on the way. Significant buoyage changes have actually been few and far between since the first edition was published, but marina facilities are improving all the time to provide comfortable and convenient bases from which to explore these magnificent cruising grounds.

In the Channel Islands area, Diélette and Carteret are now fully established as attractive marinas on the west side of the Cotentin Peninsula. Both are accessible for about 2½ hours each side of high water, although for a first visit you should time your arrival for as near high water as possible.

The new Elizabeth Marina at St Helier is an impressive development that has extended the harbour area considerably. Although the new basin is occupied mostly by residents and long-term berth-holders, the extra space has freed up the original St Helier town marina for many more visitors. Together with the marinas at Diélette and Carteret, these new facilities increase the scope for cruising the previously rather neglected east side of the Channel Islands area, between Sark, Jersey and the Normandy coast.

St Peter Port continues to improve and develop its facilities for visiting yachts. Victoria Marina is as popular as ever and the long pontoons out in the pool now have water taps to make life easier for those who like to stay outside the sill. Several interesting new restaurants have opened in St Peter Port in the last couple of years which, with the best interests of research and accuracy in mind, I have sampled with due diligence.

Down on the North Brittany coast, the charming marina up at Plouër-sur-Rance has matured well since the first edition of this book was published. The same is true of the yacht basin at Dahouet, further west along the coast beyond Cap Fréhel and Erquy.

At Lézardrieux, the relatively new inner marina has improved the choice of berthing in this splendid river and provided more room for visiting yachts. On the debit side, there have been recent moves by some local residents of Ile de Bréhat to restrict anchoring around this charming island. Discussions on this have been heated between the local commune and the yacht clubs of the area, but I doubt whether such a restriction can actually be sustained in practice.

Tréguier, Port Blanc, Perros-Guirec and Ploumanac'h have stayed much the same, but the spacious marina at Trébeurden, which had not been completed as the first edition went to press, is now well established and a popular port-of-call on a fascinating corner of the North Brittany coast.

Further west, no great navigational changes have taken place between Morlaix and the Chenal du Four, and there are no new marinas on the horizon as far as I know. But details of the port facilities, weather forecast sources and restaurants have all been updated, and I have also included the latest information on visitors' moorings at Ushant.

Down at the south end of the Four, Le Conquet used to be a handy passage bolt-hole if you ran out of fair tide, but the port has steadily become much more focused on commercial fishing and yachts are no longer allowed to anchor in the outer harbour.

But if you can take the ground safely, there's usually plenty of room in the drying area beyond the inner mole.

One thing is certain. The appeal of the cruising area covered by this book is timeless. I have long held the view that a cruise to North Brittany and the Channel Islands provides an almost perfect blend of navigational challenge, the exhilaration of passage-making and the satisfaction of arriving. The landfalls that await you are some of the most enchanting in Europe.

Yachtsmen who know this area well soon get used to rocky outcrops, fast tidal streams and a dramatic rise and fall, but newcomers can find the prospect a little daunting. Navigators certainly need to be on the ball in these waters, but GPS has smoothed much of the tension from passage-making and pilotage. One of the prime objects of this book is to welcome yachts to the area and show how accessible it is most of the time. I have therefore tried to provide safe, clear directions for the main harbours and passages without (I hope) digressing into too much fine detail and without dwelling gloomily on all the hazards that could possibly befall you if everything went wrong. The pilot charts in this companion have been designed to clarify harbour approaches and to highlight navigational features that are important to yacht navigators. They do not contain the same level of detail as British Admiralty or French SHOM charts, either above or below water, and they are certainly not intended to replace them. As in the first edition, I have included carefully selected approach waypoints for all the main entrances.

For most visitors, the culinary attractions are an important part of a Brittany cruise. As before, restaurants feature prominently in the port guides, although it's important to remember that the whole question of eating out is an extremely personal business. What appeals to one person on a particular occasion will not necessarily delight others who follow. But I have eaten well and widely in an attempt to cover the ground, so I sincerely hope that you'll have pleasurable experiences most of the time.

A book like this is always hungry for new information from those on the spot. If, therefore, you should come across any instances where buoyage, port information or restaurant information needs updating, I'd be grateful if you could spare the time to write me a quick note c/o the publishers.

Peter Cumberlidge
January 2001

ACKNOWLEDGMENTS

The author is extremely grateful to the following (in alphabetical order) for their assistance in preparing this book:

Monsieur Alain Blancheton, Directeur du Port at Carteret; Julie Baker; Roger Bowns; Colin and Joyce Bradshaw; James Briggs; Peter Carnegie in Jersey; John Carre, harbourmaster at Sark; Tony Dawson of the Guernsey Tourist Board; Fran Elliott; John Elliott of the Guernsey Sailing Trust; Liliane Faustin at Plouër-sur-Rance; Tony Garrett; Brett Lewis; Simon Macphail, Assistant Harbour Master at St Peter Port; Rowland Neal of Mainbrayce Marine, Alderney; Peter Wilson, Marinas and Moorings Manager for Jersey Harbours; and all the Channel Island and North Brittany harbourmasters who have kindly passed on their up-to-date local knowledge about buoyage, lights, pilotage and facilities.

ABOUT THE AUTHOR

Peter Cumberlidge is a well-known yachting journalist and the author of several books on pilotage and seamanship. He and his wife Jane have cruised widely under sail and power, but always return with affection to Brittany and the Channel Islands. The Cumberlidges' gaff cutter, Stormalong, has been in the family for many years and is normally moored at Dartmouth. She was designed by William Kelly and built as a yacht in 1936 at Gostelow's, a small yard at Boston on the Wash. Traditionally rigged and aesthetically simple, Stormalong has explored most European cruising grounds between the Baltic and Mediterranean, but is particularly at home among the anchorages and harbours described in this book.

CRUISING NORTH BRITTANY
& THE CHANNEL ISLANDS

I can still remember my first nervous landfall on the Channel Islands. After a 14 hour passage from Dartmouth, mostly overnight, we were approaching the north end of the Little Russel (or so I hoped) in a morning haze and fairly quiet sea. The tides were nearer neaps than springs, but we'd passed a couple of crab-pot markers lying hard over in a stream which seemed to be sluicing west rather faster than we were sailing south-east. My confidence in the carefully drawn triangles on the chart took a bit of a knock. I swung our trusty old Seafix RDF set (this is going back a bit) between the Casquets, Alderney and Guernsey and managed a set of bearings which produced a narrow cocked-hat about 10 miles long.

After breakfast, my crew sighted a smudge on the horizon to the south and I adjourned to the foredeck with the binoculars. The excitement of a landfall never palls, but I don't think it's too romantic to say that arriving was even more satisfying in those pre-

GPS days when you really weren't sure where you were. Guernsey seemed to finish well over to the west and I altered about 15 degrees to starboard for the final leg. An hour later, Platte Fougère lighthouse and the low north-east coast emerged from a patch of mist on the port (wrong) bow and I learnt the old lesson of trusting your estimated position until confronted with reliable evidence to refute it. There was just enough wind for us to claw back to the east – the engine didn't feel like starting that morning – and catch the last dregs of tide down the Russel. We felt like a million dollars as we

ghosted in between St Peter Port pierheads.

Now that most of us know precisely where we are most of the time, the quality of landfalls has changed in character. There is never quite the same tension about approaching a rocky coast, even for the first time, when the GPS is keeping careful track of things, perhaps flashing a reassuring blip on a chart plotter screen. But this facility has been good for cruising, on the whole. Safety has been greatly increased and GPS has given countless yachtsmen the confidence to cruise to places they might not otherwise have reached, sometimes in weather conditions they certainly wouldn't have contemplated without reliable navigation electronics.

This has certainly been the case for North Brittany and the Channel Islands. GPS has eased the way into many of the previously quite tricky corners of this incomparable cruising area, especially for those working to a fairly tight ration of holiday time. Summer fog and mist used to bring passage-making to a virtual standstill, but nowadays we can still get about with confidence and save a day that would have otherwise been lost. Now that GPS takes a lot of the navigational strain, navigators are more free to enjoy the character of Brittany and the Channel Islands to the full, and can be more adventurous about trying new places and new passages. This book is intended to assist that process and to convey some of the local knowledge that should make cruising this coast safer and more rewarding. Above all, it is intended as an aid to enjoyment which, in the end, is surely what cruising is all about.

THE CHANNEL ISLANDS

Fast tides, with rocks everywhere, is the picture that comes to mind when you think about the Channel Islands. Quite rightly too, for the spring tidal range can be as much as 35 feet and the streams correspondingly swift; Jersey has the highest rise and fall in the islands, and the north end of the Alderney Race can boast the fastest recorded rates of eight to nine knots. The rocks are indeed copious, with many covered at high water and unmarked by buoys and beacons. But adversity is not without its comforts, and the trick when navigating hereabouts is to use both tide and rocks to your advantage.

The first rule is always to work your passages around the Channel Islands so that the streams are in your favour. Try, if possible, to allow a generous margin of error in your timing, so that you don't pick up a strong foul tide right at the end of a trip which could easily delay your arrival by several hours. Sailing between Alderney and Guernsey, for example, you will need to carry the tide right down through the Little Russel when southbound, or up through the Swinge or the Race when northbound. The same is true on the passage from Guernsey to Jersey, when you ought to arrange for a favourable if slackening stream along the south coast of Jersey between Corbière and St Helier.

As for all the off-lying chunks of granite, it's noticeable that the Channel Islanders tend to treat rocks as navigational friends rather than enemies. Whereas you or I might turn a few shades paler at the close-up view of a weed-covered outcrop being licked by a heavy swell, a local would probably say: "Ah yes, that's the Demie du Nord – we know where we are now, eh?" I wouldn't go as far as to say that rocks are all in the mind, but you can certainly use them positively, to help you find your way about.

Each of the islands has its own distinctive character. Alderney is wild and windswept, its large harbour restful in fine weather but uneasy when things are cutting up rough. Alderney is the least developed of the three main islands and feels much more English and rural than Guernsey or Jersey. Guernsey is larger and more densely populated than Alderney and seems to be steadily filling up with cars, but it still retains a small town atmosphere and everybody seems to know everybody else. St Peter Port harbour is always a fascinating place to lie, with its continual bustle of ferries, ships, yachts and fishing boats. A few miles opposite St Peter Port are Herm and Jethou, exquisite miniatures and part of the Bailiwick of Guernsey. Sark, a few miles further to the south-east, often looms mysteriously out of a haze, its craggy outline somewhat forbidding from a distance. Yet this most individual of the islands is not difficult to approach and its inhabitants are very friendly when you make their acquaintance. Sark is almost self-governing and, that apart, is a law unto itself.

Jersey, the largest and most sophisticated of the Channel Islands, lies about 15 miles south-east of Guernsey. The pace of life is a shade faster here, the economy diverse and more solidly prosperous, and the airport one of the busiest in Europe. It doesn't feel as though you are on an island as you wander round the main town of St Helier, nor when you are driving along the busy dual carriageway between St Helier and St Aubin. But away from the hectic south coast, you can lose yourself in some delightful villages and quiet country lanes.

Guernsey and Jersey issue their own sterling currency, although English notes and coins are accepted throughout the islands. It's best either to change or spend any local coins before you leave though, because most mainland banks only take Guernsey or Jersey notes, one for one. The islands

The spectacular cleft in the cliffs at Havre Gosselin, on the west coast of Sark

have their own Customs and Excise services and you must report your arrival, either from the UK or from France, as soon as possible. In St Peter Port you'll be given a Customs form and a 'Yachtsman's Guide to Guernsey' as soon as you arrive, and you should obtain a similar form from the marina office in St Helier. The local authorities are not too worried about liquor or cigarettes – duties and taxes are low over here and VAT doesn't exist. There is real concern, however, about the possible import of rabies. Customs Officers will ask whether you have any animals aboard before they inquire about whisky or cases of wine. No animal must be landed in the Channel Islands without permission; the spread of rabies would have serious consequences and the penalties for disregarding this rule are severe.

Official Ports of Entry are Braye harbour for Alderney, St Peter Port or Beaucette for Guernsey, and St Helier or Gorey for Jersey. Don't land at any of the smaller harbours or anchorages until you have cleared inwards.

Many yachts visit the Channel Islands each year with only a vague intention of carrying on down to North Brittany. There is plenty of local sailing to keep you entertained for a week's cruise, and it's always very agreeable to be based at St Peter Port for a while and make day trips to Herm, Sark and the south coast anchorages. Yet for crews with a fortnight or more to spare, the magnetism of Brittany usually proves irresistible and the islands provide a convenient stepping-stone for a passage further south.

NORTH BRITTANY

The north coast of Brittany has an amazing range of harbours, anchorages and ambience along the 150 miles from Mont St Michel to the Chenal du Four. In fact I tend to think of it as three separate cruising areas, the nearest being the Bay of St Malo and the various havens immediately accessible from the Channel Islands. Carteret, only 22 miles east of Sark, and Granville, thirty miles south-east of Jersey, are actually in Normandy, but both have excellent marinas and are useful staging-posts in a circular cruise of these parts. From Granville you can easily visit the extraordinary maze of rocks and channels which comprise Iles Chausey, or call at the bustling little port of Cancale, renowned for its oysters.

St Malo is a natural focus for this near corner of Brittany. The elegant walled town is always worth the effort of locking into the Bassin Vauban; astounding to remember that almost everything inside the ramparts has been rebuilt since 1944. When you leave St Malo, try to take a couple of days to meander up the River Rance, preferably as far as Dinan if the tides are right and your draught allows. The peaceful marina at Plouër-sur-Rance is certainly worth a visit. Converted from an old mill pool, this perfectly snug yacht basin lies out in the country on the west side of the Rance, half-a-mile above the Port St Jean road bridges and about five miles above the barrage.

There used to be a bit of a cruising gap west of St Malo until you reached Paimpol, Ile de Bréhat, and the sleepy Lézardrieux River. But St Brieuc Bay now offers a choice of three marinas, each very different but each with its own attractions and individual character. The yacht basin at Dahouet, five miles south-west of Erquy, is now well-established, an agreeable low-key spot, nicely off the usual beaten track. The locked marina at Binic remains a pleasant port-of-call on the west side of St Brieuc Bay, still a bit of a well-kept secret for many visiting yachts. A few miles north of Binic is the large marina and fishing port at St Quay-Portrieux.

Ten miles north of St Quay, the peaceful Anse de Paimpol changes little over the years, merging into that idyllic network of rocky channels adjoining Ile de Bréhat. Just inland from Bréhat, the Lézardrieux River retains its timeless rural character, despite being one of the most popular destinations on this coast for visiting yachts.

Cruising west from the Lézardrieux estuary and the tall lighthouse of Les Héaux, you reach the second distinctive section of the North Brittany coastline – the Côte de Granit Rose. The attractive pink granite really starts with Bréhat and then straggles west past Tréguier, Port Blanc, Perros-Guirec and Les Sept Iles to Ploumanac'h and Trégastel. You'll see some strange formations, especially around Ploumanac'h, providing a dramatic background to many of the anchorages. Just round the corner from Trégastel is the Bay of Lannion, an intriguing mini-cruising ground in its own right. The spacious marina at Trébeurden is an ideal base for exploring the anchorages and spectacular beaches around this bay. If the tide serves and the weather is quiet, the Lannion River is worth nosing into near high water, and you can stay afloat at neaps in the pool off Le Yaudet.

Heading west into the Bay of Morlaix, you begin to feel the third mood of North Brittany. This Atlantic end has a harder edge and the off-lying rocks can seem more hostile than photogenic in dodgy weather. The coast is even more austere beyond Roscoff and Ile de Batz but, before this, the Morlaix and Penzé Rivers are interesting to explore. The locked basin at Morlaix is a good place to change crews and a safe base to leave your boat if necessary.

There are no secure harbours west of Roscoff until you reach L'Abervrac'h, 30 miles away. Although L'Abervrac'h is low-lying and rather windswept, the estuary is easy to enter at any state of tide by day or night. The upper reaches off La Palue are fairly sheltered, with a small marina and a friendly yacht club. The smaller estuary of L'Aberbenoît, just west of L'Abervrac'h, is not quite so readily accessible but

better protected by high ground once you are in.

Once past these two Abers, you have almost reached the far corner of North Brittany, where the coast turns south and the Chenal du Four leads inside Ushant and several smaller islands to the Brest estuary and the wide expanse of L'Iroise. The small drying harbour of Portsall lies a few miles north of Le Four lighthouse, with an anchorage some way outside the harbour in quiet weather. Off the Chenal du Four itself, you have a picturesque and sheltered port-of-call at L'Aberildut, a small secret estuary with a narrow entrance. There is no marina at L'Aberildut, but the moorings are snug and the village most attractive.

Despite North Brittany's somewhat forbidding reputation for rocks and fast tides, this is not a difficult sailing area for modern boats if you plan your passages carefully and choose your weather. GPS is certainly a great friend when you are making a landfall, giving you the confidence to press on even in murky visibility. The rocks are certainly prolific and you can't afford to be slapdash, but the buoyage and lights are excellent. After a couple of seasons cruising in North Brittany, you soon get used to treating rocks as friendly marks rather than threatening enemies.

Although the tides can be powerful locally, they don't exceed more than about three or four knots along most of the North Brittany coast. You need to work the streams to best advantage, but a modern yacht which can motor at six or seven knots is not so vulnerable as the previous generation of cruising boats. Our more crusading forbears could usually only manage about four knots, and only that if the engine agreed to start. Watch out for crab-pot markers though, which are liberally strewn along this coast. A spring tide will often pull them under, making the lines almost invisible until it's too late.

You will often meet patches of overfalls, or perhaps the rather eerie swirling eddies or slicks of locally smooth water. These don't necessarily indicate dangers near the surface, but may be caused by a strong tide surging over an uneven sea-bed a long way below. They can make you edgy though, even when you know you are in perfectly safe water. Swell is quite common at the west end of the North Brittany coast, especially off L'Abervrac'h and the north end of the Chenal du Four. A heavy swell can sometimes make pilotage difficult if the rollers begin to obstruct your view of buoys or leading marks. This west end of the coast is also known for its fog or haze. On a fine summer day this will usually burn off by about lunchtime, giving you a clear spell until early evening. If there's mist or haze about in the Channel as you approach this north-west corner from seaward, you'll often find the best visibility for making a landfall at around two in the afternoon.

And don't forget that inclement weather can have its compensations along the whole coast of Brittany. If strong winds or fog keep you in port when you'd planned to be on your way, just relax and enjoy. Here is the perfect opportunity for trying another restaurant or two and exploring the menus. Remember my variation on that old maxim, sometimes applied by military men to the subject of reconnaissance:

"Time spent lunching is never wasted."

PILOTAGE AROUND THE CHANNEL ISLANDS & BRITTANY

BUOYAGE

The buoyage around the Channel Islands and North Brittany coasts is based on the IALA System A and is generally excellent in coverage and well maintained.

Lateral marks guarding the edges of navigable channels may be:

Port-hand: Tall red pillar buoys (usually offshore or in open estuaries), smaller red can buoys (usually in rivers, bays or other sheltered water), red beacon towers or red spar beacons (which actually stand on the dangers they are marking). Any of these may have square or cylindrical topmarks and red lights.

Starboard-hand: Tall green pillar buoys, green conical buoys, green beacon towers or green spar beacons. Any of these may have triangular or conical topmarks and green lights.

Cardinal marks, usually guarding specific dangers, follow the standard IALA cardinal system as shown below.

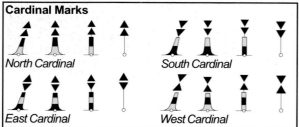

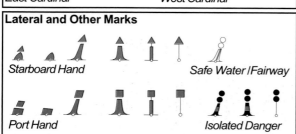

Isolated danger marks may be black and red or black-red-black buoys, beacon towers or spar beacons, usually having one or two black balls as topmarks.

Local marks: Various local marks are used around the Channel Islands and North Brittany, but their shapes and topmarks are clearly indicated on the largest scale Admiralty charts of the area. Off the south-east corner of Guernsey, for example, you'll find several spar beacons marking isolated rocks – Longue Pierre, Anfré, Moulinet and Oyster Rock. The topmarks for these spars are the initial letters of each rock's name. The same local topmark convention is used for the various spar beacons marking the approach channels west of Herm – the Alligande, Godfrey, Épec and Vermerette beacons, for example.

Out in the Little Russel, between Guernsey and Herm, the Roustel beacon tower is an unusual mark – a hollow iron lattice built on the remains of the old stone tower. A mile or so north of Herm, the beacon on Tautenay islet is a truncated stone pyramid painted with black-and-white vertical stripes.

Along the North Brittany coast, white painted stone pyramids are sometimes used as guiding marks on rocky outcrops or as leading marks for approach channels. The white Rosédo pyramid on the west coast of Ile de Bréhat doubles as a useful landmark on the east side of the Lézardrieux estuary, and as the front leading mark for the Moisie Passage. Further west, the white-painted pyramid on Ile du Château Neuf helps you identify the west side of the narrow entrance to Port Blanc.

In various shallow bays and estuaries along the Brittany coast, you'll find plenty of the rustic stakes or 'withies' often used to mark oyster or mussel beds. You should always keep well clear of these areas and never anchor over or near them.

The beacon on Tautenay islet is a truncated stone pyramid painted with black-and-white vertical stripes

The Roustel beacon tower is an unusual mark – a hollow iron lattice built on the remains of the old stone tower

The white-painted pyramid on Ile du Château Neuf helps you identify the west side of the narrow entrance to Port Blanc

Longue Pierre beacon, off the SE corner of Guernsey, has an 'LP' topmark

Vermerette beacon, a key mark when approaching Herm from the west, has an easily recognised 'V' topmark

Remember that shellfish represent an important part of the Brittany economy and that you'll probably be looking forward to a tempting selection of *fruits de mer* on the restaurant menus at the end of the day.

ABBREVIATIONS

The conventional abbreviations for the colours and characteristics of buoys, beacons and lights referred to in this book are those normally used on Admiralty charts. The most common abbreviations are as follows:

R	Red
G	Green
Y	Yellow
B	Black
W	White
BY	Black over yellow (north-cardinal)
YB	Yellow over black (south-cardinal)
BYB	Black-yellow-black (east-cardinal)
YBY	Yellow-black-yellow (west-cardinal)
BRB	Black-red-black (isolated danger)
F.R	Fixed red
F.G	Fixed green

Fl   Flashing light, period of light shorter than darkness. If followed by a number, this indicates a group of flashes e.g. Fl(3). Colour white unless followed by another colour e.g. Fl(3)G. Timing of complete sequence is given in seconds e.g.Fl(3)10s – group flash three every 10 seconds.

LFl   Long flash i.e. period of light not less than two seconds.

Oc   Occulting light, period of light longer than the period of darkness.

Iso   Isophase light, equal periods of light and darkness.

Q   Quick flashing light, up to 60 flashes per minute.

VQ   Very quick flashing light, up to 120 flashes per minute.

WEATHER AND FORECASTS

By and large, the Channel Islands and North Brittany weather is similar to that on the south coast of England. However, the Channel Islands area, in particular, does enjoy its own (usually beneficial) weather influences. The Islands, and especially south-facing Jersey, are generally a few degrees warmer than the English coast. There can also be quite marked local differences in wind strength, especially when depressions are tracking over Britain or up the English Channel.

The south of the Channel Islands area, between Jersey and St Malo, will often have more moderate winds than the north between Guernsey and Alderney. For this reason, you should take careful note of the local Jersey Radio forecast on VHF, which will give you a good idea of any significant local variations. Their excellent forecasts include a useful indication of likely sea state. In spells of brisk weather, for example, Jersey Radio may well be giving sea state differences that will help your passage-making decisions – for example: '. . . moderate in the south, rather rough in the north.' In these circumstances, a passage could well be feasible between, say, St Helier and St Malo (especially east-about the Minkies), when a trip between Alderney and Guernsey might be distinctly dodgy.

On the French coast you can usually pick up Jersey Radio on VHF at Diélette, Carteret and Granville, and along the Brittany coast between St Malo and Ile de Bréhat. But VHF reception may be lost at low tide in some marinas, and inland up some of the rivers.

The French CROSS stations broadcast useful forecasts on VHF, which cover the whole cruising area of this book. Broadcast channels and times vary from area to area, and the full details are given in the port guides for each main harbour. These bulletins are in French and repeated slowly at dictation speed. They are not difficult to follow once you get used to the terminology, and they provide the most reliable weather information for the Brittany coast once you are out of the Jersey Radio area.

Météo France provides a selection of useful telephone recorded forecasts, although your French needs to be pretty fair to follow these bulletins on the phone, especially when your money is just about to run out. The details of these telephone forecasts are given in the port guides for each main harbour, but you can pick up a handy Météo France card at most marina offices.

The west end of the North Brittany coast is noted for haze and poor visibility, especially during settled spells of anticyclonic weather. You shouldn't be alarmed by this unless you are unlucky enough to meet very thick mist or extensive fog banks. With GPS, or even without, it's usually easy enough to pick your way from buoy to buoy and get in and out of the larger harbours.

TIDAL STREAMS

Although the tides around North Brittany and the Channel Islands have a certain notoriety, they hold fewer terrors for modern yachts, with their faster cruising speeds, reliable engines and navigation electronics, than they did for the previous generation of either sailing or motor boats. In any case, anyone who has sailed in the Solent at the top of springs will know a thing or two about fast streams.

The rise and fall is a different matter though, and the possible range of over 30 feet at Guernsey, Jersey and St Malo takes a bit of getting used to. One advantage of this dramatic tidal range is that many of the attractive natural anchorages are much more sheltered at low water, making them convenient lunchtime stops especially at springs. The timing of the tides in this area is such that low water springs occur around the middle of the day and high water

springs in the mornings and evenings – handy for leaving and returning to nearby marinas.

The good news about fast tidal streams is the considerable push they can give to your passages. Cruising along the North Brittany coast, a yacht can easily pick up an extra dozen miles on a full tide. Up in the Channel Islands area, a well-timed tide can be worth a free 15 miles between Cherbourg and Guernsey.

With an average cruising speed of 5-6 knots, you should get used to thinking of passages in terms of tidal cycles i.e. units of six hours. For example, it usually takes just over a tide to get from Cherbourg to Guernsey under sail, and nearly two tides to reach St Malo from Guernsey. You can normally reckon on a full tide from St Malo to Paimpol, from Tréguier to the Morlaix estuary, and from Morlaix to L'Abervrac'h. You have to watch your average speed on full-tide passages, using the engine in good time if the wind falls light and you are keen to arrive in a tide, or accepting, if the wind is light and you prefer not to motor, that the next foul stream will bring you to a grinding halt and so finding a snug anchorage might be a good idea.

The Alderney Race has the greatest maximum rates in the area covered by this book – up to eight or nine knots at the top of springs, a couple of miles west of Cap de la Hague. As you might expect, it also has the most dangerous overfalls in a weather-going stream. If a sailing boat picks up a foul tide here, she'll soon be travelling backwards, even with a good engine. The north end of the Little Russel is another critical gateway, with streams of up to six knots in the narrows between Platte Fougère and Roustel beacon. In light airs, an early decision to start the engine can make the difference between reaching St Peter Port or not.

On the North Brittany coast, the worst corner for tidal streams is off the Lézardrieux estuary, between Les Héaux lighthouse and La Horaine tower. You can experience a good six knots across here around half-flood or half-ebb at springs, although most tidal atlases only show a maximum of about 4½ knots. This area can be tricky if you are approaching the estuary from the north, perhaps after a passage from Guernsey when the timing from St Peter Port often means that you are arriving off Lézardrieux on the early flood, just as the cross-tide is gathering strength.

Don't forget the effect of the strong streams in the Brittany rivers. Up at Tréguier, for example, the river tide runs through the marina pontoons at an alarming rate, especially during the middle ebb. Always wait until slack water before entering or leaving Tréguier marina, or you'll be in much greater danger than you will ever experience offshore.

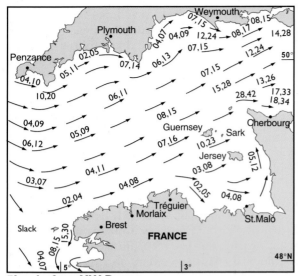

5hrs before HW Dover

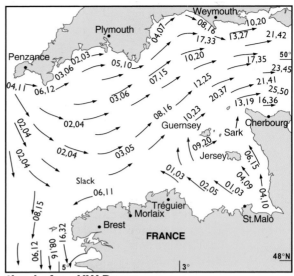

4hrs before HW Dover

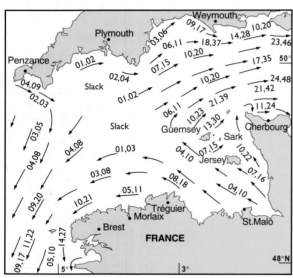

3hrs before HW Dover

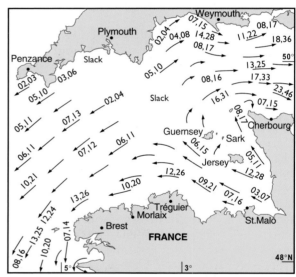

2hrs before HW Dover

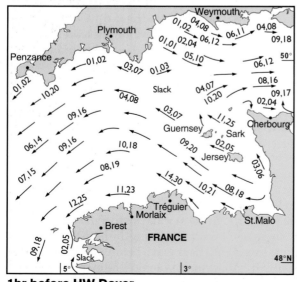

1hr before HW Dover

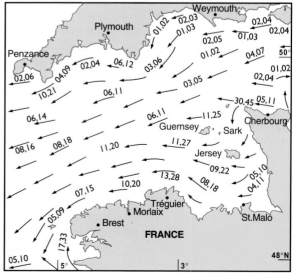

HW Dover

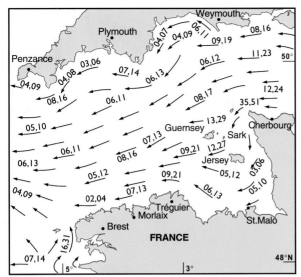

1hr after HW Dover

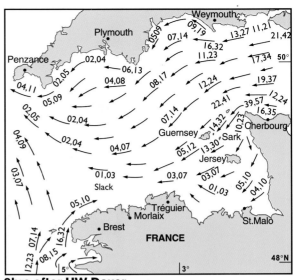

2hrs after HW Dover

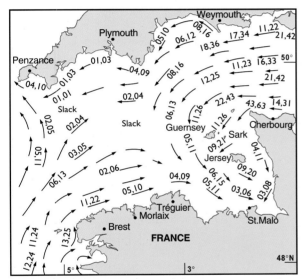

3hrs after HW Dover

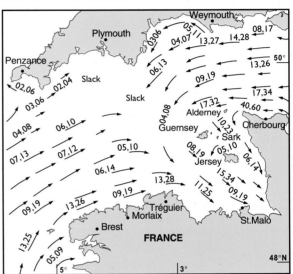

4hrs after HW Dover

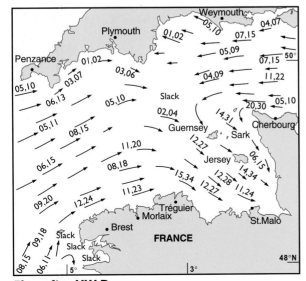

5hrs after HW Dover

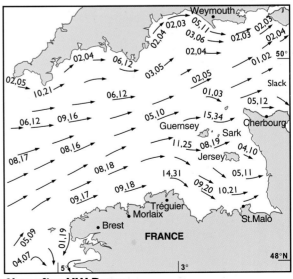

6hrs after HW Dover

EATING IN BRITTANY

For many yachtsmen, one of the important attractions of a French cruise is the opportunity to enjoy some of the food and wines which, despite growing internationalism in our own shops and restaurants, you can only really savour by crossing the Channel. Traditional Breton cooking

reflects, to a large extent, the hard country way of life that this independent and relatively isolated province has always demanded from its generations of farmers, growers and fishermen. The rocky coastal landscape and the shallow, not particularly fertile soil of the interior mean that crops and livestock, like the Bretons themselves, have to be pretty robust to survive. So this is not, on the whole, a region for delicate haute cuisine, although some of the more fashionable tourist restaurants cater for metropolitan tastes. The genuine local cooking is hearty and generous, and often based on simple ingredients, whether you are talking about meats, vegetables or the incomparable *fruits de mer*.

Lamb and mutton are often associated with Brittany, although the area actually produces very little of France's sheep meat. The genuine *pré-salé* comes from lean sheep which have been grazed on coastal salt marshes and has a distinctive full flavour, rather as though it had already been seasoned. The time-honoured way of serving *Gigot d'Agneau* – leg of lamb – is with white or green beans and whole cooked tomatoes. The lamb is liberally spiked with garlic cloves before roasting and will emerge in

good time from the oven so as to be pink and succulent in the middle.

Poultry – *volaille* – is also popular in Brittany, and you'll find that a free-range chicken bought from a Breton butcher, usually complete with head and feet, looks more yellow and has much more flavour than we've become accustomed to in England. With typical French pragmatism, even many battery producers let their chickens run free in meadows for a few weeks before killing, so that they acquire something of a free-range character. If you haven't a practical sized oven on board, much can be done with a good jointed chicken, a large casserole, garlic and mushrooms, and a cooking liquor based on red wine or Brittany cider.

Pork is still the most important meat in Brittany farming. You can understand the reasons for this when you peruse the tempting counters of a charcuterie in even a small country town and realise that similar, or more elaborate selections of cold meats, pork-based pâtés and saucisses will be on display all over France every day. Some of the offerings may look a bit suspicious though. *Boudin*, which is more or less the same as our black pudding, is something of an acquired taste. *Andouille* or *Andouillette*, a white pudding made from pork chitterlings, has a drier texture than boudin and can make a quick and savoury supper on board. With a sharp knife, cut a large *Andouille* sausage diagonally into half-inch thick slices and fry in a very small quantity of butter and oil in quite a hot frying pan. Serve with grilled bacon, a buttery potato purée, and a full red wine.

North Brittany is well known for field vegetables, particularly artichokes, cauliflowers, early potatoes and those famously splendid pink onions. Firm Breton onions keep well on board a boat if you have a cool, dry, airy space where you can hang them either as a string or loose in a net bag. Early Nantes carrots are first class, especially when cooked whole with white wine in a chicken casserole.

FRUITS DE MER

Of course seafood, and especially shellfish, is probably the most popular culinary speciality of Brittany. Oysters, mussels, langoustines, crabs and lobsters are ready and waiting on the menus of most restaurants anywhere near the coast. Brittany oysters (*huîtres*), in particular, are well worth the tribulations of a few chilly night watches, some slightly edgy pilotage, or a spell of fresh head-winds.

Oysters: You find oysters cultivated all the way round the Brittany coast, but Cancale, on the west side of the Baie de Mont St Michel, is the most important oyster area on the north coast. Oyster farming is a long-term business, with most varieties taking at least four years to mature, fatten and cleanse before they are ready for the table. At Cancale they mature the delicious *plates* oysters, bred down on the south coast of Brittany in the Gulf of Morbihan, and also the *Bélons* which start life not far from the Morbihan in the Bélon River. There are various delicious ways of

serving oysters, but to my mind you can't beat a dozen of these noble molluscs *au naturel*, with just a quick squeeze of lemon juice on each before they slip down. As a fine accompaniment to a plate of Breton oysters, choose a good well-chilled *Muscadet sur lie*, a Sancerre or the more local Gros Plant du Pays Nantais. On board, if the wine locker happens to be low, whisky and water goes rather well with oysters.

If you pass through the Channel Islands on the way down to Brittany, you should try some of the local Herm oysters, which are cultivated off the rocky west coast of the island to the north of the harbour. The best place to buy them is at the co-operative retail shop over on Castle Emplacement at St Peter Port, and you'll find the Herm oyster a worthy match for its Brittany rival.

Mussels: Brittany *moules marinière* or *moules au cidre* make a delicious (but quite filling) first course. I'm never sure whether it's the mussels themselves that are filling, or whether it's all the French bread that you dip into the sauce, but it's a good idea to choose a fairly light main course if you start with moules. Mussels are easy to cook on board if you get a chance to buy some in a local market. First make sure the mussels are clean on the outside, by scrubbing the shells with a kitchen brush and rinsing them in clean sea-water (not marina water). Also gently pull off any of the 'beard' which often attaches between the two halves of the shells. Throw away any mussels which stay open as you scrub them, as they'll probably be dead and therefore a risky proposition. It only takes one dodgy mussel to floor the hardiest of mariners.

The basic *moules marinière* recipe is quite simple, but you need a decent sized pan or casserole. Gently fry three finely chopped shallots (or a medium-sized onion) and a couple of chopped cloves of garlic in butter in this large pan. Stir in a little fresh parsley and a pinch of thyme before adding the mussels, as much white wine as it takes almost to cover them (usually about three or four good glasses), a bay leaf and some black pepper. Cook at a fairly high heat until the liquid just starts to bubble and the mussels open – but no longer.

Remove the mussels from the pan, discarding any rogues which are still closed, and put them in a bowl which has been warmed. Then strain the wine into a clean pan and reduce quickly and vigorously by about a third. For a basic marinière sauce, simply pour this reduced liquor over the mussels and serve. For a somewhat richer dish, remove the reduced liquor from the heat, add a knob of butter, and then slowly stir in 2-3 ounces of double cream until you have a smooth sauce. Pour this over the mussels and garnish with a little chopped parsley. Voilà!

For *moules au cidre*, use a medium or slightly sweet (*doux*) Brittany cider instead of the white wine. If you reduce the cider considerably, say by more than a half, the sauce will be rich and syrupy.

Langoustines: These popular shellfish look rather like miniature lobsters and are usually slightly bigger than large prawns. Langoustines often appear on restaurant menus in Brittany, either as a first course in their own right or as part of a *plateau de fruits de mer*. They are normally served with mayonnaise and can be excellent, but tend to vary in size and quality from restaurant to restaurant. Langoustines are particularly easy to overcook and I think it's best to buy them alive and fresh in a market and do them yourself on board.

Ideally, langoustines should be dropped into clean boiling seawater for two minutes only. Then fish them out quickly and allow to cool before serving. We like to eat them for lunch in the cockpit, when the empty shells can quickly be returned whence they came.

Lobster and crab: Lobster (*homard*) is normally extremely reliable in Brittany restaurants. Any plateau which includes this king of shellfish will be on the pricey side, but not as expensive as in England. So if you really appreciate lobster, make the most of it while cruising. I certainly enjoy lobster myself, although the price, even in Brittany, tends to make me wince and somehow takes the edge off the appetite. Crab, on the other hand, is excellent value, and a good *tourteau* (the flat-back

Spider crabs fresh from the quay

crab with a large shell) contains several different types of delicious meat. The French are also keen on *araignée de mer* (spider-crab) which is tasty enough but generally rather more trouble to pick at than the results are worth.

When you are buying crab to eat on board, make sure that it's cooked and ready to eat. Trying to boil live crabs in the confines of a galley can be a stressful business. We normally serve crabs in their shells and pick them at the table in French fashion. It's worth having a set of shellfish picks on board for a Brittany cruise, and a reasonably clean set of mole-grips that you can pass round for claw-cracking.

But before you serve a cooked crab you must first remove the 'dead man's fingers'. This process is more difficult to describe than to do. Hold the main crab shell in the flat of one hand and first break off the two main claws, which should come away easily. These are an excellent source of meat, but will need cracking with the mole-grips before you can get in amongst it. Then, still holding the main shell in one hand, prise open the 'flap' on the bottom of the crab's body, which should come away as a whole piece with all the smaller legs attached. This lower part is a bit like the 'chassis' of the crab, while the main shell forms the bodywork.

Around the inside of this chassis, you'll see a number of off-white, slightly hairy and rather puffy tendrils or 'fingers', which you should carefully pull away one by one and discard. Also check the main shell for stray fingers that may already have become detached. When all dead man's fingers have been safely despatched, the two halves of the crab can be brought to the table with the large claws. A good 2-3lb flat-back crab should keep two enthusiastic diners busy for at least an hour. The inner recesses of the main shell can be emptied completely. The small claws are a bit of a fiddle to pick, but often contain some of the sweetest meat. Once you have broken away all the smaller claws, the main part of the chassis is best dealt with by cutting it in half with a large, sharp kitchen knife. This will reveal many more crevices from which a surprising quantity of white meat can be picked.

A good mayonnaise goes well with crab, but I also like to make a slightly sharp vinaigrette to serve with the richer meat. Finely chop two shallots, put

them in a small bowl and pour over about half a cup of red wine vinegar. Stir in a generous pinch of paprika, season with salt and pepper and let the mixture stand for about half-an-hour before using. A little of this vinaigrette spooned over some freshly picked meat is just the job.

Coquilles St Jacques: Scallops are caught on the North Brittany coast, especially in the east part of the area between St Malo and Paimpol. They are often served in their shells in a cream sauce with cheese or mushrooms, but the simpler the sauce the better. The flavour of a scallop is very subtle and should not be obscured by too many other ingredients. I like them lightly sautéed in butter with chopped bacon, and then served as a warm salad over chopped lettuce or rocket leaves with a walnut oil dressing and small toasted croutons. Fry the bacon in the butter first, and add the scallops when the bacon is almost done.

BRITTANY WINES AND CIDER

There are only two wines, both white, which can be said to be local to Brittany – Muscadet and Gros Plant, which come from the lower Loire near Nantes. In fact this area is just on the edge of Brittany, so many dedicated Bretons don't really count either of these wines as drinks of the region at all, being more inclined to cite their local ciders. Some of the Brittany *cidres bouchés* are excellent drinks, dry and crisp and not unlike, if you can

imagine such a thing, a rough country champagne.

The most interesting Muscadets come from Sèvre-et-Maine, the département to the south-east of Nantes which encompasses the two river valleys of the Sèvre and the Maine. You will also come across Coteaux de la Loire and plain Muscadet. The Muscadet grape itself originally came from Burgundy, where it was known as the Melon de Bourgogne. It has a low natural acidity and is an early ripener. With the traditional method of producing Muscadet – 'Sur Lie' – the new Muscadet is left in its barrels at the end of fermentation and then bottled direct. This process is supposed to avoid oxidation and impart a fresh flavour to the wine. Nowadays though, not all the vineyards interpret Sur Lie in the traditional way and you'll find that only a small proportion of Muscadets have that exciting full favour alongside the dryness.

The secondary white grape of the Muscadet area is the Gros Plant or Folle Blanche, and the wine produced from it – Gros Plant du Pays Nantais – is sharper than Muscadet and often quite green in colour. Gros Plant is generally regarded as a bit of a poor relation to Muscadet, being a Vin Délimité de Qualité Supérieure rather than an Appellation Controlée wine. You often see it in French supermarkets in the litre *vin de table* bottles. You can, however, strike lucky with Gros Plant and find a clean tasting wine which is refreshing, quite fruity and not too sharp. In North Brittany, the locals

will often drink a Gros Plant with oysters and then move on to a fuller Muscadet with a white fish such as sole. It's worth remembering that even the better Gros Plant wines don't travel well, especially not in the bilge-lockers of a yacht at sea.

CRÊPES

These excellent thin pancakes are a Breton speciality and you can eat them, with a wide range of fillings, at the crêperies which are found in almost any small village. Crêpes made from white flour are normally served with sweet fillings while the buckwheat versions, often known as galettes, generally have savoury fillings. At a crêperie you can enjoy a delicious meal consisting entirely of crêpes, starting perhaps with a seafood galette, moving on to ham and mushroom, then maybe sampling a cheese galette before finishing with a sweet crêpe such as chocolate or strawberry. It's traditional – and just right – to drink Brittany cider with savoury crêpes, and this is usually served in pottery bowls rather than glasses.

You can buy packets of pre-cooked crêpes at any supermarket, and these are handy to have on board when you are cruising. They need to be lightly moistened, just by dipping quickly into a saucer or shallow bowl of water, before heating them gently in a well-buttered frying pan. You only really need do them on one side, so you can add your chosen filling while the crêpe is still in the pan, and then turn the pancake in half just before serving.

Hand-made crêpes the traditional way

PASSAGES
TO THE CHANNEL ISLANDS AND NORTH BRITTANY

FROM THE DOVER STRAIT

Yachts from the Thames Estuary or the East Coast rivers have a longish haul down to the cruising grounds of Brittany and the Channel Islands. Even with a fair easterly and sailing direct, you can reckon about 200 miles from Ramsgate to St Peter Port. A north-westerly gives

you a useful slant, but westerlies or south-westerlies are bad news, as they have been for generations of sea captains bound down-Channel under sail. With head winds in particular, it can be difficult to break up this passage into manageable legs. Many yachts coast from Ramsgate to

The snug marina at Dover is two or three days' cruising from the Channel Islands area

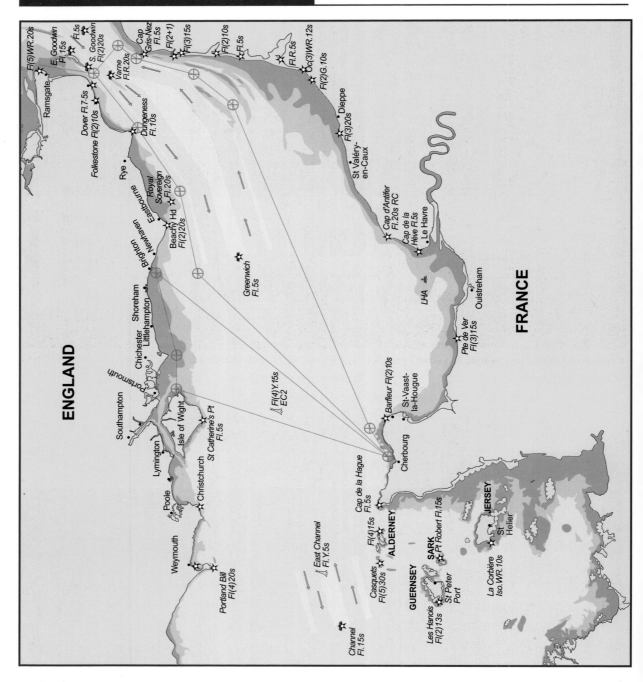

Eastbourne or Newhaven first – a rather inhospitable 60 miles to Eastbourne's Sovereign Harbour or 75 miles to Newhaven, with no real scope for shelter on the way. From Newhaven or Brighton you can either cross the Channel to Cherbourg, a little over 90 miles direct, or work along to Bembridge, about 46 miles, and take your departure for Cherbourg or the Alderney Race from there.

From the Dover Strait, unless you have plenty of time to spare, there's usually no strategic advantage in crossing over to the French side of the Channel early on and coasting westwards via Normandy. On the contrary, the distances are rather greater because you have to negotiate the Dover Strait shipping lanes at right-angles and then work well south if you are bound for Dieppe or Fécamp. A settled north-westerly, which is a reasonably fair wind if you keep to the English side of the Channel first, becomes an increasingly tighter slant as you drop south and west along the French coast.

In practice, yachts from the east end of the English Channel will need to allow two or three days cruising to reach the Channel Islands area.

Cherbourg's Port Chantereyne is a useful staging-post on a cruise to the Channel Islands

FROM BRIGHTON, NEWHAVEN OR EASTBOURNE

From Brighton, Newhaven or Eastbourne towards the Channel Islands and Brittany, the choice of strategy is usually whether to set off to cross direct to Cherbourg, a passage of just over 90 miles as the gull flies, or to coast along to the Solent first, with the aim perhaps of taking your cross-Channel departure from Bembridge or the St Helen's Road anchorage. The second plan adds about 20 miles to the Cherbourg trip, but gives you a shortish Channel crossing of only 65 miles which can generally be covered in daylight. Bembridge to Cherbourg also cuts the shipping lanes at a much safer angle than the direct passage from Brighton or Newhaven.

If you do make for Cherbourg direct from Brighton or Newhaven, care is needed with the French landfall in poor visibility. From either starting point, the direct line of approach brings you in from the north-east at an acute angle to the extensive off-lying dangers between Cap Lévi and Pointe de Barfleur.

With the powerful tides off the Cherbourg peninsula and around Barfleur, you need to keep a close eye on your track and be sure to stay outside the various buoys that guard this stretch of coast. With a stronger than expected east-going tide, you can be in amongst the rocks off Barfleur before realising it.

If freshening westerlies or south-westerlies make the last part of the passage hard-going, you have the option of falling off a little towards St Vaast-la-Hougue and the sheltered east side of the Cotentin peninsula. The race to the ENE of Pointe de Barfleur should be given a wide berth – up to five miles off the headland in any strong wind-over-tide conditions.

FROM THE SOLENT AREA, INCLUDING POOLE AND WEYMOUTH

Although the 60-70 mile Channel crossing from the Solent area to Cherbourg is probably one of the most well-trodden sailing routes around Britain, it is certainly not without its hazards and difficulties. The powerful tidal streams provide the main navigational complication, especially towards the French side of the Channel. In the days before GPS, many a boat ended up off Cap de la Hague or Barfleur wondering what went wrong, and even with GPS you have to keep ahead of the tidal game. Peak spring rates can reach 4-5 knots in this part of the Channel, but even the more modest 2-3 knots between springs and neaps is not exactly negligible if you are cruising at five or six. You need to work out the likely net set with some care, but there'll also be some strategic questions to keep in mind when deciding on your course to steer. These will hinge on what the tide and weather are likely to be doing as you approach the French coast. It's usually a good idea to keep some easting or westing in reserve, depending on which of the elements you think will have the upper hand as you make your landfall.

Other things being equal, the coast west of Cherbourg is more straightforward to approach than the Barfleur side, especially in poor visibility. Pointe de Barfleur is a bleak headland indeed, with its notorious race extending 3-4 miles to the ENE. Between Cap Lévi and Pointe de Barfleur there are various rocks and shoals up to 2½ miles offshore, marked by a W-cardinal and two N-cardinal buoys. These shoals create some boisterous overfalls at springs, even in quite moderate weather.

For a night landfall, the north coast of the Cherbourg peninsula has a good spread of powerful lights. Working west to east you have the main Gros du Raz lighthouse on Cap de la Hague (*Fl.5s23M*), with the much weaker (and somewhat unreliable) light on La Plate beacon tower (*Fl(2+1)WR.12s9/6M*) a mile to the east; the Cherbourg Fort de l'Ouest light (*Fl(3)WR.15s22/19M*); Cap Lévi (*Fl.R.5s22M*); and Pointe de Barfleur-Gatteville (*Fl(2)10s.29M*). If you are approaching the Cherbourg peninsula well to the Cap de la Hague side, Alderney's Quenard Point light (*Fl(4)15s28M*), or its loom, will probably be visible off to the west. On a clear night though, you usually pick up the bright lights of the Jobourg Atomic Energy Centre, about 10 miles west of Cherbourg, before seeing any of the lighthouses. In poor visibility, day or night, one of the main dangers as you approach Cherbourg is the fast-moving cross-Channel ferry traffic approaching and leaving the harbour.

As far as the rise of tide is concerned, it doesn't much matter when you arrive at Cherbourg, since the harbour and marina are accessible at any state of tide, by day or night. On the English side though, you need a fair stream for coming out of Hurst Narrows and the Needles Channel, and this will probably be the main constraint on your departure time. With the wind at all fresh from the west or south-west, it's best to negotiate the four miles between Hurst and the Bridge buoy in the hour before HW Dover, just as the weather-going stream is about to start. By thus slipping out on the very first of the ebb, you should avoid the steep wind-over-tide chop that can soon build up in the west entrance of the Solent.

ACROSS FROM POOLE

The passage from Poole harbour leads you out through the Swash Channel to Poole fairway buoy, south-east for about a mile to clear the overfalls off Handfast Point, and then seawards past Peveril Point, Durlston Head and Anvil Point. The timing of your departure is not too critical, although it's preferable to carry an outgoing tide past Brownsea Castle and through the narrows between Sandbanks and South Haven Point. The most

Old Harry, a familiar landfall and departure for boats based at Poole

Alderney is only a day sail across from Poole or Weymouth

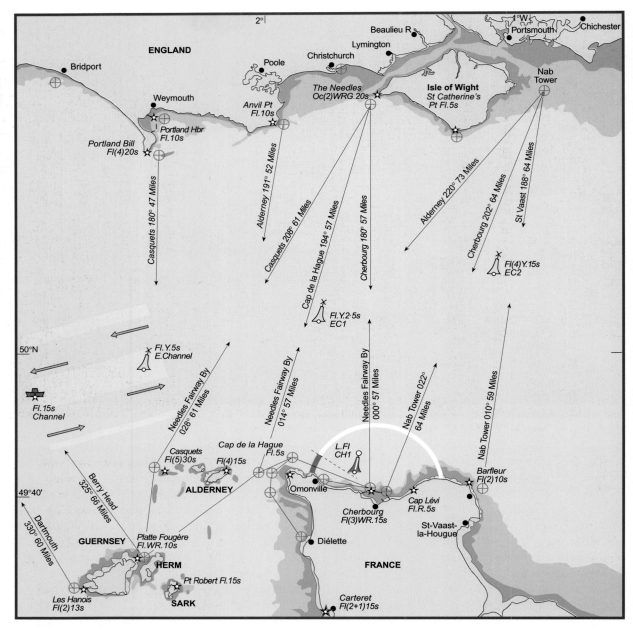

common strategy is simply to make the crossing during daylight and therefore to leave Poole as soon as convenient after the early morning shipping forecast and an early breakfast.

Since Poole is that much further west than the Solent, it usually makes sense to cross to Alderney rather than Cherbourg, which then gives you a head start on the next leg down to St Peter Port or St Helier. Assuming you can lay the course, the 57 miles from Poole fairway buoy to Alderney's Braye harbour can easily be completed in daylight. You can enter Braye at any state of tide, so the time of high water, of itself, has no bearing on this aspect of the passage planning. If possible though,

there's much to be said for making the final approach to Alderney near slack water, either 5-6 hours after or 1-2 hours before HW Dover. For a first visit, it's also preferable to avoid spring tides, both for this landfall and for any planned passage on to Guernsey or Jersey in the next day or two. These factors, taken together, point to a dead neap period when HW Dover is around 1930 GMT and LW Poole is near midday.

ACROSS FROM WEYMOUTH

Perhaps the most efficient start to a Channel Islands and North Brittany cruise from Weymouth is to make a passage direct to Guernsey keeping

Weymouth harbour is well-placed for a cross-Channel passage to Guernsey

west of the Casquets. This crossing is about 75 miles from Weymouth harbour to St Peter Port, and the timing is a bit critical if you want to catch slack water off the Casquets and pick up a fair tide down the Little Russel.

Other things being equal, the best time to arrive off the Casquets is about an hour before HW Dover, right at the end of the Channel flood. The streams just west and south-west of the Casquets rocks will be relatively slack and you can expect reasonably quiet conditions near the banks. You'll have five hours of south-going stream left to run down towards Guernsey and through the Little Russel to St Peter Port, which is about 17 miles from the Casquets.

Working backwards to the Dorset coast with an average cruising speed of five knots, you'd have to leave Weymouth pierheads on the previous high water Dover and take five hours of Channel ebb and six of flood to arrive off the Casquets at the most useful period of slack. Off Portland, you'd pass over the Shambles bank in quiet weather but probably stay east of Shambles E-cardinal buoy if the wind was at all fresh from the west. Leaving at HW Dover, your track would take you close to the East Channel light-buoy, at

the east end of the Casquets separation scheme. You can pass fairly close west of the Casquets rocks so long as the main stream is setting you safely off, although unpredictable tidal eddies and overfalls are likely anywhere in the vicinity. I must say I prefer to see the distinctive white lighthouse and the cluster of towers and buildings from a good mile or two off.

From the Casquets to the north end of the Little Russel is not quite 13 miles and a convenient landfall waypoint is a position three quarters of a mile due east of Platte Fougère lighthouse (white with a black horizontal band) off the north-east corner of Guernsey. A Channel ebb stream is broadly favourable on this leg, but it will also be trying to set you westwards along Guernsey's rocky north coast.

In fresh westerly weather, especially near springs, you should avoid the heavy overfalls over the Casquets SW bank, four miles south-west of Casquets lighthouse. At night, the white sectors of Platte Fougère (*Fl.WR.10s16M*) to starboard and Tautenay beacon (*Q(3)WR.6s7M*) to port should keep you on line for the entrance to the Little Russel until you can pick up the St Peter Port leading lights.

FROM THE
SOUTH DEVON HARBOURS

From any of the South Devon harbours, including the popular stretch between Torbay and Plymouth, the North Brittany coast is a longish haul direct, 90-100 miles depending on your destination and where you leave from. Many yachts make for St Peter Port first, a 70 mile passage from Dartmouth or Salcombe, a little over 75 from Tor Bay, which you can usually complete in daylight by making an early start. But if your main objective is France rather than the Channel Islands, there is much to be said for crossing to Brittany straightaway, perhaps returning 'anti-clockwise' via Guernsey if time allows.

From Dartmouth to Lézardrieux or Tréguier is about 95 miles direct, or for only another 20 miles you could be tucked up in the L'Abervrac'h estuary, with the object of cruising gently back eastwards towards Lézardrieux via Morlaix, Trébeurden and Perros. Also within easy reach of L'Abervrac'h, a morning's sail to the west and south, you have the various small harbours of the Chenal du Four as well as the off-lying islands of Ushant and Molène.

Of course the winds and forecast at the time of departure will probably have most influence on your strategy. Dartmouth to L'Abervrac'h, for example, is a good reach in a north-westerly but a bit tight in a due westerly, when Morlaix is a close reach and Tréguier or Lézardrieux an easy reach. In a south-westerly even Lézardrieux is a tight slant from Dartmouth or Salcombe and you may prefer to make for Guernsey in the hope of a veer in the next couple of days.

In westerly weather, with a series of Atlantic lows moving in, the usual response to freshening and backing winds on a Brittany passage is to fall off for a more easterly landfall: if you were heading towards L'Abervrac'h, to make for Morlaix or Trébeurden instead; if you were bound for Morlaix, to ease off for Perros; if you were hoping for Tréguier or Lézardrieux, to bear away for St Peter Port if conditions should harden in mid-Channel.

However, poor visibility is the greatest curse when approaching the North Brittany coast, and mist or haze is quite common in summer, especially at the western end. GPS navigators may feel partly immune to this threat, but you still have to be careful to approach landfall waypoints from a safe direction. As you draw inshore, the strong Brittany tides can soon turn what was a safe approach line into a dangerous one if you relax your concentration prematurely. You always need to be aware of what the tide is doing and is about to do when making a landfall, or your friendly digital display, having brought you safely across the Channel, can lead you into a tight corner right at the end of the passage. The approach to Le Libenter buoy, off L'Abervrac'h, is a case in point. For the last mile or two you need to approach this W-cardinal buoy from due north or west of north. Arriving from any of the South Devon harbours though, your natural approach track will be from east of north unless, for example, you set an offshore waypoint a couple of miles north of Le Libenter.

A night landfall on the North Brittany coast is no great problem in reasonable visibility, and most of the main harbours in this pilot are well lit for entry at night. Morlaix basin is an exception – you can enter the estuary and reach the Pen Lann anchorage and moorings at night, but the upper reaches of the river are only navigable by day and Morlaix lock is only worked during daylight hours.

Dartmouth is less than 70 nautical miles from St Peter Port

Taking departure from Start Point lighthouse

Passing La Corne lighthouse at the entrance to the Tréguier River

Arriving off La Palue in L'Abervrac'h

From Fowey
or Falmouth

From Falmouth to L'Abervrac'h is about 95 miles and the direct track, just east of south, gives a cracking reach in a westerly and a splendid run in a north-westerly. From Fowey you can reckon 105 miles either due south to L'Abervrac'h or SSE to the Morlaix estuary. Any of these passages leads

somewhat obliquely across the broad band of shipping between the busy Ushant and Casquets separation zones, so you have to be on your guard for a good part of the crossing. Even in fine weather, this west end of the Channel can feel rather exposed and lonely as you draw away from the Cornish coast. Out to the west there is nothing but empty ocean for thousands of miles, and a long, slightly menacing Atlantic swell often makes its presence felt as you approach the north-west corner of Finistère. Near landfall time you'll probably be conscious that, not very far away on the starboard bow, are the notorious tide-swept waters around Ushant.

However, these westernmost passages to Brittany

at least have the advantage that there's plenty of room to fall off to leeward if the weather picks up from the Atlantic. With a south-westerly, for example, Falmouth to Morlaix is pretty much a dead reach, with an even freer slant if you don't bear away until somewhere in mid-Channel. With very hard south-westerlies, there's scope to fall even further away to the east until you come under the lee of the Brittany coast.

In normal conditions though, a practical plan is to set a landfall waypoint near the Grande Basse de Portsall W-cardinal buoy, which lies right on the north-west corner of Brittany a little over five miles west of L'Abervrac'h entrance. You then have a choice of turning left for the last leg to Le Libenter buoy and going into L'Abervrac'h or L'Aberbenoît,

From St Anthony Head to L'Abervrac'h is about 95 miles

or, if the tide serves, of carrying on down the Chenal du Four to one of the attractive small harbours or anchorages between Portsall and Pointe de Saint-Mathieu. L'Aberildut, for example, is well worth a visit and will give you a quieter (and cheaper) first night in France than L'Abervrac'h, which is used by many more visiting yachts. You could make directly for Ushant if the weather and tide were right, although I always think this rather austere island is best visited on a short passage from the mainland, after a good night's rest and some careful homework with the tidal atlases and French charts.

In good visibility, a night landfall on the NW corner of Brittany is straightforward enough using the well-spaced and powerful lights of Ile Vierge (*Fl.5s27M*), Le Four (*Fl(5)15s18M*) and the two powerful Ushant lights – Le Stiff (*Fl(2)R.20s24M*) and Créac'h (*Fl(2)10s34M*). Neither L'Abervrac'h entrance nor the Chenal du Four are difficult to negotiate at night.

In murky conditions it's often worth using Grande Basse de Portsall W-cardinal buoy as your landfall waypoint, even if you are making for L'Abervrac'h. The short, five-mile leg from Grande Basse de Portsall to Le Libenter buoy then approaches L'Abervrac'h entrance at the safest angle, although in real mist or fog you have to make sure of identifying Le Libenter before pressing on any further east.

Plâtresses tower is a key mark in the Chenal du Four

FROM THE BRISTOL CHANNEL AND LAND'S END

A good many yachts based in the Bristol Channel, as well as the far-ranging Irish fraternity, often look towards Brittany for their summer cruising. These crews have a rather more substantial and daunting passage to get down to L'Abervrac'h or Morlaix than those of us starting from the Devon or Cornish coasts, or even the Solent. From Bristol itself, for example, a yacht faces a long haul of 110 miles through some tricky waters and against the prevailing weather, just to reach Padstow, which is the last sheltered haven before Land's End. From Padstow round the exposed tip of Cornwall to the Longships is another 45 miles.

Having arrived off the Longships lighthouse, you can either take a departure direct for L'Abervrac'h, a passage of near enough 100 miles to the SSW, or carry on round Land's End for 15 miles into Penzance Bay and rest up in Penzance basin or Newlyn before setting off across the Channel. Yachts which start from the Welsh side of the Bristol Channel often find an easier slant down to Land's End. From Penarth Port marina to the Longships is about 140 miles, from Swansea yacht haven 120 miles and from Milford Haven entrance 100 miles.

Because the track to Brittany from either Penzance Bay or the Longships is well east of south, any westerly weather will give you a free wind and even a south-westerly is no worse than a close reach. You cut the Ushant shipping lanes more or less at right angles, whereas the passages from further east along the Cornwall and Devon coasts are more oblique. Many Bristol Channel and most Irish yachts bound for Brittany call at the Isles of Scilly at least in one direction. The passage from the Scillies to Brittany looks long and lonely on the chart, but St Mary's to L'Abervrac'h is the same distance – 105 miles – as from Salcombe to L'Abervrac'h. The slant, almost exactly south-east, is good in westerlies on the way out but not usually such fun coming home.

The shipping lanes around Land's End and south of the Scillies are often busy and this whole area is distinctly inhospitable in poor visibility or heavy weather. The tides can be surprisingly strong and, because the streams are divided by the islands and by Land's End, their directions are difficult to predict. Given the choice, I think I'd rather be caught down off the North Brittany coast in a sudden mist than sculling about off the far end of Cornwall.

For a night landfall, you have a well-spaced array of good lights: of Ile Vierge (*Fl.5s27M*), Le Four (*Fl(5)15s18M*) and the two powerful Ushant lights – Le Stiff (*Fl(2)R.20s24M*) and Créac'h (*Fl(2)10s34M*).

Longships lighthouse is a familiar turning point on a passage between the Bristol Channel and Brittany

THE CHANNEL ISLANDS

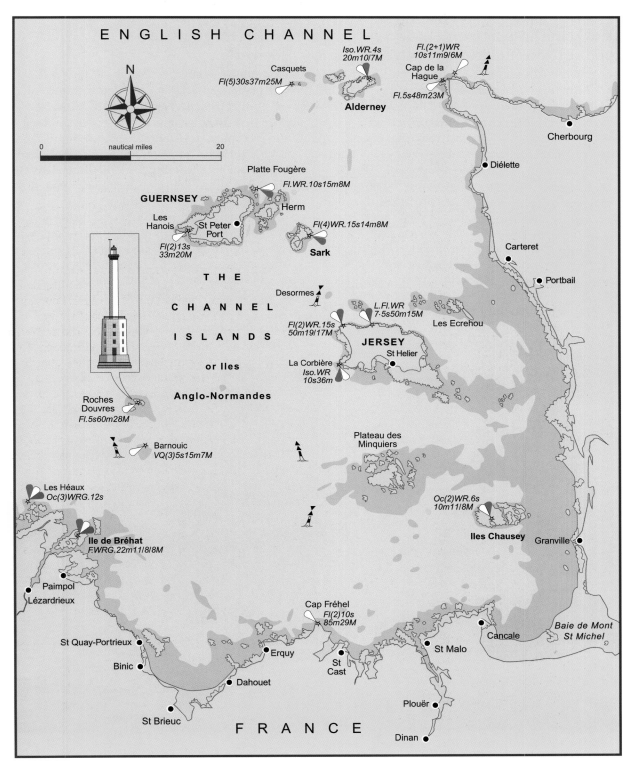

ENGLISH CHANNEL

Iso.WR.4s
20m10/7M

Fl.(2+1)WR
10s11m9/6M

Casquets
Fl(5)30s37m25M

Cap de la
Hague

Fl.5s48m23M

Alderney

Cherbourg

Diélette

Platte Fougère
Fl.WR.10s15m8M

GUERNSEY

Herm

Les
Hanois

St Peter
Port

Fl(2)13s
33m20M

Fl(4)WR.15s14m8M

Sark

Carteret

Portbail

THE

CHANNEL

Desormes

L.Fl.WR
7·5s50m15M

Fl(2)WR.15s
50m19/17M

Les Ecrehou

ISLANDS

JERSEY

St Helier

or Iles

La Corbière
Iso.WR
10s36m

Anglo-Normandes

Roches
Douvres
Fl.5s60m28M

Barnouic
VQ(3)5s15m7M

Plateau des
Minquiers

Les Héaux
Oc(3)WRG.12s

Oc(2)WR.6s
10m11/8M

Ile de Bréhat
F.WRG.22m11/8/8M

Iles Chausey Granville

Paimpol

Lézardrieux

Cap Fréhel
Fl(2)10s
85m29M

Baie de Mont
St Michel

St Quay-Portrieux

Erquy

Cancale

St
Cast

St Malo

Binic

Dahouet

Plouër

St Brieuc

Dinan

FRANCE

ALDERNEY

The third largest of the Channel Islands, Alderney is the most northerly and the closest to France. It makes an interesting port-of-call at the start or finish of a Channel Islands and North Brittany cruise, lying only 57 miles from Poole fairway buoy and just over 60 miles from the Needles. Braye, Alderney's

only harbour, is on the north coast of the island and accessible at any state of tide by day or night. The harbour area is mainly protected from seaward by the large stone breakwater, but is open from between north and north-east. Braye has not yet been invaded by marina pontoons and yachts either lie at anchor or use the visitors' moorings (over 60 yellow buoys). Mainbrayce Marine Services are based in the Inner Harbour and provide a full range of yard facilities.

Despite lying only eight miles west of Cap de la Hague, Alderney is somehow the most English of the Channel Islands. The diminutive capital of St Anne has a country village atmosphere, and cobbled Victoria Street looks as though it could happily accommodate a band of Morris dancers or the stalls of a WI fête. Braye, Alderney's only harbour, is a popular staging post for yachtsmen

bound south for the other Channel Islands or the North Brittany coast. Braye harbour entrance is just over 60 miles from the Needles and less than 50 miles S by E from Portland Bill. The passage along from Cherbourg is not quite 25 miles, a comfortable coastal leg after a Channel crossing from the Solent. Given reasonable visibility, Braye harbour is easy to approach from any of these directions, provided you take good account of the tides.

Unfortunately though, Braye is open to the north-east and is best avoided in winds from this quarter. In winds from due east, limited shelter can be found in the south-east part of the harbour, by anchoring under the lee of Albert Fort and to the south of Toulouse Rock. Even sustained north-westerlies can send in a persistent swell, which somehow manages to curve its way round the long breakwater – the 'Alderney' roll is a well-known phenomenon. But in

Braye near high water. Mainbrayce are just inside the entrance to the inner harbour

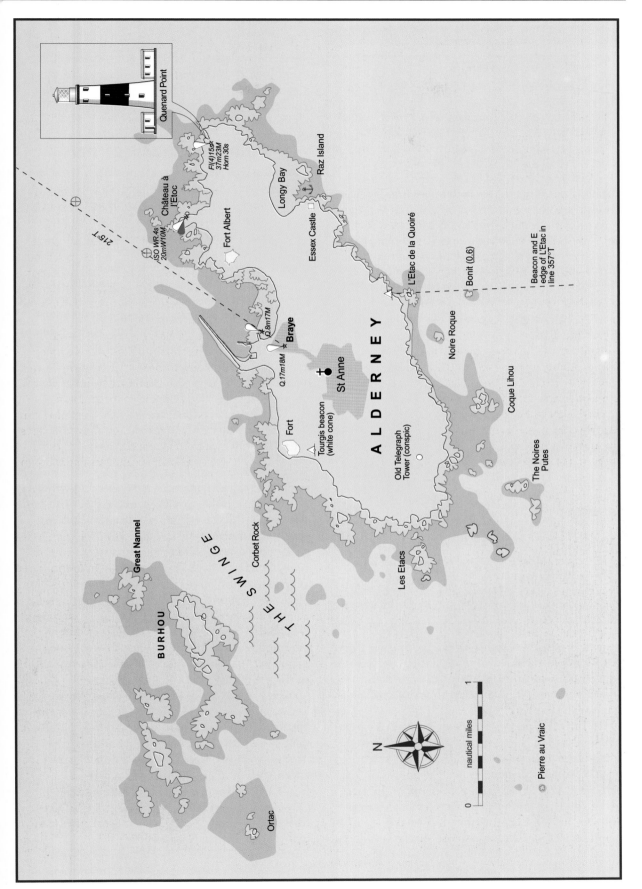

Quenard Point

Fl(4)15s*
37m23M
Horn 30s

Château à
l'Etoc

215°T

iSO WR 4s
20m W10M

Fort Albert

Longy Bay

Raz Island

Essex Castle

L'Etac de la Quoiré

Bonit (0.6)

Beacon and E
edge of L'Etac in
line 357°T

Noire Roque

Q.8m17M
Braye

Q.17m18M

St Anne

Fort

Tourgis beacon
(white cone)

Coque Lihou

Old Telegraph
Tower (conspic)

A L D E R N E Y

The Noires
Putes

Corbet Rock

Great Nannel

T H E   S W I N G E

Les Etacs

BURHOU

Ortac

N

nautical miles

Pierre au Vraic

TIDES

HW Alderney is at HW St Helier +0045, or HW Dover -0405.

In the Race, the SW-going stream runs from about 4hrs 35mins after HW St Helier for 5½ hours. The NE-going stream starts about 1hr 15mins before HW St Helier, starts to ease off 3hrs 45mins after HW St Helier, and falls slack half an hour later. Spring rates reach 5-6 knots through most of the race, but 8-9 knots locally.

In the Swinge, the SW-going stream starts 4hrs after HW St Helier and runs until 2¾hrs before the next HW St Helier. The NE-going stream starts 2¼hrs before HW St Helier and runs until 3½hrs after HW St Helier. Spring rates can reach 7 knots between Alderney and Burhou. Slack water in the Swinge is about half-tide (up or down) at Braye Harbour.

CHARTS

Admiralty: 3653 (for the Alderney Race), 60 (Alderney and Casquets), 2845 (Braye).

HAZARDS

The most important factor when approaching Alderney is timing the tide, either in the Alderney Race or the Swinge. The overfalls in the Swinge can be dangerous on a weather-going stream, when it's safer to leave for or arrive from Guernsey east-about Alderney.

WAYPOINTS

NE approach waypoint, 6½ cables due N of Château à l'Étoc Point – 49°44.65'N, 02°10.65'W
Inner approach waypoint, 4 cables WNW of Château à l'Étoc Point – 49°44.14'N, 02°11.10'W

seven days a week and a couple of good pubs. St Anne is a 20 minute walk up the hill and, not far beyond the town, Alderney airport offers regular connections with Southampton and the other Channel Islands.

APPROACH AND ENTRY

From the E or NE: Arriving round the NE corner of Alderney, either from Cherbourg or from the south via the Race, keep at least half a mile off the NE coast to avoid Grois Rocks (drying 5.5m), which extend north for a quarter of a mile from Château à l'Étoc Point. A useful clearing line for these dangers is Casquets lighthouse open to the north of Burhou bearing 262°T or less, and it's convenient to use this line until Braye harbour opens up. From Cherbourg, time your approach to miss the strongest hours of tide in the Alderney Race between Cap de la Hague and Quenard Point – a good time to be crossing this gap is about 4 hours after HW St Helier, which means leaving Cherbourg a good hour earlier than you would if bound SW through the Race.

From the SW: Arriving from the south-west, after a passage up from Guernsey say, you can either skirt south-about Alderney via the Race or, if conditions allow, cut through the Swinge between Burhou and Alderney. The Swinge is a temperamental stretch of water and can kick up some nasty overfalls when even a light wind is blowing over the tide – in a fresh wind-over-tide it is dangerous. If in doubt, come south-about Alderney.

The south coast has only two dangers that you can't see – Bonit Rock (dries 0.6 metres) lies three quarters of a mile east of Coque Lihou and 4 cables south of L'Étac de la Quoiré point. A useful striking line for Bonit is a white pyramid beacon on the south coast in transit with the east side of L'Étac de la Quoiré bearing 357°T. Sailing up the Race, therefore, you will have safely passed Bonit when the white pyramid is well open to the east of L'Étac de la Quoiré.

At the east end of the south coast, the Brinchetais Ledge extends nearly half a mile south-east from Houmet Herbé fort. This danger can be avoided by using a clearing line astern – keep the most northerly of the Coque Lihou rocks open to the south of L'Étac de la Quoiré bearing more than 240°T. Once clear of Brinchetais, follow round Quenard Point ½-¾ mile off, to avoid Sauquet Rock (dries 0.9m), until you bring Casquets lighthouse open to the north of Burhou.

The Swinge: This is the shortest route between Braye and Guernsey and, despite its reputation, is

quiet or southerly weather, Braye is a charming and restful haven, mercifully free of marina 'facilities'. If you'd rather not anchor, you can use one of the numerous heavy-duty visitors' moorings, which all have yellow buoys.

Mainbrayce Marine Services are based in the Inner Harbour and offer a full range of yard facilities. Their water taxi is useful if you have a large party to go ashore in dodgy weather. Call Mainbrayce Taxi on Ch 37(M) or Ch 80. With your own dinghy, land at the dinghy pontoon just opposite the Alderney Sailing Club. Not far from the Club, on the commercial quay, the States of Alderney run an excellent shower block with its own laundrette. Braye village is nearby, with Jean's Stores open

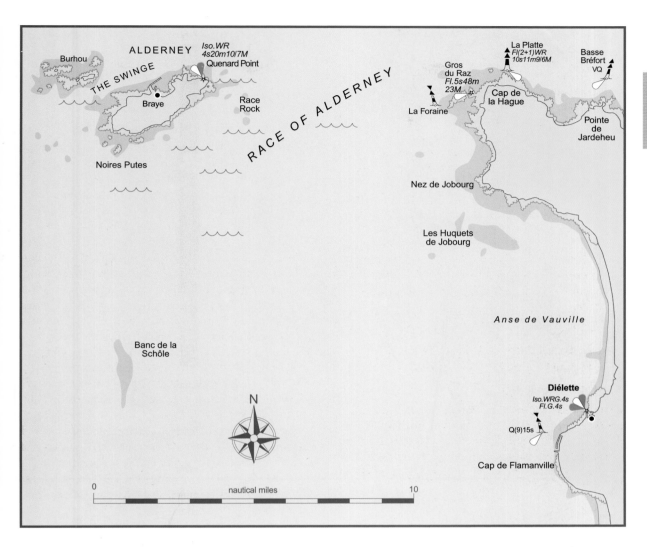

no problem on a quiet summer day or when wind and tide are together. The important thing is to stay right in the middle of the passage between Burhou and Corbet rock ($\frac{1}{2}$ metre high), the latter marking the seaward edge of a wide area of dangers extending half a mile NW from the Alderney coast between Roque Tourgis Fort and Fort Clonque.

Sailing south-westwards from Alderney, leave Braye harbour 2$\frac{1}{2}$ hours after HW St Helier. Having cleared the submerged end of the breakwater, set off westward towards Burhou; the tide should start to carry you down through the Swinge, but keep the north end of Château à l'Étoc point open to the north of the breakwater end i.e. bearing more than 080°T, until you are nicely between Burhou and Corbet rock. Then sail south-westward out into open water.

About two miles WSW of the SW tip of Alderney, there is an isolated and unmarked drying rock – Pierre au Vraic (dries 1.2m). This is left safely to the south by keeping Tourgis white conical beacon open to the north of the north edge of Fort Clonque and bearing more than 063°T; or left safely to the north by keeping the Tourgis beacon open to the south of the southern edge of Fort Clonque and

Quenard Point lighthouse at the NE tip of Alderney

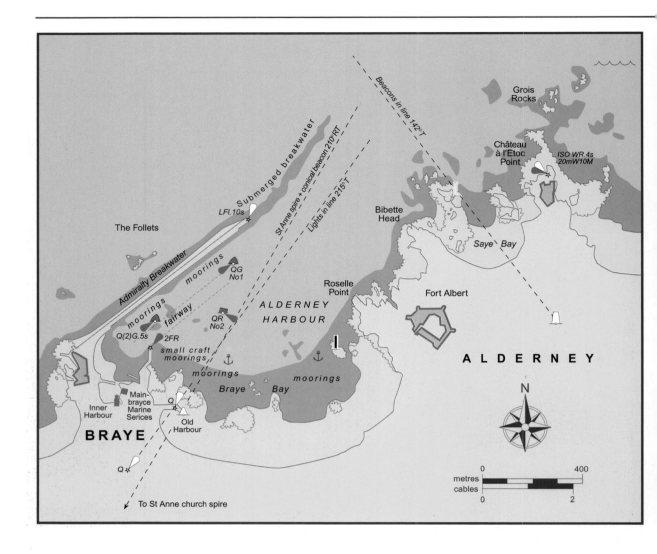

bearing less than 057°T. You are clear of Pierre au Vraic when Ortac rock (22m high) bears east of north true.

When approaching the Swinge from the southwest, there will usually be plenty of water over Pierre au Vraic if you have carried the tide up from Guernsey. Steer towards Burhou initially, but don't let the NE-going stream bring Great Nannel rock open to the east of Burhou until Corbet rock bears due east true. Then turn NE through the Swinge but start working east towards Braye when Château à l'Étoc point is open to the north of the breakwater end.

At night: It is not prudent to use the Swinge in either direction at night, because there are no lights that enable you to judge the middle of the Swinge safely.

From the NW: Approaching Braye from the NW, after a passage from the West Country for example, you'd normally leave the Casquets about five miles to the south-west and then Burhou about 1½ miles to the south-west. The

Nannels rocks lie close NE of Burhou and Great Nannel is 15 metres high. The most northerly outlier of this group is L'Emproué, a patch awash at datum, which lies 3 cables due north of Great Nannel. All the dangers off Burhou are left safely to the west by keeping Fort Albert (on the east side of Braye harbour) open to the east of Braye breakwater head, bearing more than 115°T.

Final approach and entry to Braye: Braye harbour is entered from the north-east, leaving the submerged foundations of the old Admiralty breakwater to starboard and the various rocks to the north of Bibette Head to port. Arriving from the east by day, keep the Casquets lighthouse just open to the north of Burhou until the entrance opens up and Château à l'Étoc point bears a shade east of south. Then make good south-west towards the inner part of the harbour and try to line up the leading marks – a white conical beacon on Old Harbour pierhead just open to the north of St Anne church spire up on the hill bearing 212°T. This line

Braye inner harbour dries and the fuelling berth is accessible for about 2½ hours either side of high water

leads right into the harbour, leaving the submerged part of the breakwater 100 metres to starboard.

Arriving from the Swinge or from the north-west, you have to clear the end of the submerged breakwater before turning SW into the harbour. From the Swinge, you can keep Quenard Point lighthouse (white with a black horizontal band) just open to the north of Château à l'Étoc Point bearing 112°T or more until the St Anne church leading line comes on. From further NW, keep the white beacon on Homet des Pies rock (a cable NE of Bibette Head) in line with a black-and-white beacon on shore behind it bearing 142°T until the St Anne leading line comes on.

At night: The Braye leading lights – front (*Q.17M*) in transit with rear (*Q. 18M*) bearing 215°T – bring you in from the NE, just south of the daylight line. These lights are visible when bearing between 210°-220°T. When arriving from the east, say from Cherbourg, keep the Casquets (*Fl(5)30s24M*) bearing less than 260°T until the Braye leading lights come into line.

To clear the end of the submerged breakwater when arriving from the NW, stay in the white sector of Château à l'Étoc light (*Iso.WR4s10/7M*) until you can line up the leading lights. The main lighthouse on Quenard Point (*Fl(4)15s28M*) marks the north-east corner of the island.

Alderney Harbour

MOORINGS AND ANCHORAGES

Braye harbour visitors' moorings: Visiting yachts can use any of the yellow buoys in Braye harbour, but make sure you are well secured with two good warps or chain and warp. Guard carefully against chafe because there is often a persistent swell in Braye.

Anchoring in Braye: You can anchor clear of the moorings, especially in the south-east part of the

harbour, but use heavy ground tackle, veer plenty of chain and set a riding light at night.

Alderney anchorages: You have to be careful about anchoring around Alderney, because the strong tides can make it difficult to leave in a hurry if weather conditions change. However, there are several possible

anchorages for quiet summer days, which can be picked out from Admiralty Chart No 60. The two most suitable for strangers are Longy Bay and Saye Bay, using the larger scale Admiralty Chart No 2845.

Longy Bay: This wide shallow bay lies on the SE side of Alderney just east of prominent Essex Castle, and is well protected in north-westerlies. Enter from due south, preferable either $2\frac{1}{2}$ hrs before HW St Helier or about 3 hrs after, leaving Queslingue rock (14m high) close to port. Fetch up on a line between Essex Castle and Raz Island fort, but much closer to the Essex Castle side. Near neaps, you can edge a bit further NNW.

Saye Bay: This attractive sandy cove lies just E of the harbour entrance and is a pleasant spot to lie during the day with the wind anywhere in the south. It is best entered from the NNW an hour or two after HW St Helier, by following the St Anne church leading line in or out of Braye until Homet des Pies white beacon is a little open to the W of the black-and-white beacon on the shore behind it. Approach Saye Baye on this line, leaving Homet des Pies rocks only 50 metres to starboard. Fetch up

Alderney Port Guide

(All telephone numbers below are Alderney code 01481).

Harbour control: Harbourmaster Steve Shaw, The Harbour Office, Braye (Tel: 822620).

VHF: For Port Control call Alderney Radio on VHF 16 or 74 from 0800-1800 between 1st May and 30th September, seven days a week.

Weather forecasts: Posted at the Harbour Office. Comprehensive Jersey Radio forecasts on VHF Ch 25 and 82 at 0645, 0745 and 0845 local British time, then at 1245, 1845 and 2245 GMT.

Yacht Club: Alderney Sailing Club at the harbour (Tel: 822758 and 822959).

Fuel: Diesel alongside from Mainbrayce Marine Services in the inner harbour, fuel berth accessible for about $2\frac{1}{2}$ hrs either side of HW. Depth gauge at inner harbour entrance.

Water: Alongside at the fuelling berth, or from Braye jetty.

Showers and laundrette: In the shower block near the Alderney Sailing Club. Use of these facilities is included in the mooring charges.

Chandlery: From Mainbrayce Marine Services, Inner Harbour, (Tel: 822772, Fax: 823683 or call VHF Ch 80).

Gas: From Mainbrayce Marine Services (as above).

Chart agents: Mainbrayce.

Repairs: Mainbrayce.

Marine engineers: Mainbrayce.

Electronics: Mainbrayce.

Tourist information: States Office, St Anne's (Tel: 822811, Fax: 822436).

Water Taxi: Call Mainbrayce Taxi on Ch 37(M).

Taxis: Alderney Taxis (Tel: 822992). ABC Taxis (Tel: 823760). JS Taxis (Tel: 823181). Island Taxis (Tel: 823823).

Bike hire: JB Cycle Hire (Tel: 822294). Puffin Cycles (Tel: 823725). Pedal Power (Tel: 822886). Top Gear (Tel: 822000).

Moped or Buggie Hire: Alderney Moped and Car Hire (Tel: 823352).

Car Hire: Braye Hire Cars (Tel: 823881). Central Car Hire (Tel: 822971). Alderney Moped and Car Hire (Tel: 823352). Mermaid Rent-a-Car, Braye Garage (Tel: 822460)

Shopping: In Braye, near the harbour, Jean's Store is open 7 days a week. Up in St Anne, 15 minutes walk up the hill, there are two self-service shops – Le Cocq in Marais Square and the Riduna in Victoria Street. Ebenezer Wrinklies is a useful delicatessen-cum-bakery, also in Victoria Street. Half-day closing is Wednesday.

Banks: Several in St Anne, but no automatic cash machines.

Air connections: To Southampton, Guernsey and Jersey via Aurigny Air Services (Tel: 822886, 822609). New Celtic West services planned to Exeter, Bristol and Rennes.

Chapter 2

about 100 metres SE of Homet des Pies or a bit further inshore at neaps.

FACILITIES

Although Braye harbour has no marina and is uncomfortable in north-easterlies, the moorings are perfectly snug in westerly weather. Mainbrayce Marine have a good chandlery and full repair facilities and can cope with most breakdowns. There are showers at the harbour, next to the Alderney Sailing Club. Braye itself has a couple of shops and the town of St Anne is about 20 minutes walk up the hill.

Victoria Street feels more English than England

A DAY ASHORE

Provided your boat is securely moored, you can spend a pleasant day either walking or cycling round Alderney (there are several local bike and moped hire shops). The island is peaceful and unspoilt, with some spectacular coastal paths. There are several quiet beaches where you can lose yourself for a peaceful lunch and a siesta. The local bus makes a regular circuit round the island, so you can easily get out to all the beaches and back. Buses leave from Butes car park near the Belle Vue Hotel. The Alderney train runs excursions from Braye to Mannez Quarry on the north side of the

island and is great fun if you have children to entertain.

Alderney is well known for its extensive fortifications. Some date back to Victorian times but even more dramatic are the more recent World War II works from that difficult period when the island was completely evacuated and occupied by German forces. This was not a pleasant part of Alderney's history. The local museum tells the story well, and then you can climb over and explore the forts all along the cliffs.

Bird-watchers will find much of interest around the Alderney coast. The off-lying rocks and islets around the west end of the island are particularly spectacular when the gannets are nesting.

Restaurants

Handy for the harbour in Braye, the **Sea View Hotel** and Rita's famous **First and Last** are both good for lunch or dinner. The First and Last is probably the most popular Alderney restaurant with visiting yachtsmen, many of whom make a reservation by mobile phone as soon as the island lifts above the horizon. **The Braye Chippy**, just behind the sailing club, is a traditional fish-and-chip restaurant where real fresh seafood is given just the right treatment – not licensed but you can bring your own bottle.

Bumps Restaurant in Braye Street (Tel: 823197) is popular with visitors, but on the pricey side. **The Harbour Lights** pub and restaurant in Newtown has excellent fresh seafood and mariner-sized steaks (Tel: 822168). Up in St Anne, the **Belle Vue Hotel** has a tempting bistro-style menu. **Gannets**, at the bottom of Victoria Street, offers good value in a continental style. **The Georgian House** restaurant (Tel: 822471) in

Victoria Street is under new management and will be well worth a spin. **The Albert** pub has a reliable menu at attractive prices. **Nellie Gray's** in Victoria Street (Tel: 823333) is still a sound choice if you like Indian food. **Ingrid's Café** serves meals all day from breakfast to dinner – not licensed, bring your own bottle. **The Courier** Italian restaurant is open from May to October.

In Marais Square, the **Marais Hall** pub does food in the evenings. Down at the bottom of Longis Road, past the golf club on the right, the **Old Barn Restaurant** is set in its own magnificent gardens and is definitely worth visiting. The **Albert House** in High Street is under new management and looks a sound bet for lunch or supper. If you fancy eating on board, the **China Garden** in High Street turns out reliable take-aways, but you can also make for Nellie Gray's, the Braye Chippy and the Belle Vue bistro.

GUERNSEY

Second largest of the Channel Islands, Guernsey enjoys a special place in the affections of UK yachtsmen. The attractive main harbour of St Peter Port has a friendly bustling atmosphere and makes a convenient staging-post for a cruise to North Brittany. St Peter Port can be entered at any state of tide, by day or night,

and in almost any weather. The sheltered visitors' marina, accessible for about 2-2½ hours either side of HW for 1.5m draught, is right next to the town centre. The privately owned Beaucette Marina, at the NE tip of the island, is a pleasant alternative to St Peter Port if you like a bit of peace and quiet. Beaucette is accessible for about 3 hours either side of HW for 1.5m draught, except in easterly swell.

Guernsey is the most westerly of the Channel Islands, roughly triangular in shape with the west coast about eight miles long and the south and east coasts six miles each. The low-lying west coast is rather inhospitable for yachts, with drying reefs and shoals straggling out for a good two miles. You should keep at least three miles offshore when sailing anywhere along this stretch between Platte Fougère lighthouse, at the north-east end of the island, and Les Hanois lighthouse, which guards the dangers off the south-west corner. The higher south coast of Guernsey is comparatively steep-to and has a much gentler character similar to parts of South Devon. There are various fair-weather anchorages

towards the east end near St Martin's Point, notably at Petit Port, Saint's Bay and Icart Bay. These attractive and largely unpopulated bays offer good shelter in any winds from the north, although all are subject to a slight rolling swell above half-tide and are quietest near low water.

St Peter Port, Guernsey's principal town and harbour, lies two miles north of St Martin's Point on the island's east coast, with its back to the prevailing winds. The harbour looks out across the south end of the Little Russel channel towards the neighbouring islands of Herm and Jethou, less than three miles away. Unless the weather is hazy, you can also see the more mysterious and rugged outline of Sark, six miles to the ESE.

The skyline of St Peter Port has a slightly foreign flavour, which adds quixotic spice to this welcoming Channel Island landfall. Stacked up behind the harbour, among the elegant town mansions of Guernsey granite, pockets of old colonial stucco mingle with Normandy style cottages, making you wonder if English is spoken here. Some of the white-

The unmistakable waterfront at St Peter Port

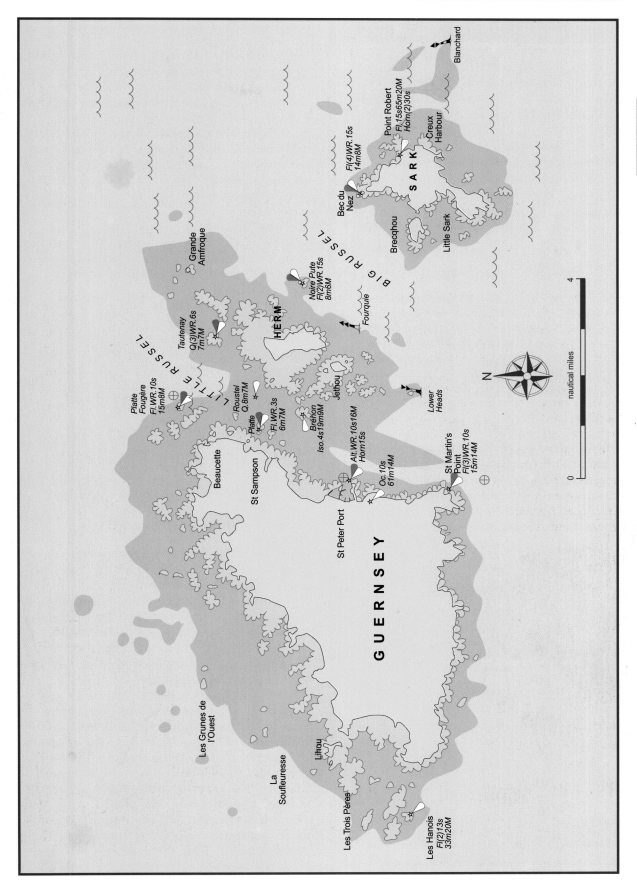

Blanchard

Point Robert
Fl.15s65m20M
Horn(2)30s

Creux
Harbour

Bec du
Nez
Fl(4)WR.15s
14m8M

S A R K

Brecqhou

Little Sark

Grande
Amfroque

BIG RUSSEL

Noire Pute
Fl(2)WR.15s
8m6M

Fourquie

Tautenay
Q(3)WR.6s
7m7M

HERM

Jethou

Lower
Heads

N

nautical miles

Platte
Fougère
Fl.WR.10s
15m8M

LITTLE RUSSEL

Roustel
Q.8m7M

Platte
Fl.WR.3s
6m7M

Bréhon
Iso.4s19m9M

Alt.WR.10s16M
Horn15s

Oc.10s
61m14M

St Martin's
Point
Fl(3)WR.10s
15m14M

Beaucette

St Sampson

St Peter Port

G U E R N S E Y

Les Grunes de
l'Ouest

La
Soufleuresse

Lihou

Les Trois Pères

Les Hanois
Fl(2)13s
33m20M

TIDES

HW St Peter Port is at HW St Helier +0010 or HW Dover -0440. Heights above datum: 9.0m MHWS, 1.0m MLWS, 6.7m MHWN, 3.5m MLWN. The tidal streams are strong around Guernsey, with spring rates reaching 5-6 knots at the N end of the Little Russel, 4 knots off the NW coast and 3 knots off the S coast. In the Little Russel opposite St Peter Port, the N-going stream runs from about 3 hrs before to 3 hrs after local HW and the S-going from 3 hrs before to 3 hrs after local LW.

CHARTS

For a passage from Cherbourg or Alderney use Admiralty 2669 or Imray C33A. Coming up from Lézardrieux, St Malo or Jersey use Admiralty 2669. For the final approach to St Peter Port use Admiralty 3654 and 808. You should have the Admiralty Tidal Stream Atlas for the Channel Islands and adjacent coasts of France (NP264).

HAZARDS

The NW coast of Guernsey is fringed with drying rocks for up to two miles offshore and should be given a wide berth. At the SW corner of the island, there are rocks up to ¾ mile NW of Les Hanois lighthouse. The northern approach to the Little Russel requires care – the streams are strong and drying rocks extend for 2½ miles NE of the north end of Herm.

WAYPOINTS

Little Russel NE outer, 2.2M 013°T from Tautenay beacon tower: 49°32.30'N 02°25.98'W

Little Russel North, 6 cables 065°T from Platte Fougère lighthouse: 49°31.14'N 02°28.22'W

Roustel, 1 cable due west of Roustel beacon tower: 49°29.29'N 02°28.88'W

St Peter Port entrance, 1 cable 065°T from Castle pierhead: 49°27.41'N 02°31.20'W

Little Russel South, 6 cables 110°T from St Martin's Point lighthouse: 49°25.16'N 02°30.75'W

Little Russel SE, 1.57M 098°T from St Martin's Point lighthouse: 49°25.16'N 02°29.23'W

Lower Heads, 1 cable due south of S-cardinal buoy: 49°25.79'N 02°28.47'W

washed villas look distinctly Mediterranean and a green copper dome brings a whiff of the orient. The prominent belfry of St James could almost be a minaret, especially seen through shimmering haze.

There's no doubt you are approaching a busy island harbour. Fast launches and ferries dart out with local panache. You might see a coaster turning in from Jersey, or meet one of the racy Condor wave piercers, which cut a mean 40 knots across from Poole or Weymouth. At weekends there are sails everywhere.

St Peter Port is a honeypot for all this action, a sociable haven for all comers, where there's always room for one more boat. The spectacular ramparts of Castle Cornet are floodlit at night, adding a Riviera touch to harbour life.

Two miles to the east, across the Little Russel, the exquisite miniatures of Herm and Jethou complete the picture with a masterstroke. Seen from St Peter Port, the peaceful rural slopes of Herm look like the far side of a lush farming valley, an enticing contrast to the rocky fringes of the sea. Jethou is even smaller, separated from Herm by the narrow Percée Passage.

Sailing through the Little Russel, intent on marks and beacons, you often don't notice the full effect of Herm and Jethou on the scene. It's not until you gaze out from Peter Port that these tiny islands assert their character. As mysterious outlines in early mist, they often promise another idyllic cruising day. In strong north-easterlies or southerlies, when the Russel tides are fighting the wind, the seething white water opposite Herm underlines the charms of luxuriant dry land, with good restaurants within easy reach.

As you arrive through St Peter Port pierheads, a harbour dory will sprint alongside with a friendly greeting and a copy of the local guide. A buoyed channel leads round the south edge of the outer harbour towards Victoria Marina entrance and the waiting pontoons just outside.

Visitors either berth in Victoria Marina or raft alongside the long pontoons in the outer harbour. Victoria is accessible for about 2½ hours each side of high water and has the advantage of being right on the waterfront near the centre of town. The outer pontoons are quieter and cooler in high summer. They now also have fresh water laid on, which makes this option rather attractive.

For yachts starting a Brittany cruise, St Peter Port is a convenient jumping-off point for St Malo, St Quay, Paimpol, Lézardrieux or Tréguier. Homeward-bound crews often linger here before returning

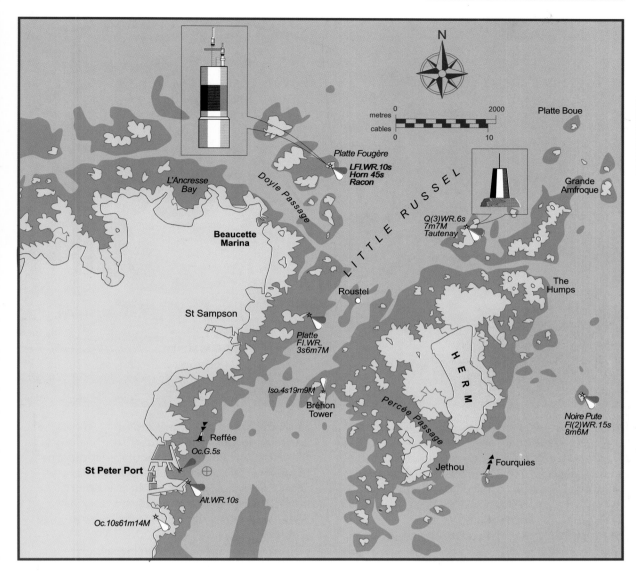

across the Channel, drawing out the holiday for as long as possible. Others base themselves in St Peter Port for a while to enjoy some local cruising and make day trips to Herm or Sark.

At the north-east tip of Guernsey, just south of Fort Doyle, peaceful Beaucette Marina is sheltered by the solid rock walls of an old coastal quarry and entered through a narrow cleft which is almost invisible from seaward. Beaucette is privately run and well worth a visit if you prefer to sample a quieter side of Guernsey than St Peter Port provides. The start of the entrance channel into Beaucette lies about three-quarters of a mile south of Platte Fougère lighthouse, and you head just north of west to follow a pair of leading marks and a line of large channel buoys. In quiet weather, the marina is accessible for a good 3 hours either side of high water for $1\frac{1}{2}$ metres draught, but any swell from the east makes the entrance a bit more tricky.

Midway between St Peter Port and Beaucette, the drying harbour of St Sampson is used mostly by small coasters and local boats. Visiting yachts rarely call here at the moment, although there are ambitious plans afoot to convert St Sampson into a sizeable marina. A long-established shipyard is based on the north side of the harbour, and at present there is usually room alongside one of the inner quays to dry out, either for a scrub or for running repairs.

APPROACHES AND ENTRY

St Peter Port is a summer crossroads for yachts on passage between the UK and Brittany. Many Solent boats cross the Channel to Cherbourg and then catch the tidal escalator down to Guernsey through the Alderney Race. For boats from Poole, a crossing via Alderney is usually more efficient.

Weymouth boats normally reach Guernsey either

Castle Cornet

via Alderney or by a direct passage west of the Casquets. Boats from Torquay, Brixham or Dartmouth usually make for the north end of the Little Russel and a waypoint off Platte Fougère lighthouse. Boats from Salcombe, Plymouth or the Yealm often arrive south-about Guernsey via Les Hanois and St Martin's Point.

St Peter Port from northward: The Little Russel channel, between Guernsey and Herm, is the most commonly used route to St Peter Port from the north. It is entered between Platte Fougère lighthouse (white with a black horizontal band) which stands nearly a mile off the NE tip of Guernsey, and Tautenay beacon tower (black-and-white vertical stripes) which marks a large drying reef just over a mile north of Herm. There are rocks to the south and north-west of Platte Fougère, and the lighthouse should be left about three quarters of a mile to starboard as you come into the Little Russel.

Tautenay is on the north-west edge of an extensive area of rocks which straggles north and east from Herm for nearly 3 miles. The outlier of these dangers, Platte Boue (dries 1.8m), lurks about 1½ miles north-east of Tautenay and three quarters of a mile NNW of Grande Amfroque islet (17m high). The transit of the two beacons on Grande Amfroque leads across Platte Boue as a danger line, bearing 151°T from seaward. When approaching the Little

Russel from the direction of Alderney, it is best to keep over towards the Guernsey side, making towards Platte Fougère on about 230°T to clear Platte Boue by a good 1¼ miles. You will have to allow for any cross-set across the north end of the Little Russel until you are nicely south of Platte Fougère and the stream starts to follow the line of the channel.

From an approach waypoint three quarters of a mile E of Platte Fougère, make good 198°T for not quite 1½ miles towards Roustel beacon tower, with Roustel in line with Bréhon fort behind it on this bearing. When you are a couple of cables from Roustel, come to starboard towards Castle Cornet, prominent just S of St Peter Port, steering to make good 220°T and leave Roustel a cable to port, Platte green beacon tower two cables to starboard and Bréhon fort not quite half a mile to port. St Peter Port entrance is then only 1½ miles to the south-west.

Bear in mind that the streams in the Little Russel can be strong, up to 5 or 6 knots at springs, so you should time your passage to carry a favourable tide. With a weather-going stream, you can experience some vicious overfalls in the north part of the Little Russel, especially in the vicinity of Roustel tower. Some of the worst conditions occur in a fresh north-easterly during the middle hours of the NE-going stream.

Because the NE corner of Guernsey is very low-

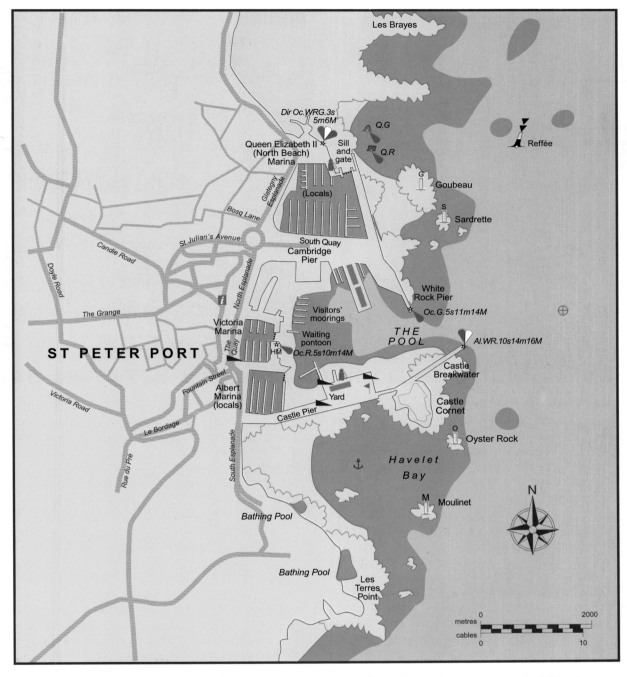

Les Brayes

Dir Oc.WRG.3s
5m6M

Q.G

Reffée

Queen Elizabeth II
(North Beach)
Marina

Sill
and
gate

Q.R

G Goubeau

S Sardrette

(Locals)

Glategny Esplanade

Bosq Lane

St Julian's Avenue

Candie Road

Doyle Road

The Grange

Victoria
Marina

North Esplanade

South Quay
Cambridge
Pier

Visitors'
moorings

Waiting
pontoon
Oc.R.5s10m14M

White
Rock Pier
Oc.G.5s11m14M

THE
POOL

Al.WR.10s14m16M

ST PETER PORT

The Quay

HM

Albert
Marina
(locals)

Castle Pier

Yard

Castle
Breakwater

Castle
Cornet

O Oyster Rock

Victoria Road

Fountain Street

Le Bordage

Rue du Pré

South Esplanade

Havelet
Bay

M Moulinet

N

Bathing Pool

Bathing Pool

Les
Terres
Point

metres   2000

cables   10

lying, you often pick up the much higher southern end of the island before the land actually nearest you lifts above the horizon. Be careful about jumping to early conclusions about your line of approach when arriving from the NE. It can sometimes seem as if you are coming in too far to the west, because the SE end of Guernsey appears fine on your port bow and you mistakenly assume that this is the NE coast. An early alteration of course to correct this 'error' would then take you too close to the dangers NE of Herm.

This illusion can work in reverse when you are

approaching the Little Russel from the NW. Picking up the high southern part of Guernsey before the low NE corner, it can seem as if you are making a landfall too far to the east. If you make a premature 'correction' to bring the left-hand edge of the visible land nicely on your starboard bow, Platte Fougère will probably turn up later well off to port.

Yachts arriving off Platte Fougère from the West Country should avoid cutting too close to the Braye rocks, which extend nearly a mile north-west of Platte Fougère lighthouse. Bring the south tip of Sark just open to the east of the north end of Herm

St Peter Port's Victoria Marina on a quiet day

CUSTOMS
DOUANE

when approaching Platte Fougère from the north-west; you should see Guernsey, Herm and Sark as separate islands.

At night: The Little Russel leading lights – Castle Breakwater light (*Alt.WR.10s16M*) in transit with Belvedere light (*Oc.10s14M*) behind it bearing 220°T – bring you straight in from the north-east to leave Platte Fougère (*LFl.WR.10s16M*) just over a mile to starboard and Tautenay beacon (*Q(3)WR.6s7/6M*) only half a mile to port. This line passes closer to the dangers north and east of Herm than you would normally risk by day, so it's important to keep in the white sector of Tautenay once you are within 4 miles of Herm and to stay dead on the Little Russel leading lights as you get near Platte Boue. The main marks in the Little Russel are lit – Roustel (*QFl*), the Platte beacon tower (*Fl.WR.3s7/5M*), and Bréhon fort (*Iso.4s9M*).

Approaching the entrance to the Little Russel from the NW at night, perhaps when arriving from Dartmouth or Torbay, stay in the white sector of Platte Fougère to clear the various rocks which lie up to three quarters of a mile NW of the lighthouse. When Platte Fougère bears due west three quarters of a mile off, make good 198°T towards Roustel light (*Q.7M*) until you are well into the white sector of the Platte beacon tower and you can start to line up the Little Russel leading lights at 220°T.

The Big Russel: When approaching Guernsey from the NE by day in boisterous weather or poor visibility, the Big Russel – between Herm and Sark – can be a safer and easier route than the Little Russel. This channel is two miles wide, the streams are not quite so powerful and the overfalls usually not quite so steep. You enter the Big Russel from the NE between Noire Pute, a low isolated above-water rock with a small light-beacon nearly a mile east of Herm, and Bec du Nez, the most northerly point of Sark. It's usually best to keep well over towards Sark at first, to avoid being set too close to the dangers NE of Herm. Most prominent of these rocks from this direction is Grande Amfroque islet, with its two small beacons, which should be left a good two miles to the west.

If bound for St Peter Port, continue south-west through the Big Russel to leave Noire Pute and then the Fourquies N-cardinal buoy each about three quarters of a mile to the west, and then edge a bit further west to round the Lower Heads S-cardinal buoy. St Peter Port entrance then lies only $2\frac{1}{2}$ miles to the NW.

At night: The Big Russel is not so well lit as the Little Russel, so you need reasonable visibility to come through safely at night. The most prominent lights as you approach from the NE will be Platte Fougère (*LFl.WR.10s16M*), well over to starboard in the Little Russel, and Point Robert (*Fl.15s20M*) on the east side of Sark, which should be off on your port bow. These two lights are useful for fixing your position before you pick up Noire Pute (*Fl(2)WR.15s6M*) and Bec du Nez on the north tip of Sark (*Fl(4)WR.15s8M*).

Also useful is the red sector of Tautenay light (*Q(3)WR.6s.7/6M*), which can give you quick transits with Platte Fougère and then Noire Pute. You should see Bréhon light (*Iso.4s9M*) as you pass the gap between Herm and Jethou, and the Lower Heads buoy has a reasonable light (*Q(6)+LFl.15s*) and a bell. Once round this buoy steer due west for half a mile to be sure of clearing the Lower Heads rocks, and then head NW towards St Peter Port Castle Breakwater light (*Alt.WR.10s16M*).

St Peter Port from southward: The approach from southward is straightforward in good visibility. Enter the broad channel anywhere between St Martin's Point and the Lower Heads S-cardinal buoy, giving either a berth of at least 4 cables. Then steer towards St Peter Port with Castle Cornet nicely on the port bow, staying two cables east of Castle Breakwater head until the harbour entrance has opened up.

The streams can be strong down off St Martin's Point, so the two miles up to St Peter Port can be hard-going if the tide is foul. Note that there are various drying rocks, some marked by spar beacons, up to three cables offshore on a direct line between St Martin's and Castle Cornet.

At night: St Martin's Point (*Fl(3)WR.10s14M*) shows red if you are approaching the SE corner of Guernsey from the SW, and then white as you open up the south end of the Little Russel and pick up the Castle Breakwater light (*Alt.WR.10s16M*). Coming round from the west or south-west, you should keep at least three quarters of a mile off St Martin's at night, to be sure of clearing Longue Pierre beacon (unlit) which lies close east of the point, and of staying well outside the various unlit rocks between St Martin's and Castle Cornet. You can head for St Peter Port, keeping the Castle Breakwater light nicely on the port bow, when the latter bears 348°T.

The east side of the approach is marked by the Lower Heads buoy (*Q(6)+LFl.15s*). Be careful not to be set too far over towards the Lower Heads if you are rounding St Martin's Point on a NE-going tide. To check this, make sure that the light on Bréhon fort is always bearing east of north as you pass St Martin's and make for St Peter Port.

Approach from the north-west via Les Hanois: The south-west corner of Guernsey is a simpler landfall than the north end of the Little Russel, especially in poor visibility. Yachts arriving from the West Country often approach St Peter Port 'south-about', thereby avoiding any problems with tide or overfalls in the Russel. Les Hanois

lighthouse stands a mile west of Pleinmont Point, the SW tip of the island, and there are drying rocks up to three quarters of a mile NW of the lighthouse. Coming from the N or NW, you should therefore aim to pass at least 1½ miles W of Les Hanois before coming round to the SE and then E along the S coast of Guernsey.

The south coast is comparatively steep-to, although there are various drying dangers up to half a mile offshore. You should therefore keep a good mile offshore between Pleinmont Point and Icart Point, then edging north a bit to round St Martin's Point by three quarters of a mile.

At night: Hanois has a good powerful light (*Fl(2)13s.20M*), but it can sometimes be tricky to gauge a safe distance off. As you come round to the south of Les Hanois, you can cross bearings of the lighthouse with the fixed red lights marking the radio masts on Pleinmont Point. The red sector of St Martin's Point lighthouse (*Fl(3)WR.10s14M*) won't appear until it bears more than 081°T, or when you are passing just over a mile south of Pleinmont Point. To be approaching the south coast a safe distance off, you must have seen the red sector of St Martin's before the fixed red radio mast lights on Pleinmont bear west of north true.

Entering St Peter Port harbour: Entry is straightforward, coming in from just north of east to leave White Rock pierhead (*Oc.G.5s*) with its port control tower to starboard, and Castle Breakwater (*Alt.WR.10s*) to port. Avoiding traffic is the main consideration, so watch out for coasters or fast ferries coming and going. A red light on White Rock pierhead means entry or exit prohibited, and this signal is shown when a large ship or ferry is about to leave or arrive. Once through the pierheads, keep to port and follow the buoyed channel into the pool, leaving the local moorings to starboard. You'll probably be met by a port control dory and given a customs form and directions. The fairway turns to starboard opposite the fishing jetty and you follow round

Looking out over the sill at Victoria Marina

Restaurants

St Peter Port is packed with restaurants and bistros of all styles and price ranges. You could stay a month and eat somewhere different each evening. This selection contains some of my favourites, but is certainly not exhaustive:

Da Nello's, at 46 Lower Pollet, is justifiably one of the most popular bistros in St Peter Port (Tel: 721552). Nello is a genial host.

Court's Restaurant is in Le Marchant Street (up behind Smith Street). Peter Stables keeps you amused while he's char-grilling your steaks (Tel: 721782).

The Merchant House Restaurant, at 38 High Street, is an elegant dining room run by David and Gina Mann. The Mann's previously ran the only Good Food Guide listed restaurant in Guernsey. Now you can enjoy their excellent and innovative cooking right in the centre of town (Tel: 728019).

Four Seasons Restaurant on South Esplanade is a slightly hushed establishment for serious eating (Tel: 727444).

Da Bruno on North Esplanade is excellent for lunch or dinner. Book early and try for the table in the window (Tel: 721880).

La Perla, just behind the bus station, is a lively metropolitan café-restaurant. Creative cooking (Tel: 712127).

Pacifica is next to Guernsey Brewery on South Esplanade. Extensive cosmopolitan menu (Tel: 713157).

Dix Neuf in the Arcade has a relaxed brasserie atmosphere where you can start the day with coffee and a croissant. Good for lunch or dinner, often accompanied by a live jazz band (Tel: 723455).

Christies, in the Pollet, is a well-run brasserie where you can enjoy a coffee, drink or bar snack watching the world stroll by. Also excellent for lunch or dinner on the terrace overlooking the marina (Tel: 726624).

The Absolute End is one of my favourites, 20 minutes stroll north along the Esplanade beyond Salerie Corner. Seafood is the speciality – fresh crab and lobster, local scallops, good brill and sole, succulent Herm oysters (Tel: 723822).

Simply Ireland is on Glategny Esplanade before the Absolute End. Interesting Irish dishes and a touch of the Blarney from Máire and Seamus (Tel: 725554).

Bertie's Landing is handy for the marina on Albert Pier (Tel: 720823).

La Frégate is one of the culinary stars of St Peter Port, up at Les Cotils. Quite formal, on the pricey side, first-class cooking (Tel: 724624).

Le Nautique, near the marina at Quay Steps, is under new management and is now one of the best restaurants in St Peter Port. Innovative cuisine, impeccably presented, seafood a speciality (Tel: 721714).

The Wellington Boot at Havelet Hotel is a bit of a hike up Havelet, off the far end of South Esplanade. Excellent Sunday lunch (Tel: 722199).

Rosario's in Mansell Street is a reliable Italian Restaurant. Walk south-west along Market Street and keep climbing up Mill Street (Tel: 727268).

The Waterfront, off North Esplanade, is casual and quick (Tel: 721503).

Sawatdi at North Plantation is an excellent Thai restaurant, with live Thai dancing on Tuesdays (Tel: 725805).

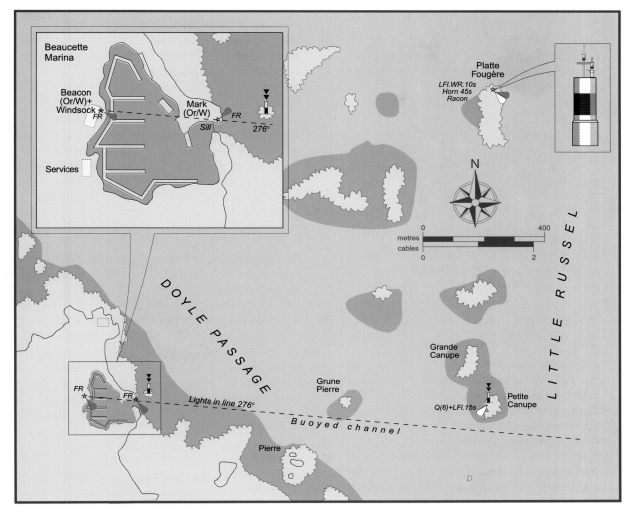

towards the waiting pontoon just outside Victoria marina entrance.

Beaucette Marina: This rather fascinating yacht basin lies right at the NE tip of Guernsey, two cables south of Fort Doyle (marina Tel: 01481 245000). It has all the usual facilities, including a diesel fuelling berth, a laundrette and a good marina restaurant. You can also hire cars and bicycles. The narrow entrance to Beaucette crosses a natural sill and there is a depth gauge just outside. You can reckon on about 2.7 metres in the entrance at half-tide, which means that in reasonably quiet conditions the marina is accessible for three hours either side of high water for 1.5 metres draught. However, in any significant swell from between north and east, you should enter or leave as near to high water as possible; in heavy swell from this quarter, strangers should avoid Beaucette altogether.

The outer end of the Beaucette approach channel lies not quite three quarters of a mile due south of Platte Fougère lighthouse, just south of a S-cardinal spar beacon marking the Petite Canupe rock.

Coming from the north, leave Platte Fougère between a quarter and half a mile to the west and head due south until you spot the Petite Canupe beacon. To reach Petite Canupe when coming from the south, make good due north for just over three quarters of a mile from Roustel beacon tower. Make the final approach to the beacon from the east, aiming to leave it about 120 metres to starboard.

You should now be able to line up the Beaucette leading marks: front – a red vertical stripe on a white background on the north head of the entrance; rear – a similar red stripe on top of the white clubhouse building. Keep these marks exactly in transit bearing 276°T and pass between the prominent line of green and red buoys leading to the entrance. Edge over towards the south side of the fairway as you draw close inshore, to line up for the narrows. Just outside the north head of the entrance, a pole beacon on a drying rock is left to starboard on the way in. The entrance itself makes a dog's-leg to port and then you leave the inner breakwater to starboard. The visitors' berths are on the south side of the basin. If

you arrive off Beaucette a bit early on the tide, there are two yellow visitors' waiting buoys just outside the entrance during the season.

At night: There's no problem about entering Beaucette at night in quiet weather and reasonable visibility, so long as you are sure of your navigation in the Little Russel. You should be immediately opposite the outer end of the entrance channel when Tautenay light (*Q(3)WR.6s7/6M*) bears due east true. The Petite Canupe beacon is lit (*Q(6)+LFl.15s*) and the Beaucette leading marks have fixed red lights. The red and green channel buoys are unlit.

MOORINGS AND ANCHORAGES

St Peter Port, Victoria Marina: St Peter Port visitors' marina is on the west side of the harbour, immediately facing you as you come in through the main pierheads. Follow the buoyed fairway right around the south side of the harbour. The sill dries 4.2 metres and the marina is accessible for 2-2½ hours either side of HW for 1½ metres draught. The sill has a depth gauge but it's important not to cut things too fine when the tide is ebbing.

The south side of the marina (to port going in) has long pontoons, where boats berth alongside each other. The north side (to starboard going in) has individual finger pontoons. Victoria marina can become very crowded in high season, especially at weekends. Boats wait outside for sufficient rise of tide to enter, either moored alongside the waiting pontoon just opposite the entrance, or one of the long pontoons in the pool. You can also lie fore-and-aft between a pair of the large yellow visitors' buoys. Note that the town end of the waiting pontoon has only ½ metre at datum, whereas the seaward end has about a metre. The port control dories direct boats in and out of the marina at tide time.

St Peter Port, in the Pool: Visitors can raft alongside the long pontoons in the outer harbour, using a dinghy or the local harbour taxi to get ashore. These outer pontoons are quieter and cooler in high summer, and they also have fresh water laid on. There are dinghy landing pontoons alongside the quay just north and south of the marina entrance. The charges for the pool pontoons are the same as for Victoria marina. If the pontoons are full, you can lie fore-and-aft between a pair of the large yellow visitors' buoys.

St Peter Port, Queen Elizabeth II Marina: This large marina basin has its own entrance about four cables north of the main harbour entrance. Although most of the berths are for local residents only, you can make arrangements to moor at 'R' pontoon if you are staying in St Peter Port for several days. 'R' pontoon has water and power, although there are no shower facilities in this marina as yet. However, visiting yachts must not enter the QEII directly, without having cleared customs and made the necessary arrangements with the harbour office.

St Peter Port, Havelet Bay: Havelet Bay, just outside the harbour to the south of Castle Pier, offers a useful 'overflow' anchorage in high season, so long as the wind isn't in the south or south-east. Enter from eastward between two spar beacons – Moulinet (with topmark 'M') and Oyster Rock (with topmark 'O'). During the summer, two pairs of port and starboard-hand buoys (lit at night) lead in from Moulinet and Oyster Rock towards the anchorage, where you fetch up 200-250 metres SW of Castle Cornet, or as space allows. You'll need to buoy the anchor because there are several private moorings. A patch of drying rock lurks on the south side of the bay, about 100 metres offshore opposite Belvedere light. Even in quiet weather, you often get a persistent rolling swell in Havelet near high water.

Beaucette Marina: Although Beaucette has limited space for visitors, it's often a good bet when St Peter Port is overcrowded. The north-east corner of the island is quiet with some good beaches and coastal walks. You can catch a bus into St Peter Port from near the marina.

Anchorages between Havelet Bay and St Martin's Point: This short but attractive stretch of coast south of St Peter Port is perfectly sheltered in westerly weather and offers four possible anchorages – Soldiers Bay, Fermain Bay, Bec du Nez and Divette – which are ideal for family beach expeditions on a fine summer day.

Soldiers Bay: Enter from due east a cable south of Les Terres Point, leaving Anfré spar beacon a good cable to the south. Near low springs avoid Boue Sablon, a rock awash, which lies two cables NW of the Anfré beacon.

Fermain Bay: This is an attractive but popular holiday beach, just over a mile south of St Peter Port entrance and immediately south of Fermain Point. Approach from due east and anchor well clear of where the Fermain launches land at the beach.

Bec du Nez: This small cove lies a couple of cables south of Fermain Bay and is best approached by making for Fermain first and then edging south along the coast close inshore. This strategy avoids Gabrielle Rock (dries 2.1m) which lurks a quarter of a mile due east of Bec du Nez. There is a useful danger line for Gabrielle Rock – Doyle's column up on the hillside in transit with Divette red-and-white beacon down on the shore bearing 237°T.

Divette: This anchorage is just south of Bec du Nez, on the opposite side of a short promontory separating the two. You can approach from due east, keeping the Divette red-and-white beacon well open to the north of Doyle's column to avoid Gabrielle Rock (dries 2.1m).

GUERNSEY SOUTH COAST ANCHORAGES

(Use Admiralty Charts 807 or 808)

Icart Bay: This wide unpopulated bay lies a couple of miles W of St Martin's Point and offers three possible anchorages in quiet weather or when the wind is settled anywhere in the north.

Le Gouffre, on the far west side of Icart Bay, is approached from the SSE, leaving Pointe de la Moye just over a cable to the west. Watch out for Rousse de Moye rock (dries 6.1m) which lies a cable SSE of Pointe de la Moye, and Vieux Poulain (dries 7m) on the east side of the anchorage.

Petit Bôt, in the NW corner of Icart Bay, is approached from just east of south. Keep the Martello Tower at the head of Petit Bôt bearing 347°T, to avoid Fourquie de la Moye rock (dries 3.3m) which lies right in the middle of the entrance to Icart.

NE corner of Icart Bay, opposite a sandy beach. Approach from due south to leave Icart Point a couple of cables to the east, so long as you have enough rise of tide over Baleine Rock (dries 0.9m) which lies ¼ mile SW of the south tip of Icart Point. Near low water, you can enter Icart Bay as though you were making for Petit Bôt, leaving Fourquie de la Moye a good cable to starboard and then heading just north of east for the NE anchorage.

Petit Port: Half a mile west of St Martin's Point, between Icart and Jerbourg Points, Petit Port bay has two possible anchorages in quiet weather or northerlies. The anchorage actually known as Petit Port is in the NE corner of this bay and is approached from due south, leaving Jerbourg Point to starboard and Mouillière rock (dries 8.5m and usually showing) to port.

The narrow inlet known as Saint's Bay is in the NW corner of Petit Port bay, close east of Icart Point. A number of local running moorings are laid off the quay on the west side of Saint's Bay, so you need to anchor towards the east side near the mouth.

FACILITIES

St Peter Port has all the facilities you would expect of a busy yachting and commercial harbour, with a full range of yacht services, marine engineers and chandlers. Although food and general household shopping tends to be more expensive than on the mainland, Guernsey's lower tax regime makes topping-up the drinks locker a slightly cheaper operation than in the UK.

EXPLORING ASHORE

St Peter Port is a colourful lively town with all the easy familiarity of an amiable village. The bottom of the High Street is only a few minutes stroll from Victoria Marina, across the Quay and in past the town church. Everything is close to hand and you can meander for an hour or two without walking far.

Around mid-morning, I often follow the smells of fresh baking towards Mange-Tout in the Arcade, where the home-made bread and croissants take some beating. The delicatessen is packed with tempting possibilities for lunch. Another tantalising counter is Giovanni's Delicatessen, just behind the market in Fountain Street. This specialist Italian deli is also the place for real French baguettes, which come in each day from St Malo.

Bucktrout and Co is a famous name in St Peter Port for stocking the cellar and the Marina Corkscrew on the Quay is also a useful emporium. For some unusual wines, I generally stroll north along the waterfront, past the QEII residents marina and Salerie Corner onto St George's Esplanade. Here you'll find the Wine Alley and the Grapevine (my favourite), where the mouth-watering choice of bins is enhanced by the proximity of France.

The magnificent Castle Cornet is often taken for granted as part of the harbour scenery, and as the venue where the famous noonday gun is fired from the ramparts. However, Castle Cornet is open to the public and worth a visit. Spanning eight centuries, the ancient buildings house several fascinating

Guernsey Port Guide

(Telephone numbers below are Guernsey STD code 01481).
Harbour control: Harbour Master Capt Robert Barton, Harbour Office, St Julian's Emplacement, St Peter Port (Tel: 720229). Port Control VHF Ch 12.
St Peter Port Radio works on Ch 20, with a link call facility on Ch 62.
Weather forecasts: Forecasts updated regularly at Victoria Marina office. Comprehensive Jersey Radio forecasts on VHF Ch 25 and 82 at 0645, 0745 and 0845 local British time, then at 1245, 1845 and 2245 GMT. For telephone recorded forecasts for the Channel Islands area, dial 09006 650022 from Guernsey or Alderney, or 01481 80000 from outside the islands.
Yacht clubs: Guernsey Yacht Club, Castle Emplacement (Tel: 722838). Royal Channel Islands Yacht Club, Quay Steps (Tel: 723154).
Fuel: Diesel and petrol at Boatworks+ fuel pontoon (Tel: 726071) in the outer harbour – accessible about 4hrs each side of HW. Also at QEII Marina fuel pontoon (Tel: 713947) – accessible 3hrs each side of HW.
Water and electricity: At all marina pontoons and at some of the Pool pontoons.
Calor and Camping Gaz: Boatworks+, Castle Emplacement (Tel: 726071). Herm Seaway, Castle Emplacement (Tel: 726829).
Refuse: On the quay above the marina.

Showers, laundrette, telephones: At the main Victoria Marina facilities block on Albert Pier and on the north side of the marina at Victoria Pier. Entry to the facilities blocks is by code number, obtainable when you pay your harbour dues.
Banks with cashpoints: Numerous banks with cashpoints in High Street.
Post Offices: In Smith Street and the States Arcade.
Tourist information: Guernsey Information Centre at North Plantation (Tel: 723552, Fax: 714951).
Doctor: Pier Steps Surgery, High Street (Tel: 711237).
Hospital: Princess Elizabeth Hospital, Le Vauquiedor, St Andrews (Tel: 725241).
Chandlers: Boatworks+, Castle Emplacement (Tel: 726071). Marquand Bros on North Quay (Tel: 720962). Seaquest Marine,

13 Fountain Street (Tel: 721773).
Sail repairs: Warren Hall, North Side, St Sampson (Tel: 249090). Also at Island Yachts, St Helier (Tel: 01534 725048) or Jackson Yacht Services, Le Boulevard, St Aubin (Tel: 01534 743819).
Rigging and mast repairs: Boatworks+, Castle Emplacement (Tel: 2726071).
Boatyards and repairs: Boatworks+ (as above). Andrew Dorey (Tel: 252123). Marine and General Boatyard, St Sampson (Tel: 245808).
Lift out: Boatworks+ (as above). Harbour Office (Tel: 720229).

Also an excellent 16-ton boat hoist at Beaucette Marina (Tel: 245000)
Engine repairs: Chicks Marine Ltd (Volvo Penta), Collings Rd (Tel: 723716/724536). Herm Seaway (Yanmar and Perkins), Castle Emplacement (Tel: 726829).
Electronics: Advantage Marine Electronics, Rue Colin, Vale, Guernsey (Tel: 716964). Radio and Electronic Services, Les Chênes, Rohais (Tel: 728837). Sea-Tech Marine Electronics, at Marquand Bros on North Quay (Tel: 710999 or mobile 07781 123121).
Shops: Food shopping in St Peter Port has become rather limited with the expansion of out-of-town supermarkets. Near the marina you have a small Co-op in Market Street and a compact M and S on the ground floor of Creasey's Department Store. Good fresh bread and delicatessen at Mange-Tout in the Pollet (Tel: 724529). Specialist Italian foods and fresh French bread at Giovanni's Delicatessen, 42 Fountain Street (Tel: 727302).
Bike hire: Millards Bikes, Victoria Road (Tel: 720777). Quay Cycle Hire at the ferry terminal (Tel: 714146). SOS Mountain Bikes, States Arcade (Tel: 712621).
Car hire: Economy Car Hire, North Plantation (726926).
Taxis: Bluebird Taxis (Tel: 244444).
Water Taxi: Terry Hodson, VHF Ch 10 or phone mobile 07781 108767.
Changing crews: Guernsey Airport has flights to all main UK airports except Heathrow. Buses C1 and C2 to airport. Condor fast ferries to Poole, Weymouth, Jersey and St Malo (Tel: 726121). Emeraude car ferries to St Malo and Jersey, and passenger ferries to Carteret and Granville (Tel: 711414).

museums and a tea-room. There are also four quite extraordinary period gardens.

The Maritime Museum traces the colourful history of Guernsey's sea trading and includes an arresting new interpretation of the story of Castle Cornet, with life-size figures and exquisite models. The Royal Guernsey Militia Museum gives some insight into the independent character of the Channel Islands.

Just 10 minutes walk from Victoria Marina at the top of St Julian's Avenue, Candie Gardens should not be missed, affording spectacular views towards Herm, Jethou and Sark. The award-winning Candie Gardens Museum describes the history of Guernsey from pre-historic times to the present day.

St Peter Port is a labyrinth of narrow streets, winding steps and old town houses leaning comfortably against each other for support. Wherever you wander, unexpected views appear round the next bend, or another mysterious alley cuts through to some hidden backwater. Secret courtyards trap the midday sun and terrace gardens flourish in these sheltered corners, where lobelia and bright fuchsias run riot. Up in Hauteville, a tricolour flies outside the elegant house where Victor Hugo lived for many years in exile.

You can explore in your own good time, but there are also some excellent new guided walks around St Peter Port, organised by Pat Kite (Tel: 07781 108769). These enjoyable tours take place Monday to Friday, starting at 10.30am from the Guernsey Information Centre on North Plantation. The walks last about 1¼ hrs and cost from £4.00–£5.50 each.

OUT AND ABOUT IN GUERNSEY

Hiring a car for a day is an inexpensive way to see the island, although increasing traffic makes driving less agreeable each year. We often take a bus or taxi to the south coast, where the cliff walks have dramatic views of rocky coves. If you catch a C1 or C2 bus to Mont Marché, a stroll through country lanes winds out to Le Gouffre, well-placed for these coastal paths. Here you can visit the art gallery at The Hollows, where local painters exhibit a great range of work. Then cross the lane to the café-bar for coffee, lunch or tea. The Hollows Restaurant is also a good choice for dinner (Tel: 264121).

Guernsey is home to several renowned artists and jewellers. Take a hire car out to visit Catherine Best at the Mill Studio in St Martin (Tel: 237771); or venture to the rural heart of the island to see father and son craftsmen Bruce and Simon Russell making fine jewellery and silverware in their restored farm buildings (Tel: 264321).

On the west coast road at Rocquaine, you can visit

Fort Grey Shipwreck Museum, housed in an old Martello Tower. Drying reefs extend two miles off Guernsey's west coast, dangers that have trapped countless victims over the centuries. A bit gruesome perhaps, but fascinating nevertheless.

The German Occupation Museum, out near the airport behind Forest Church, gives a compelling, rather poignant picture of life in Guernsey during the last war (bus routes C1 and C2).

DAY CRUISING FROM GUERNSEY

St Peter Port is often used as a staging-post for passages down to Brittany, but it also provides a convenient base for some splendid local cruising. The magnificent beaches on the east coast of Herm make a relaxing day away – a gentle sail across the Little Russel followed by some rock-hopping through the Alligande and Percée Passages.

For exploring ashore on Herm, it's best to take one of the ferries from St Peter Port, leaving your boat in the marina. Herm is owned by the States of Guernsey and has been leased to the Wood family since 1949. Under their thoughtful custody, Herm has prospered as a community and as a tourist attraction, yet retains its special rural character. The White House Hotel is excellent for lunch or dinner, and the Mermaid Tavern does good bar meals.

Sark lies out on its own, a few miles beyond Herm across the Big Russel. This stark granite plateau can seem aloof even on a clear sunny day, but is not difficult to approach. Havre Gosselin is usually the best daytime anchorage if you are coming from St Peter Port. Sark drifts you back in time as you wander ashore, with its horse-drawn carriages and dusty main street. However, a good foray ashore takes longer than you should leave your boat at anchor. For a worthwhile exploration of this fascinating and unique island, it's best to leave your boat safely moored in St Peter Port and take one of the Sark Shipping Company launches across in the morning, returning to St Peter Port in the late afternoon. You can hire bikes in Sark, stride around on foot, or take one of the carriage tours.

HERM & JETHOU

The smallest Channel Islands of Herm and Jethou lie just three miles opposite St Peter Port on the east side of the Little Russel. Herm is $1\frac{3}{4}$ miles long by half a mile wide – at high tide. At low water springs its area seems to double, as the extensive drying plateaux to the west and north are exposed.

The island has been owned by the States of Guernsey since just after the last war and has been leased to the Wood family since 1949. Under their thoughtful custody, Herm has prospered as a community and as a tourist attraction, yet retains its special rural character. The White House Hotel is excellent for lunch or dinner, and the Mermaid Tavern does good bar meals. Tiny Jethou, only three cables from end to end, lies a similar distance south-west of Herm's southern tip, across the Percée Pass. Jethou is owned by the Crown and has provided a retreat for a succession of wealthy leaseholders seeking perfect seclusion. No landing is allowed and the jetty at the north end is private – you can only admire from afar!

The miniature stone harbour on Herm's west coast was built, in the early 19th century, from local granite. It is used by the St Peter Port launches above half-tide, and often by Guernsey yachtsmen who come over at weekends or in the evenings for a meal at the White House Hotel. From a visitor's point of view, this picturesque, almost Lilliputian haven is quite feasible for an overnight stop, so long as you can find room inside.

The harbour dries to muddy sand at half-ebb and you need to be able to take the ground easily, either alongside one of the walls or on legs. The bottom is mostly clear of obstructions, but a few large stones lurk in the outer part, near the four mooring buoys. You are sheltered from all easterly winds, and from the south and west, but open to the north and NW. There is a fresh water tap at the top of the slip, near the Island Administration Office. Basic provisions and gas can be obtained from the shop near the Mermaid Tavern, but there is no diesel or petrol.

APPROACHES

There are several approaches to Herm through its various off-lying dangers, for which the best chart is Admiralty No 808. The two most commonly used

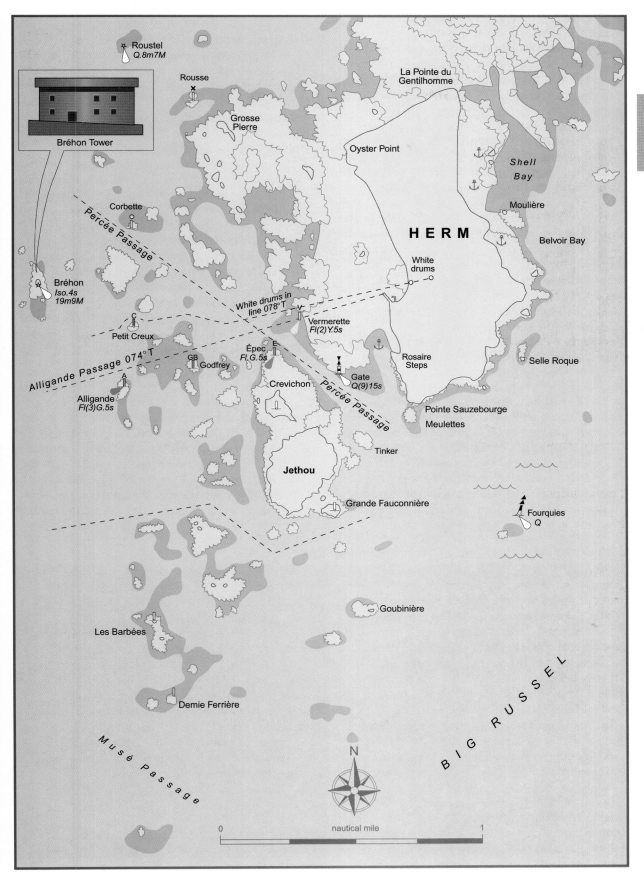

Roustel
Q.8m7M

Rousse

Grosse
Pierre

La Pointe du
Gentilhomme

Oyster Point

Shell
Bay

Moulière

H E R M

White
drums

Belvoir Bay

Bréhon Tower

Corbette

White drums in
line 078°T

Vermerette
Fl(2)Y.5s

Selle Roque

Bréhon
*Iso.4s
19m9M*

C

Petit Creux

Épec
Fl.G.5s

Rosaire
Steps

GB Godfrey

E

Gate
Q(9)15s

A

Alligande
Fl(3)G.5s

Crevichon

Pointe Sauzebourge

Meulettes

Tinker

Jethou

Grande Fauconnière

Fourquies
Q

Goubinière

Les Barbées

Demie Ferrière

B I G   R U S S E L

N

0 nautical mile 1

are the Alligande Pass from the Little Russel and the Percée Pass from the Great Russel.

The Alligande Pass: This passage is best taken at least two hours above low water. Coming from St Peter Port say, first reach a position not quite half a mile south of Bréhon Fort. Then make good 074ºT to leave Alligande beacon (green with an 'A' topmark, *Fl(3)G.5s* at night) about 150 metres to starboard, Petit Creux beacon (red with a 'C' topmark, unlit) a good 250 metres to port, and Godfrey beacon (green with a 'GB' topmark, unlit) 120 metres to starboard.

The leading line for the Alligande Pass is Vermerette beacon (a yellow spar beacon well ahead of you with a 'V' topmark, *Fl(2)Y.5s* at night) in line with Herm harbour pierhead at 074ºT. Three cables after the Godfrey beacon, as you draw north of Épec beacon (green with an 'E' topmark – *Fl.G.5s* at night), turn to starboard into the Percée Pass. Now head south-east for not quite half a mile, leaving a W-cardinal spar beacon to port before turning east and then north towards Rosaire steps.

The Percée Pass: This is the most straightforward approach to Herm and can be taken at any state of tide, but it should not be used at night without local knowledge. Come in dead between Herm and Jethou from the south-east (don't get too close to either Herm or Jethou) having avoided the Fourquies, a nasty isolated patch of rocks (drying 2.3m) three quarters of a mile east of the south end of Jethou. The Fourquies are marked close on their north side by a small N-cardinal buoy. When Sauzebourge Point (the south tip of Herm) bears north-east, head due north, parallel with the south-west corner of Herm, towards the Rosaire anchorage or the harbour.

ANCHORAGES

Rosaire: You can anchor a cable WNW of Sauzebourge Point, or further north near Rosaire Steps, the island's low water landing, but keep well clear of the Guernsey launches coming and going. Herm harbour is a couple of cables north of Rosaire, but you can only approach it within two hours of high water.

Belvoir Bay and Shell Bay: In quiet or westerly weather, you can anchor off the east coast of Herm in either Belvoir Bay or Shell Bay. The easiest approach to either of these anchorages is simply to follow round the south-east and east sides of Herm keeping a good quarter of a mile off. If you are coming in from the Great Russel, watch out for Noire Pute rock (2m high with a small light beacon) and the drying tail up to 1½ cables north of it. These dangers lie nearly a mile off the east coast of Herm. When entering or leaving Shell Bay, keep well south to avoid the various drying rocks which form the south-east outliers of the extensive dangers fringing the north end of Herm.

ASHORE

Herm is a delightful island and well worth exploring on foot, but perhaps the best way to see it properly is by catching a launch from St Peter Port, with your boat safely tucked up in Victoria marina. Take a good lunch basket and a bottle of wine, and stroll round the north end of the island to finish up on Shell beach by yardarm time. A swim before lunch, a siesta afterwards, and back to St Peter Port on a late afternoon launch. Sounds OK to me.

Belvoir Bay, off the east coast of Herm

SARK

Inimitable Sark, probably the most independent of the Channel Islands, lies about 16 miles SSW of Alderney, only six miles ESE of Guernsey and just over ten miles NNW of Jersey. Sark is a granite plateau of an island, 300 feet above the sea. Seen from Guernsey, its brooding profile can seem aloof

even on a clear day, and rather sinister across rough water in murky visibility. Yet Sark is not difficult to approach and Havre Gosselin is probably the simplest first anchorage if you are coming from St Peter Port.

Sark's off-lying rocks, although numerous, are mostly isolated and sheer. In good visibility, preferably near neaps, pilotage is fairly straightforward using Admiralty Chart 808, so long as you work your tides carefully. The times and heights of tide, for all practical purposes, are the same as for St Peter Port. The streams round Sark can be strong, up to 4 or 5 knots at springs off the east and west coasts, up to 6 knots in the Goulet between Creux and Les Burons, and up to 7 knots in the Gouliot Passage between Brecqhou and the west coast. Slack water is at half-tide up or down. Night navigation around Sark is not advisable unless, perhaps, you are leaving one of the west coast anchorages in calm conditions with a good moon.

Sark takes you back in time, not just because

bicycle, tractor, and horse-drawn carriage are the only forms of transport, but also because of the essential feudalism of its community. The island has a hereditary governor – the Seigneur – and is administered by a local parliament called the Chief Pleas. Most of Sark is divided into 40 tenements, originally small farms, whose owners are tenants to the Seigneur and entitled to a seat in the Chief Pleas. Also sitting are twelve deputies voted by the electorate of Sark.

The small town is clustered in the centre of Sark. Most of the shops are in the Avenue, the narrow main street that has something of an outback flavour. Even when the day seems quite still, the wind moans in the telephone wires, lifts the dust around the unmade roads, and sets the hanging signs creaking. At the end of the Avenue are two miniature banks and then the road drops down to the Bel Air tavern, the comfortable Aval de Creux hotel, and thence to tiny Creux harbour and Maseline jetty where the ferries land.

Visiting yachts in tiny Creux harbour

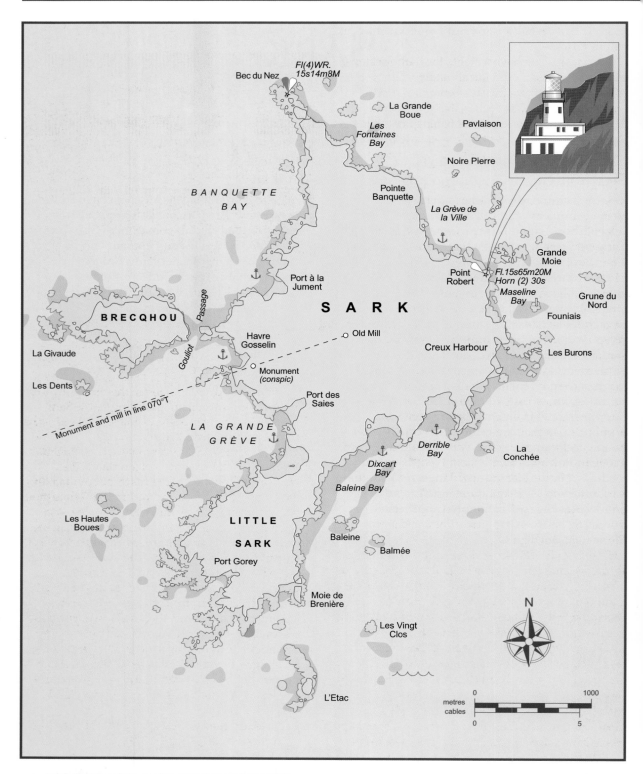

Fl(4)WR.
15s14m8M

Bec du Nez

La Grande
Boue

Pavlaison

Les
Fontaines
Bay

Noire Pierre

Pointe
Banquette

*BANQUETTE
BAY*

La Grève de
la Ville

Grande
Moie

⚓

Point
Robert

Fl.15s65m20M
Horn (2) 30s

Grune du
Nord

Port à la
Jument

⚓

*Maseline
Bay*

Founiais

S A R K

Passage

BRECQHOU

Gouliot

Havre
Gosselin

⚓

Old Mill

Creux Harbour

Les Burons

La Givaude

Monument
(conspic)

Les Dents

Monument and mill in line 070°T

Port des
Saies

*LA GRANDE
GRÈVE*

⚓

Derrible
Bay

⚓

La
Conchée

*Dixcart
Bay*

Baleine Bay

Les Hautes
Boues

LITTLE

Baleine

Balmée

SARK

Port Gorey

Moie de
Brenière

Les Vingt
Clos

N

L'Etac

metres
cables

0   1000

0   5

MOORINGS AND ANCHORAGES

Yachts must keep clear of the ferry and launch activity at Maseline and are not permitted to anchor in the harbour area or approaches. However, there are two clearly marked visitors' buoys a little way north-west of the jetty (don't use any of the other moorings though, which are all private). Not far south of Maseline, Creux harbour is enclosed by stone piers and sheltered in any winds from the west. Yachts can use Creux in quiet weather, entering within a couple of hours of high water and mooring stern or bow-to the north wall. You must keep clear of the harbour steps though, which are in continual use.

At low neaps you have water to the harbour steps, but at springs Creux dries at about two-thirds ebb to a firm sandy bottom. Yachts are not allowed to anchor or moor in Les Lâches, the cove just outside Creux harbour where the local fishing boats lie. If in doubt about any aspect of calling at Sark, contact the Harbourmaster John Carre (Tel: 832000) who will be pleased to advise.

There are two attractive and secluded bays just a mile SW round the coast from Les Lâches – Derrible Bay and Dixcart Bay. You can tuck close into either of these coves to escape the strong tidal streams which set along the east side of Sark past Creux and Maseline. Derrible and Dixcart are ideal in north-westerly winds, when it's possible to stay safely at anchor overnight. From Dixcart Bay, there's a pleasant walk up the valley to the Dixcart Hotel (Tel: 832015) and Stock's Hotel (Tel: 832001), both having comfortable restaurants serving a good selection of quick meals.

Half a mile north round the coast from Maseline, just past the prominent Point Robert lighthouse, is a broad bay known as La Grève de la Ville. A few local boats are moored here and visiting yachts may anchor clear of these moorings. Grève de la Ville offers good shelter in south-westerlies and you can get up to Sark by climbing the cliff path from the beach. The bay itself is clear of dangers, but there are various drying and above-water rocks off the entrance to the east. The simplest approach is from due north, between Banquette Point and Noire Pierre rock (3m high).

The west side of Sark has three useful anchorages: Port à la Jument, half a mile ENE of Brecqhou; Havre Gosselin, a steep sided cove close south-east of the Gouliot Passage which separates Sark and Brecqhou; and La Grande Grève, the wide bay just a quarter of a mile south of Havre Gosselin opposite La Coupée, the narrow ridge of cliff between Sark and Little Sark. These anchorages are straightforward to approach from the Big Russel, so long as you avoid the drying rocks fringing Brecqhou and the west side of Little Sark. Havre Gosselin usually offers the best shelter of the three, but all are subject to some swell above half-tide.

All three anchorages allow access up to the island, but the most practical if you need supplies is Havre Gosselin. The cliff path up from Port à la Jument needs care and is not recommended in the dark. La Grande Grève has one of the best swimming beaches, mostly of sand. It's also the most convenient for exploring Little Sark and its convivial hostelries.

The horse-drawn carriages on Sark

ASHORE

From wherever you land, it's a long climb up to the main plateau of the island, but then the walking is fairly level and you'll have splendid sea views from over 300ft above sea level. Havre Gosselin is one of my favourites, a dramatic cleft in the cliffs still used sometimes as an emergency landing by the Sark Shipping Company in easterly gales. You land at the old stone jetty and then keep climbing.

At the top of the winding steps you reach Pilcher's monument, built in memory of Jeremiah Giles Pilcher (a London merchant), his three companions and their boatman who drowned in 1868 while their sailing gig was trying to return to Guernsey. The monument is prominent as you approach from the west, a reminder to treat the sea with respect. Even if you don't have time to explore the rest of the island, it's worth the long haul up from the Gosselin landing for the panoramic view back down to your boat and across to Herm, Jethou and Guernsey.

Heading inland towards the small town, you pass the island duck-pond and soon reach the Avenue, which has various food and tourist shops as well as a post office and a couple of banks. The Gallery Stores has petrol and paraffin, and various items of hardware. Bikes can be hired from Avenue Cycle Hire (Tel: 832102).

The Aval du Creux Hotel (Tel: 832036) is a good bet for lunch or dinner, down the hill a little way towards the harbour. Beau Sejour Guest House (Tel: 832034) has a small but very good restaurant using fresh local produce. The restaurant at the Hotel Petit Champ is a sound choice, on the west coast between Havre Gosselin and Port à la Jument (Tel: 832046). La Moinerie Hotel (Tel: 832089), just behind the Seigneurie, specialises in seafood and the proprietor is a local fisherman.

JERSEY

Largest and most southerly of the Channel Islands, Jersey enjoys an enviable position in the Gulf of St Malo, with a climate a notch or two warmer than the south coast of England and a fascinating selection of Normandy and Brittany harbours only a short day's sail away.

Facilities for yachts are now first class and Jersey is increasingly popular as a staging post in a Channel Islands and North Brittany cruise. The main visitors' marina at St Helier is right near the centre of town and is accessible via an automatic sill for three hours either side of high water

Jersey often conjures up a curious mix of images, none of which is ever wholly representative: a holiday retreat where the shellfish is fresh and you still receive change with a round of drinks; a tax haven for best-selling authors; an offshore centre for financial manoeuvring; Bergerac, of course – remember him? These strands are all part of Jersey, but there is also a close local community which a casual visitor only glimpses in passing. Many island families can trace their line back to Norman roots, and a strong sense of tradition and independence exists among Jerseymen.

Jersey has a special constitutional relationship with Britain. Various events after '1066' resulted in the Channel Islands attaching directly to the crown and not becoming part of the UK. The effect today is

that Jersey remains self-governing, with the island parliament raising its own taxes and enacting its own laws. Duties are low and there is no VAT.

The island appears substantial from seaward, especially if you approach via Guernsey, Herm or Sark, and the high cliffs of the north coast can seem a mite forbidding against the afternoon light. Grosnez lighthouse perches right up on the north-west tip and the broad sweep of St Ouen's Bay curves south towards La Corbière.

If you make a landfall from the south, the signs of a bustling population are much more obvious. The main town of St Helier stands out as a built-up area, complete with blocks of high-rise flats and a prominent power-station chimney that serves as a useful mark for navigators. St Helier is a busy commercial port, handling large Ro-Ro ferries from England and France, fast inter-island and St Malo wave-piercer ferries, fast catamarans, and busy coasters, container ships, tankers and fishing boats of all shapes and sizes. You need to take care when approaching or leaving St Helier, especially in the

The visitors' pontoons at the north end of St Helier Marina

Small Roads just outside the harbour entrance.

La Collette yacht basin is just outside the harbour entrance to the south and is accessible at all states of tide. La Collette can accommodate up to 60 visiting yachts and serves as the main holding area for the two St Helier marinas.

The main St Helier visitor's marina is close to the town centre, with berths for up to 200 visitors. The automatic sill allows access for three hours each side of high water. Facilities are excellent, with good showers close to hand and a useful selection of boatyards, chandlers and engineers.

The new Elizabeth Marina is outside the main harbour area north of the car ferry terminal. It is reached by a buoyed channel from the Small Roads and, like the visitors' marina, is accessible for three hours each side of high water. A one-way system operates through the relatively narrow entrance and you must always obey the signal lights. Elizabeth Marina has berths for more than 560 boats, available to non-residents on one, five and ten-year leases. Monthly rates are also available, which can be useful if you deliver your boat down to Jersey from the UK and then leave her there for a while before starting a holiday cruise.

The south-east of Jersey is low-lying and fringed with drying rocks for several miles. The south-west corner is rather attractive and the Western Passage to St Helier, between the south coast and various drying rocks which lie up to $1\frac{1}{4}$ miles offshore, takes you close past La Corbière, St Brelade and St Aubin Bays, and the imposing ramparts of Elizabeth Castle. This is the natural way in if you are coming from Guernsey, direct from the Alderney Race west-about Jersey, or up from Lézardrieux or Tréguier.

The Eastern Passage to St Helier is the obvious route if you arrive from Granville or Iles Chausey, or from St Malo east-about the Minkies. The outer mark is Demie de Pas S-cardinal beacon tower, $1\frac{1}{2}$ miles SSE of Elizabeth breakwater head. Other passages cut through the off-lying dangers from the SSW, but are not much used by visiting yachts except near high water. The 'red-and-green' passage can be handy at night if you are coming up from the NW Minkies buoy, so long as you keep dead on the leading lights (023°T) once you are within 3 miles of St Helier.

Jersey has a number of smaller harbours, all of which dry below about half-tide. Nearest to St Helier is St Aubin, only two miles away on the W side of St Aubin Bay. This delightful pier harbour has a restful, almost continental waterfront. The entrance is well protected by St Aubin Fort, which is built right out into the bay and shelters a number of local moorings. Gorey, on the east coast of Jersey, is naturally sheltered from the

TIDES

St Helier is a standard port for the Channel Islands and North Brittany area. HW St Helier is at HW Dover -0450 approx. Heights above datum: 11.0m MHWS, 1.4m MLWS, 8.1m MHWN, 4.0m MLWN.

The streams are powerful around Jersey near springs, when you can experience a maximum rise and fall of more than 11 metres. The flood flows eastward and the ebb westward along the south coast at up to 5 knots and it can be a slow haul from Corbière to St Helier if you miss the tide. The ebb sets north along the east coast and then north-westward between Rozel and Les Écrehou at up to 5 or 6 knots at top springs.

CHARTS

Admiralty: 3655, 1137, 1138, 1136.

HAZARDS

The SE corner of Jersey is the most dangerous, where the rocky Violet Bank straggles for three miles off La Rocque Point and two other areas of drying rocks – Plateau de la Frouquie and Plateau de l'Arconie – lurk another mile offshore to the SE. There are various drying rocks off the south coast of Jersey, to the south of St Aubin Bay and Noirmont Point, and the buoyed Western Passage to St Helier leads close inshore inside these dangers. Drying rocks extend up to half a mile W of Corbière lighthouse.

WAYPOINTS

Western approach WP 1.4 miles due W of La Corbière lighthouse – 49°10.87'N, 02°17.00'W
Western Passage WP ½ mile WNW of Passage Rock N-cardinal buoy – 49°09.82'N, 02°12.90'W
Eastern Passage WP 2 ca S of Demie de Pas S-cardinal beacon tower – 49°08.86'N, 02°06.08'W

west and north, and is partly protected from the east by its long stone breakwater. Mont Orgueil castle overlooks the picturesque harbour and village. Many local craft are moored here, with some deep-keeled yachts taking the ground on legs. There are some visitors' buoys near the harbour entrance (drying at low springs) or you can anchor in suitable weather outside the breakwater. From a visitor's point of view, Gorey is well placed for a passage across to the west coast of the Cotentin Peninsula, perhaps to Carteret or Portbail; or as a base for a day trip to Les Écrehou, a fascinating group of rocky islets about seven miles to the NE.

Just 1½ miles north of Gorey is St Catherine's Bay,

protected on its north side by a substantial breakwater nearly half a mile long. You can anchor or sometimes find a vacant mooring just south of the breakwater and as far inshore as your draught and the tide permit. St Catherine's is a peaceful, unspoilt anchorage, with good shelter in any westerly winds but subject to a roll near the top of the tide even in calm weather. South of the main mooring area the bay is shallow and littered with drying rocks. Approach from due east, steering to leave the breakwater close to starboard (watch out for cross-tide around the breakwater head as you come in or out).

A couple of miles round from St Catherine's on the NE tip of Jersey, tiny Rozel harbour is worth anchoring off, or nosing into near high water if the weather is quiet or south-westerly. If you can find room among the local boats, you can dry out on firm sand. The anchorage is snug in south-westerlies, but always subject to roll near the top of the tide.

Bouley Bay lies 1½ miles west of Rozel, with Bouley Pier protecting a few local fishing boats which take the ground at low water. The anchorage off the pierhead is best with some south in the wind and somewhat prone to swell from the north-west, but makes a pleasant overnight stay in fine weather. Bonne Nuit Bay, two miles further west, has a similar set-up on a smaller scale. Give Belle Houge Point and Les Sambues rocks a wide berth on the way round and avoid Cheval Rock (dries 10.1m and shows at most states of tide) on the final approach to Bonne Nuit. The west half of the north coast is rather exposed, although quite straightforward to navigate on a sail round the island. Keep well clear of the Paternosters, an extensive plateau of drying rocks two miles north of Grève de Lecq bay.

APPROACHES AND ENTRY

St Helier from the W: The Western Passage is the 'big-ship' channel to St Helier, leading close along Jersey's SW coast inside the various off-lying rocks. When rounding Corbière Point from the north to line up for the Western Passage, it's important to

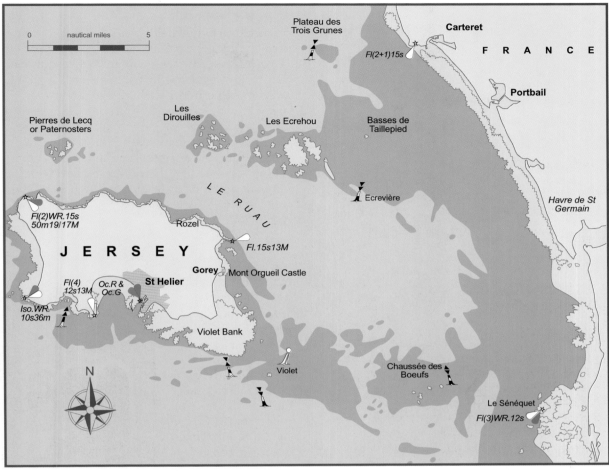

stay at least ¾ mile west of the lighthouse until you have passed nicely south of it; there are one or two isolated drying rocks which extend offshore for a good half mile. Once you are clear of these dangers, turn east and start to follow the coast about half a mile off.

Pass north of Passage Rock N-cardinal buoy and make for Noirmont Point lighthouse, a black tower with a white horizontal band. Keep between Noirmont and Les Fours N-cardinal buoy three cables south of it and then make good 082°T towards St Helier. Elizabeth Castle breakwater head, marked with black-and-white stripes, is now 1¾ miles away, and the prominent power station chimney will be fine on your port bow. When crossing St Aubin Bay, you leave Pignonet S-cardinal beacon and then two red can buoys to port, and Ruaudière green conical buoy to starboard. A second green conical,

East Rock, lies on the east side of the entrance to the Small Roads. Just before you reach East Rock buoy, turn to port on about 023°T to leave Oyster Rock thin spar beacon, La Platte red lattice beacon and Elizabeth breakwater head to port. St Helier harbour pierheads are half-a-mile in from La Plate.

Elizabeth Marina sill at low water. The tide runs strongly through the entrance during the first hour after opening

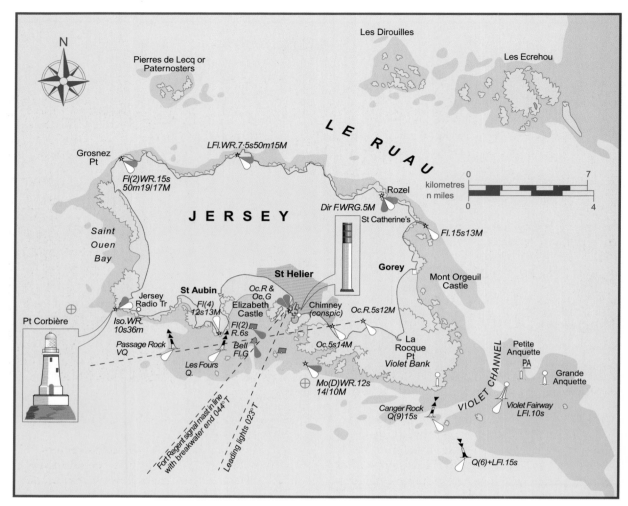

La Corbière lighthouse at the south-west corner of Jersey

At night: La Corbière has a powerful light (*Iso.WR.10s18/16M*), although it's difficult to gauge your distance off as you come round from the north. You are safely south of its off-lying rocks when Noirmont Point (*Fl(4)12s13M*) bears 097°T, when you can start making good about 100°T to pass north of Passage Rock N-cardinal buoy (*VQ*). The

leading lights for the Western Passage are La Grève d'Azette light (*Oc.5s14M*) in transit with Mont Ubé light (*Oc.R.5s12M*) behind it bearing 082°T. Just before reaching East Rock green buoy (*Q.G*), you pick up the Small Roads leading lights – front (*Oc.G.5s*), rear (*Oc.R.5s*) – which take you in at 023°T to St Helier pierheads.

St Helier from the E and S: First make for a waypoint half a mile south of the Demie de Pas S-cardinal beacon tower, which lies 1½ miles SSE of Elizabeth breakwater head. As you come up with the Demie, steer to leave it 2-3 cables to the east and then head NW to leave Hinguette red can buoy a cable or so to port. Continue north-westward towards the centre of St Aubin Bay until East Rock green conical buoy is about 1½ cables to the NE, and then turn in for the harbour entrance as above. Near low water, watch out for Les Tetards, a patch awash at datum ¾ mile W by S of Demie de Pas.

At night: There are no leading lights for the Eastern Passage. Simply leave the Demie de Pas (*Mo 'D'.WR.12s14/10M*) a good cable to the east and make good 314°T for a mile, leaving

Elizabeth Castle and the approaches to St Helier harbour entrance

Hinguette buoy (*Fl(4)R.15s*) two cables to port, until the Small Roads leading lights – front (*Oc.G.5s*), rear (*Oc.R.5s*) – come into line at 023°T. This transit takes you up to St Helier pierheads leaving East Rock buoy close to starboard and La Platte beacon (*Fl.R*) to port.

The 'Red-and-Green' passage: This passage approaches St Helier from the SSW, passing between Grunes St Michel (drying 1.5m) and Hinguette rocks (drying up to 3m), and right over the Fairway Rock (with 1.2m over it). Strangers should only use the red-and-green within an hour of high water, leaving Hinguette red buoy three cables to starboard before making for the black-and-white stripes of Elizabeth breakwater head.

At night: The red-and-green passage can be useful at night if you are approaching St Helier from the direction of the NW Minkies buoy, when the Small Roads leading lights – front (*Oc.G.5s*), rear (*Oc.R.5s*) – in transit at 023°T lead between Grunes St Michel and Hinguette. Even with the advantage of the leading lights though, only come in this way above half-tide and keep dead on the transit once you are within three miles of St Helier entrance.

Entering St Helier harbour: Yachts must obey the following traffic signals which are shown from the Victoria pierhead control tower:

● A flashing green light on the control tower roof and / or an occulting green light on the side of the tower means that vessels may enter the harbour but not leave.

● A flashing red light on the control tower roof and / or an occulting red light on the side of the tower means that vessels may leave the harbour but not enter.

● When both red and green lights are showing, no vessel may enter or leave.

● A quick flashing amber light shown from the Victoria pierhead control tower means that craft less than 25m long, and under power, may enter or leave contrary to the displayed signal lights, keeping well to starboard between the pierheads.

You have to take account of other traffic reacting to these signals when entering or leaving La Collette basin, the approach to which lies just outside the harbour entrance. You also need to watch for ferries arriving at or leaving the Ro-Ro berths, just outside the harbour entrance to the north-west. If in doubt about traffic movements, call St Helier Port Control on VHF Ch 14. Note that the marina channels 37(M) or 80 are not used in St Helier.

Entering St Helier Marina: Once into the harbour you turn to port for the visitors' marina, but then keep over to starboard on the approach. You'll see the marina traffic lights up ahead at the north end of the main basin:

● Green light – boats can enter the marina but not leave

Gorey harbour has a timeless, salty atmosphere and is overlooked by the imposing ramparts of Mont Orgueil castle. Gorey starts to dry soon after half ebb

- Red light – boats can leave the marina but not enter
- Red and green lights together – marina closed
  These signals must always be obeyed, or else you risk going aground on the automatic sill. A digital gauge at the entrance shows the depth (in metres) over the sill.

St Helier to Gorey via the Violet Channel: Gorey harbour, on the east side of Jersey, is often avoided because of the apparently tortuous passage round the dangers off the SE corner of the island. This area seems pretty horrific when you first glance at the chart, but the passage from St Helier to Gorey is much easier than it looks. The Violet Bank, although extensive, is reasonably compact on its south side. It is best to leave St Helier 1½-2 hours before high water. Take the Eastern Passage until you are half a mile S of Demie de Pas beacon tower and then turn ESE towards Canger Rock west-cardinal buoy, about 4 miles away.

Aim to pass a mile S of Icho Tower, prominent among the rocks with its whitewashed top, and enter the Violet Channel midway between La Conchière beacon and Canger Rock buoy. From here, make good a little S of E true towards Violet red-and-white fairway buoy (the name on this buoy is simply 'Jersey', but it's the only fairway buoy around the Channel Islands) keeping it fine on your port bow. Just before the Violet buoy, turn to make

good due N true for two miles, taking a back bearing on the buoy every so often to stay on this track. Thereafter, follow the buoys and beacons NW towards Gorey and Mont Orgueil castle – Le Giffard red can buoy left to port, Horn Rock red spar beacon to port, Gorey Roads green conical buoy close to starboard and then a green spar beacon to starboard. The visitors' moorings lie near and east of the harbour entrance, most of them dry. To enter Gorey harbour, carry on round the breakwater head. In suitable weather, you can anchor and stay afloat to the east of Gorey breakwater, but take careful soundings if you are staying over low water.

MOORINGS AND ANCHORAGES

St Helier visitors' marina: The town marina is accessible for about three hours either side of high water (the sill opening and closing times are posted at the head of the pontoons outside the marina office). If you arrive outside this period, or wish to leave the marina without departing from St Helier, you moor in La Collette holding basin (see below) which is always available. The marina has good showers and facilities and is well-placed for the centre of St Helier.

Elizabeth Marina: This smart new yacht harbour is outside the main harbour area just north of the car ferry terminal. Elizabeth Marina is reached by a buoyed channel from the Small Roads and, like the

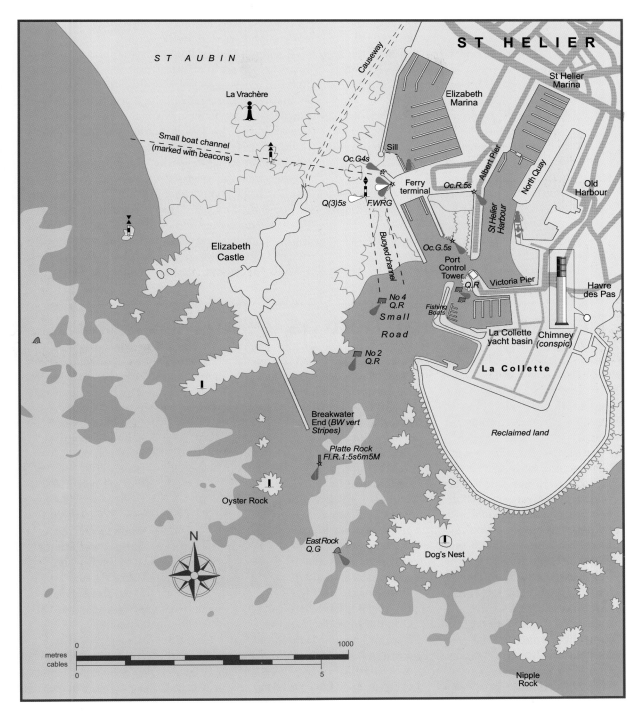

ST HELIER

ST AUBIN

Causeway

La Vrachère

Small boat channel
(marked with beacons)

Oc.G4s

Sill

Ferry
terminal

Oc.R.5s

Elizabeth
Marina

St Helier
Marina

Albert Pier

North Quay

Old
Harbour

Q(3)5s

F.WRG

Buoyed channel

Oc.G.5s

St Helier
Harbour

Elizabeth
Castle

Port
Control
Tower

Q.R

Victoria Pier

Havre
des Pas

No 4
Q.R

Small

Road

Fishing
Boats

La Collette
yacht basin

Chimney
(conspic)

No 2
Q.R

Reclaimed land

La Collette

Breakwater
End (BW vert
Stripes)

Platte Rock
Fl.R.1·5s6m5M

Oyster Rock

N

East Rock
Q.G

Dog's Nest

metres
cables

0

1000

0

5

Nipple
Rock

visitors' marina, is accessible for about three hours
each side of high water. A one-way system operates
through the relatively narrow entrance, with a set of
signal lights on each side of the entrance. These signals
operate as follows and must always be obeyed:

When the marina gate is closed, 3 red vertical
lights show on both sides of the entrance and vessels
must not proceed.

For the first ten minutes after the gate is open, three
green lights show on the inside while three red lights

still show on the outside, allowing boats to leave the
marina during this period but not enter. Boats
waiting to enter must wait in the holding area near
the waiting buoys until the exiting period has
finished.

There follows a one-minute separation period,
with three red lights showing on both sides of the gate
– no boat must leave or enter against the red lights.

Then three green lights appear on the outside,
with three red lights still showing on the inside –

boats can then enter but not leave. This 10 minute, one minute, 10 minute sequence continues until closing time, when a warning siren sounds as the gate is coming up. When the sill gate is closed, three red vertical lights again show on both sides of the entrance.

Whenever possible, avoid entering or leaving Elizabeth Marina during the first hour after opening, as the current can be powerful through and near the entrance at that time, reaching a good four knots over the sill at springs.

Yachts waiting for sufficient rise of tide to enter Elizabeth Marina can either moor in La Collette basin or use one of the yellow holding buoys near the entrance to the buoyed approach channel, just outside the west breakwater. A repeater for the Elizabeth Marina signal lights – a single red or a single green – is mounted on the west breakwater, conveniently placed for the holding buoys.

Elizabeth Marina has berths for more than 560 boats, which are available to non-residents on one, five and ten-year leases. Monthly rates are also available, which can be useful if you plan to deliver your boat down to Jersey from the UK and then leave her there for a while before returning to start a holiday cruise.

La Collette: Just outside the main harbour pierheads on the south side, La Collette is St Helier's holding basin and accessible at any state of tide by day or night. La Collette has berths for 60 visiting boats, with showers and facilities ashore. You enter the basin close alongside the outer pier, leaving the two red can buoys to port. If you are waiting in La Collette for one of the main marinas to open, you'll

---

Restaurants and bistros

Near the marinas: One of my favourites for lunch near the marina is **La Bastille** wine bar, perhaps after a drink in **'The Office'** next door. Also in Wharf Street is the **Belgo** bistro, specialising in moules-frites and some interesting Belgian beers (Tel: 729100). **The Wharf** pub does excellent well-priced bar lunches, opposite Belgo's on the corner of Wharf Street and Conway Street. The **Royal Yacht Hotel**, just opposite St Helier Marina next to the bus station, is always a reliable retreat, with hearty bar food and a carvery restaurant. A little further along the Weighbridge, the **Jersey Museum Bistro** is very agreeable (Tel: 510069).

O'Fados, on the Esplanade, is a sound choice for an inexpensive evening meal. **Banks Bistro** and wine bar is very convivial, in King Street not far from the Post Office (Tel: 759420). Also don't forget that **St Helier Yacht Club**, on South Pier, serves good food at reasonable prices in convivial surroundings.

The **Pomme d'Or Hotel**, just opposite the marina on Liberation Square, is good for breakfast (in **Le Pommier Coffee Shop**), for lunch (in the **Harbour Room Carvery**) or for dinner (in the Harbour Room Carvery or **La Petite Pomme** restaurant – Tel: 880110). **The Sailor's Rest Café,** on the quay just opposite the head of the pontoons, turns out an excellent value breakfast from early in the morning.

Further into St Helier: **The Original Wine Bar**, near the Odeon Cinema in Bath Street, is a convivial haunt for locals working in St Helier (871119). This is one of my favourite Channel Island bistros, with a comfortably clubby atmosphere, good food and wines, and restful armchairs and sofas. Food served only on weekday lunchtimes.

If you have just one evening out in St Helier, I would make for **Nelson's Eye**, overlooking the beach at Havre des Pas (Tel: 875176). Excellent seafood, but also first class if you fancy some red meat. From St Helier marina, walk through the road tunnel and turn right at the roundabout (down Green Street) for Havre des Pas.

From La Collette basin, cut through south of Mount Bingham. Best to book.

Out of town: If you fancy a taxi ride away from St Helier, it's worth the trip out to **Longueville Manor** at St Saviour (Tel: 725501). An excellent Michelin rated restaurant in a splendid 13th century manor house.

In the opposite direction, St Aubin village, on the west side of St Aubin's Bay, is a pleasant spot for an evening out. My favourite here is **La Barca** on the waterfront, a very agreeable Italian restaurant with a view over the harbour. Best to book (Tel: 744275).

At the south end of the harbour, **The Old Court House Inn** (Bergerac's regular haunt) is also a good bet, especially for lunch (best to book in the evenings – Tel: 745103).

Picturesque Rozel harbour, on the north-east corner of Jersey. Bilge-keelers can dry out here on firm sand in quiet weather

probably be shepherded in at the right time by one of the Port Control dories.

St Aubin: This delightful harbour on the west side of St Aubin Bay is used mainly by local boats and dries at about half-ebb. You should enter St Aubin within an hour either side of high water, mooring alongside the north quay wall immediately to starboard as you go in. St Aubin is interesting for a short visit on the tide or, if there's room, you can dry out on a good sandy bottom against the north quay. Close to hand is Battrick's Boatyard, the comfortable Royal Channel Islands Yacht Club, and various pubs and restaurants. The Old Court House is a good bet for supper. For a relaxing afternoon, I can recommend tea and scones at the Panorama Guest House in High Street. The sheltered garden overlooks the bay and you can choose from forty different teas!

Gorey: Despite its popularity with tourists, I always find Gorey a restful spot. The harbour, with its solid stone quays and running moorings, has a timeless salty atmosphere which offers a welcome antidote to marinas and mod cons. Bilge-keelers or yachts with legs can dry out on the firm sand if there's no swell, but don't anchor too close to local boats because the harbour bottom is a maze of ground chains. You can stay afloat at neaps at the visitors' moorings just outside the harbour entrance or anchor a little way east of the breakwater and stay

afloat at all tides if you choose your spot carefully. There are shops and several good restaurants ashore. I like the Seascale and the Mont Orgueil, but you can also get a good meal at the Galley, the Moorings Hotel and the Dolphin Hotel.

Rozel: From half a mile offshore, bring Rozel pierhead to bear 245°T and head in on this line towards the fishing boat moorings until you pick up the small red and green buoys which mark the final approach. The entrance is narrow, leaving the pierhead close to starboard and a west-cardinal spar beacon to port. Bilge-keelers or yachts with legs can dry out on firm sand in Rozel if there is no swell, anchoring fore-and-aft a little to the west of the local boats and facing the quay as they do.

You can stay afloat outside Rozel, clear of the fishing boat moorings, although an uneasy scend usually finds its way in near high water. One sound reason for stopping overnight is to sample the cooking either at Le Couperon de Rozel or at the Granite Corner. The latter is notable if you can get in, but the dining room is intentionally small and it's best to book ahead.

Bouley Bay: Just 1½ miles west of Rozel, the small pier harbour at the head of Bouley Bay shelters a few local fishing boats which take the ground at low water. The anchorage off the pierhead is snug in any winds from the south but somewhat prone to swell from the north-west.

St Helier Port Guide

(All telephone numbers below are for the Jersey STD code 01534).

Harbour control: Harbourmaster Capt Brian Nibbs, Harbour Office, Weighbridge, St Helier, Tel (01534) 885588.

VHF: St Helier Port Control Ch 14 (not the marina channel). Jersey Radio Chs 25 or 82.

Marinas: St Helier Marina (Tel: 885508); Elizabeth Marina (Tel: 885530); La Collette yacht basin (Tel: 885529).

Weather forecasts: The local forecast for the Channel Islands area is posted outside the marina offices. Comprehensive Jersey Radio forecasts on VHF Ch 25 and 82 at 0645, 0745 and 0845 local British time, then at 1245, 1845 and 2245 GMT.

Yacht Clubs: St Helier Yacht Club, South Pier, St Helier (Tel: 732229 office, 721307 bar, Fax: 720849). Royal Channel Islands Yacht Club, St Aubin (Tel: 741023).

Fuel: Diesel and petrol at the South Pier fuelling berth (Tel: 519700) in the outer harbour (available up to 4-4½ hours either side of high water within opening hours) or at the Elizabeth Marina fuel berth (Tel: 626930), just inside the entrance on the starboard hand (marina accessible 3 hours each side of high water. Good low-tax prices.

Water and power: At all marina pontoons.

Showers: At both marinas and at La Collette.

Laundrettes: In St Helier and Elizabeth Marinas. Also the McClary Laundrette at 13 Burrard Street, St Helier (Tel: 25077).

Banks with cashpoints: St Helier town centre probably has as many banks as pubs.

Post Office: In Broad Street, 10mins walk from St Helier Marina.

Tourist information: St Helier tourist office (Tel: 500777) in Liberation Square, just across the road from St Helier Marina.

Gas: From the Marina Shop or at South Pier Shipyard (Tel: 519700), next to the St Helier Yacht Club.

Chandlery: St Helier Marina Shop; South Pier Shipyard, South Pier (Tel: 519700); Channel Island Yacht Services, 8 Commercial Buildings, St Helier (Tel: 871511); IS Marine, 15-16 Commercial Buildings, St Helier (Tel: 877755); JE Marine Services, Elizabeth Marina, La Route du Port Elizabeth, St Helier (Tel: 626930).

Chart agents: South Pier Shipyard, as for 'chandlery' above.

Sail repairs: Island Yachts, St Helier (Tel: 725048); Jackson Yacht Services, Le Boulevard, St Aubin (Tel: 743819).

Rigging and mast repairs: South Pier Shipyard (Tel: 25077).

Repairs: South Pier Shipyard (Tel: 25077); Jackson Yacht Services, Le Boulevard, St Aubin (Tel: 743819); Battricks Boatyard, North Quay, St Aubin (Tel: 743412).

Marine engineers: D K Collins Marine Ltd, South Pier, St Helier (Tel: 732415); Fox Marine Services, Unit 4, La Folie Quay, St Helier, Tel 721312, or 744516 after hours; Bill Keating Marine Engineering Ltd, Unit 3, La Folie Quay, St Helier (Tel: 733977).

Electronics: Jersey Marine Electronics, Unit 2, La Folie Quay, St Helier (Tel: 721603); Marine and Vehicle Electrics Ltd (contact Steve Bottomley), Lowland Cottage, St Catherine's Hill, St Martin (Tel: 853717 or mobile 07797 716853): Auto Electric Ltd, 5-7 Byron Road, St Helier (Tel: 730311).

Yacht guardiennage: If you plan to leave your boat in St Helier for a month or two, it can be useful to employ a local agent to keep an eye on things and check the warps and fenders periodically. Contact either: Bill Hibbs Marine Ltd (Tel: 725526) or Channel Islands Marine Ltd at St Helier Marina (Tel: 767595).

Shopping: St Helier town centre is close to the marina, and you can buy groceries at all hours at the Marina Shop (Tel: 736955).

Bike hire: Zebra Cycle Hire, 9 Esplanade, St Helier (Tel: 736556). Also Jersey Cycle Tours at St Mary (Tel: 482898) who will deliver bikes to the marina.

Car hire: Holiday Autos, 77 Don Road, St Helier, but also on Albert Pier (Tel: 888700).

Taxis: At the rank next to the bus station, opposite Liberation Square, or phone 'Hail a Cab' on 629600.

Air and ferry connections: Jersey airport is 40 minutes from St Helier marina by bus and 20 minutes by taxi. There are flights to almost every UK airport and most European capitals.
From St Helier harbour there are regular fast ferries to and from Poole, Guernsey and St Malo.

Local boats dried out at Gorey harbour

Bonne Nuit Bay: A couple of miles W of Bouley Bay, Bonne Nuit Bay also has a small pier harbour. Give Belle Houge Point and Les Sambues rocks a wide berth on the way round and avoid Cheval Rock (dries 10.1m and shows at most states of tide) on the final approach to Bonne Nuit.

Beau Port: An attractive anchorage on the W side of St Brelade Bay, sheltered in winds with north in them and a good spot for an easy day trip in the boat from St Helier. Approach from the SSE using Admiralty Chart 1137, steering to leave Grosse Tête rock on the W side of Beau Port a cable to port. Near low water, avoid Fournier Rock (dries 0.3m) which lies 2 cables S of Beau Port.

FACILITIES AT ST HELIER

Elizabeth Marina has all the facilities you'd expect of a modern yacht harbour. The fuel berth is just inside the entrance on the starboard hand and the chandler is near the marina office and showers on the east side of the marina.

St Helier visitors marina has power and water at the pontoons, excellent showers and a handy marina shop where you can buy basic stores and wines at all hours. There's a scrubbing grid in the north-east corner of the basin. South Pier Shipyard, 15 minutes walk from the marina, have an excellent chandlery shop and comprehensive repair facilities. They are also chart agents and operate the fuelling berth just opposite the harbour entrance, which has sufficient

water for 3-4 hours either side of high tide. There are marine engineers at La Folie, halfway along the road between the marina and South Pier Shipyard. St Helier Yacht Club, just above the fuelling berth, welcomes visiting yachtsmen and serves excellent bar meals.

St Helier town centre is only a short walk from the visitors' marina, with a wide range of shops and restaurants. The bus station and taxi rank are just opposite the marina in Caledonia Place. You should allow forty minutes to the airport by bus and twenty minutes by taxi. The ferry terminals are on the south-west side of the harbour near the entrance.

A DAY AWAY

Ashore: There is plenty to occupy the family ashore if you linger in St Helier for a few days. The award-winning Maritime Museum on New North Quay, next to St Helier Marina, is a magnificent celebration of the sea and Jersey's colourful nautical heritage. The Jersey Museum is also handy for the marina, up at the Weighbridge. The sports facilities and swimming pool up at Fort Regent are excellent, especially for keeping an active family occupied.

Remember that you can hire a car cheaply and easily in St Helier (don't forget your driving licence) for an excursion of the island. Any of the small harbours I have mentioned are interesting to visit by

St Aubin harbour near high water

land, and you get a good view of the west coast by driving out to Corbière point. Some local attractions particularly worth visiting are the Jersey Pottery (good for a light lunch), the Jersey Lavender Farm, the German Underground Hospital (more intriguing than it sounds), La Mare Vineyard (which makes its own wine and cider), and the famous Jersey Zoo out at Trinity, established by the naturalist Gerald Durrell in the magnificent grounds of an old Jersey manor.

Around the island: You can enjoy some interesting day cruising around Jersey, which many visitors miss in their enthusiasm to reach France or their haste to return to England at the end of a holiday. There is much to be said for allowing a few days to savour Jersey's spectacular coast and sample one or two of its smaller harbours and anchorages.

St Helier Marina visitors' pontoons are handy for the town

A day trip to Les Écrehou:
From Gorey, it is worth taking a day out to visit Les Écrehou if the weather looks settled. This tiny archipelago is officially part of the Jersey parish of St Martin. The main islet, Marmotière, harbours a cluster of small cottages once inhabited by fishermen and now leased by a select group of local yachtsmen for summer use. Much of the surrounding plateau dries at low water, with individual outcrops merging into a fascinating maze of narrow channels, rocky pools, seaweed and sand. It's best to arrive off Les Écrehou at half-tide down, when there is plenty of water in the approaches but enough of the key rocks exposed to make them easily visible. Leave Gorey two hours after HW if you can average 5 knots. The tide will be setting strongly north-westwards, so allow carefully for this set during the short passage across to Maître Ile.

The approach to Les Écrehou is from the SSW, leaving Maître Ile to port. From a position where Maître Ile bears 005°T, just over a mile off, bring Bigorne rock between La Grande Galère and La Sablonière rocks bearing 022°T. The tip of Bigorne looks like a large inverted tooth at or above half-tide, whereas the other two seem much flatter. Follow this transit until you are about $\frac{1}{2}$ mile from Bigorne and then alter to the north-west to keep the white flagstaff on Marmotière in line with two vertical black marks bearing 330°T. This transit leads to the anchorage south-east of Marmotière.

LES ÉCREHOU

On a clear day, from the high cliffs at the NE tip of Jersey, it almost looks as though you could heave a line across the dozen tide-troubled miles to the Normandy mainland, or at least reach the small plateau of reefs known as Les Écrehou, midway between Jersey and Carteret. This miniature

archipelago is officially part of Jersey's parish of St Martin. The central islet, Marmotière, harbours a cluster of stone cottages once used by fishermen and now leased by a select band of local yachtsmen as summer retreats. Maître Ile, the largest islet, lies a quarter of a mile south of Marmotière. Its only man-made features are a post beacon and a solitary cottage built from the ruins of a much larger house. Its only occupants are densely packed colonies of sea birds.

There's a slip on the north side of Marmotière, from which you can scramble up between the closely packed cottages, most of them not much larger than beach huts. The view from the highest rock near the flagstaff is strangely unreal. It feels odd to be standing on such a tenuous vantage point and seeing Jersey, Normandy and, to the NW, the distinctive outline of Sark, all at the same time. Close to the north is Blanche Ile, connected with Marmotière by a shingle bank that covers at high water. Blanche Ile has a couple of small buildings of its own. To the west are more reefs; first Les Dirouilles and then, five miles beyond them, the low black teeth of the Paternosters.

Near high tide, the frail looking settlement on Les Écrehou seems to huddle more tightly as most of the terra firma vanishes. But as the ebb drops away, individual outcrops merge into a fascinating maze

of narrow channels, rocky pools, seaweed and sand. On a low spring in the Écrehou, the tiny cottages on Marmotière perch far above the anchorage like a fortress and your boat lies perfectly sheltered in an almost landlocked lagoon. Then you can take the dinghy ashore in almost any direction and wander among fascinating reefs, untouched stretches of sand, limpid rock-pools and winding channels which, only a few hours before, were submerged under megatons of fast-moving water.

The tranquillity of the place is truly restful, perhaps more so for knowing that the idyll is predictably temporary. You can reckon on maybe three hours of complete peace – an hour and a half each side of low – before fingers of tide start creeping back among the reefs. Then the channels steadily widen and spill over to join small pools into larger pools, and large pools into sounds. It's time to recover your dinghy and get back on board before the stream works up to its full four or five knots through the main body of reefs. Then it's up anchor and off again. Very soon, only the highest heads will be left above the cold run of the tide, with a few slicks and whirlpools as ominous clues to the dangers below.

TIMING THE TIDES

The rise and fall at Les Écrehou is $9\frac{1}{2}$ metres at mean springs and $4\frac{1}{2}$ metres at neaps. The stream runs NW

The Écrehou anchorage close south-east of Marmotière

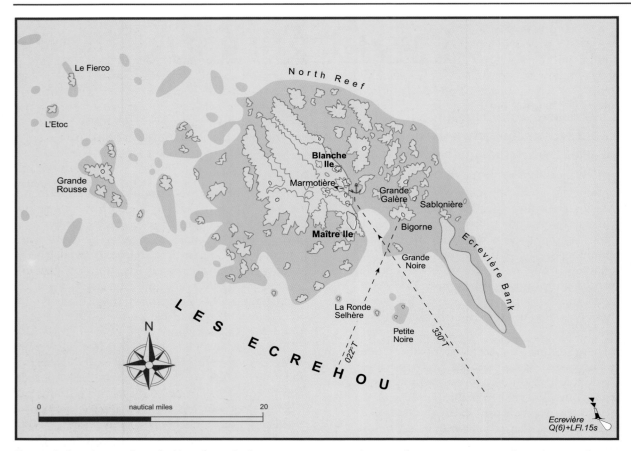

Le Fierco

L'Etoc

Grande
Rousse

North Reef

Blanche
Ile

Marmotière

Grande
Galère

Sablonière

Maître Ile

Bigorne

Grande
Noire

Ecrevière Bank

La Ronde
Selhère

Petite
Noire

022°T

330°T

N

L E S   É C R E H O U

0   nautical miles   20

Ecrevière
Q(6)+LFl.15s

through the plateau from half-an-hour before HW St Helier until half-an-hour before low water, and then SE from low water St Helier until half-an-hour before high water. The streams are at their strongest at half-ebb and half-flood, sometimes reaching $4\frac{1}{2}$-5 knots at springs in the approaches to Les Écrehou but more like 6-7 knots locally in the Sound close east of Marmotière.

Although neaps make for easier navigation, it's more interesting to visit Les Écrehou near springs, when you can explore ashore for an hour or so either side of an afternoon low water. You should only consider Les Écrehou on a quiet day, with a settled forecast and no swell. Marmotière affords only minimal protection near high water, when the sea surges uneasily across the covered reefs. As the tide falls, however, the anchorages become almost landlocked, with only a south-easterly able to penetrate with any persistence.

A good time for a day trip is two or three days after a moderate spring i.e. just as the tides are taking off. This gives you a civilised start from Jersey and an afternoon low with plenty of rocky interest. Gorey harbour, on Jersey's east coast, is usually the best place from which to start and finish a day trip. In this case, you should plan to leave Les Écrehou again by half-flood. The strong SSE stream through the Sound will carry you quickly down past Maître Ile,

so make sure that you turn to starboard in good time to line up the outer transit.

APPROACHES AND ENTRY

Although Les Écrehou seem fairly compact on the chart, most of the outer rocks are covered at high tide and you need to get your bearings before coming too close. The streams can reach $4\frac{1}{2}$-5 knots between Jersey and the French coast, and are stronger through the reefs, especially in the Sound just east of Marmotière. You can only approach Les Écrehou by day. Gorey, that pleasant drying harbour on Jersey's east coast, makes a convenient point of departure. Leave Gorey two hours after local high water if you average five knots, allowing carefully for the strong set to the NNW. Aim to arrive $1\frac{1}{2}$ miles south by west of Maître Ile at about half-ebb, when there's plenty of water in the approach channel but enough of the key rocks exposed to make them clearly visible.

The cottages and flagstaff on Marmotière are the most easily identified features from a couple of miles off, but they merge behind Maître Ile as you draw nearer. Maître Ile has a beacon at its highest point. About half a mile ENE of Maître Ile, three above-water rocks – Bigorne (5m high), Sablonière (2m high) and Grande Galère (4m high) – provide the first leading marks into the plateau. The narrow

Écrevière Bank stretches SE from these rocks for more than a mile, with Écrevière S-cardinal buoy another mile beyond its tip. There are various above-water rocks on the W side of Les Écrehou, of which the outlier is Grande Rousse (8m high), two miles W of Marmotière. The two above-water rocks of Les Dirouilles group – Les Burons and Frouquie – are a couple of miles W of Grande Rousse.

Don't pass the outer waypoint i.e. 1½ miles south by west of Maître Ile, before lining up the first set of marks – Bigorne rock, four cables east of Maître Ile, brought between Grande Galère and Sablonière rocks behind it bearing 022°T or a shade over. Bigorne looks like a large inverted tooth jutting out of the water. Grande Galère and Sablonière have a much flatter profile and appear as a matching pair at half-tide.

Follow this transit NNE, allowing for cross-tide. Don't stray south of a line with Bigorne midway between Grande Galère and Sablonière, since this will bring you very close to La Ronde Selhère (dries 2.7m) and La Petite Noire (dries 4.8m). You can err to port until Bigorne touches the north edge of Sablonière. When half a mile from Bigorne, locate the second set of marks before they come on – Marmotière flagstaff in line with a vertical black board behind it bearing 330°T. A white-painted rock below the flagstaff makes the transit easy to pick out. Stay exactly on these marks until within two cables of Marmotière and then borrow slightly to the east to clear the drying ledges which extend northward from Maître Ile.

MOORINGS AND ANCHORAGES

There is an outer anchorage close SE of Marmotière and an inner anchorage in a shallow pool a little way WSW of Marmotière. The outer area has a large 'States of Jersey' mooring buoy which you can use if vacant, and a couple of smaller moorings laid by local yachtsmen. There are also several private moorings in the pool. When using the outer anchorage, tuck well under the south side of Marmotière to avoid the powerful stream in the Sound.

The pool should only be entered within four hours of high water, or so long as Pommère rock (dries 3.2m) in the entrance is covered. To enter the pool from the outer anchorage, edge round the south and west sides of Marmotière in order to clear Le Fou and Pommère rocks (both covered within four hours of high water) before turning to port to fetch up just west of Pommère. Once into the pool, you have about 1½ metres at MLWS.

You can leave the outer anchorage at any state of tide, but most yachts will be hemmed into the pool for two hours either side of low water, until

Pommère rock has covered again. It's not safe to leave (or enter) Les Écrehou at night, since there are no lights anywhere on the plateau.

You must clear out of Les Écrehou in good time with any hint of deteriorating weather. Even on a fine summer day, keep an eye on visibility and get to sea post-haste if mist or fog looks likely. Gorey is easy to reach on the flood and well protected in any winds from the west. If you are forced to leave while the ebb is still running hard, the anchorage off Rozel harbour, on the NE corner of Jersey, may be easier to fetch than Gorey.

St Helier is 16 miles from Les Écrehou via the Violet Channel, although you really need to leave Marmotière as near half-flood as possible in order to make the best of this passage. Carteret, a restful drying harbour on the Normandy coast, lies about eight miles to the NE; it should only be entered near high water, preferably on making tides.

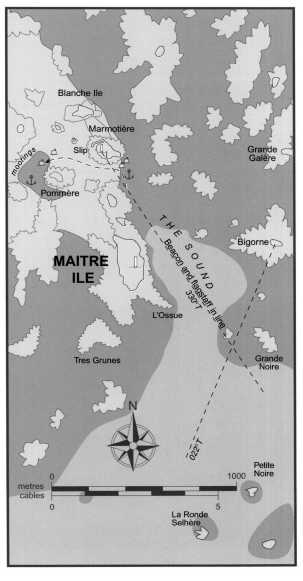

THE PLATEAU DES MINQUIERS

It's strange how some of the most sinister navigational dangers, be they notorious reefs, wreck-strewn sandbanks or vicious tide races, can exert a magnetic fascination at the same time as you are telling yourself to keep well away. You can often feel the vibes when perusing the chart, tempting you to edge up close and have a look, just to see if reality lives up to reputation. There is a nefarious expanse of reefs 10 miles south of Jersey which has this mysterious compelling aura – the Plateau des Minquiers, often known as the Minkies.

A glance at the Channel Islands chart reveals that the total extent of the Minkies is almost as large as Jersey itself, with the main drying areas of sand and rock comprising some 25 square miles. The extremities of the plateau are guarded by cardinal buoys, and the only rock high enough to count as an islet is Maître Ile, near the eastern edge of the reefs.

For years there was dispute between Britain and France over the sovereignty of the Minkies, but in 1953 the International Court at The Hague resolved the matter in favour of Britain. Since then, all the buoys have been maintained by the States of Jersey and the half dozen old fishermen's cottages on Maîtresse Ile are leased by various Jersey families as occasional summer retreats.

If you happen to be lying in St Helier Marina during a quiet settled spell when visibility is reasonable, it can be interesting to venture down to the Maîtresse Ile anchorage for a day trip – so long as you appreciate the potential dangers of the operation. A good time to arrive off the Minkies is at half-ebb, when there's still plenty of depth over many of the deeper rocks and shoals but you are starting to feel the benefit of the natural breakwaters that the larger reefs provide as the sea level falls. To approach Maîtresse Ile from the north, you first have to find Demie de Vascelin green conical buoy,

Approaching Maîtresse Ile from northward

The cottages on Maîtresse Ile

which is moored off the northern edge of the plateau about 8 miles at 175°M from St Helier's Demie de Pas S-cardinal beacon tower.

Useful steering marks in good visibility are the tall power station chimney in line with Demie de Pas once you have cleared the Eastern Passage out of St Helier. The back-bearing of this transit is 351°T and it leads to a position $\frac{1}{2}$ mile east of the Demie de Vascelin. When you spot the buoy, aim to leave it close to the west, allowing for the stream which will be sluicing across your track at up to four knots near springs. Maîtresse Ile, dead ahead, seems rather an insubstantial destination from four miles away. Other rocks should come into view on the starboard bow, perhaps just lifting above the horizon in a slight swell. You begin to feel the graveyard atmosphere which permeates the Minkies even when the sun is shining, a sensation well-known to generations of local sailors and fishermen.

From Demie de Vascelin, you need to pick up the first pair of leading marks – Jetée des Fontaines de Bas red-and-white striped beacon in line with the tall flag-staff in the centre of Maîtresse Ile at 161°T. If you can't identify the transit straightaway, steer to

Maîtresse Ile seen from the west

approach Maîtresse Ile on this bearing, keeping the green buoy at 341°T astern and compensating for the strong cross-tide. There will be rocks to starboard now as far as you can see, with evil patches of overfalls on both sides where hitherto unseen dangers are starting to surface. You should just be able to make out the silhouette of the cottages on Maîtresse Ile.

A couple of cables from Jetée des Fontaines, turn to starboard towards Grune Tar white beacon before coming back to the SSE on a second transit – a spar beacon with two balls and a white beacon behind it

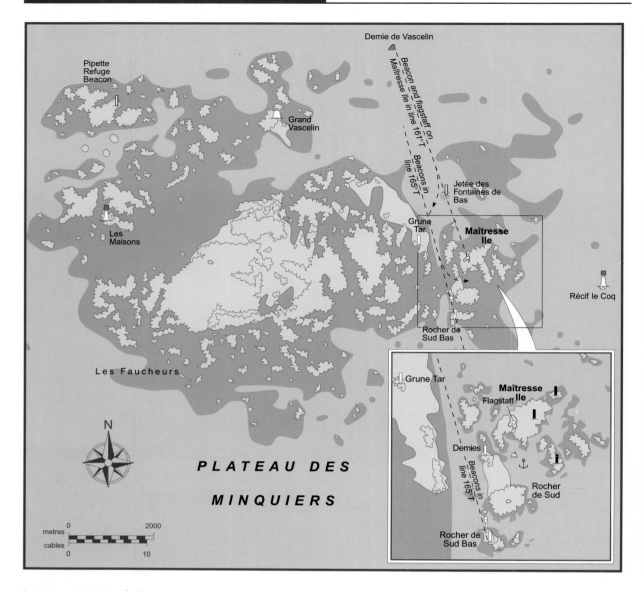

bearing 165°T. Both these marks are built on Rocher du Sud Bas and it's important to have them lined up before passing Grune Tar. You soon appreciate this by the proximity of a swirling tide rip to starboard as you shave within 50 yards of a gravel bank. Follow this second transit for three quarters of a mile before swinging to port past the Demies beacon to enter the anchorage. The States of Jersey maintain a heavy-duty mooring here for their buoyage tender, but you can make fast to one of the smaller yacht moorings.

There is a landing slip just below Maîtresse Ile's huddle of cottages and it's usually safe to go ashore when Rocher Nord-Est is sufficiently exposed to protect the slip from any surge outside. Up behind the cottages is a helicopter landing pad, an austere vantage point from which you can appreciate the full extent of this haunted seascape.

It's an eerie experience to be quite alone amidst 25 square miles of tide-swept rock, sand and weed. On a clear day, Jersey stands out sharply to the north. Off to the west, the main expanse of reefs will be uncovering fast, the powerful ebb pouring through a maze of narrowing channels. The several isolated beacon towers, far from being reassuring, are starkly reminiscent of headstones: Les Maisons, Grand Vascelin, Pipette Refuge Beacon – RIP. You can see Iles Chausey to the south-east, Cap Fréhel to the south-west, and between them the Brittany coast and the Rance estuary. Down in the anchorage, your boat should be lying quietly, increasingly protected by Rocher Nord-Est as the sea drains away. If you have only a moderate draught and conditions still look settled, you can stay in the anchorage through low water and leave again at about half-flood, following the above directions carefully in the reverse order.

CHAPTER 3

PASSAGES
BETWEEN NORTH BRITTANY AND THE CHANNEL ISLANDS

THE ALDERNEY RACE

This somewhat notorious stretch of water between Alderney and the north-west corner of the Cherbourg Peninsula is about eight miles wide between Cap de la Hague and Quenard Point, the east tip of Alderney. The potential malevolence of the Race derives from a combination of locally very strong tidal streams and an uneven sea-bed. The streams can reach eight or nine knots at peak springs in parts of the Race, and often touch six or seven knots at ordinary springs. Although the various rocky shoals and banks to the south and east of Alderney and west of Cap de la Hague have plenty of water over them for navigation, they can cause nasty areas of overfalls on the surface, which are accentuated when the tide is weather-going.

The Alderney race is therefore one of those passage 'gateways' at which you must always time your arrival carefully, both to carry the stream in your favour and to avoid the worst of the overfalls.

When bound south through the Alderney Race, the best time to arrive at a position two miles NW of Cap de la Hague is $4\frac{1}{2}$ hours after HW St Helier (or about half-an-hour before HW Dover). It is then slack water in the Race, but the SW-going

Looking north across The Swinge in quiet conditions

stream will be just about to start in your favour. Coming north through the Race, most yachts will have carried a fair-tide up from Guernsey or Jersey and need to arrive off Quenard Point no later than four hours after HW St Helier (an hour before HW Dover).

When holiday cruising down to the Channel Islands from the south coast of England, many yachts cross to Cherbourg first. It's then fairly easy to time the short passage from Cherbourg to the Race to best advantage. You can reckon about 14 miles from Cherbourg west entrance to the Cap de la Hague waypoint so, with a five knot cruising speed, you should leave the west entrance 1½ hours after HW St Helier i.e. at 3½ hours before HW Dover, aiming to cast off from the marina half-an-hour before that.

Now at 3½ hours before HW Dover, the main English Channel stream is still east-going, and will be for the next 3 hours. However, a west-going eddy runs close inshore between Cherbourg and Cap de la Hague, starting about 3 hours before HW Dover off Cherbourg and much earlier further west. It's important to use this favourable current rather than wait for the main ebb, otherwise: (a) you'll arrive in the Alderney Race when the stream is at its strongest and the overfalls at their most boisterous, and (b) if you are heading for

St Peter Port on Guernsey, you won't reach the Little Russel channel before the tide turns foul again. In westerly weather it may be preferable to leave Cherbourg even earlier than 3½ hours before HW Dover, to allow for working to windward and so as to arrive in the Race while the stream is still trickling north. This will help minimise your exposure to the most critical wind-over-tide conditions.

From Cherbourg's Fort de l'Ouest, head fairly close along the coast towards Pointe de Jardeheu. A track of 292°T for 8½ miles takes you to Basse Bréfort N-cardinal buoy, which marks the end of a rocky ledge extending three quarters of a mile north of Jardeheu. About 3½ miles along this line you will leave Bannes Rocks N-cardinal beacon tower half a mile to the south. This tower stands at the NE corner of quite a wide plateau of shoals and so, when tacking westwards, you should not stand in within a mile of the shore until the Bannes tower is itself one mile east of your own longitude. Once up with the Basse Bréfort buoy, make good 288°T for four miles to a position about 1¾ miles north of the tall Gros du Raz lighthouse; this course should leave the smaller La Plate light-tower a good half mile to the south.

Now alter course to just south of west, steering, if you can see it, for Quenard Point at the east tip of

The sleepy English charm of Alderney's Victoria Street

Alderney. Assuming you have arrived at the best time of tide, the trick is to head towards Quenard Point but then allow the first of the SW-going stream to suck you into the Race. This should allow you to pass well to the north of a sometimes heavy patch of overfalls lying about 3½-4 miles W by S from Gros du Raz. The best line through the Race usually lies 2-2½ miles south of, and roughly parallel with, the south coast of Alderney. Another heavy area of overfalls often builds up over Alderney South Banks, which this track should leave a mile or so to the north.

At springs, and following the line just described, the SW-going stream will accelerate you through the Race and past the south coast of Alderney at anything from 2½ to about 6 knots more than your sailing speed, depending on how long after slack water you make the passage. Peak spring rates can exceed 9 knots locally, but this alarming maximum is usually only attained an hour or so after HW St Helier (4 hours before HW Dover) at a position between 2-3 miles SW of Gros du Raz lighthouse.

When deciding whether or not to make a passage through the Race, bear in mind that a moderate wind against the tide will have a marked effect on sea conditions. The Race can be taken at night in reasonable visibility, but the navigator will have a busy time keeping a track of your position when the speed over the ground might easily exceed 10 knots. Remember, also, that the psychological effect of any overfalls will be that much greater when you can't see them coming. Sailing through overfalls at night is always an eerie business, even if you think you know exactly where you are. There's always that uneasy feeling of doubt when you hear the hissing of breaking water at night, and your imagination can soon conjure up dangerous reefs and banks just below the surface dead ahead, despite the confident GPS display or the reassuring cocked-hat from a good set of bearings.

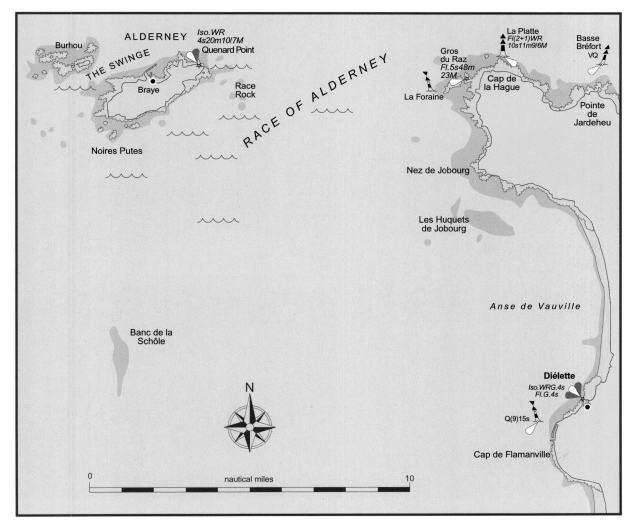

Platte Fougère lighthouse is the key mark at the north end of the Little Russel

ALDERNEY RACE TO GUERNSEY

Once you are clear of Alderney, the tide will continue to help you towards Guernsey at up to 3½knots at springs, with the best of the stream running from six hours after to four hours before HW St Helier. So if you have slipped past Quenard Point more or less according to plan

at around 5½ hours after HW St Helier, and maintained an average speed of 5 knots, you can expect to be approaching the Little Russel channel only 2 hours later at springs, perhaps 2½ hours at neaps.

THE LITTLE RUSSEL

The Little Russel lies between the NE tip of Guernsey and the 3-mile stretch of drying rocks which string out NE from the north end of Herm.

The most northerly of these dangers are unmarked – Platte Boue (which dries 1.8 metres) and Boufresse (dries 3.4 metres). Platte Boue, the outer of these two, lies three quarters of a mile NNW of Grande Amfroque (17 metres high), a small islet which in turn lies just over two miles NE of Herm. Grande Amfroque has two beacons built on it, one white and one black-and-white; their transit leads across Platte Boue as a danger line, bearing about 151°T from seaward.

Platte beacon, on the west side of the Little Russel (this and following photos in section 3.2 by Peter McMahon)

Corbette d'Amont yellow beacon, about half a mile NW of Roustel on the west side of the Little Russel

Roustel beacon tower in line with Bréhon fort

On the Guernsey side of the Little Russel, Platte Fougère lighthouse lies not quite a mile NE of Fort Doyle, the island's NE tip. When approaching the Little Russel from the direction of Alderney, it is best to hold a track which heads towards Platte Fougère on about 230°T. This line clears Platte Boue by a good 1¼ miles and makes for a safer landfall than that provided by the Herm side of the Russel. Platte Fougère lighthouse is conspicuous from seaward in good visibility, white with a black horizontal stripe.

When you are about 1½ miles NE of Platte Fougère, steer SSW into the Little Russel, keeping Roustel beacon tower in line with Bréhon fort behind it, bearing 198°T. This part of the channel can be subject to steep overfalls if the tide is weather-going. When a couple of cables from Roustel, make good 220°T to leave Roustel a cable to port, the Platte beacon 2 cables to starboard, and Bréhon fort not quite half a mile to port. Then make for Castle Cornet and St Peter Port south breakwater. Having followed these directions, and of course weather permitting, you should be arriving off St Peter Port just as the south-going tide between Guernsey and Herm is starting to ease off. This will be at about four hours before HW St Peter Port, so you'll have an hour or two to wait in the outer harbour before you can safely cross the sill into Victoria Marina.

Chapter 3

Bréhon tower, seen here from rather too close

Try to pick some quiet weather for a first passage through the Alderney Race and the Little Russel. Even quite a moderate south-westerly or southerly against a spring tide will make for hard sailing when you are trying to concentrate on marks and bearings. If, however, you are through the Race and the wind draws ahead and freshens, you can either bear away for Jersey or continue towards Guernsey via the Big Russel, between Herm and Sark.

THE BIG RUSSEL

The Big Russel is much wider than the Little Russel and is relatively steep-to on the Sark (east) side. There are still patches of heavy overfalls on a weather-going tide, but the pilotage is much simpler and there's more room to manoeuvre. Once you are south of Herm and abreast of Brecqhou, pass to the south of the Lower Heads S-cardinal buoy and then head NW for St Peter Port.

In quiet conditions, reasonable visibility and above half-tide, there is a route to St Peter Port between Herm and Jethou, by way of the Percée Pass and Alligande Pass. When making for the Big Russel from the Alderney Race, pass N and W of the sometimes turbulent Banc de la Schôle, which lies about halfway between the two.

Vivian beacon tower is on the west side of the Little Russel, close south of St Sampson

La Corbière lighhouse, on the SW corner of Jersey

ALDERNEY RACE TO JERSEY

Most yachts bound for the Channel Islands from the south coast of England head for Guernsey after having crossed to Cherbourg, either in one hop or via Alderney. But if your cruising plans include Granville, Iles Chausey or St Malo, there is much to be said for making directly from the Alderney Race to Jersey's St Helier Marina. From here it is an easy day's sail to anywhere in the Gulf of St Malo, and the passages to the French coast are generally more sheltered than those made from Guernsey.

The best timing from Cherbourg through the Alderney Race is the same as for the passage to St Peter Port, arriving off Cap de la Hague at $4\frac{1}{2}$ hours after HW St Helier (or about half-an-hour before HW Dover). It is then slack water in the Race, but the SW-going stream will be just about to start in your favour. The line through the Race is a bit different though. Having reached a waypoint about $1\frac{3}{4}$ miles due north of Gros du Raz lighthouse, skirt round Cap de la Hague about this distance off, finally setting off due south along the west side of the Cherbourg Peninsula to leave Gros du Raz and La Foraine W-cardinal beacon tower to port.

Once abreast Nez de Jobourg and clear of the temperamental areas of the Race, the easiest route to St Helier is to set a course for the NW of Jersey and then pass west-about the island round La Corbière lighthouse. From a position two miles west of Nez de Jobourg, make good 209°T for 25 miles down to the Banc Desormes W-cardinal buoy, which lies four miles NNW of Jersey's Grosnez Point. This track leaves Blanchard E-cardinal buoy three miles to starboard and Sark itself five miles to starboard. When approaching the vicinity of Banc Desormes, be sure you are well clear of the Paternosters, a nasty plateau of drying and above-water rocks 2-3 miles NE of Grosnez Point.

When sailing down the west coast of Jersey, keep outside Rigdon Bank and a good mile west of La Corbière lighthouse. There are drying rocks up to half a mile W and NW of Corbière, so don't turn along the south coast of Jersey until Noirmont Point light-tower bears less than 097°T. The Western Passage to St Helier is straightforward and well-marked. By keeping up an average of five knots from the Alderney Race, you should carry a fair tide all the way to St Helier, arriving near high water.

PASSAGES TO CARTERET

Many yachtsmen are only familiar with the two extremities of the west coast of the Cotentin Peninsula – the north tip around Cap de la Hague, often glimpsed in passing as you are sucked through the Alderney Race, and Granville's Hérel marina at the south end. However, Diélette marina is only a dozen miles south of Cap de la Hague, and the attractive marina at Carteret lies only 15 miles north-east of Jersey's Gorey harbour. The shallow approaches to Carteret can be rough even in quite moderate onshore winds, so choose quiet conditions or a spell of easterlies for a first visit.

FROM GUERNSEY

St Peter Port to Carteret is 30 miles. With the Victoria Marina access about $2\frac{1}{2}$ hours each side of HW and the Carteret window much the same, you'll need to leave St Peter Port from the outer harbour. Aim to arrive off Carteret an hour before HW there.

A convenient time to leave St Peter Port is a couple of hours before low water, when the Little Russel tide is south-going. Make for the Lower Heads buoy south of Jethou and then for a waypoint three-quarters of a mile SW of L'Étac, the southern tip of Sark. The broadly south-west going stream will help keep you off the dangers around this corner of Sark.

From L'Étac to Carteret is 23 miles, just south of east. The tide will be more or less south-going, slackening off two hours before HW. Five miles west of Carteret, a W-cardinal buoy marks Plateau des Trois Grunes, whose southern edge dries 1.6m. This shoal is no problem near HW, when you can use the buoy as a landfall waypoint and then steer for a position half-a-mile south of Cap Carteret.

FROM SARK

A passage from one of the Sark anchorages simply means leaving at the right time to arrive off Carteret an hour before HW. Dixcart Bay, on the south side of Sark, is a convenient departure point if conditions are OK for lying there.

FROM JERSEY

A direct passage to Carteret from St Helier round the SE corner of Jersey can be tricky to time. It's usually best to leave from one of the fine-weather anchorages off the east coast of the island – off Gorey perhaps, or St Catherine Bay. From St Catherine to Carteret is just 13 miles via L'Écrevière buoy.

FROM THE ALDERNEY RACE

Given that one is usually trying to pass the Alderney Race near slack water, a direct passage down to Carteret is almost impossible to time to advantage. Coming from Cherbourg, the best strategy is to slip round Cap de la Hague on the last of the south-west going tide, tuck into Diélette (just 12 miles south of La Hague) and go on to Carteret next day.

Carteret marina is perfectly snug and is now one of the most popular ports of call in the Channel Islands area

CHANNEL ISLANDS TO BRITTANY

Skippers making a Brittany cruise by way of the Channel Islands often find they begin to relax and feel that their holiday has really started once they've arrived safely at Guernsey's St Peter Port or Jersey's St Helier. From either of these secure and convenient marinas, a fascinating range of cruising lies close to hand, subject to wind, weather and tide, and how far you feel like travelling each day. Given the time, it can be pleasant to spend a while day-sailing from St Peter Port, exploring various anchorages off the nearby islands of Herm and Sark and, indeed, around Guernsey itself. If you are keen to press on for France, there are three useful passages starting from St Peter Port:

- A short hop to Jersey, bringing you within easy reach of Iles Chausey, Granville, Cancale or St Malo.
- A somewhat longer haul SSE straight to St Malo.
- A day passage SW to Lézardrieux or Tréguier, which leaves you well placed to continue west along the Brittany coast or to cruise east towards St Malo and home via Granville or Chausey.

With St Helier now well-endowed with marina facilities, many English yachts make for Jersey direct from Cherbourg, without calling at Guernsey first. The scope for local sailing out of St Helier is not so varied as from Peter Port, but you have a choice of fairly straightforward day passages to Chausey, Granville, Cancale or St Malo, or a more open leg WSW to Lézardrieux.

ST PETER PORT TO ST HELIER

This inter-island trip is 25 miles from pierhead to pierhead. If you average five knots, a good time to leave St Peter Port is soon after low water, which will mean coming out of the Victoria Marina within a couple of hours of high and waiting outside in the pool, either alongside the marina holding pontoon or moored between two of the large visitors' buoys.

The main part of this passage, from just outside St Peter Port harbour to a position a mile due west of La Corbière lighthouse, involves making good 150°T for 19 miles. The tide will be setting S and then SSW in the first hour, S in the second hour, SSE in the third hour and SE as you approach Corbière. With a fair wind and the more or less favourable stream, you ought to arrive off Corbière within 3½ hours of leaving St Peter Port, and probably a bit earlier at springs. There should then be plenty of fair tide in hand for the last six miles to St Helier.

The reason for staying a mile off Corbière is to give a safe berth to the various drying rocks which extend W and NW from that headland. But once Noirmont Point light-tower (3½ miles ESE of Corbière on the

The St Peter Port skyline is one of the most attractive landfalls in Europe

Le Grand Jardin lighthouse at the entrance to St Malo

Roches Douvres lighthouse, seen rather closer than you would normally pass it on passage between Guernsey and Lézardrieux

Approaching the old skyline of St Malo

south coast of Jersey) bears about 095°T, you should make good in that direction, allowing at first for the strongish SE-going stream which will be trying to set you southward until you are well east of Corbière and tucked under the coast.

The Western Passage to St Helier leads four cables N of Passage Rock N-cardinal buoy and then between Noirmont Point light-tower and the Four N-cardinal buoy. From here make good 082°T for not quite two miles towards the end of Elizabeth breakwater (which is marked by black-and-white stripes) leaving Raudière green conical buoy close to starboard and two red cans to port. Pass between La Platte red lattice beacon (off the end of Elizabeth breakwater) and East Rock green conical buoy before turning NNE into the Small Roads towards St Helier harbour entrance.

ST PETER PORT TO ST MALO

The direct passage from St Peter Port to St Malo is a longish leg of 55 miles, which takes you seven miles west of Jersey and then west-about the notorious Plateau des Minquiers, known colloquially as the Minkies. You skirt the Minkies soon after the midway point of the passage, leaving the NW Minkies buoy about half a mile to the east and then the SW Minkies buoy close to the east. The NW and SW Minkies buoys are just over five miles apart.

Having reached and identified the SW Minkies buoy, alter to the SE to make good 150°T for 15 miles towards the St Malo fairway buoy.

There's often much to be said for a night passage, aiming to set off from St Peter Port at around 1700. In good visibility, bearings from the powerful lighthouses of La Corbière, Roches Douvres and Cap Fréhel give a good cut near the NW Minkies buoy, which you must be sure of leaving well to the east. The NW and SW Minkies buoys are both lit and it's useful to sail fairly close to the SW Minkies buoy to take a new departure for St Malo. You should be able to identify lights on the French coast as you make your landfall, but the final approach to St Malo can be timed for soon after dawn. The Chenal de la Petite Porte is the natural entrance channel when coming from this direction, but the Chenal de la Grande Porte is better if you make your landfall much further west than the St Malo fairway buoy.

Cruising at an average of five knots, this passage spans two tides, so your departure time from St Peter Port will probably be determined as much by your own schedule as by the streams. However, it is useful to have a south-going run in the Little Russel when you leave, and to have a slack or west-going stream when passing the Minkies. You can achieve these objectives by leaving St Peter Port about an

La Chambre anchorage off the SE corner of Ile de Bréhat

hour after local low water, arriving off the NW Minkies near high water.

ST PETER PORT TO LÉZARDRIEUX OR TRÉGUIER

A direct line from the SW tip of Guernsey to the outer marks of the Lézardrieux River is something like 35 miles to the SSW. Unfortunately, the extensive rocky plateau of Roches Douvres lies right in the way, so your passage will consist of a dog's-leg on one side or the other. About 4½ miles south of Roches Douvres is a much smaller patch of drying rocks, Plateau de Barnouic, which has a shallow bank, the Banc du Moulec, a couple of miles to the WNW. The tide runs strongly in the vicinity of all these dangers and the navigator's problem is to skirt them by a safe distance while staying close enough to take advantage of the marks. My own strategy is usually to pass Roches Douvres down-tide with plenty of room to spare. When sailing west-about, I prefer to view the gaunt stone lighthouse from a distance of at least three miles.

The Roches Douvres plateau is about two miles wide from west to east and nearly 1½ miles from north to south. The lighthouse is 200 ft high and even in daylight, given reasonable visibility, you can often see the tower before losing the south coast of Guernsey. Summer haze permitting, Roches Douvres should then remain in sight until you pick up those first enigmatic smudges of North Brittany.

When sailing from St Peter Port towards the Lézardrieux estuary near spring tides, and trying to make the best of the powerful streams between Guernsey and the Brittany coast, it usually works out that you pass west of Roches Douvres, having left Victoria Marina about 1½ hours after a morning high water with a safe margin over the sill. You then push the foul but slackening tide down to St Martin's Point before setting a course towards a corner waypoint some 3-4 miles WNW of Roches Douvres lighthouse. This leg is 24 miles and the tide will be setting broadly west for about 4½ hours after your departure, with some south in it towards local low water. It is prudent, therefore, to make good at least five knots, so that you are well past Roches Douvres before the new flood starts running east.

From the Roches Douvres corner waypoint, set a course for a position one mile NW of Basse du Nord N-cardinal buoy, which marks the north extremity of the dangers extending seaward from La Horaine tower. This track leads about 1½ miles west of Roche Gautier W-cardinal buoy and then down onto the Grand Chenal de Trieux leading line, but it's vital to allow generously for the powerful flood stream, which will be setting ESE across the entrance by the time you arrive. Spring rates here can reach 6 knots locally, somewhat in excess of the estimates given in

Chapter 3

Granville's Port de Hérel marina sill at low water

the tidal atlases. You should keep continual track of progress on your way in, since it's all too easy to be set too far to the east.

When planning this passage, bear in mind that the outer dangers of the Trieux extend up to four miles from the mainland, which in any case is low-lying hereabouts. GPS can give you confidence to press on if conditions close in, but don't forget the old adage about returning to the open sea rather than groping shorewards if uncertain of your position.

From the corner waypoint west of Roches Douvres, it's about five miles further to Basse Crublent buoy and the entrance to the Tréguier River than it is to the outer approaches of the Trieux. However, when the tide is east-going and more or less contrary, those extra miles will be hard-gained.

ST HELIER TO GRANVILLE

The attractive old town of Granville lies right down in the SE corner of the Gulf of St Malo and makes an interesting and convenient day's sail from St Helier. The passage leads SE for 30 miles, keeping well NE of the Minkies and then skirting fairly close to the north of Iles Chausey. By leaving St Helier soon after local low water, you will carry the flood for most of the way, finally meeting a weak north-going stream between Chausey and

Roche Jaune, in the lower Tréguier River

Visiting yachts rafted up in Chausey Sound near low water

Rounding Maîtresse Ile to the westward. This is the only real island within the Plateau des Minquiers

the Normandy coast. However, in order to set off at low water, you have to come out of St Helier marina within three hours of high water and then wait at the holding pontoon in La Collette, the basin just outside the main harbour on the south side of the entrance.

Follow the Eastern Passage out of the Small Roads and take your departure from the Demie de Pas S-cardinal beacon tower, aiming to make good a track of 133°T. This line leads nearly a mile NE of the NE Minkies E-cardinal buoy, not quite 1½ miles NE of Les Ardentes E-cardinal buoy, a similar distance NE of L'État black-and-white beacon on the NE edge of Chausey, and finally between two E-cardinal buoys a little way east of Chausey. From a position midway between these buoys, steer SSE to round Pointe du Roc and La Fourchie red beacon tower by a good half mile before turning east towards Granville's Hérel marina.

In good visibility, other useful marks on the way down are: Gorey Castle on Jersey's east coast; L'Enseigne black-and-white beacon, standing on a low hump-backed islet about a mile N by W of Chausey's Grande Ile; Grande Ile lighthouse itself, which stands on Pointe de la Tour at the SE corner of the island; and three rather similar E-cardinal beacon towers which guard the eastern perimeter of the Chausey plateau.

Low water pottering at Chausey

ST HELIER TO CHAUSEY, CANCALE AND ST MALO

These are variations on the passage from St Helier to the NE Minkies buoy and then east-about the Minkies but west of Chausey. The navigation and pilotage are fairly straightforward, but there are several strategic points to bear in mind, both on the first part of this route and later, depending on your destination.

On the leg between the NE Minkies buoy and Chausey, aim to pass at least two miles west of Les Ardentes E-cardinal buoy, bearing in mind that there are drying rocks for nearly a mile west of the buoy.

If bound for St Malo, leave St Helier about three hours before local high water if you can average five knots. You will carry a fair tide down to the NE Minkies buoy, push a weak foul stream between the Minkies and Chausey, and then pick up the first of the west-going ebb for the final stretch to St Malo. If bound for Chausey Sound, either west-about Grande Ile or via the more intricate northern entrance, leave St Helier no later than two hours after local low water, aiming to arrive near high water when the stream in Chausey Sound is relatively slack.

If bound for Cancale, leave St Helier at around low water, aiming to arrive off Pointe du Grouin soon after high water, while the stream is slack and you have plenty of depth in the approaches to Cancale.

ST HELIER TO ST MALO WEST-ABOUT THE MINKIES

Although this route is a couple of miles longer than skirting east-about the Minkies, it can be more convenient during periods of springs when the tide will be ebbing as you leave St Helier in the morning and then making in the afternoon and evening. You will therefore carry a fair stream through the Western Passage to Passage Rock N-cardinal buoy and have a broadly favourable set down to the NW Minkies buoy. The tide should still be trickling away from danger as you pass between the NW and SW Minkies buoys, but the new flood will provide some help as you head SSE towards St Malo.

The streams off St Malo are strong at springs. As you approach the coast on this last leg, it's better to over-compensate for an east-going tide rather than under-compensate, because you can always pass west of the two Vieux Banc buoys and enter the St Malo estuary by the Chenal de la Grande Porte.

ST HELIER TO LÉZARDRIEUX

For this passage, it's convenient to take a departure from the Passage Rock N-cardinal buoy and then set a course to make good about 243°T for 32 miles, towards a landfall waypoint half a mile due N of Basse du Nord (sometimes called Nord Horaine) N-cardinal buoy. This track leads four miles S of Barnouic E-cardinal beacon tower. If you leave St Helier half an hour or so before local high water, the tide will be fairish throughout the trip so long as you can average five knots or more, but you should aim to reach the Basse du Nord buoy before the new flood starts setting east.

THE BAY OF ST MALO

Le Grand Jardin lighthouse, at the entrance to St Malo

DIÉLETTE

This attractive Normandy marina lies 11 miles SSE of Cap de la Hague and can be a useful staging-post for yachts bound to or from the Alderney Race. Diélette gives you the option of coming round from Cherbourg to arrive north of Cap de la Hague $2\frac{3}{4}$ hours *before* HW St Helier

(not quite five hours after HW Dover), in order to catch the more delicate slack water between the south-going and north-going streams in the Race. If you can slip through at *le moment juste* and head straight for Diélette without hanging around, you can enter the marina near local high water and be well placed for pressing on next day either to Carteret, Jersey, Sark or Guernsey.

This way into the Channel Islands area is an interesting alternative to the more traditional route from the Alderney Race direct to Guernsey. The immediate approaches to Diélette are shallow and can be inhospitable in sustained fresh winds from between NW and SW, but in light or moderate summer weather there's no problem about either finding the place or getting in. The outer harbour is accessible in practice for most of the tide except near low springs, when you need about two hours rise to get in or out safely. The channel between the

pierheads is dredged from time to time to just above chart datum, but there's a tendency to silt just outside and between the outer breakwaters, so don't cut things too fine. The Bassin de Commerce is dredged to two metres below datum, so yachts can stay afloat alongside the waiting pontoon on the NE side, immediately ahead as you come in through the entrance. The marina basin has an automatic sill with a depth gauge and is normally accessible for three hours each side of high water. Least depths in the marina vary from between $1\frac{1}{2}$ and $2\frac{1}{2}$ metres.

APPROACH AND ENTRY

Conspicuous from offshore are the two squat dome towers of the large nuclear power station at Flamanville, just over a mile south-west of Diélette. A pier harbour just below the power station is strictly for the use of work vessels. Close north of the power station, looking like a well-worn wreck, are

Chapter 4

TIDES

HW Diélette is at HW St Helier –0005 approx, or HW Dover –0440.
Heights above datum: 12.2m MHWS, 1.6m MLWS, 9.2m MHWN, 4.3m MLWN. The streams off Diélette run more or less north-south and reach about $2\frac{1}{2}$ knots at springs.

CHARTS

For Diélette approaches or passages to or from the Alderney Race use Admiralty 3653. For passages between Diélette and Guernsey use 3653 and 3654. For passages from elsewhere in the Channel Islands area use 2669.

HAZARDS

Sustained fresh westerlies cause steepening seas in Diélette's shallow final approaches. Avoid Diélette altogether in strong onshore weather, and in marginal conditions be sure to enter or leave as near HW as possible.

WAYPOINTS

Diélette NW offing, 3.2 M 326°T from north power station dome tower – 49°34.97'N, 01°55.52'W
Diélette entrance, 2 ca 320°T from Jetée Ouest pierhead light – 49°33.39'N, 01°51.93'W

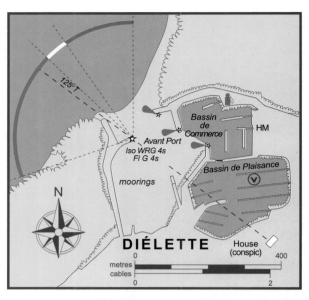

DIELETTE MARINA

The marina has developed gradually over recent years, but is now well established with comfortable pontoon space for over 400 boats. There's usually plenty of room, with 80 visitors' berths reserved on pontoons A, B and C. The minimum depth in the marina basin is 1.50m, but you'll find up to $2\frac{1}{2}$ metres between pontoons B and C. If in doubt about tides or access times, call *Port Diélette* on VHF Ch 9.

The waiting pontoon on the east side of the Bassin de Commerce has two metres at low water and you can stay overnight there if the tides aren't convenient for the marina basin. Enter or leave the marina when the signal lights show two greens and a white. Three red lights mean that entry or exit is forbidden. A gauge at the entrance shows the depth in metres over the sill.

The marina has a shower block at the east side of the basin, and you can eat well at the friendly yacht club – *Le Raz Blanchard* – which is open every day during the season. Just below the yacht club is a useful chandler, *Diélette Nautic*. On the quay near the harbour office, the popular *moules-frites* café, *L'Escale*, has a small general store that stocks basic food and some wines. A colourful market is held at the port every Sunday during the summer.

The restful Diélette waterfront is overlooked on the south side by traditional stone cottages with the classic French flavour of rural Normandy. Inland to the east you soon wander into unspoilt country, whose gentle slopes and winding lanes are alive

for loading iron ore onto waiting ships. This obstructed shoal area is guarded by Flamanville west-cardinal buoy, which lies offshore about three quarters of a mile west of the ruins.

First-time visitors should approach Diélette well above half-tide, avoiding fresh onshore winds or periods of heavy onshore swell. The final line of approach is from the north-west – simply make for the prominent pierheads from this direction and drive in. Watch out for the numerous small crab-pot floats just outside the entrance. The entrance section of Diélette harbour dries at datum, but the commercial basin just to the east is dredged to two metres below. The marina is entered in the south-west corner of the commercial basin and boats with 1.50m draught can normally cross the marina sill for a good three hours each side of local high water.

The lively Sunday market at Diélette marina

with skylarks and buzzing insects on a hot summer afternoon. The sleepy charm of Diélette makes it popular with Guernsey-based yachts, especially at weekends, whose crews enjoy the place as a familiar home from home. You can reckon about 27 miles from St Peter Port to Diélette.

Diélette Port Guide

Harbour office: Bureau du Port, Terre-Plein Est, Port de Diélette, 50340 Treauville (Tel: 02.33.53.68.78, Fax 02.33.53.68.79, VHF Ch 9).
Weather forecasts: Local forecasts posted at the Bureau du Port. Comprehensive Jersey Radio forecasts on VHF Ch 25 and 82 at 0645, 0745 and 0845 local British time, then at 1245, 1845 and 2245 GMT.
Fuel: Petrol and diesel at the fuel berth just outside the marina sill.
Water and electricity: At the marina pontoons.
Showers and washing machines: At the amenities building just north of the yacht club.
Gas: Camping Gaz from the café *L'Escale*.
Chandlery and repairs: At the friendly Diélette Nautic

(Tel: 02.33.53.26.27), below the yacht club. The marina has a 30-ton travel-lift.
Sail repairs: Nearest at Cherbourg – Rémy Cousin at Port Chantereyne (Tel: 02 33 93 64 81).
Shopping: Small general store for basics at the café *L'Escale*, which usually keeps a fair selection of wines. There's a popular quayside market just opposite *L'Escale* on Sundays (try the spit-roasted chickens or succulent basted lamb-joints). The nearest large supermarket is the *Super U* at Les Pieux, a short taxi ride (6km) inland from Diélette.
Yacht clubs: *Le Raz Blanchard* on east side of marina basin, with convivial restaurant (Tel: 02.33.93.10.24).
Local taxi: Serge Lecrosnier (Tel: 02.33.52.53.53 or 06.80.25.52.49).

Restaurants

The moules-frites at **L'Escale** are just the job for lunch, especially in warm weather when you can eat on the terrace. **Le Raz Blanchard** is convivial at midday or in the evenings, and just a short stroll from the pontoons.

If you walk eastwards past the amenities block, cross the road and head off down a lane into the country, you'll soon reach the restaurant **Le Fer de l'Anse**, which is well worth a spin. My preference though, especially for Sunday lunch, is to take a taxi out to **Le Sémaphore** (Tel: 02.33.52.18.98), which is right on the cliff-top not quite a mile south of the power station. Good food and spectacular sea views west towards Sark.

CARTERET

I'm rather fond of Carteret and its attractive, well-run marina. The shallow, picturesque entrance opens up between long stretches of dunes about three quarters of a mile east of the distinctive lighthouse and signal station on Cap Carteret. Inside the breakwaters, the harbour area is a long natural inlet which dries mostly to firm sand, but the marina just beyond the town retains about 2.3m at low water. This perfectly sheltered basin looks across the low dunes and sands of the upper estuary and is accessible for about 2½ hours each side of high water. The exact sill opening and closing time are given in a booklet published annually by the harbour office. The pleasant town at Carteret has a restful atmosphere, a few small shops and a good selection of restaurants. There are more shops, including a large supermarket, a mile inland at Barneville.

Since the harbour entrance is open from between south and west, you should only approach Carteret in quiet weather or easterlies for a first visit, and even then time your arrival for the hour before high water. In brisk winds from any westerly direction, the approaches to Carteret are generally rough as you close with the shelving lee shore.

The long west coast of the Cotentin peninsula is still a well-kept secret for most British boat-owners. Channel Islanders know it well, but yachts coming down from England usually hop on the tidal escalator of the Alderney Race, get tucked up in St Peter Port and then look south towards St Malo or Lézardrieux.

Yet a circular cruise on from Guernsey could nicely take in the period charms of Sark and then, just another 23 miles to the east, the delightful harbour at Carteret. Before the marina was built at Carteret, only a few hardy drying-out types ventured in; bilge-keels, legs or leaning against the quay were the order of the day. But the Port des Isles, completed in 1995, has become one of the most successful yacht harbours on the French coast.

The sheltered basin looks across the low dunes and golden sands of the estuary, where oyster-catchers forage in the pools. On the marina quay, the

The entrance sill at Carteret marina

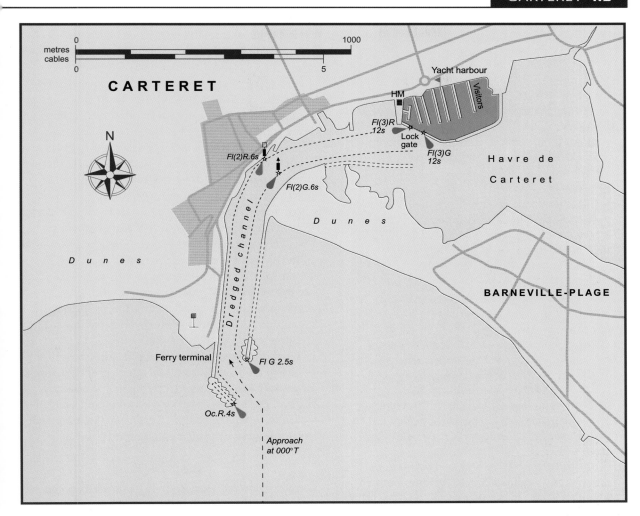

*carefully planted shrubs and borders are starting to
mature and the yacht club is now an established part
of the waterfront. Behind the gardens, the
traditional stone houses have a four-square solidity,
reminding you that this is rural Normandy, where
the country and sea meet on equal terms.*

On a fine summer afternoon, the approaches to
Carteret are truly idyllic in that summer holiday
way the French carry off to perfection. The beaches
look almost Mediterranean and the sea curls
enticingly along the sand. Swimmers splash in the
shallows, windsurfers tack about with élan and
brightly coloured kites soar high in the thermals
above the cliffs.

Barneville and Carteret belong to the same
commune, and the marina's full name is *Le Port des
Isles de Barneville-Carteret*. The 'Isles' in the title, spelt
in the English way, comes from Carteret's close
affinity with the Channel Islands. This is partly a
question of proximity, but also reflects shared
Normandy roots. The ancient Dukes of Normandy
had much to do with how the Channel Islands have

developed. Many Jersey families, in particular, can
trace their ancestors back to the Norman mainland.

Wandering along the waterfront, you sense the flux
of history through this intriguing natural harbour,
which has been used for centuries as a working port.
Shell-fishing remains important to Carteret and,
until the early part of this century, small sailing
vessels – *goëlettes* – traded between Carteret and the
islands. The first passenger service to Jersey began in
1881 and the *Gare Maritime* now handles 50,000
passengers each year.

APPROACHES AND ENTRY

As you study the charts, the broad fringes of drying
green make this coast seem rather unapproachable,
but above half-tide most shoals are safely covered
and local boats sail around without any problems.
As you approach Carteret from the west, it's easy to
see where the gap in the coast will appear. North of
Cap Carteret, with its prominent radio mast, signal
station and lighthouse, the cliffs are quite high
behind the dunes and long beach stretching towards

TIDES

HW Carteret is at HW St Helier –0005 approx, or HW Dover –0440.
Heights above datum: 11.2m MHWS, 1.5m MLWS, 8.5m MHWN, 4.1m MLWN.
The streams off Carteret run more or less north-south and reach about two knots at springs.

CHARTS

For Carteret outer approaches or a passage from Jersey use Admiralty 3655 or French SHOM 7133. For passages to Carteret from elsewhere in the Channel Islands use Admiralty 2669.

HAZARDS

Snug though the marina is once you are inside, remember that Carteret entrance is exposed to the west. In moderate to fresh onshore winds, the shallow approaches throw up short steep seas, while any significant swell becomes more menacing as the water shoals. For a first visit, wait for quiet conditions or offshore winds. Gentle summer westerlies or north-westerlies are no problem, and due northerlies are not too bad. In any event, aim to arrive off the pierheads about an hour before high water.

Five miles west of Carteret, a W-cardinal buoy marks Plateau des Trois Grunes, whose southern edge dries 1.6m. This shoal is no problem near HW, when you can use the buoy as a landfall waypoint and then steer for a position half-a-mile south of Cap Carteret.

WAYPOINTS

Les Trois Grunes W-cardinal buoy, actual position:
49°21.88'N   01°55.11'W
Les Trois Grunes north clearing, 6 cables N of W-cardinal buoy:
49°22.48'N   01°55.11'W
Les Trois Grunes south clearing, 6 cables S of W-cardinal buoy:
49°21.28'N   01°55.11'W
Cap Carteret offing, 6 cables 240°T from lighthouse:
49°22.16'N   01°49.13'W
Carteret entrance, 2 cables due S of east pierhead beacon:
49°22.03'N   01°47.22'W

Flamanville. To the south, the coast is much lower, with salt marshes and shallow inlets not far behind the holiday seafront.

The entrance jetties jut out almost due south, the west jetty overlapping a little so that you curve round to enter from the south-east before straightening up to follow the harbour channel. The long east jetty and the outer part of the west jetty both cover at high springs, but a line of posts keeps you clear. On the port hand you pass the high straight quay of the *Gare Maritime*, where regular ferries come in from Gorey, on Jersey's east coast. Then you reach the fishing quay, where crabbers and scallopers lie aground at low water. To starboard are open dunes and golden sand, with sailing school dinghies drawn up above the tideline.

The channel is well marked by substantial red and green beacons – if the marina sill is open, there's enough water in the channel. You pass the prominent Hôtel La Marine and then the two drying inlets where local boats take the ground. Ahead you will see the two red and green beacons marking the marina entrance. Beyond the marina, the estuary creeps inland behind the low sandy coast towards the sleepy village of Barneville.

The marina is accessible for about $2\frac{1}{2}$ hours each side of high water, but the exact sill opening and closing times are given in a booklet published annually by the harbour office. Try to visit Carteret mid-week if possible, when the visitors' berths on the east side of pontoon F have more breathing room.

ASHORE

Strolling downstream from the yacht club, you pass the Bureau du Port where Normandy and Channel Island flags fly above the office, a true symbol of *entente cordiale*.

Following the waterfront along Avenue Barbey d'Aurevilly, past the old drying part of the harbour, you reach the friendly Bar du Port, which has the most agreeable terrace in town for a cold beer or a *kir*. The main shopping street – Rue de Paris – runs west from the Bar du Port, with all the basics for food shopping. On the south side, the local vintners – Cave Dubégny – is worth browsing. The butcher is near the post office on Rue des Quatre Volontaires.

On the estuary side of Rue de Paris, the Hôtel La Marine has an excellent dining room and a sunny terrace overlooking the harbour. The local sailing school has its base just opposite, and parties of youngsters pile into dinghies at the slipway next to the hotel.

The French run plenty of summer activities for schoolchildren, and it's always encouraging to see tiny eight-year olds in lifejackets and sunhats tacking their Optimists deftly across the harbour – the next generation of Gallic cruising folk seems assured. Following the promenade seawards, you soon reach

At low water in Carteret marina you float high above the drying sand outside

the Hôtel L'Hermitage and the wide quays where the fishing boats moor. Stroll here on Sunday mornings to eye up the shellfish stalls.

Following Rue du Port out to the sea, you reach the attractive south-facing beach just west of the harbour entrance. This is a good spot for those who like swimming, closer to the marina than the long west-facing beach north of Cap Carteret.

A cliff path meanders out to Cap Carteret, a surprisingly dramatic headland for a coast that is generally low-key. The signal station – still known as Le Sémaphore in French – flies the tricolour with panache and the lighthouse is a powerful affair with a 25 mile range. From this vantage point, you have fine views out towards the reefs and islets of Les Écrehou and the substantial outline of Jersey.

INLAND TO BARNEVILLE

The nearest village for reasonable shopping is Barneville Bourg, a good mile inland from Carteret marina. Barneville lies on the east side of La Gerfleur river, and you can reckon about 35 minutes stroll from the marina, but a bit longer coming back if you've overloaded your bags at the supermarket.

From the head of the pontoons, walk east past the travel-lift and boat park, look for a gap in the hedge and follow the footpath along the shore (you can't use this short cut at HWS when the path is covered – follow the main road instead).

Cross a small stream coming down from one of the old sluices, keep to your left up a slight slope and then double back on a narrow path leading to the footbridge over the river. Cross the bridge and turn left along Chemin du Tôt, which brings you to the edge of Barneville village.

Market day in Barneville is Saturday. For the *Champion* supermarket take the left (north) turning

Carteret marina sill at low water

The distinctive radio mast and signal station on Cap Carteret

out of the square and follow Rue du Pont Rose down the hill for about 300 yards. The *Champion* has pretty well everything you need.

The harbour channel at Carteret

On the way back towards Carteret, coming down from the square, keep an eye open for the left turn and blue sign to Le Tôt. If you miss this turning to the footbridge, it's a bit further walking back to Carteret along the main road.

Carteret has quite an active fishing fleet and on Sunday mornings it's fun to wander down to the fish quay along Promenade Abbé-Lebouteiller. Here you'll find all kinds of shellfish stalls where you can select the makings of a leisurely lunch on board. The local crabs are particularly succulent. Don't forget to put a bottle or two of *Gros Plant du Pays Nantais* in the fridge before you go.

BY TRAIN TO PORTBAIL

A fascinating tourist train runs along a preserved line from Carteret to Portbail, leaving Carteret station at 10am on Tuesdays and arriving at Portbail half-an-hour later. Tuesday is market day in Portbail, and you have two hours in which to browse the stalls and catch the atmosphere of this charming old town. Portbail harbour, which dries, is half a mile from the town at the end of a long causeway. An intriguing spot for intrepid bilge-keelers.

The train leaves Portbail at 1230 and arrives in

Carteret Port Guide

Harbour control: Directeur du Port Alain Blancheton, Bureau du Port, Quai Barbey-d'Aurevilly, 50270 Barneville-Carteret (Tel: 02 33 04 70 84, Fax: 02 33 04 08 37). VHF Ch 09 – call 'Port de Carteret'.

Weather forecasts: Local forecasts posted at the Bureau du Port. Comprehensive Jersey Radio forecasts on VHF Ch 25 and 82 at 0645, 0745 and 0845 local British time, then at 1245, 1845 and 2245 GMT. The signal station on Cap Carteret normally repeats these forecasts in French on Ch 09, 15mins after the Jersey Radio broadcasts.

Fuel: The fuel berth may not always be in service. If not, the nearest diesel and petrol alongside is at Gorey Harbour, on the east coast of Jersey, for three hours each side of HW until 1900.

Water and electricity: At the visitors' berths – the east side of Pontoon F.

Showers: At the yacht club just above the marina.

Laundrette: In Place de l'Église at Barneville.

Gas: From the Carteret mini-supermarket, or from the 'Champion' supermarket in Barneville.

Chandlery: Carteret Marine, 1 bis, Avenue de la République (Tel: 02 33 53 82 00).

Sail repairs: Nearest at Cherbourg – Rémy Cousin at Port Chantereyne (Tel: 02 33 93 64 81).

Engineers: Carteret Marine (as above). Dubois Marine, 60 Avenue de la République (Tel: 02 33 04 90 54).

General repairs: Carteret Marine (as above) with 45T travel-lift and 24T crane at the marina.

Shopping: Basics in Carteret, but best in Barneville, a half-hour walk inland. Useful 'Champion' supermarket and food shops in Barneville. Carteret has a good baker and a serviceable mini-supermarket in the main street (Rue de Paris). The butcher is just behind Rue de Paris near the post office.

Bank: Small Crédit Agricole with cash machine in Rue de Paris. Also a cashpoint outside the post office.

Yacht clubs: Yacht Club de Barneville-Carteret, Quay Barbey d'Aurevilly (Tel: 02 33 52 60 73).

Tourist information: Tourist office in Place Flandres-Dunkerque (Tel: 02 33 04 94 54).

Local taxi: Garage Tollemer at 18 Rue du Cap (Tel: 02 33 04 95 22).

Car hire: Budget Car Hire – ask at the Yacht Club (or Tel: 02 33 94 32 77).

Bike hire: Claude Éliard at Barneville, in Place de l'Église (Tel: 02 33 53 88 03).

Changing crews: From Carteret it's about 40 minutes by taxi to Cherbourg and the cross-Channel ferries. Regular passenger ferries from Carteret *Gare Maritime* to Gorey, on the east coast of Jersey, and then by taxi to Jersey Airport.

Restaurants

Both Carteret and the inland village of Barneville have an interesting selection of eating places. In Carteret, the **Hôtel La Marine** is a sound three-star choice, overlooking the harbour at 11 Rue de Paris (Tel: 02 33 53 83 31). Further downstream, opposite the fishing quay, **L'Hermitage** is always reliable (Tel: 02 33 04 46 39), and the *moules marinière* are particularly good. L'Hermitage is my favourite choice for Sunday lunch, but be there soon after midday.

Not far beyond L'Hermitage, the **Hôtel de la Plage et du Cap** (Tel: 02 33 53 85 89) is just the right distance from the marina to settle the digestion after four excellent courses. Nearer the marina, at 5 Avenue de la République, the **Hôtel Le Carteret** has a tempting *menu gastronomique*.

In fine weather, it can be pleasant to stroll inland to Barneville and eat at **Le Gohan** in Rue des Rivières (Tel: 02 33 04 95 33).

Excellent grilled meat over a wood fire.

Carteret at 1300. Carteret station is not far behind the tourist office on Avenue de la République.

OUT TO LES ÉCREHOU

Carteret is a handy base for visiting Les Écrehou, an extraordinary archipelago of reefs and islets seven miles SW of the harbour entrance. The Écrehou anchorage is just south of the central island, Marmotière, on which there are a few summer cottages. On a warm summer day, preferably near springs with low water in the early afternoon, this is a magical place to lie, hemmed in by drying rocks.

From Carteret you come south-about L'Écrevière bank to make this approach. Leave Carteret pierheads half-an-hour after HW there and allow for the strongish north-going stream as you make for L'Écrevière buoy. Use Admiralty Chart 3655.

PORTBAIL

The entrance to Portbail lies four miles SSE along the coast from Carteret. This rather fascinating natural inlet is bordered by low ground and marshes and approached by crossing several off-lying shoals and a coastal fringe of shallow drying rocks. Portbail is most suitable for bilge-keelers or boats with lifting keels, but intrepid keel-boat navigators can enter with care and dry out alongside the jetty.

For a first visit, choose a period just before springs and time your entrance for an hour before high water. A small red-and-white fairway buoy is moored about 1½ miles south-west of the mouth of

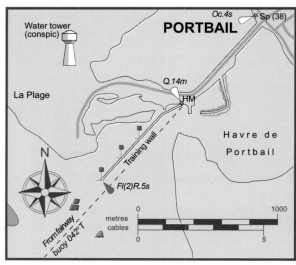

the inlet, from which make good about 048°T to pass between a red and a green buoy just before the entrance itself. Thereafter, leave the red post beacons along a training wall fairly close to port before altering to starboard towards the head of the stone jetty. Round up behind the jetty head and lie alongside its south-east side, where you'll dry out about 2½ hours after high water. Bilge-keelers can use a vacant mooring and dry out in the harbour.

Portbail is most easily visited from Carteret or from Gorey harbour, only 15 miles away on the east coast of Jersey. Although there are leading lights and

the outer beacon on the training wall is lit, I wouldn't recommend entering Portbail at night unless you know the entrance and this stretch of coast reasonably well.

The rather charming old town is about half a mile from the harbour across the long causeway. Portbail has a useful selection of shops and restaurants and Tuesday is market day.

GRANVILLE

Granville is an attractive, unassuming old Normandy port in the south-east corner of the Gulf of St Malo, on the north fringes of the Baie du Mont Saint Michel. Granville's sheltered and spacious marina, Port Hérel, is accessible via a sill for about three hours either side of high water.

The marina and harbour offer a full range of facilities and the various marine services can deal with most kinds of repair. The town itself is quite large, with an interesting selection of shops and restaurants. Granville is a useful and agreeable staging post in a cruise down to the St Malo area and Iles Chausey via Jersey. The 30 mile passage between St Helier and Granville makes a convenient leg in either direction, usually taking just under a tide. The approaches to Granville are shallow and the bay outside the harbour dries out to a line between Pointe du Roc and Le Loup.

Granville is often avoided by newcomers to the Channel Islands area. A quick glance at Admiralty Chart 2669 can give the impression that this south-east corner of the Gulf of St Malo looks rather vulnerable if the weather should freshen from the west, with its shallow approaches adding a nasty edge to what would be a tricky lee shore. Yet although Granville is exposed to the west, it is more snug and approachable that you might at first think. On the passage down from St Helier, for example, Plateau des Minquiers and then Iles Chausey provide a fair degree of shelter from a hard south-westerly. Although the final approach to Granville will be rough-going, the fetch from the south-west is not all that great and the sea should only start to turn really malevolent at force 7 and above. In fresh north-westerlies you obtain some lee from Chausey in the approaches to Pointe du Roc, so it's really only in strong winds from due west that Granville becomes a fully exposed lee shore.

The approaches to Granville are straightforward navigationally, so long as you work the tides carefully and arrive near high water. In reasonable visibility you are never out of sight of land, either arriving from St Helier or from St Malo. There are various useful beacon towers around the eastern edge of Chausey. Pointe du Roc, just off Granville, is fairly high and easy to identify.

TIDES

HW Granville is at HW St Helier −0020 approx.
Heights above datum: 12.8m MHWS, 1.4m MLWS,
9.6m MHWN, 4.6m MLWN.
The streams off Granville are only moderate, rarely
exceeding 1½ knots even at springs between Pointe
du Roc and Iles Chausey.

CHARTS

Admiralty: 3659, 3672 (large-scale)
French SHOM: 7341

WAYPOINTS

Approach waypoint ½ mile SW of Pointe du Roc:
48°49.69'N, 01°37.30'W

HAZARDS

The shallow approaches to Granville can be rough in
fresh winds from the west, when you need to arrive or
leave as near high water as possible. There are rocks
up to three cables NW of Pointe du Roc, even just
seaward of La Fourchie red beacon tower, so give
the headland a wide berth when arriving from Jersey.
When entering Port de Hérel, keep close to the main
breakwater head which has the illuminated depth
gauge, leaving to starboard the red posts marking
the bathing beach wall.

Granville's Port de Hérel marina is accessible for
about 3½ hours either side of high water in quiet
weather, but you should reckon on 3 hours as a
working maximum and two hours if the wind is
moderate onshore. The marina lies a little way east
of the Vieux Port, of which the outer part dries and
the inner wet basin is used mainly by fishing boats.
Although the marina is large with all modern
facilities, it nevertheless has a friendly and rather
restful atmosphere. The attractive façades of the old
walled town – La Haute Ville – rise behind the
harbour area, and Granville's two large and ornate
churches dominate the skyline. The town centre is
only 15 minutes walk from the marina and has a
good selection of shops and restaurants. Granville,
of course, is just out of Brittany, and has more in
common with some of the harbours further up-
Channel than with the Breton ports a few hours
sailing to the west.

APPROACHES AND ENTRY

The approaches to Granville are shallow for several
miles offshore, especially to the north-west between
Pointe du Roc and Chausey. There is plenty of water
above half-tide in quiet weather, but you should
arrive or leave as near high tide as possible in fresh
onshore winds. Granville harbour and marina lie
close south and east of Pointe du Roc, a prominent
headland with a lighthouse and signal station. La
Fourchie red beacon tower stands 1½ cables NW of

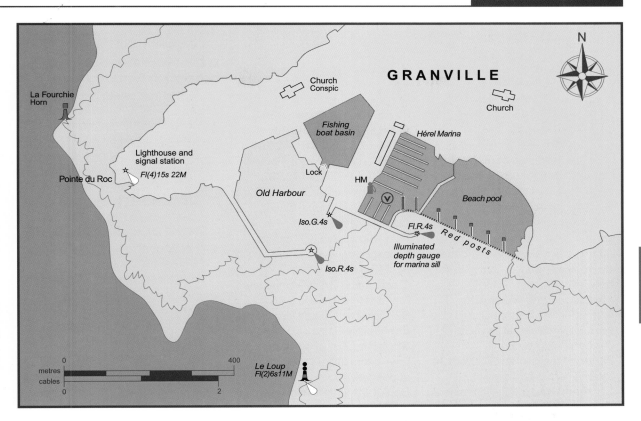

GRANVILLE

La Fourchie Horn

Pointe du Roc

Lighthouse and signal station
Fl(4)15s 22M

Church Conspic

Church

Fishing boat basin

Hérel Marina

Lock

HM

Old Harbour

Beach pool

Iso.G.4s

Fl.R.4s

Iso.R.4s

Illuminated depth gauge for marina sill

Red posts

metres

cables

0   400

0   2

Le Loup
Fl(2)6s11M

N

Pointe du Roc and there are several drying rocks a little way seaward of the beacon tower.

Coming from Jersey east-about Chausey, pass midway between Basse du Founet and Anvers E-cardinal buoys and then make good about 145°T towards an outer waypoint half a mile SW of Pointe du Roc. This line passes close to a wreck shown on the chart as exposed at LAT, but having plenty of water over it near high water. From the Pointe du Roc waypoint, steer just north of east to pass midway between the first breakwater head (Jetée Ouest) and Le Loup isolated danger beacon tower. Then continue ENE to round the second breakwater (Jetée Est) which has a large illuminated depth gauge at its outer end. The gauge shows metres and tenths, so that 93 represents 9.3 metres over the sill at that moment. Keep fairly close when rounding the marina breakwater, leaving to starboard a line of red posts marking a retaining wall for the beach bathing pool. Watch out for other yachts coming out. Once round the breakwater head and through the outer entrance, you'll see the sill gateway between a red and a green beacon – make sure you keep dead between these two. The visitors' pontoons are straight ahead as you cross the sill.

Coming from Iles Chausey, St Malo or Cancale, it's usually convenient to make for the same outer waypoint and proceed as above, although you can leave Le Loup beacon tower on either hand.

Granville's Hérel marina

Granville Port Guide

Harbour control: Capitainerie du Port, Port de Plaisance de Hérel, Granville (Tel: 02 33 50 20 06, Fax: 02 33 50 17 01). VHF Ch 9

Weather forecasts: Posted at the Capitainerie during the season. Recorded forecast from Météo France Tel 08 36 68 08 50. If your French is fairly fluent and you are uncertain about whether conditions are suitable for a passage, it can be worth walking up to the signal station on Pointe du Roc and having a chat with the duty officer.

Fuel: Diesel and petrol at the marina fuelling berth, just opposite the bureau de port at the head of the visitors' pontoon.

Water: At the pontoons or from the fuelling berth.

Showers: Next to the Capitainerie.

Calor and Camping Gaz: Comptoir Maritime, 75 Rue du Port (Tel: 02 33 50 18 71).

Chandlery: Comptoir Maritime (as above); Granvil'Eole, Port de Hérel (Tel: 02 33 51 09 56); Granville Plaisance, Port de Hérel (Tel: 02 33 50 23 82). Lecoulant Marine, Port de Hérel (Tel: 02 33 50 20 34). Manche Ouest Marine, Port de Hérel (Tel: 02 33 50 74 10).

Chart agents: La Marine, 2 Rue St Sauveur (Tel: 02 33 50 71 31, Fax: 02 33 50 29 83).

Sail repairs: Voilerie Granvillaise, Port de Hérel (Tel: 02 33 50 62 28).

Engineers: Méca Services (Volvo Penta, Yanmar, Nanni), Rue Clément Desmaisons (Tel: 02 33 90 19 67, Mobile 06 07 23 65 81). SMMIG (Volvo Penta), Port de Hérel (Tel: 02 33 50 16 79).

General repairs: Chantier Anfray (wood repairs), Quai Ouest, Granville (Tel: 02 33 50 18 14); Hurel Services (GRP repairs), Cale d'Hacqueville, Granville (02 33 51 03 11).

Electronics: Granville Plaisance, Port de Hérel (Tel: 02 33 50 23 82); Manche Ouest Marine, Port de Hérel (Tel: 02 33 50 74 10).

Shopping: Good shopping in town centre, with several useful supermarkets.

Banks with cashpoints: Several in town centre.

Yacht club: Le Yacht-Club de Granville (Tel: 02 33 50 04 25).

Tourist information: Office de Tourisme, 4 Cours Jonville, 50400 Granville (Tel: 02 33 91 30 03, Fax: 02 33 91 30 19).

Local taxi: Radio-Taxis Granvillais (Tel: 02 33 50 50 06).

Changing crews: Rail connections to Cherbourg and the cross-Channel ferries. Passenger ferries to Jersey and Guernsey.

Restaurants

My favourite bistro in Granville is still **Chez Pierrot** at 16 Rue Clément Desmaisons (Tel: 02 33 50 09 29), near the town centre. Another good bet is **Le Phare**, 11 Rue du Port (Tel: 02 33 50 12 94), whose 1st floor restaurant has a fine view over the outer harbour. The **Hôtel Normandy Chaumière** is always reliable at 20 Rue Paul Poirier (Tel: 02 33 50 01 71), not far north of Chez Pierrot. **Le Borsalino** is handy for the marina on Promenade Lavat (Tel: 02 33 50 02 99). If you feel like pushing the boat out, I recommend lunch or dinner at the **Hôtel Grand Large** at 5 Rue de la Falaise (Tel: 02 33 91 19 19), where the **Restaurant La Frégate** overlooks the sea. Stylish cooking – best to reserve a window table.

MOORINGS AND ANCHORAGES

Port de Hérel marina: The marina offers the only snug berth for visiting yachts. If you just miss the sill, 3½ hours after high water, you are also rather late for getting into the Avant Port and finding a drying berth alongside one of the quays. In quiet summer weather, if you arrive off Granville near low water, you can edge in and anchor to wait for the tide about a cable NW of Le Loup beacon tower.

FACILITIES

Granville marina has excellent facilities, with water and electricity at the pontoons, good showers, and a travelift, engineers and chandlers to cope with all kinds of repairs. The town is quietly elegant and good for shopping, with some particularly mouth-watering charcuteries and a colourful market. You'll also find quite a catholic selection of restaurants.

ILES CHAUSEY

Charming Iles Chausey lie down in the crook of the Gulf of St Malo, 20 miles SE of Jersey, eight miles WNW of Granville and 16 miles NE of St Malo. The plateau is compact and practically steep-to – almost a perfect oval on the chart – about six miles from east to west and $2\frac{1}{2}$ north to south. On all sides except

the far east, you can edge in safely towards the outer reefs until you pick up your bearings from Admiralty Chart 3656. The main island, Grande Ile, has a hôtel-restaurant, a small general store and bar, and a few holiday cottages. The small local population are mostly involved with fishing and in dealing with the tourists that pile in by vedette from Granville during the season.

It's always fascinating to visit Chausey, especially during spring tides when, at low water, much of the plateau dries out to a maze of rocks and sand-pools. At anchor in Chausey Sound, you are practically landlocked for several hours until the flood returns. At high water springs though, you can feel rather exposed as many of the natural breakwaters are submerged and any outside swell is liable to penetrate into the Sound. But springs give you a morning and evening high water, when it's easy to make a day trip out from Granville. If you leave Port de Hérel marina an hour or so before high water and get over to Chausey before mid-morning, you can enjoy the best of the day, and the tide, at anchor before returning to Hérel in the evening.

APPROACH FROM THE SOUTH

The southern approach to Chausey Sound is quite straightforward, since the plateau is more or less steep-to. Simply sail in from the south-east to leave a green conical buoy to starboard and three E-cardinal beacons off Pointe de la Tour to port. After the green buoy leave a W-cardinal beacon and then a N-cardinal beacon to starboard, after which you can anchor or moor on the east side of the fairway (but keep clear of the large moorings used by the vedettes and fishing boats). There are also moorings further up the Sound, opposite the north end of Grande Ile.

The island gives good shelter from strong winds from between south and west, and the off-lying reefs and islets provide limited protection from the north-east and east. The streams are very strong in Chausey Sound near half ebb or flood and you have to be very careful when going ashore with the dinghy. The landing slip is just opposite La Crabière beacon, and it's only a short walk up to the Hôtel du Fort et des Iles.

APPROACH FROM THE NORTH

The north approach to Chausey Sound through the reefs and shoals of the plateau needs some care, but

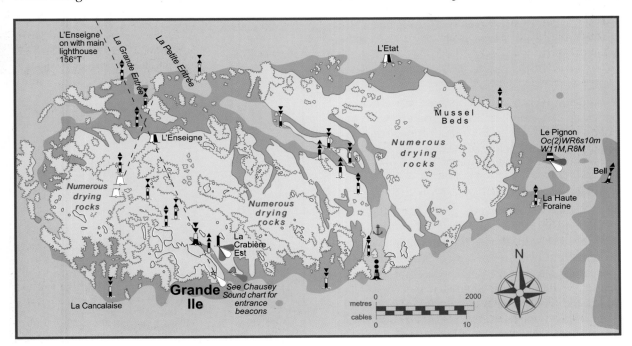

is not difficult in quiet weather and good visibility. It should only be taken above half-flood, since the shallowest part dries nearly five metres. The leading line for La Grande Entrée passes just clear to the W of Les Ardentes, which has enough water over it above half-tide in calm conditions.

The transit is L'Enseigne beacon tower in line with Pointe de la Tour lighthouse on Grande Ile, bearing 156°T. L'Enseigne is white with a black top, looking needle-like from the north on its low hump of islet. Pointe de la Tour lighthouse looks wider and more squat and will be seen as the easternmost feature on Grande Ile. If you can pick up these marks before reaching Les Ardentes, keep L'Enseigne well open to the east of Pointe de la Tour lighthouse until you have passed safely clear of the reef, and then edge down onto the leading line with the east-going stream.

On the final approach to the plateau, keep the lighthouse just touching the east side of L'Enseigne and leave the outer E-cardinal spar beacon fairly close to starboard. Stay on the leading line, steering to leave Les Longues W-cardinal beacon close to port and a second E-cardinal beacon about a cable to starboard. Once abreast the latter, alter 45° to starboard onto the inner leading line - La Massue cylindrical white beacon in transit with a similar beacon on Le Chapeau bearing 201°T. This second line leaves L'Enseigne 1½ cables to port and then a third E-cardinal spar beacon close to starboard.

When abreast this third E-cardinal beacon, turn to the south to leave La Massue beacon tower to starboard and then steer SE as if to leave the W-cardinal spar beacon just south of La Saunière rocks close to port. However, just before Le Chapeau white beacon tower comes abeam to starboard, take

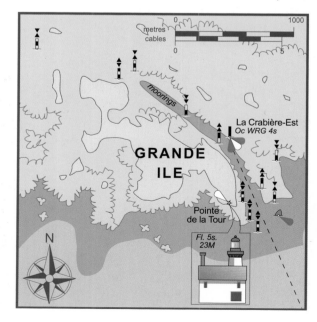

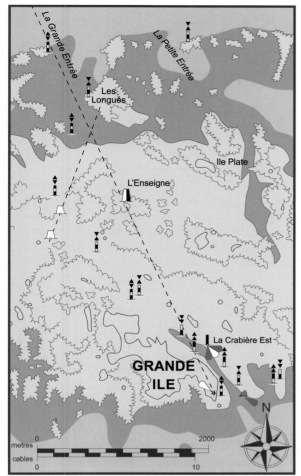

Chapter 4

AT NIGHT

The northern entrance to Chausey Sound cannot be used at night (or by day in poor visibility). However, the south entrance is straightforward at night in quiet weather, using Pointe de la Tour lighthouse (*Fl.5s23M*) to bring yourself in from seaward and then steering into the Sound on the narrow white sector of La Crabière-Est (*Oc.WRG.4s*).

ASHORE

Like most small islands, Grande Ile is fascinating to wander round, especially in early or late season. Be there mid-week if you can, to avoid the weekend invasion of launch visitors and local yachts. From the landing slip, the path winds up to the Hôtel du Fort et des Iles, which has a bar and restaurant (Tel: 02.33.50.25.02). From the terrace you can look back over the anchorage and across the main body of reefs towards the French coast north of Pointe du Roc.

South from the hotel, a sandy track leads out to the lighthouse from where, on a clear day, you can see the cliffs east of St Malo between Pointe du Meinga and Pointe du Grouin before the land drops away towards Mont St Michel. A little way north-west of the lighthouse is a sandy cove edged with gorse. This can provide a daytime anchorage in moderate weather from between NW through N to NE. The approach from due south is clean, but there are rocks drying 4.4 metres not far to the south-west. The holding is a bit unreliable, over sand and rock.

Chausey has an uplifting atmosphere of restful independence, protected from the outside world by its natural barrier of rock and sand. Entering the plateau is like crossing a frontier into a private domain. Many yachts miss this port-of-call on the usual run between St Malo and Jersey or Guernsey. It's well worth a visit and not at all as daunting as the charts may at first suggest.

an echo-sounder reading. You need at least three metres more than your draft at this point in order to get over the shallowest part of the Sound a little further on, a patch just before the W-cardinal beacon which dries 4.9 metres at datum. If you are early on the tide, you can anchor opposite Le Chapeau until there is sufficient depth over this bar. The height of tide will increase quickly at and just after half-flood.

Once past the bar and the W-cardinal beacon, steer towards the next pair of beacons – an east and a west – keeping the east beacon (i.e. the starboard-hand one) in line with Pointe de la Tour lighthouse until you are about 50 metres from the beacon. Then edge to port to pass through the gateway, when you will see the line of moorings ahead to starboard.

When coming down from Jersey, bear in mind that you have the option of passing west-about Chausey and then approaching the Sound from the south. This will be preferable to attempting the north entrance if visibility turns out to be worse than expected.

Chausey Sound near low water

CANCALE

This small drying harbour is tucked well into the north-west corner of the wide expanse of the Baie du Mont Saint-Michel, sheltered in most conditions except strong winds from between south and east. Mention Cancale to a Frenchman and he will think of oysters, assuming, of course, that

he's not thinking about them already. Cancale specialises in these most succulent of shellfish, and the harbour front is lined with restaurants offering tantalising menus of fruits de mer and dégustation de huitres. You can also buy oysters and mussels from stalls on the quay, for those odd peckish moments during the day.

Two stages of oyster cultivation are carried out at Cancale – maturing and cleaning. The beds well out in the bay are used for maturing, and the oysters stay there for two years in mesh sacks, known as poches, which are supported above the mud in wooden racks. The cultivators go out frequently in their distinctive flat-bottomed boats to turn the poches when the tide is out. Later, the oysters are moved to the cleaning parcs (or dégorgeoirs) just below the harbour, where they gradually flush themselves with mud-free water. The mud is cleaned off the shells by passing the oysters along a conveyor through a jet of water.

It's a long patient process, but then eating shellfish is a serious business in France. The delicious plates oysters, most of which are bred down in the Gulf of Morbihan, are usually four or five years old when they appear on your plate. Think of that next time you enjoy a dozen, as they slip down in little more time than it takes to sip a couple of glasses of chilled Chablis or perhaps a crisp Gros Plant du Pays Nantais. If you get a chance, try a few of the véritables Cancales, which are sometimes called pieds de cheval. These are large, specially cultivated oysters, horseshoe-shaped and a meal in themselves. They were apparently a great favourite with Louis XIV.

APPROACH AND ENTRY

Cancale lies not quite three miles south of Pointe du Grouin, close to the east of which the long narrow Ile des Landes (51m high) seems only just separated from the mainland by the Chenal de la Vieille Rivière. About four cables NNE of Ile des Landes is the above-water rock known as Herpin (21m high) with Ruet W-cardinal bell-

buoy (unlit) a quarter of a mile NW of it. Three quarters of a mile NE of Herpin is Pierre d'Herpin rock and lighthouse. The passage between Herpin and the lighthouse is called Le Grand Ruet, through which the stream runs strongly at half-tide, often with uneasy eddies and overfalls. Four cables NE of Pierre d'Herpin, a small dying rock called La Fille (dries 3.8m) is marked on its north side by an unlit N-cardinal buoy.

When arriving from Chausey or Granville, you'd normally pass east of La Fille buoy and Pierre d'Herpin lighthouse before heading SSW for Cancale via the narrow channel between Ile des Rimains and Pointe de la Chaîne. When coming from St Malo, it can be useful to cut through Le Grand Ruet if the tide is favourable and not weather-going. Note the shallow patch (with only 1.1m over it) about four cables WSW of Pierre d'Herpin lighthouse.

Because of its fast streams, Chenal de la Vieille Rivière is only passable at dead slack water (low or high) and you should give a wide berth to the drying rocks which extend up to a cable north and east of Pointe du Grouin. A rocky shoal (drying 1.6 metres) lies three cables NW of Pointe du Grouin, marked on its north side by Grande Bunouze unlit N-cardinal buoy.

It's a mile from Pointe de la Chaîne narrows to Cancale harbour. This stretch dries at low springs and has a good many oyster beds marked by withies. At neaps you can anchor and stay afloat within two cables south of Pointe de la Chaîne, but don't drop your hook in the oyster beds whatever you do. The harbour itself is accessible for about two hours either side of high water. Bilge-keelers or yachts with legs should settle down in the middle of the harbour if possible. Although you can lie against the inner side of the breakwater, this is usually busy with fishing boats on the tide.

ANCHORAGES

Between Pointe de la Chaîne and Pointe du Grouin there are two shallow bays – Port Mer and Port Pican, respectively just north and south of Pointe Chatry. Keel boats can anchor and stay afloat off these bays,

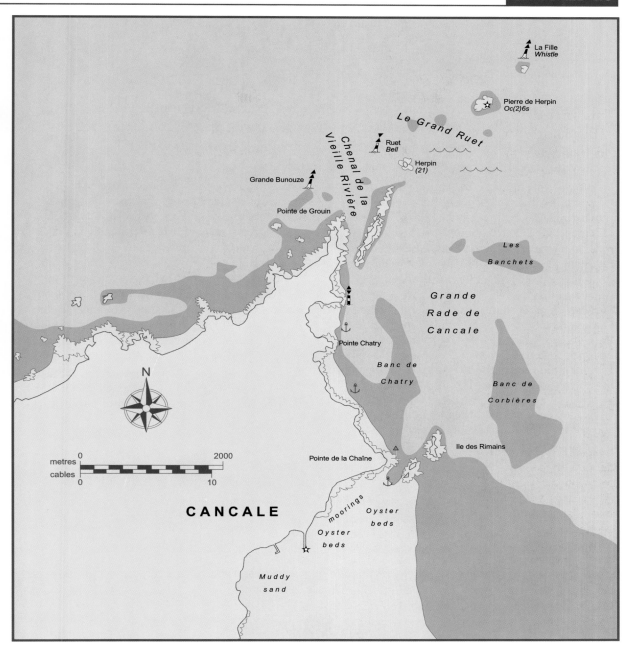

sheltered from between NW through W to S. The holding is good over sandy mud and you can leave at night with care using Pierre d'Herpin light (*Oc(2)6s*). You can also anchor a little way west or south-east of Ile des Rimains, although both these spots are prone to an uneasy scend even in quiet weather.

ASHORE

Cancale is a pleasant little tourist town, although often quite crowded in high season. You can buy Camping Gaz at Mr Bricolage or at the Super-U supermarket. There's also a laundrette near Super-U and you can hire bicycles from the Hôtel Nuit et Jour. Diesel or petrol are only available by jerrycan. You can buy oysters from the Marché aux Huîtres at the seaward end of Quai Thomas and there's a good fish market on Quai Duguay-Trouin.

RESTAURANTS

There's a choice of restaurants on the quayside at Cancale. For a copious Plateau de fruits de mer, Le Continental on Quai Thomas is pretty reliable (Tel: 02 99 89 60 16). For some interesting oysters, I like L'Huîtrière at 14 Quai Gambetta (Tel: 02 99 89 75 05) – try their 'Huîtres chaudes à la crème de poireau'. If you feel extravagant and enjoy a little exercise before dinner, you'll be well rewarded for the 15 minute stroll up the hill to the Relais Gourmand at 1 Rue Duguesclin (Tel: 02 99 89 64 76).

ST MALO

Always a favourite with British yachts, St Malo is a natural focus for the east end of Brittany. Although the entrance is rocky and quite narrow near Grand Jardin lighthouse, the main channels are well marked and easily navigable by day or night. The elegant walled town is always worth the effort of

locking into the Bassin Vauban, and it's astonishing to remember that almost everything inside the ramparts has been rebuilt since 1944. Outside the lock at St Servan, the spacious Port des Sablons marina is accessible for most of the tide. Just upstream from St Malo, the River Rance offers some delightful sailing and makes a useful cruising retreat in bad weather.

St Malo doesn't change much over the years. Once you have passed Le Grand Jardin lighthouse, the last couple of miles of this dramatic rocky approach often give you a cracking good sail. The famous silhouette of the old walled town seems to beckon a welcome, even though the massive ramparts were built to keep out marauders and withstand serious siege. Elegant houses peer out above the parapet, suggesting a world of gracious living within. The steep pitched roofs and shuttered windows are almost an emblem of Brittany, which even first-time visitors find curiously familiar, as if they always knew this was how St Malo would look.

The tall cathedral spire is a kind of visual pivot, about which the grand façades rotate as you come up the long estuary towards the breakwater.

Over on the west shore just opposite St Malo, the traditional old resort of Dinard changes little over the years. The seafront has a rather Victorian flavour, with its quaint mix of rambling family houses and comfortable, slightly peeling seaside hotels.

The motley crew who help with the warps as you lock through into the Bassin Vauban never seem to get much older, although their noses are an even darker shade of red than they used to be. The club pontoons at the north end of the Bassin Vauban are still a pleasant place to lie and just close enough to the bustle of the town. If you arrive late on the tide for locking through, you can usually get into Port des Sablons marina, immediately outside the lock-gates on the south side. Even at springs, the long sill is generally passable for a good four hours either side of high water.

APPROACH AND ENTRY

The two main channels into St Malo, both to the west of Ile Cézembre, are the Chenal de la Grande Porte and the Chenal de la Petite Port. Either can be used by day or night, at any state of tide and in most weathers,

The snug pontoons at the north end of St Malo's Bassin Vaubin

although the Chenal de la Grande Porte is slightly easier going in strong onshore winds. A secondary channel – Chenal du Décollé – leads close inshore from the west, but is only really suitable for leaving St Malo near high water.

There are three approach channels to the east of Ile de Cézembre – Chenal de la Grande Conchée, Chenal des Petits Pointus and Chenal de la Bigne. They can only be used by day and with sufficient rise of tide over the shallow area between Ile de Cézembre and St Malo. Of these three, the Chenal des Petits Pointus is the most useful if you are arriving from the east from Granville, Cancale or Chausey.

Chenal de la Grande Porte: This straightforward channel leads practically due east towards Le Grand Jardin lighthouse leaving Pierres des Portes and Les Courtis rocks a couple of cables to the north. The outer mark, No 2 red whistle buoy (*Fl(3)R.12s*) lies 1¾ miles west of Le Grand Jardin and not quite 2¼ miles

SE of Le Vieux Banc W-cardinal buoy (*VQ(9)10s*).

After passing close south of No 2 red buoy, make good 089°T towards Le Grand Jardin to leave No 4 red bell buoy (unlit) close to port, No 6 red buoy (unlit) a good 100m to port and No 1 green whistle buoy (*Fl.G.4s*) close to starboard. Then edge a little south of east to leave Le Sou E-cardinal buoy (*VQ(3)5s*) to starboard before turning SE to follow the buoyed channel into the estuary. Le Buron green beacon tower is prominent just over a mile to the SE, and you should steer to leave it about 100m to starboard. When half a mile from Le Buron, make sure you are well in the middle of the channel and not about to shave too close to the Pierre Salée rocks on the west side.

At night: The Chenal de la Grande Porte leading lights are both red – Le Grand Jardin (*Fl(2)R10s15M*) in line with Rochebonne (*DirF.R.24M*) beyond it bearing 089°T. About 250 metres from Le Grand Jardin, turn SE into the estuary when Les Bas-

TIDES

HW St Malo is at HW St Helier –0020 approx
Heights above datum: 12.2m MHWS, 1.5m MLWS,
9.3m MHWN, 4.2m MLWN
Streams are powerful off St Malo, especially during
the middle flood, reaching 4 knots at springs across
the outer part of the Chenal de la Petite Porte. Rates
reduce markedly inside Le Grand Jardin.

CHARTS

Admiralty: 2700
French SHOM: 7130

HAZARDS

There are numerous drying and above-water rocks in
the outer estuary, but they are all well marked and fall
into place as you approach one of the three
waypoints above. The strong cross-tides provide the
main hazard, especially if you are approaching the
Chenal de la Petite Porte around mid-flood.

WAYPOINTS

Outer approach to Chenal de la Grande Porte, a
cable due W of No 2 red buoy
– 48°40.27'N, 02°07.63'W
Outer approach to Chenal de la Petite Porte, a cable
due E of the fairway buoy
– 48°41.42'N, 02°07.06'W
Outer approach to Chenal des Petits Pointus, ½M NE
of St Servantine green buoy
– 48°42.30'N, 02°00.32'W

Sablons (*DirF.G.22M*) comes into line with La Balue
(*DirF.G.25M*) bearing 129ºT. This second transit
leads right up to the breakwater head.

Chenal de la Petite Porte: This is the main
shipping channel into St Malo and leads south-east
towards Grand Jardin lighthouse from a position
close east of the St Malo red-and-white fairway
buoy. From the fairway buoy waypoint, make good
130ºT towards Le Grand Jardin, allowing carefully
for any cross-tide and aiming to leave Les Courtis
green beacon tower (*Fl(3)G.12s7M*) 1½ cables to
starboard. Near low water springs, be sure to avoid
La Grande Hupée rock (with 1.3 metres over it) just
on the east side of the fairway and Basse Nord-Est
des Portes (with 1.9 metres over it) a cable ENE of
Les Courtis.

Once you are safely past Les Courtis, steer SSE
between Le Grand Jardin and Le Sou E-cardinal buoy
(*VQ(3)5s*) before following the buoyed channel
towards St Malo. Aim to leave Le Buron green beacon
tower, a mile into the estuary, about 100m to starboard.

At night: From a position close east of the fairway
buoy (*LFl*), bring Le Grand Jardin light (*Fl(2)R.10s*)
into line with La Balue (*F.G*) bearing 130ºT. Follow
the daytime directions but bring Les Bas-Sablons
(*F.G*) into line with La Balue (*F.G*) at 129ºT when you
are midway between Le Grand Jardin and Le Sou E-
cardinal buoy (*VQ(3)5s*). This second transit takes
you right up to St Malo breakwater head.

Chenal des Petits Pointus: This channel to the east
of Ile de Cézembre can only be taken be day, in
reasonable visibility and above half-tide, but is a
convenient way into St Malo if you are arriving from
Chausey, Granville or Cancale. The key mark is the
Rochefort W-cardinal beacon tower, which lies 1½
miles NW of Pointe du Meinga. Pass a good half
mile seaward of Rochefort before making for the
approach waypoint half a mile NE of La St
Servantine green bell buoy. At this point, Les Grands
Pointus rocks (3 metres high) will be about half a
mile away to the SE.

From this outer waypoint, make good 202ºT to
leave the St Servantine buoy a quarter of a mile to
starboard and Les Petits Pointus red beacon tower a
cable to port before edging west a little to leave La
Plate N-cardinal tower a quarter of a mile to
starboard and Le Bouton S-cardinal buoy 2 cables to
starboard. Continue SSW to pass midway between
Le Grand Dodehal red spar beacon and Les Roches
aux Anglais green conical buoy before turning to
starboard to leave Les Crapauds du Bey red can
buoy close to port and so enter the estuary to the
west of Le Petit Bey fort.

The three other channels into St Malo – Chenal de la
Grande Conchée, Chenal de la Bigne and Chenal du
Décollé – are not included here for reasons of
simplicity, but can be followed fairly easily using the
excellent Admiralty Chart No 2700.

MOORINGS AND ANCHORAGES

St Malo has two sets of berths for visitors: The
pontoons at the north end of Bassin Vauban,
reached by the main shipping lock that leads
through to the docks, and the large Port des
Sablons marina at St Servan, just outside the lock.
If you enjoy locks and have the time, it's worth
entering Bassin Vauban and mooring just outside
the old city walls. If you prefer a finger pontoon, if
time is pressing or you need fuel, Sablons is the
best bet. Each is very pleasant in its own way and
both have good showers, with water and
electricity at the pontoons.

Bassin Vauban: The large shipping lock for the
Bassin Vauban is worked continuously for 2½ hours
each side of high water. There are some moorings
just south of the main breakwater which can be used
while you are waiting for the gates to open. Some of

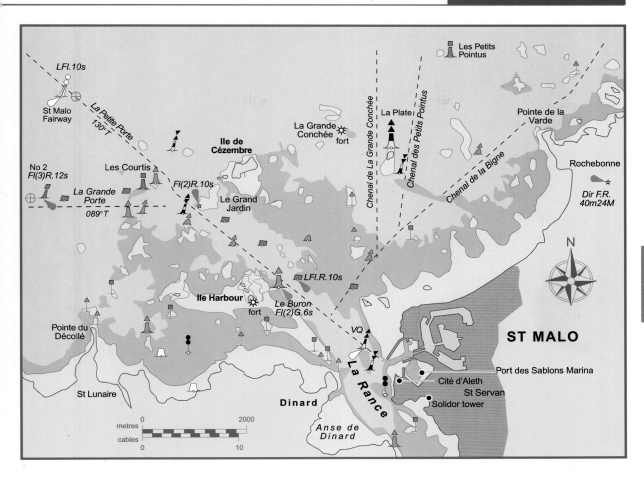

these moorings dry, so edge in carefully if you arrive at or soon after low water. Before entering the lock, have a long bow and stern warp ready with a large bowline in each, because the lock-crew will take your warps as you come alongside the wall, using their heaving lines if necessary. The Lockmaster listens on VHF Ch 12.

As you emerge into Bassin Vauban, turn to port and make for the snug pontoon berths at the north end of the basin. These pontoons are pretty full in high season and you usually have to raft alongside another boat, but there always seems to be room for one more.

St Malo lock-times: The Bassin Vauban lock is worked for 2½ hours each side of HW St Malo. There are five inward lockings (*Entrées*) and five outgoing (*Sorties*). The first inward lock starts 2½ hours before HW and the lockings then alternate at half-hourly intervals until the last outgoing lock opens two hours after high.

	Entrées	*Sorties*
1	HW −2½ hrs	HW −2 hrs
2	HW −1½ hrs	HW −1 hr
3	HW −½ hr	HW
4	HW +½ hr	HW + 1 hr
5	HW + 1½ hrs	HW + 2 hrs

Remember to look up high water in French time. There are no lock charges and your lines are normally taken by warp-handlers. The traffic lights work on the usual international system.

Port des Sablons: You enter this large marina across a low fixed sill which is only two metres above datum. The window of access is therefore generous. Depending on draught, you can usually get in or out of Port des Sablons up to four hours each side of high water at springs and for most of the tide at dead neaps. Depth over the sill is displayed at the entrance.

The marina has a full range of facilities, but the visitors' berths are subject to swell in strong north-westerlies. If you arrive at St Malo late in the evening, it's often convenient to berth at the marina overnight and then lock into the Bassin Vauban next morning. When approaching or leaving Sablons, watch for ferries either leaving or approaching the Ro-Ro terminal on the east side. Also remember that the tide can be strong through the narrow entrance, especially during the middle hours of the flood. The visitors berths are hard to starboard as you come in, so allow room to round up.

Anchorages: There are two possible anchorages between St Malo and the Rance barrage; off St

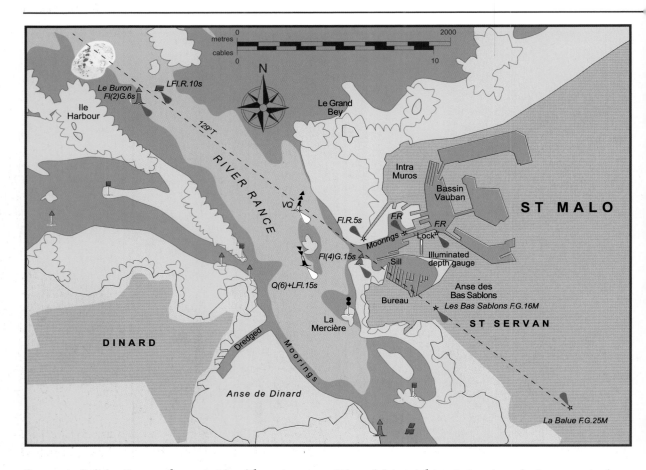

Servan in Solidor Bay, on the east side of the estuary, or off the Anse de Dinard on the west side. The best spot in Solidor Bay is about a cable west of Pointe des Corbières, inside the Solidor Bank. The Anse de Dinard dries right out at springs, but you can tuck fairly well in at neaps.

ASHORE

You normally enter St Malo through Porte St Vincent, the main east gate of the town. Even dodging cars and velos, one half-expects to hear rumbling carriage wheels and the ring of hooves on cobbles. The ancient gate opens into Place Guy la Chambre, where spacious brasserie terraces invite you to take things easy.

First on your left is the well-known restaurant À La Duchesse Anne. Beyond La Duchesse, a whole string of dining rooms vie for attention along Rue Jacques Cartier. Opening north from Porte St Vincent, Place Châteaubriand has more bistros ranged opposite the Hôtel de Ville. The expansive frontage of the Hôtel de France et Châteaubriand adds a note of grand style to this main square, which teems with tourists in summer.

Rue St Vincent takes you towards the centre, with stylish shops on both sides as you wander into Rue Porcon de la Barbinais and on towards Place du Pilori. Butchers and bakers seem few and far between, and even the supermarket lurks in a basement. St Malo intra-muros seems too chic to sell

St Malo breakwater and the old walled town

you a couple of pork chops, but the choice of restaurants is prodigious.

One great attraction of St Malo is a stroll round the ramparts. From St Vincent you have a fine vantage over the basin and quays, where a motley collection of sailing ships, old and new, is usually moored. As you turn west, the ferry terminals and lock come into view, and beyond them St Servan, Port des Sablons and the wooded peninsula of Aleth.

The seaward ramparts are the most spectacular, with commanding vistas of the channels you picked your way through to get here. In heavy weather, the sea breaks white over the outer reefs and it's rather pleasant to be up on the walls looking out.

ST SERVAN

The attractive quarter of St Servan is part of St Malo yet quite distinct, with an atmosphere all its own. You'll find a tempting range of food shops in St Servan's main street – Rue Ville Pépin – and the walled town of St Malo is only 20-25 minutes walk around the bay past the two ferry terminals.

Above Port des Sablons are the old ramparts of Cité d'Aleth, with some pleasant walks round the Aleth peninsula to the Rance estuary. Here you'll find the distinctive Solidor tower and a snug beach where local boats moor. The 'Cape-Horners' museum in the tower is worth a visit, if only for the spectacular river views from the top. Quai Solidor has some agreeable cafés and bistros, among them one of my favourite retreats – the Restaurant L'Atre. Le Cancalais is particularly good for a morning coffee. From the café terrace, you look across to the Rance barrage and the lock that leads to the charming upper reaches of this special river.

DINARD

This traditional French seaside resort lies just opposite St Malo on the west side of the estuary. With its popular casino, quaint mix of houses and large rambling hotels, Dinard waterfront has that special period flavour common to once-fashionable watering places. For a day trip from St Malo, take the passenger ferry which leaves regularly from the long landing slip – La Cale de Dinan – near the Gare Maritime.

Dinard has one or two interesting picture galleries and some notable restaurants. For dinner I'd make for the Grand Hôtel at 46 Avenue George V (Tel: 02.99.88.26.26). For lunch I rather like Le Printania at 5 Avenue George V (Tel: 02.99.46.13.07). If you

The Solidor Tower is unmistakable on the St Servan waterfront

GMT. CROSS Corsen forecasts go out in clear French on VHF Ch 79 from Cap Fréhel at 0545, 0803, 1203, 1633 and 2003 French local time. You can ring the Météo France recorded forecast on 08.36.68.08.35.

SHOPPING IN ST MALO

Near Port des Sablons, the best food shopping is in the main street at St Servan (Rue Ville Pépin), which has a fine selection of delicatessens, charcuteries and pâtisseries. At the top of the high street, at 2 Place de la Roulais, you'll find the excellent Poissonnerie de la Roulais just opposite some traffic lights, with its mouth-watering selection of fish and shellfish (Tel 02.99.81.31.16).

Near Bassin Vauban, the Marché Plus supermarket is handy and useful. From the Bureau du Port, enter the St Malo walls through Porte St Vincent, head straight across into Rue St Vincent and Marché Plus is not far along on the right, on the basement floor of the Vetmod clothes shop. Remember, though, that it's only about 20 minutes brisk walk across to St Servan and the temptations of Rue Ville Pépin – follow Quai St Louis past the entrance lock and bear right at the roundabout just beyond the Gare Maritime du Naye.

Banks and cashpoints: There are plenty of banks with cashpoints in St Malo and St Servan. Nearest to Bassin Vauban is the Crédit Mutuel de Bretagne on the north side of Rue St Vincent – go straight ahead through Porte St Vincent and it's just up on the right. From Port des Sablons, walk into St Servan and continue up the main street (Rue Ville Pépin). The first cash machine is at the Banque Populaire de l'Ouest, on the right opposite the Codec supermarket.

FINDING WHEELS IN ST MALO

Bike hire: From Diazo Velocation at 47 Quai Duguay Trouin (Tel 02.99.40.31.63), 10-15 minutes walk from the Bassin Vauban pontoons past the Casino. At Port des Sablons, ask at the Bar de la Capitainerie about hiring from Malocavelo (Tel 02.99.56.22.02).

Car hire: From Assistance Auto de la Côte d'Emeraude, near the station at 34 Boulevard de la République (Tel 02.99.20.21.95).

Taxis: Call Allo Taxis Malouins on 02.99.81.30.30

A DAY AWAY

The Rance is the best destination for a day excursion in the boat (see the next chapter). If, however, your crew seem in need of a day ashore, it can be fun to take the ferry over to Dinard and have lunch at one of the large hotels there. Dinard also has some good beaches for the family.

are feeling flush, I recommend La Salle à Manger at 25 Boulevard Féart (Tel: 02.99.16.07.95).

Dinard Yacht Club has old ties with England and you always eat well at the restaurant there. The inner moorings don't have plug-in convenience, but make a pleasant change from marinas. The non-drying trots are concentrated into a narrow dredged pool, reached by a marked channel starting three cables south-west of 'Plateau Rance Sud' S-cardinal buoy. The pool is reckoned to have two metres at datum, but check the depth carefully before the tide runs away.

LOCAL WEATHER FORECASTS

Local forecasts are posted daily at Bassin Vauban and Sablons Bureaux du Port. Jersey Radio forecasts broadcast on VHF Ch 25 and 82 at 0645, 0745 and 0845 local British time, and then 1245, 1845 and 2245

St Malo marina services

St Malo marina services (Telephoning St Malo from the UK dial 00 33 299 etc)

Harbourmaster at Bassin Vauban: Monsieur Roland Machard (Tel: 02.99.56.51.91, Fax 02.99.56.57.81). VHF Ch 9.

Harbourmaster at Port des Sablons: Monsieur Yorik Lucas (Tel: 02.99.81.71.34, Fax 02.99.81.91.81)

Fuel: Diesel and petrol alongside the fuelling berth at Port des Sablons, between pontoons H and I. Ask at Bureau du Port during office hours (0700–2100 during the season). 24-hour self-service operation is only for holders of French credit cards.

Water: At all pontoons in the Bassin Vauban or at Sablons.

Camping Gaz: Bassin Vauban – from Marché Plus supermarket on the corner of Rue St Vincent and Rue Sainte Barbe (see 'Shops' below).

Port des Sablons – Camping Gaz at Sablons Yachting, near the Bureau du Port.

Chandlers: Near Bassin Vauban – The best bet is Chantier de la Ville Audrain at Avenue Louis Martin, St Malo (Tel 02.99.56.48.06). From the Bureau du Port, head south-east towards the station (away from town) along Avenue Louis Martin.

At Port des Sablons – My favourite chandler in St Servan is Voilerie Richard at 3 Rue du Glorioux, just inland from Quai Solidor on the River Rance side of the peninsula (Tel 02.99.81.63.81).

Yacht clubs: La Société Nautique de la Baie de Saint Malo has its clubhouse just opposite the Bassin Vauban pontoons. The club bar is open every day from 1730–2130 local time (Tel 02.99.20.22.97).

Showers: At Bassin Vauban and Sablons – both use a code-number entry system.

Laundrettes: Good washing machines and dryers in the Bassin Vauban facilities block. Useful laundrette not far from Sablons marina on the south side of Rue des Bas Sablons, just east of the Service Alimentation and opposite a good boulangerie.

Repairs: Best at Port des Sablons, where lifting out is easy. Sumalo Yachting and Key West SA are both near the head of the pontoons.

Engineers: Most of the local mechanics are mobile, so can be contacted either from Bassin Vauban or Port des Sablons. Chatelais et Le Gall are long established, at Quai Surcouf, St Malo, along the south side of Bassin Duguay Trouin (Tel 02.99.56.14.67, Fax 02.99.40.55.71) – and also at Sablons (Tel 02.99.81.73.30). Chantier Naval de la Plaisance, at Sablons, are Volvo Penta service agents (Tel 02.99.82.62.97, Fax 02.99.82.81.87). Also at Sablons you have Key West SA and Pascal Houery, Mécanique Marine.

Restaurants

There are so many restaurants in St Malo that recommendations can be tricky. However, this small selection includes some of my favourites:

In St Malo

Restaurant La Porte St-Pierre at 2 Place du Guet, St Malo, is just inside Porte St-Pierre on the north-west side of the town walls (Tel 02.99.40.91.27, Fax 02.99.56.06.94). This reliable hôtel-restaurant has been run by the Bertonniere family since 1936 and has a strong tradition of good eating at reasonable prices. Just the right distance to stroll to and from Bassin Vauban.

À La Duchesse Anne in Place Guy la Chambre, just inside Porte St Vincent on the left, is the most notable of a tempting line of restaurants along Rue Jacques Cartier (Tel 02.99.40.85.33, Fax 02.99.40.00.28). In season it's worth booking a table in advance, whether for lunch or dinner. A Sunday lunch à la Duchesse Anne is a real treat that pleasantly absorbs most of the day.

La Coquille d'Oeuf is at 20 Rue de la Corne de Cerf (Tel 02.99.40.92.62). This interesting traditional restaurant has some good country meat dishes which can sometimes hit the mark if your cruise menus have concentrated on fish and fruits de mer.

Crêperie Le Corps de Garde at 3 Montée Notre Dame is a good bet for a light lunch or supper (Tel 02.99.40.91.46). Le Corps de Garde has a commanding position on the ramparts facing the sea, not far north of Porte St Pierre. In fine weather, you can sit out on the terrace and enjoy traditional Breton galettes and crêpes, sipping a good chilled local cider the while.

At St Servan

Restaurant l'Atre, facing the Rance on Quai Solidor, is my favourite eating place in St Servan (Tel 02.99.81.68.39). From Port des Sablons, cut through Rue du Dick towards the Rance and then turn left to reach Restaurant l'Atre.

Dào-Viên is an unusual Vietnamese restaurant, just past the laundrette on Rue des Bas Sablons. A definite change from Breton fruits de mer.

Le Hoggar, at 7 Rue Amiral Magon, is just round the corner from Dào-Viên on the road up to Place Bouvet and St Servan town centre. Le Hoggar is a Moroccan and oriental restaurant and a good place for couscous.

THE RIVER RANCE

The Rance is one of the most restful rivers in Brittany, and no cruise in the St Malo area would be complete without a trip at least as far up as the sleepy village of St Suliac. And if heavy weather curtails your offshore passage-making at sea, at least you'll be able to enjoy some good sailing on the Rance.

If the tides are right, there's plenty of room in the river for tacking about for a good six miles above St Malo.

But the Rance has some eccentricities, which are caused by the tidal generating barrage across the river about three quarters of a mile above St Malo. In fact the Rance 'tides' are largely controlled by the power-station engineers, who open the turbine sluices according to a timetable which is published a month in advance. The principle of this hydro-electric system is that the tide is allowed to flow through the barrage generators in both directions, but in practice this means that the effect of the tide in the upper Rance lags well behind the outer estuary tides by up to three hours, with both ebb and flood concentrated into a three to four hour

period instead of the usual six. The important point for visiting boats is that the streams flow swiftly in the Rance when they are running, especially at springs; the level also rises and falls almost visibly during this compressed period. Remember this when anchoring or making dinghies fast to quays or slips.

For information about tide times and levels inside the Rance, ask at the barrage lock for a timetable. This information is published a few days ahead in the local paper Ouest France. You can also phone a recorded message on 02.99.16.37.33 or ring the barrage lock-keeper direct on 02.99.16.37.37.

THE RANCE BARRAGE LOCK

The sea-lock into the Rance is right at the west end of the power-station barrage, only three quarters of a mile above St Malo. Most of the estuary immediately above and below the barrage is cordoned off by buoys to prevent boats straying too close to the turbine sluices. The approach channels to the lock are well over on the west side of the river. The lock operates every hour, by day only, from four hours before high water until four hours after. Yachts headed upstream enter the lock on the hour, as soon as the road bridge opens and the down-going boats have come out.

Yachts coming downstream can enter the lock at about twenty minutes to the hour, but will not lock through until just before the hour, when the road bridge is lifted to let boats out of and then into the lock. If you are planning to go right upriver to the upper tidal lock at Le Châtelier, it's a good idea to check the Rance tide times with the barrage lock-keeper here, to make sure you'll have sufficient rise to continue upstream to Châtelier. However, if you take the first lock out of St Malo's Bassin Vauban, two hours before high water there, you can usually carry the flood stream all the way to Châtelier lock, and can certainly arrive there before the river ebb starts. Le Châtelier lock normally operates between 0600 and 2100 during the season, for as long as there's at least 8.5 metres of tide outside the gates.

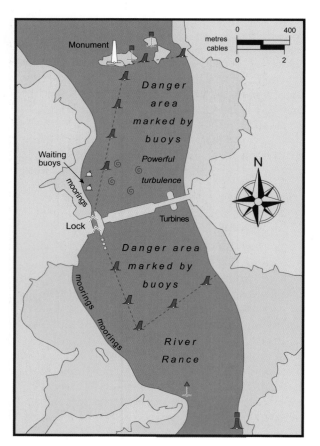

Above the barrage: The Rance feels spacious just above the barrage, although a large area is marked off by buoys to stop boats straying near the sluices. The first impression is of sheltered rural water safely cut off from the sea. For the first two or three miles there are plenty of local moorings in the various bights and inlets, and you can often find an empty buoy in a quiet corner. You pass a waterside hotel with its own landing pontoon, and then the sleepy boatyard at La Landriais. The villages are set well back from the river until you reach St Suliac on the east bank, three miles above the barrage.

There's just about room to anchor outside the moorings at St Suliac, if you stay near the downstream trots where the soundings are deeper. Ashore, you have a waterfront restaurant and a few useful shops in the village. In quiet weather, St Suliac is a delightful place to linger a couple of days and just absorb the atmosphere of the river.

Above St Suliac, a buoyed channel leads across this wide reach and cuts close to the west shore before curving south-east into the narrow gorge below the two road bridges at Port St Jean. Once past the bridges, the channel lies just outside the moorings opposite Plouër-sur-Rance, but then swings across towards the old stone quay and landing slip at Mordreuc.

Plouër Marina: The sheltered marina at Plouër lies on the west side of the Rance, half-a-mile above the Port St Jean road bridges and about five miles above the barrage. Converted from an old mill pool, Plouër is one of the most charming ports-of-call in Brittany. Access is through a narrow sill gate and you can enter or leave when the red and green sill lights are on. The pontoons have water

and electricity, and there are showers and washrooms at the Bureau du Port. The village is a good 20 minutes walk inland, but the Bar-Restaurant de la Cale is handy near the river landing slip.

On the east side of the Rance, half a mile above Plouër, the village of Mordreuc has a friendly bistro on the quayside, useful if you are moored at Plouër marina and don't mind a trip across (and back) in the dinghy.

Reaching Le Châtelier lock: Above Plouër and Mordreuc, the river narrows and the channel winds from side to side dodging steep mud banks. These higher reaches have a mysterious jungle quality, accentuated by the ancient rustic fish traps at the river's edge.

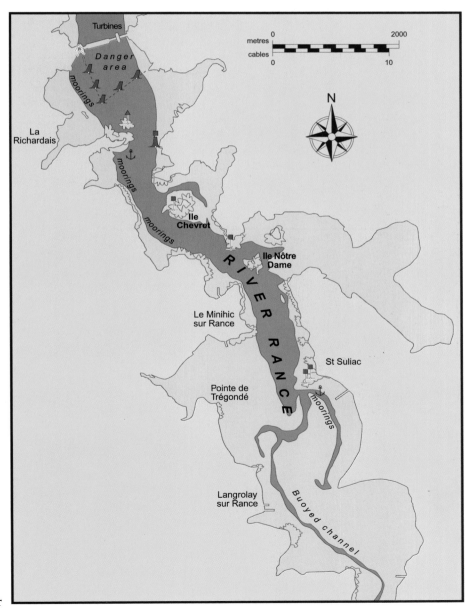

The last few hundred yards before Châtelier lock are narrow and tortuous, marked by spar beacons rather than buoys. It's best to arrive on the last of the Rance flood or during the high water stand, creeping up slowly, especially if another boat is coming down. The lock normally operates between 0600 and 2100 (local time) during the season, so long as there's at least 8.5 metres of tide outside the gates. You can phone Châtelier on 02.96.39.55.66.

THE CANAL TO DINAN

Just above Châtelier lock are the peaceful pontoons at Port de Lyvet. This is the limit of navigation for deeper draught boats, because the next three miles up to Dinan are only navigable safely if you draw less than about 1.3 metres.

However, the final stretch up to Dinan is rewarding if you can make it. The port area has pontoons alongside the quays and there are several good restaurants within a short stroll. A narrow cobbled street winds up from the port past some splendidly preserved timbered houses. The old medieval town overlooks the Rance valley, surrounded by ramparts and guarded by an imposing 14th century castle.

Although St Malo and Dinan are both tourist areas, the river between them is one of the most untouched waterways in Brittany. Here you can savour that unique, timeless world of rural France as you meander past rich farmland, small country cottages and one or two elegant châteaux which recall the French knack for civilised living.

THROUGH THE BRITTANY CANALS
ST MALO TO THE VILAINE RIVER

For smaller, shallow draught boats, the Brittany canal route between St Malo and the Vilaine River can be a useful way of getting down to the Biscay coast while avoiding the more open passages around the rocky north-west corner of France.

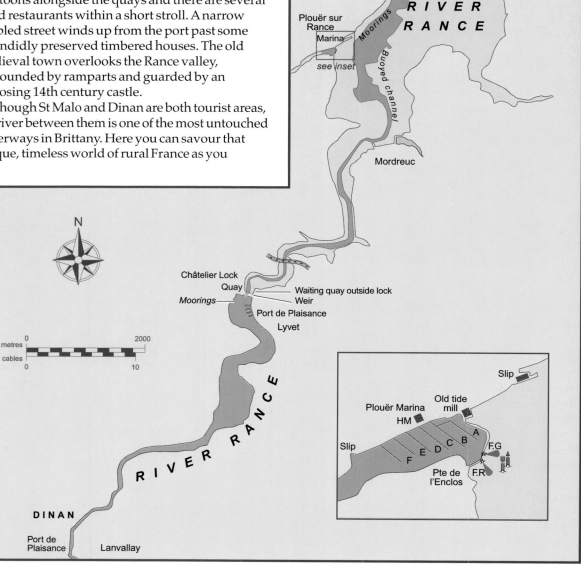

The restful country marina up at Plouër-sur-Rance

Although these canals cut off quite a lot of distance right across the narrowest part of Finistère, they are not really time-saving unless bad weather along the Brittany coast would have kept you tucked up in harbour for several days if you'd been going round by sea. However, French inland waterways are a delightful experience in themselves and not to be rushed. I can think of no finer way of getting to know the true character of Brittany than by meandering gently through these sleepy canals and rivers, mooring each evening way out in the country or perhaps near a small village shop or café.

Distance and time: The navigable distance between the Rance barrage and the mouth of the Vilaine is about 250 kilometres (135 nautical miles) and there are 63 locks including the sea-locks at either end. This trip can be covered in less than a week if you are in a hurry or easily stretched to a more languid fortnight. Much depends on how relaxed or pressed you feel and how long you like to linger for lunches and siestas.

There are three distinct stages which, working from north to south, are as follows:

1   The canalised River Rance from the barrage lock just above St Malo to Châtelier lock a couple of miles below Dinan; Distance 23 kilometres (12½ NM) with a lock at either end.

2   The Canal d'Ille et Rance, from Le Châtelier lock to Rennes and the junction with the Vilaine River; Distance 85 kilometres (46 NM) with 47 locks above Châtelier.

3   The Vilaine River from Rennes to the mouth just below Tréhiguier. The Vilaine is canalised as far as the barrage lock at Arzal, which is only five miles from the sea; Distance 140 kilometres (75½ NM) with 14 locks.

Maximum draught: The shallowest sections of the route are the Canal d'Ille et Rance and the upper Vilaine between Rennes and Redon. Although the official draught limit for the through-route is 1.3 metres (just over 4 feet), you should reckon on *not much more than a metre*, especially during a dry summer.

Headroom: The lowest fixed bridges are on the Canal d'Ille et Rance, just above Dinan, with a least headroom of 2.75m (9 feet) in the centre of arches and 2.3m (7ft 6ins) at the sides. The maximum headroom under the Vilaine bridges is 3.2m (10ft 6ins) above normal water level, but this can be reduced if the river is in flood.

The best places for raising and lowering your mast are Dinan at the English Channel end and La Roche Bernard at the Biscay end. Both these attractive and restful inland ports have hand-cranes on the quay.

ST CAST

The small resort and harbour of St Cast lies about eight miles west along the coast from St Malo, tucked under the south-east side of Pointe de St Cast. The harbour is protected by a breakwater from the north, by land from the west and south, and by a rocky outcrop called Bec Rond from the south-east.

St Cast harbour is occupied mostly by trot moorings, of which the inner trots dry out and the outer buoys used by the fishing boats have about two metres at low springs.

The final approach to Port de St Cast is straightforward from the north-east, usually leaving Les Bourdinots E-cardinal buoy about a quarter of a mile to the west and then making for the breakwater head. You enter the harbour between the breakwater head and the north-east tip of Bec Rond, which is marked by a red spar beacon. At night, the light on the breakwater head (IsoWG, 4s) has two white sectors leading in from the north-east, one each side of Les Bourdinots rocks. Yachts that can take the ground easily may lie to one of the moorings in the first two lines of trots, drying out on firm sand. You might find a vacant fishing boat mooring in deeper water for an hour or two, but you'd be lucky to stay on one overnight without an early morning interruption.

ASHORE

St Cast is quite a pleasant little town with a few basic shops and quite a good choice of restaurants. Rouxel Marine and the Co-opérative Maritime are both useful chandlers, and Rouxel can organise engine repairs. You can buy Camping Gaz at Maison Blanche in Rue Piétonne or at Maison Ohier on Boulevard Duponchel. There's a laundrette in Place Charles de Gaulle.

The restaurants and crêperies are geared to summer tourists, but you will certainly eat well in most of them. I rather like the Hôtel Bon Abri in Rue du Sémaphore (Tel: 02 96 41 85 74) and Le Suroît on Boulevard Duc d'Aiguillon (Tel: 02 96 41 80 95). The Crêperie Le Bretan'or on Place Anatole Le Braz is good for lunch or a light supper (Tel: 02 96 41 92 45).

ANCHORAGES

In quiet weather there's a pleasant anchorage outside the harbour area in the attractive Anse de St Cast, within two to three cables south-east of Bec Rond in about 1.4 metres LAT. You can also fetch up close south-east of Pointe de la Garde, which lies about a mile SSE of St Cast breakwater head. The Pointe de la Garde anchorage has a clear approach from the north-east and about 1.2 metres depth at LAT with fair holding over sand. There's a landing slip on the south-east side of the point.

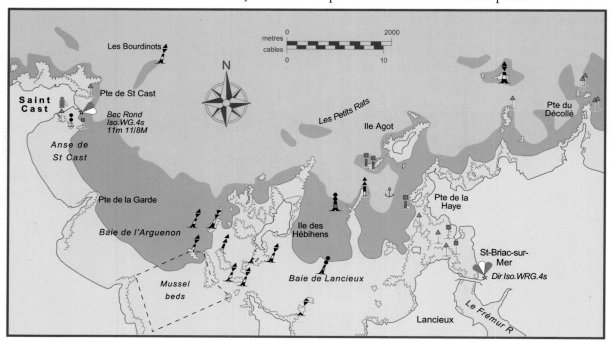

ERQUY

The small resort and scallop-fishing port of Erquy lies about eight miles WSW along
the coast from Cap Fréhel, open to the west but well sheltered from the east.
The harbour area dries to just outside the outer mole, but you can stay
afloat at anchor a cable or two west of the end of the mole.

The approach to Erquy requires care from any
direction, because this stretch of coast is well
peppered with off-lying rocks.

APPROACH AND ENTRY

From the NE: Coming from Cap Fréhel in reasonable
weather and visibility, and by day only, the best
approach is by the Chenal d'Erquy, inside the
extensive plateau of rocks which straggles offshore to
the north of Cap d'Erquy. Having rounded Cap
Fréhel by half a mile or so and skirted seaward of
Amas du Cap islet, bring Amas du Cap just touching
the north edge of Fréhel. Follow this transit (bearing
077°T astern) for four miles until Les Justières S-
cardinal buoy is four cables abeam to starboard, and
then continue for another half mile until Le Verdelet
islet (42 metres high, 3½ miles SW of Cap d'Erquy) is
just open to the north of the large above-water rocks
immediately off Cap d'Erquy, bearing 228°T. Come
round to the SW on this transit, but edge seaward of
the line as you get near Cap d'Erquy, to leave Basses
du Courant S-cardinal buoy fairly close to starboard.
Skirt round Cap d'Erquy at least a quarter of a mile off
to enter Erquy harbour from the NW.
From the NW: You would approach Erquy from the

NW if arriving from Paimpol or Bréhat. Make for Le
Petit Léjon W-cardinal buoy first, aiming to leave it
about half a mile to the north. At this point, Rohein
islet with its prominent W-cardinal beacon tower
will be 2½ miles to the south. Now make good 119°T
towards Erquy, keeping Cap d'Erquy fine on the
port bow and aiming to leave L'Evette N-cardinal
beacon tower half a mile to starboard. Although the
tides are fairly weak in this southern part of the Baie
de St Brieuc, don't allow yourself to stray too far
south of this track, or you'll come a bit too close to
the various dangers which extend eastward from
Rohein for about 2½ miles. Once L'Evette beacon
tower is safely abaft the beam, drop south a little so
that you make the final approach to Erquy harbour
from more or less due west.
At night from the NW: It is straightforward to enter
or leave Erquy at night in this direction, using the
north-west white sector of the harbour light at the
head of the outer mole (*Oc(2+1)WRG.12s11M*), but
keep right on the south side of the white sector (i.e.
at the green edge) as you make the final approach
past Cap d'Erquy.
From the W: You'd approach Erquy from this
direction i.e. sailing south of Rohein islet, if arriving

Chapter 4

from St Quay-Portrieux, Binic, Le Légué, or from Dahouet just round the corner on the other side of Pointe de Pléneuf. Simply leave Rohein W-cardinal beacon tower at least three quarters of a mile to the north and Petit Bignon W-cardinal beacon tower at least three quarters of a mile to the south while heading due east true towards Erquy. A couple of miles from Erquy, leave the Plateau des Portes rocks (drying 9.4 metres and usually showing) 3-4 cables to port and L'Evette N-cardinal beacon tower half a mile to port and then make for the end of Erquy's outer mole.

At night from the W: It is straightforward to enter or leave Erquy at night in this direction, using the west white sector of the harbour light at the head of the outer mole (*Oc(2+1)WRG.12s11M*), but keep on the south side of the white sector i.e. towards the red edge, as you pass Plateau des Portes rocks.

ASHORE

The best chandler nearest the harbour is Le Comptoir Co-opératif at 88 Rue du Port (Tel: 02 96 72 32 39). For engine repairs contact Régina Plaisance out at La Croix-Rouge (Tel: 02 96 72 13 70). The shops and main part of the town are 15 minutes stroll from the harbour area on the south-east side of the bay, although there are several good hôtel-restaurants conveniently near the inner mole and overlooking the beach at the head of the harbour. In town there are two excellent fish shops worth making for –

Poissonnerie du Centre at 12 Rue Clémenceau or Poissonnerie Rhoegineenne at 8 Rue Foch.

One of my favourite restaurants at Erquy is still L'Escurial on Boulevard de la Mer (Tel 02 96 72 31 56), where Véronique Bernard works wonders with the local Coquille Saint-Jacques (L'Escurial is closed on Sunday evening and Monday). It's also worth taking a taxi out to Relais St-Aubin (Tel: 02 96 72 13 22), south on the D68 between Erquy and La Bouillie, where Monsieur and Madame Josset will look after you well (for local taxis Tel: 02 96 72 49 58 or 02 96 72 32 32).

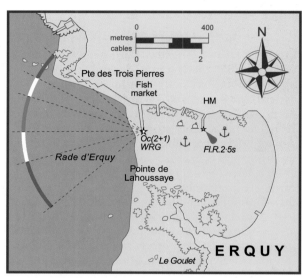

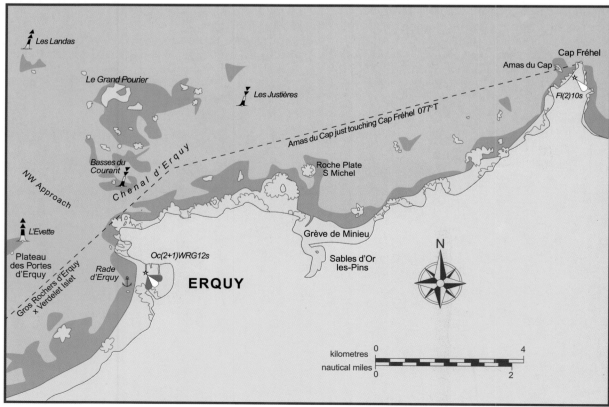

The drying part of the harbour at Dahouet. The marina is just off the picture to the right

PORT DE DAHOUET

Dahouet inlet is tucked into the south-east corner of Baie de St Brieuc about five miles west of Erquy, next to the small seaside town of Pléneuf-Val-André.

The snug marina basin makes an interesting port-of-call if you are coast-hopping between St Malo and Paimpol. The marina is retained by a sill across the southern part of the head of the inlet and offers complete shelter once you are inside. Access is for 2-2½ hours either side of high water for 1½ metres draught, although Dahouet inlet should not be approached in fresh onshore winds above about force 5.

APPROACH AND ENTRY

The entrance to Dahouet is just over a mile south-west of Pointe de Pléneuf and its off-lying islet of Le Verdelet (42m high). The final approach is made from north-westward, to avoid Plateau des Jaunes rocks, which extend a good mile seawards from Le Verdelet, and to clear the various drying dangers lurking up to nearly a mile offshore to the west of the mouth.

Approach from seaward: When approaching Dahouet from outside the Baie de St Brieuc, it's convenient to make for an outer waypoint a mile

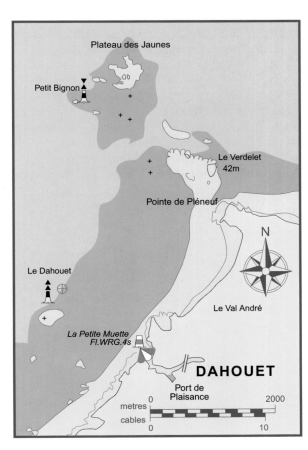

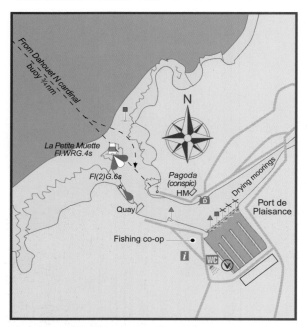

La Petite Muette
Fl·WRG.4s

From Dahouet N cardinal
buoy 3/4nm

N

Fl(2)G.6s

Quay

Pagoda
(conspic)
HM

Drying moorings

Port de
Plaisance

Fishing co-op

i

WC

due west of Rohein W-cardinal beacon tower and then track 143°T for 4½ miles towards an inner waypoint which leaves Le Dahouet N-cardinal buoy close to starboard. The entrance lies three quarters of a mile south-east of Le Dahouet buoy. The Rohein waypoint is a shade over six miles south of Grand Léjon lighthouse, which is the outer mark for the bay.

Approach from St Quay or Binic: If you are coming from the marina at St Quay-Portrieux, your departure waypoint will be just south of La Roselière W-cardinal buoy, at the south-east end of the Rade de St Quay. Le Dahouet buoy bears 106°T from Roselière, distant 7½ miles. From Binic, the pleasant yacht harbour three miles south of St Quay-Portrieux, Le Dahouet buoy lies a little south of east, nine miles across the head of the bay.

Approach from the E: When approaching Dahouet along the coast from the east, either from

Erquy or from St Malo via Cap Fréhel and the Chenal d'Erquy, you have to round Plateau des Jaunes by a good half mile and then leave Petit Bignon W-cardinal beacon well clear to the east before heading south for Le Dahouet N-cardinal buoy.

Entry: Dahouet entrance is tricky to identify from a distance, but the gap in the cliffs opens up as you reach the N-cardinal buoy. La Petite Muette green and white beacon tower stands right in the mouth of the inlet and a distinctive stone Calvary marks the east headland of the narrow entrance. Dahouet should only be approached within two hours of high water, and for a first visit you should come in during the last 1½ hrs of the flood. Entry is not advisable at night or in fresh onshore winds, say from between WNW through N to NNE.

Steer to come in at about 158°T, leaving La Petite Muette about 50m to starboard and then heading for the middle of the narrow dog-leg entrance. Keep towards the east side of the harbour until you reach the marina basin, which is to starboard just before the main area of drying moorings. The sill is passable with 1½ metres draught for about 2½ hours either side of HW at springs and 2 hrs either side at neaps.

FACILITIES

In the first instance, visitors should berth on the outside (east) face of pontoon 'O', in the south-west corner of the marina basin. The marina has water, electricity and showers. Dahouet village has a few local shops, but the nearest town centre is at Pléneuf-Val-André, about 1½ miles from the marina. For chandlery, engine or other general repairs contact Chantier Naval du Port de Dahouet, over on the north side of the harbour at 10 Quai des Terres-Neuvas (Tel 02 96 72 97 00).

The land-locked marina basin at Dahouet

The locked basin at Le Légué

LE LÉGUÉ
AND ST BRIEUC

Le Légué is the port for the major regional town of St Brieuc, which lies right at the head of Baie de St Brieuc on the west side of the shallow Anse d'Yffiniac. Le Légué has two long connected wet basins, entered by a lock, and yachts pass through a swing bridge to moor in the inner basin.

The whole harbour area feels rather run-down and is not particularly congenial for yachts, but may be of interest to skippers of fairly shallow draught boats who enjoy ferreting into off-beat harbours and anchorages.

You should only venture into this corner of Baie de St Brieuc by day and in quiet or offshore weather. The approaches to Le Légué dry out completely for nearly two miles seaward of the harbour entrance and you shouldn't proceed south

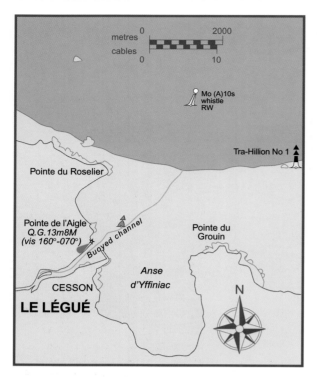

boats just outside the lock, which dry to about six metres on a soft muddy bottom. You can use a vacant mooring while waiting for the lock to open, or bilge and lifting keelers can stay outside the lock and take the ground.

You can contact the Capitainerie at Port du Légué on VHF Ch 12 / 16 (or Tel: 02 96 33 35 41). The lock times depend on the height of tide on the day, according to the following schedule:

Height of tide at St Malo	Lock gates open for the period
9–10 metres	1 hr before HW to 1 hr after
10–11 metres	1¼ hrs before HW to 1¼ hrs after
11–11½ metres	1½ hrs before HW to 1½ hrs after
Above 11½ metres	2 hrs before HW to 1½ hrs after

ASHORE

There are no special facilities for yachts, although the harbour area has a selection of chandlers, repair yards and marine engineers. St Brieuc town centre, the old part of which is quite attractive, is about a mile up the hill from the inner basin.

If you do end up in Le Légué for any reason, you may need cheering up. In this case I would strongly recommend calling a taxi and making for one of the following two restaurants to enjoy a long lunch or evening meal:

Le Quatre Saisons, 61 Chemin des Courses, St Brieuc-Cesson, Tel 02 96 33 20 38 (closed on Sundays). La Vieille Tour, 75 Rue de la Tour, St Brieuc-Plerin, Tel 02 96 33 10 30 (closed Sunday evenings and Mondays).

of Le Légué fairway buoy until about 2½ hours before high water. From the fairway buoy, make good 201°T for two miles, leaving Pointe du Roselier half a mile to starboard, until you arrive off No 1 green buoy, which is left close to starboard. The buoyed channel then leads south-west into a narrow river entrance. The lock is about half a mile in from the narrows on the south side of the harbour area. There are various moorings for local

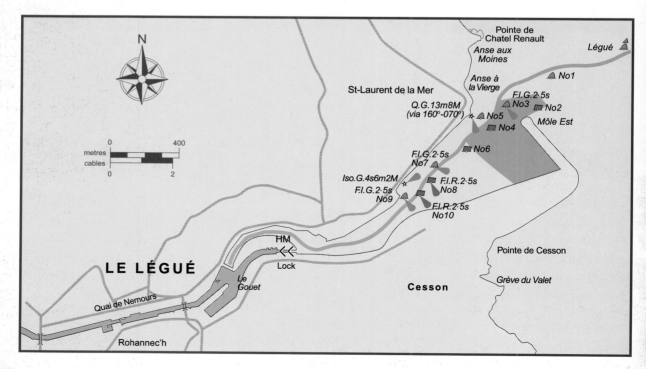

BINIC

This amiable seaside town, with its snug locked marina and wide sandy beaches, is tucked into the shallow south-west corner of Baie de St Brieuc, just $2\frac{3}{4}$ miles south of St Quay-Portrieux. The immediate approaches to Binic dry for almost a mile offshore, but the outer harbour is accessible for two hours each side of high water and the lock gate opens about an hour before high water, when the height of tide reaches 9.5 metres above datum. The gate closes again at high water.

In the days of sail, Binic was an important base for those hardy Bretons who fished for cod off the Newfoundland banks, but nowadays this gruelling occupation has been replaced by the more delicate business of cultivating oysters. There are still some local fishing boats, which moor in the outer harbour alongside the Môle du Pordic. The town caters mainly for tourists and yachts. The marina is conveniently close to the town centre, which has a varied selection of shops, restaurants and cafés.

I have always found Binic very relaxing and low-key. The friendly Club Nautique (Tel: 02 96 69 29 27) is the multi-triangular building at the root of Môle du Pordic, on the left side of the lock-gate you come in. There's a useful chandlery – Jean-Bart

Marine – on the north side of the lock near the Bureau du Port. You can call the marina on VHF Ch 9 or Tel: 02 96 73 61 86.

APPROACH AND ENTRY

From Erquy or Dahouet: Binic entrance is a couple of miles SW of the southern edge of Roches de St Quay and the approach from eastward, say from Erquy or Dahouet, is fairly straightforward. From Erquy to Binic is about 14 miles, passing south of Plateau des Portes d'Erquy and then between Rohein islet and Plateau des Jaunes before heading WSW across the southern part of the Baie de St Brieuc. From Le Dahouet N-cardinal buoy to Binic breakwater is a straight nine miles at 275°T.

From St Malo: You can either keep close inshore after rounding Cap Fréhel, following the Chenal d'Erquy, passing north or south of Plateau des

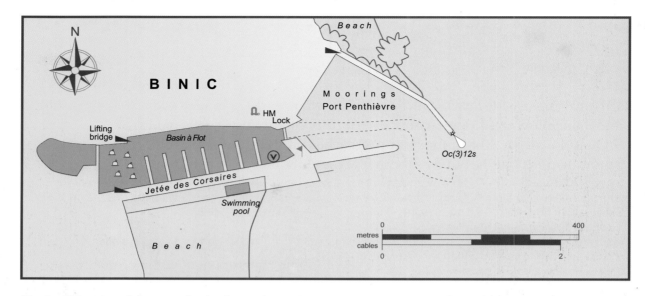

Portes d'Erquy, and then south of Rohein islet and its off-lying rocks; or you can stay outside Roches d'Erquy and Rohein, before heading SW to leave Rohein W-cardinal beacon-tower a couple of miles to the east and Caffa E-cardinal buoy close to the west and north. From the Caffa buoy to Binic entrance is just over four miles at 245°T. This second, 'big-ship' route is also the best way in if you are arriving directly from any of the Channel Islands, having first passed about half a mile either side of Le Grand Léjon lighthouse.

From Paimpol or Ile de Bréhat: The quickest route to Binic from the Anse de Paimpol or Bréhat is inside Roches de St Quay, provided you have an hour or two of rise above low water.

At night: You can reach Binic at night in good visibility, using the southern white sector of Le Grand Léjon (*Fl(5)WR.20s14/10M*) to keep safely between Roches de St Quay and Rohein. None of the dangers around the eastern and southern edges of the Roches de St Quay is lit, so you need to enter the south-west white sector of Rohein light (*VQ(9)WRG.10s*) and bring Binic east breakwater light (*Oc(3)12s12M*) to bear 250°T before quitting the Grand Léjon white sector and heading for Binic on this bearing.

Port Penthievre, Binic's drying outer harbour

RESTAURANTS

Binic is a popular seaside town and has a fair selection of hôtel-restaurants, bistros and crêperies. For dinner I rather like the restaurant in the Hôtel Le Benhuyc at 1 Quai Jean Bart (02 96 73 39 00). For lunch or a light supper we often make for the restaurant-crêperie Les Jardins de Binic, near the beach at 8 Boulevard Clemenceau (Tel: 02 96 69 28 25).

ST QUAY - PORTRIEUX

The spacious Port d'Armor marina at St Quay has made the Baie de St Brieuc a popular destination for visiting yachts. With a secure harbour to fall back to, you can contemplate visiting the whole range of fascinating anchorages and inlets around the wide bight between Cap Fréhel and L'Ost Pic.

Together with Dahouet and Binic, Port d'Armor has opened up Baie de St Brieuc as an attractive cruising ground once missed by most yachts on passage between St Malo and Paimpol. Port d'Armor is accessible at any tide, in most weathers, by day or night. The final approaches are protected from seaward by Roches de St Quay, an extensive area of offshore reefs and islets.

The popular seaside town of St Quay-Portrieux huddles behind Roches de St Quay on the west side of Baie de St Brieuc, about nine miles south-west of Le Grand Léjon lighthouse and a couple of hours' sail from Paimpol or Dahouet. The rocky approaches and old drying harbour have rather a wild, unvisited character, but Port d'Armor marina is a snug retreat, enclosed by two massive breakwaters. This large deep-water port caters for both yachting and commercial fishing interests in

an ambitious way, although the vast basin can seem rather soulless in gloomy weather. The town remains a pleasant, slightly old-fashioned resort, despite the pockets of modern development. Some of the newer, more garish cafés are somehow not quite French, yet they settle into the waterfront with distressing ease.

APPROACHES AND ENTRY

Rade de St Quay is the half-mile wide channel between St Quay and the off-lying Roches de St Quay. You can enter the Rade from the north or south, although it's important to identify the various marks carefully and not mistake one buoy or beacon tower for another. You'd normally use the north entrance if coasting down from Paimpol or Bréhat, or if you were coming in from near Grand Léjon. A useful waypoint in either case is a position

TIDES

HW St Quay Port d'Armor is at HW St Helier -0030.
Heights above datum: 11.2m MHWS, 1.3m MLWS,
8.5m MHWN, 4.1m MLWN.
The streams off St Quay can reach 3-4 knots at
springs and their directions are rather unpredictable
near Roches de St Quay.

CHARTS

Admiralty: 3674 (approaches), 3672 (harbour)
French SHOM: 7128

HAZARDS

Roches de St Quay are the main hazards in the
approach. The north-west end of these extensive
dangers is marked by Madeux W-cardinal beacon
tower and Ile Harbour lighthouse, and there are
several buoys and beacon towers around the south-
east fringes of the plateau.

WAYPOINTS

Northern approach waypoint, $\frac{1}{2}$ mile NW of Madeux
W-cardinal beacon tower
– 48°40.82'N, 02°49.28'W
Southern approach waypoint, close S of La
Roselière W-cardinal buoy
– 48°37.40'N, 02°46.38'W

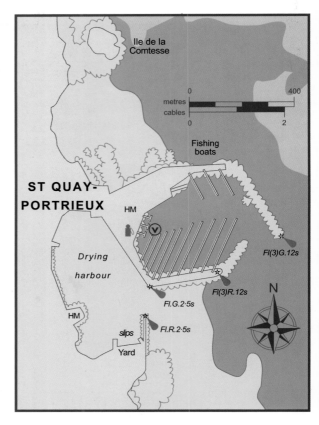

ST QUAY-PORTRIEUX

about $\frac{1}{2}$ mile north-west of Madeux beacon tower.
You would use the southern approach to the Rade
when coming up from Binic or across from
Dahouet or Erquy.

There are various shoal patches in the southern
approach to the Rade, which is best taken above
half-tide if possible. Neither approach is very
pleasant in poor visibility, even using GPS and
radar. The streams can reach 3-4 knots at springs
and their directions are unpredictable near Roches
de St Quay.

North entrance to the Rade: Leave Madeux and
Ile Harbour lighthouse each half a mile to port and
then steer to leave Moulières de Portrieux E-
cardinal beacon tower a quarter of a mile to
starboard. Port d'Armor north breakwater will be
prominent on the starboard bow and you should go
past it slightly before turning in to make the final
approach from the south-east.

South entrance to the Rade: Coming from Binic,
you can more or less follow the coast near HW,
passing outside L'Ours Seul isolated danger beacon
and Le Four white beacon tower before steering for
Port d'Armor north breakwater head. From
Dahouet or Erquy, make for the waypoint just south

of Roselière W-cardinal buoy before turning north-
west to leave La Ronde W-cardinal tower 4 cables to
starboard and an E-cardinal buoy 2 cables to port.
The marina entrance is then just over a mile to the
north-west.

At night: The south entrance to the Rade de St
Quay is easier at night than the north entrance,
because the south-east white sector of Port
d'Armor north breakwater leads you straight in
towards the marina entrance from west of La
Roselière buoy. The north entrance is slightly more
complex at night, since you have to follow a zig-
zag trail of three white sectors, but the approach
isn't difficult so long as you have reasonable
visibility and are careful about identifying which
light is which.

First make for the north approach waypoint, half
a mile north-west of Madeux W-cardinal beacon
tower, and pick up the white sector of Port
d'Armor north breakwater north light. Follow this
sector south until Ile Harbour is more or less
abeam and you pick up the white sector of Herflux
S-cardinal beacon. Turn south-east to follow
Herflux white sector until Ile Harbour light is
bearing almost north and its southern white sector
comes on. You can then turn to steer just west of
south keeping Ile Harbour showing white astern.
The entrance light on Port d'Armor north
breakwater head will then be showing its green

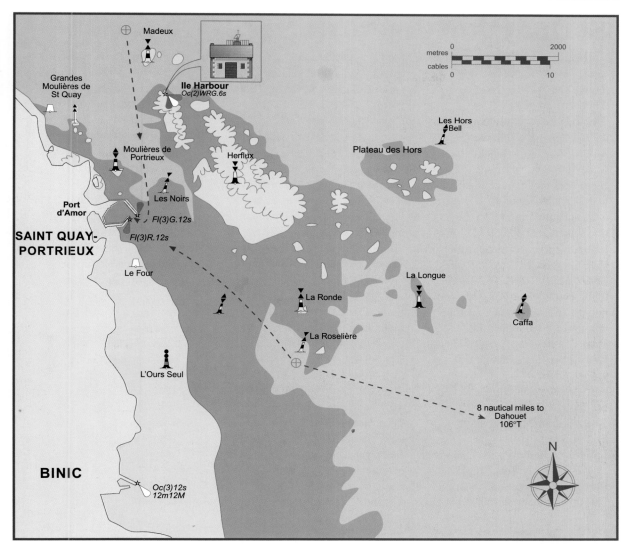

The following labels appear on the map:

Madeux

Grandes
Moulières de
St Quay

Ile Harbour
Oc(2)WRG.6s

Les Hors
Bell

Plateau des Hors

Moulières de
Portrieux

Herflux

Les Noirs

Port
d'Amor

Fl(3)G.12s

Fl(3)R.12s

SAINT QUAY-
PORTRIEUX

Le Four

La Longue

La Ronde

Caffa

La Roselière

L'Ours Seul

8 nautical miles to
Dahouet
106°T

BINIC

Oc(3)12s
12m12M

metres   0   2000
cables   0   10

N

sector, so you can simply carry on until this light is abeam, when you can turn in west towards the marina entrance.

FACILITIES

Port d'Armor is a spacious marina with fairly comprehensive facilities. There's always plenty of room for visitors, but you should first make for the reception pontoon just below the Capitainerie on the west side of the basin. The fuel berth (with both diesel and petrol) is next to this reception pontoon. Water and electricity are laid on at all berths and the showers are on the south-west side of the marina at the head of pontoon 4. The north side of the harbour is reserved for the fishing co-operative, with its landing quay and large auction market (la criée).

The town has a useful selection of shops and restaurants and the various local marine services can deal with most kinds of repair.

The distinctive picture-book lighthouse on Ile Harbour guarding the north approaches to St Quay

St Quay Port Guide

Harbour control: Capitainerie, St Quay Port d'Armor (Tel: 02 96 70 81 30, Fax: 02 96 70 81 31). VHF Ch 9.

Weather forecasts: Posted daily at Port d'Armor Capitainerie. Jersey Radio forecasts for the Channel Islands area are broadcast on VHF Ch 25 and 82 at 0645, 0745 and 0845 British local time and then 1245, 1845 and 2245 GMT. CROSS Corsen forecasts go out in clear French on VHF Ch 79 from Cap Fréhel at 0545, 0803, 1203, 1633 and 2003 French local time. You can ring the Météo France recorded forecast on 08.36.68.08.22.

Fuel: Diesel and petrol at the fuelling berth, opposite the Capitainerie.

Water and electricity: At all pontoons.

Showers: At the head of Pontoon 4.

Laundry: Laverie-Pressing du Port at 3 Rue Clemenceau.

Calor and Camping Gaz: at Chevalier, 53 bis, Boulevard Foch (walk into town from the marina and turn right at the end of Rue de la Victoire). Also at Galeries de la Plage at 6 Avenue Leclerc.

Chandlery: Co-operative Maritime, 24 Quai de la République (Tel: 02 96 70 42 06). Au Bon Cap, Esplanade du Port (Tel: 02 96 70 37 53). St Quay Plaisance, 30 Rue Paul de Foucault (Tel: 02 96 70 96 99).

Chart agents: St Quay Plaisance (as above).

Engineers: Ouest Marine Service, 73 Rue des Trois Frères Salaün (Tel: 02 96 70 41 93). Chantier CRAS (Nanni, Perkins, Volvo Penta, Yanmar), Quai Robert Richet, and at 68 bis, Rue des Trois Frères Salaün (Tel: 02 96 70 57 83 and 02 96 70 54 92).

General repairs: Chantier Mathurin CRAS (as for 'Engineers' above). Hervé Pacalet, Quai Robert Richet (Tel: 02 96 70 32 34). Alain Maintenance Nautique, 77 Rue Jeanne d'Arc (Tel: 02 96 70 48 58 or mobile 06 12 53 26 73).

Electronics: Elec Marine, 14 Rue de la Victoire (Tel: 02 96 70 92 64).

Shopping: Reasonable selection of food shops within walking distance of the marina. Small Comod supermarket at 50 Quai de la République. Several excellent Boucheries, Charcuteries and three good fish shops, of which my favourite is the Poissonnerie du Pen Hir at 9 Rue Clemenceau. The Boulangerie du Port, at 1 Rue du Commerce, is handy for the marina.

Banks with cashpoints: Several in town centre.

Tourist information:
Local taxi: P Batard, 7 Rue de la Victoire (Tel: 02 96 70 59 46 or 02 96 70 46 35).

Changing crews: Buses or taxi to St Brieuc, the provincial capital, which has good rail connections west towards Morlaix and the Roscoff-Plymouth ferry, and east via Rennes to Cherbourg, St Malo or anywhere else in France.

Restaurants

You always get an excellent meal at the three star **Hôtel Le Ker Moor**, at 13 Rue du Président Le Sénécal (Tel: 02 96 70 52 22). Le Ker Moor is splendidly situated on the cliffs north of the harbour area, 10-15 minutes stroll from the marina. Along the front, not far south of the marina, I also rather like the **Hôtel Le Gerbot d'Avoine**, at 2 Boulevard du Littoral (Tel: 02 96 70 40 09). For lunch, we often make for **Ar Mor** at 42 Rue des Trois Frères Salaün (02 96 70 30 32).

A DAY AWAY

Because Port d'Armor is accessible at all states of tide, it can be rather pleasant to base yourself at St Quay for a while and make day trips out to the nearby beaches. A pleasant spot in quiet weather is the Plage du Châtelet, just a mile NW of the marina entrance on the other side of Pointe de St Quay. You enter the bay from due north, leaving La Hergue white pyramid to starboard and Grandes Moulières green beacon to port.

Port d'Armor marina at St Quay

PAIMPOL

Paimpol is a charming old Breton town, clustered around a sheltered locked harbour at the head of the shallow Anse de Paimpol, a few miles south of Ile de Bréhat. The lock usually works for abour $2\frac{1}{2}$ hours each side of high water and the pontoon berths are handy for the town centre.

The Anse de Paimpol dries for almost two miles from the harbour, so you have to anchor well out in the bay until there's enough rise of tide to negotiate the inner channel. The town has good shops and several interesting restaurants.

As you come in from the east past the white, four-square tower of L'Ost Pic lighthouse to approach the shallow Anse de Paimpol, you can appreciate the full flavour of the North Brittany seascape. To starboard there are rocks everywhere, an amazing tangle of granite and seaweed which stretches away to the north and west towards Ile de Bréhat. You usually have to edge into the bay and anchor, and then wait for sufficient rise of tide to enter Paimpol basin. The low-tide anchorage is two miles short of the harbour entrance, but you won't be able to cross the drying flats and oyster beds to reach the lock-gate until an hour or two before high water. Once inside the basin though, you'll find perfect shelter at

the convenient pontoon berths just opposite the Maison des Plaisanciers.

This old Breton port has had a varied seafaring history. In the 17th and 18th centuries, the St Malo privateers sometimes used Paimpol as a local base for their sorties against British ships. In the 19th century, the local métier was fishing for cod, not in the relative comfort of the Channel approaches but way up in the freezing north off the banks of Iceland – and under sail of course. Nowadays, the main business of the Paimpolaise, no less successful, is cultivating succulent oysters from the extensive beds in the Anse de Paimpol. You'll see the forests of withies on either hand as you approach, and it's important to stay well clear of these areas when anchoring anywhere in the outer bay.

The Anse de Paimpol dries for two miles from the harbour breakwater, a dramatic and rather eerie sight on a low spring tide. The wet dock has two

TIDES

HW Paimpol is at HW St Helier −0030
Heights above datum: 10.9m MHWS, 1.4m MLWS, 8.3m MHWN, 3.9m MLWN.
The streams are fairly weak in the Anse de Paimpol, but can reach 3–4 knots at springs just offshore to the east and 2–3 knots in and near either end of the Chenal de la Trinité.

CHARTS

Admiralty: 3673 (good large-scale)
French SHOM: 7127

WAYPOINTS

Approach WP $\frac{1}{4}$M NE of Les Calemarguiers E-cardinal buoy – 48°47.18'N, 02°54.50'W
Inner WP 3 cables due N of Gouayan red beacon tower – 48°47.58'N, 02°56.74'W

HAZARDS

The N side of Anse de Paimpol is bordered by a string of rocks and islets, marked at their E end by Les Charpentiers E-cardinal beacon tower. These rocks are fairly steep-to and can be left a couple of cables to starboard as you come into the bay from the E. Two shoal areas lie to the east of L'Ost Pic lighthouse – Les Calemarguiers and Basse St Brieuc – marked at their E ends by E-cardinal buoys; you should pass outside these buoys if arriving below half-tide.

which has had some pontoons added. Because of its restricted access times, Paimpol doesn't become so crowded as some North Brittany harbours, even in high season. But it does attract a fair number of British regulars who, appreciating the ambience of the harbour and town, return year after year. Because Paimpol is on the same branch railway as Pontrieux, which connects with the main line at Guingamp, it has useful potential as a delivery base or a point for changing crews.

APPROACH AND ENTRY

From the Baie de St Brieuc: Coming across from St Malo, or up from Erquy, Dahouet, Binic or St Quay, the easiest approach to the Anse de Paimpol is to pass close east of the two E-cardinal buoys marking Les Calemarguiers and Basse St Brieuc shoals, and then make good about 285°T from Les Calemarguiers buoy for a mile until you are lined up to enter the Anse de Paimpol between the string of rocks leading out to Les Charpentiers E-cardinal beacon tower, which are left to starboard, and Gouayan red beacon tower, Roche Gueule red buoy and La Jument red beacon tower, which are left to port. You may have to allow for a strong cross-tide until you are safely west of Les Charpentiers and into the bay.

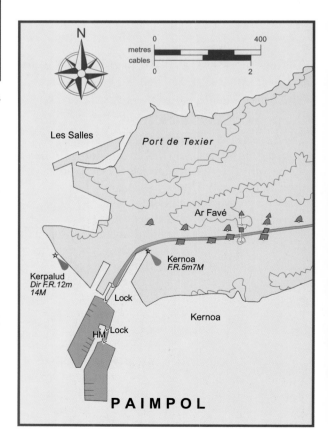

largish basins, entered via a lock from about 2½ hours before high water to 2½ hours after. The port de plaisance is in No 2 basin, straight ahead as you come through the lock and handy for the old town centre. The usual visitors' berths are at the end of pontoon A.

The small building next to the Maison des Plaisanciers has showers, wash-basins and toilets (not many though, so it's worth getting up early). There's a laundrette not far away in town. Perhaps because of its salty traditions, Paimpol is well endowed with boatyards, engineers and chandlers, most of which are located on the east side of the harbour along Quai de Kernoa. On the west side is the Paimpol base of the famous Iles de Glénan sailing school and you often see their small boats, crammed with willing apprentices, tacking around the rocky channels between Paimpol and the Trieux River.

To my mind, Paimpol's working harbour gives the place a congenial atmosphere. The port de plaisance is not so much a marina as simply a dock basin

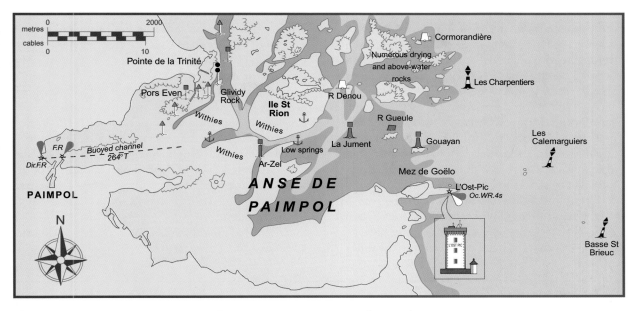

Direct from Guernsey or Jersey: When approaching the Anse de Paimpol from the direction of Guernsey, you should pass a mile east of Men-Marc'h E-cardinal buoy and the Plateau de Men-Marc'h and then make good due south for four or five miles before turning in towards Les Charpentiers. Coming from Jersey, you can head directly towards the outer waypoint a quarter of a mile NE of Les Calemarguiers E-cardinal buoy, until Les Charpentiers beacon tower bears north of west and you can head west into the Anse de Paimpol. You will probably have to allow for a strong cross-tide until you are safely west of Les Charpentiers and into the bay.

From Lézardrieux or Bréhat: The quickest and most straightforward route to Paimpol from anywhere in the Lézardrieux estuary is by way of the Chenal de la Trinité, which is reached from the roadstead immediately south of Ile de Bréhat. This channel may look a little intricate at first sight, but it's actually well marked and easy to follow above half-tide using Admiralty Chart 3673. You enter the north end from a position 1½ cables due east of Les Piliers N-cardinal beacon tower. If you reach this point a couple of hours before high tide, there will be plenty of water through the Chenal de la Trinité and across the Anse de Paimpol.

Entering the Anse de Paimpol: When the tide is well up you can sail into the Anse de Paimpol almost anywhere between the two arms of the bay – the north arm of rocks and islets culminating in Les Charpentiers beacon tower and the south arm consisting of the distinctive hump of Mez de Goëlo with the white four-square lighthouse of L'Ost Pic at the end of the off-lying rocks. In the middle of the outer

part of the bay, the two red beacon towers – La Jument and Gouayan, with Roche Gueule red buoy between them, can be left on either side near high water.

When arriving near low water, which will usually be the case if you have carried the tide along from St Malo, you should enter the Anse de Paimpol by following its north arm, thereby leaving the beacon towers and buoy to port. Pass a cable north of La

Jument and then drop south until Roche Gueule buoy is just open to the north of La Jument astern, bearing 085°T. It's then a matter of edging as far into the bay as you can before anchoring to wait for the tide. Admiralty Chart 3673 shows the shoal areas and narrow channel well.

To stay out in comparatively deep water, anchor as soon as Ile St Rion comes abeam to starboard. In quiet weather when the tide is dead low or rising and if you don't mind a 50/50 chance of nudging aground, you can follow the Roche Gueule stern transit very slowly until Roche Ar Zel spar beacon is 300 metres not quite abeam to port. Then turn NW between two areas of withies and anchor when Ar Zel is 4 cables to the SSE. You can usually start edging towards the head of the bay and the inner

buoyed channel about two hours before high water.

Above half-tide you can enter the bay by passing a quarter of a mile east of L'Ost Pic lighthouse i.e. inside Les Calemarguiers and Basse St Brieuc shoals. This will probably be a convenient approach when arriving from St Quay or Binic, or if you are working across from St Malo against a north-westerly and finish up by tacking close under Pointe de Minard.

When entering the bay by the Chenal de la Trinité within two hours of high water, leave Roche Glividy isolated danger beacon close to port and continue due south to leave the easternmost of two green spar beacons to starboard. Then turn south-west to leave Roche Saludène, a nearby green spar beacon and then Le Vahel green spar beacon each a good cable to starboard. Once abreast of Le Vahel, make good

---

Paimpol Port Guide

Harbour control: Maison des Plaisanciers, Quai Neuf, 22500 Paimpol (Tel: 02 96 20 47 65). VHF Ch 9.

Weather forecasts: Posted daily at the Maison des Plaisanciers during the season. The excellent Jersey Radio forecasts for the Channel Islands area are broadcast on VHF Ch 25 and 82 at 0645, 0745 and 0845 British local time and then 1245, 1845 and 2245 GMT. CROSS Corsen forecasts go out in clear French on VHF Ch 79 from Cap Fréhel at 0545, 0803, 1203, 1633 and 2003 French local time. You can ring the Météo France recorded forecast on 08.36.68.08.22.

Fuel: Diesel at the fuel pontoon just opposite the Maison des Plaisanciers, almost facing you as you come in through the lock.

Water: At the visitors pontoons or the fuel pontoon

Electricity: At the visitors pontoons.

Showers: At the Maison des Plaisanciers

Laundrette: At the head of Bassin No 1 in Rue de Labenne, near Quai Duguay Trouin. Also Au Lavoir

Paimpolais at 23 Rue du 18 Juin (the street opposite the station).

Calor and Camping Gaz: Le Lionnais Marine, Quai de Kernoa (Tel: 02 96 20 85 18).

Chandlery: Coopérative Maritime, 46 Avenue Général de Gaulle (Tel: 02 96 20 80 22). Dauphin Nautic, Quai de Kernoa (Tel: 02 96 22 01 72). Le Lionnais Marine, Quai de Kernoa (Tel: 02 96 20 85 18).

Chart agents: Dauphin Nautic (as above). Librarie Maritime, Rue de Romsey (Tel: 02 96 20 85 17).

Sail repairs: Le Lionnais Marine (as for chandlery above).

Engineers: Hamon Nautic (Nanni, Volvo Penta, Yanmar), Quai Loti (Tel: 02 96 20 82 00). Christian Raynaud (Perkins, Volvo Penta, Yanmar), Quai Armand Dayot (Tel: 02 96 20 82 72). SDMMP, ZA de Kerpont, 22504 Paimpol (Tel: 02 96 20 79 52).

General repairs: Chantier Naval Dauphin Nautic, Quai Armand Dayot (Tel: 02 96 22 01 72). Servimer, Quai Armand Dayot (Tel: 02 96 20 74 47).

Electronics: Servimer (as above).

Shopping: Paimpol has a reasonable selection of shops near the harbour.

Banks with cashpoints: Several in town centre.

Yacht clubs: Centre Nautique des Glénans, Quai Loti (Tel: 02 96 20 84 33).

Tourist information: At the Mairie de Paimpol, Rue Pierre Feutren (Tel: 02 96 55 31 70, Fax: 02 96 55 31 89).

Local taxi: Station taxi (Tel: 02 96 22 05 87). Bernard Omnès (Tel: 02 96 20 58 02).

Changing crews: From the station you can catch the local train to Guingamp via Pontrieux to connect with the main Brest-Rennes line. Thence west to Morlaix and the Roscoff ferry, or east to Rennes and St Malo or Cherbourg.

Restaurants

Paimpol has a wide selection of reliable eating places. The bustling **Restaurant du Port**, 17 Quai Morand (Tel 02 96 20 82 76) is always excellent value, but be there by 1215 or 1900. The three-star **Repaire de Kerroc'h** is one of my favourites, at 29 Quai Morand (Tel 02 96 20 50 13). It has a more ambitious menu, an elegant dining room and a restful atmosphere. **La Cotriade** is also a good choice, over on the east side of Bassin No 1 (Tel 02 96 20 81 08).

The distinctive lighthouse of L'Ost Pic, at the entrance to the Anse de Paimpol

263°T towards Paimpol and the head of the bay until you reach the inner buoyed channel.

At night: You need good visibility to approach Paimpol at night and it's prudent to time your arrival at the inner waypoint, north of L'Ost Pic, for two hours before high water. The red and white sectors of L'Ost Pic light (*Oc.WR.4s11/8M*) are useful for lining up your approach from offshore, but you ought to pick up the white sector of Pointe de Porz-Don light (*Oc(2)WR.6s15/11M*) before coming within three miles of the entrance to the bay. The white sector of Porz-Don leads into Chenal de la Jument to the north of Gouayan and La Jument red beacon towers and Roche Gueule red buoy, all of which are unlit. Note that Roche Gueule buoy is actually just in the south part of the white sector, so stay over to the north side of the white and keep a good lookout for the buoy as you come in. The Paimpol fixed red leading lights should come into line bearing 264°T soon after you pass Roche Gueule.

FACILITIES

Although Paimpol's friendly Port de Plaisance only has a limited number of visitors' berths, the harbourmaster usually manages to squeeze you in somewhere. The pontoons are straight ahead as you emerge from the lock. Visitors should make for a vacant space on pontoon 'A', but you can use any vacant finger if directed by the harbourmaster. In high season yachts are sometimes met by a dory as they enter the basin. The lock is worked for $2\frac{1}{2}$ hours each side of high water, although both gates are often left open for an hour or so near high water. The first locking out of the basin is $2\frac{1}{2}$ hours before high water and the last locking in is $2\frac{1}{2}$ hours after high water.

The pontoons have water and electricity, and there are showers and loos in the Maison des Plaisanciers. There is a diesel fuelling berth on the quay just opposite the showers. The town has a good selection of shops and restaurants and there are chandlers, engineers and all other yacht services over on the east side of the basin.

LÉZARDRIEUX &
ILE DE BRÉHAT

The Trieux River is quiet, deep and sheltered with wooded banks, reminiscent of the West Country in its upper reaches. The two snug *ports de plaisance* up at Lézardrieux are attractive with good facilities. Ile de Bréhat lies out in the estuary, which is wide and rocky with dangers extending several miles offshore. The tides are strong and the whole area must be treated with respect, but the channels are well marked and there are some idyllic anchorages in reasonable weather.

For many yachtsmen, this popular corner of the rocky Côte du Nord will provide a first and memorable Brittany landfall, perhaps after a pleasant day sail from Guernsey or Jersey, or maybe at the end of a slightly tense passage in murky visibility or a rising sea. The wide Trieux estuary is bounded on the west by a long sandspit, known as Sillon de Talber, and a straggling expanse of reefs guarded by the tall lighthouse of Les Héaux. To the east is Ile de Bréhat – hewn from pink granite, low-lying and scoured by the powerful tides on their way to and from the Bay of St Malo.

La Croix lighthouse, the distinctive front leading mark for the Grand Chenal

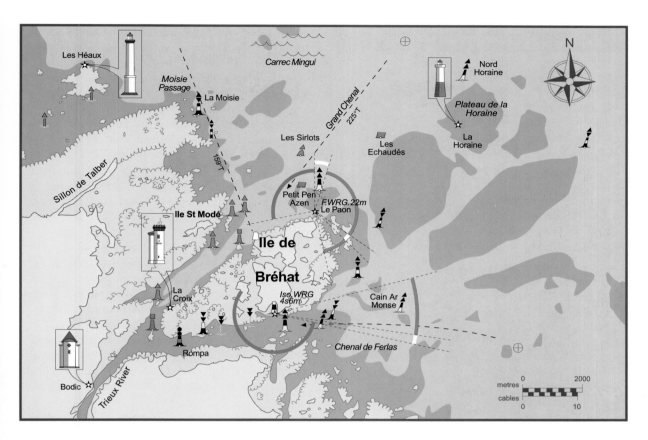

The Trieux estuary is one of the jewels of North Brittany. In the wide outer reaches where the tides run hard, the fantastic rocky channels change shape before your eyes as the extravagant ebbs and flows work their magic on the seascape. Inside the sheltering cordon of reefs, the river takes you peacefully up to the sleepy town of Lézardrieux.

The mainland is set well back and is not particularly high, so it can be difficult to get your bearings until you spot Les Héaux, or perhaps the smaller lighthouse of La Horaine which stands on the seaward side of the dangers north-east of Bréhat. Between Les Héaux and the mainland, the jagged granite seems to stretch for miles.

Once into the estuary, however, all sense of unease will evaporate. You are certainly surrounded by rocks, so that at low water it is difficult to visualise the way back to the sea. But the reefs which looked threatening from seaward now seem friendly and sheltering, a natural boundary for this picturesque and self-contained cruising area. Many of the rocks are steep-to, so you can tack reasonably close if you are working in under sail. The landmarks and beacon towers which were so enigmatic when glimpsed from offshore, now become a familiar part of your surroundings. On a fine summer's day, the

sea is a startling deep blue, a puzzling feature for which this coast is renowned.

Ile de Bréhat is the centre-piece of this unique seascape, and it has something of the same ambivalent quality. It is common enough, for example, for a skipper to be apprehensive when trying to make out the elusive marks for the Moisie Passage – a white pyramid in transit with a small chapel on a hill. It is also strange, an hour or so later, to be snugly anchored between these marks in Port de la Corderie, on the west side of Ile de Bréhat. The picture-book chapel, used by generations of seamen, casts a sympathetic aura over the anchorage, which is well protected on all sides. Bréhat is a small island, not quite two miles long and nowhere more than three quarters of a mile across. It is really two islands, which were joined by a road in the 18th century. La Corderie is the inlet between the north and south halves.

In fact everything about Bréhat is miniature – the small beaches, the narrow winding tracks, even the old women dressed in Breton black who bend double over tiny plots of potatoes and cabbages. The village of Le Bourg has a toy-town atmosphere, clustered around a diminutive square on the south island. But Bréhat is not hard on its inhabitants. It enjoys a soft local climate which, if not quite sub-

TIDES

HW Bréhat is at HW St Helier −0030 approx.
Heights above datum: 10.5m MHWS, 1.2m MLWS,
8.0m MHWN, 3.7m MLWN.
HW Lézardrieux is at HW St Helier −0030 approx.
Heights above datum MHWS 10.5m, MLWS 1.3m,
MHWN 8.0m, MLWN 3.8m.
Streams are powerful in the approaches, the ebb
setting WNW and the flood ESE between Les Héaux
and La Horaine at up to 6 knots at springs. In the
Chenal du Ferlas and the river itself above La Croix
lighthouse, spring rates can reach about 4 knots.

CHARTS

Admiralty: 3670, 3673
French SHOM: 7126, 7127

WAYPOINTS

Approach to the Grand Chenal, a mile NW of Nord
Horaine N-cardinal buoy
− 48°55.20'N, 02°56.12'W
Approach to Chenal du Ferlas, 1½ miles ESE of Cain
Ar Monse N-cardinal buoy
− 48°49.52'N, 02°54.70'W

HAZARDS

Although the estuary seems a veritable moonscape
of rocks, the main channels are deep and well
marked. When lining up for the Grand Chenal, guard
against being set east of La Horaine tower on the
flood, or too far towards Les Héaux on the ebb. When
approaching or leaving Chenal du Ferlas, check the
rise of tide and make sure that your track does not lie
too close to the various shoals east of Ile de Bréhat.

tropical, is at least mild enough to allow mimosa and
eucalyptus to flourish in the open. Landing here
during the summer, you soon become immersed in
the tranquillity of the place. The sandy soil,
sheltering pines and prosperous villas are more
reminiscent of the Mediterranean than the grey
wastes of the English Channel.

As you approach the island from seaward and line
up for the Grand Chenal, you begin to pick out the
distinctive Breton cottages which take the hard edge
off this landfall. The strange pink granite cliffs help
as well, giving Bréhat a fascinating profile which is
usually more welcoming than hostile. Yet my first
arrival off this coast had its nervous moments. We'd
come down from St Peter Port, west-about Roches
Douvres, and had seen little since leaving St
Martin's Point. We finally identified Les Héaux and

then Horaine. The navigation was probably fairly
accurate, but I was unfamiliar then with the local
strength of the tide. It wasn't long before La Horaine
had been swept well across to the starboard bow
instead of nicely on the port.

With a quiet sea and hardly any wind, this
powerful and invisible set seemed all the more
alarming, although it wasn't until we'd motored flat
out to regain Nord Horaine buoy that one could
appreciate the full force of the flood as it poured
across the estuary. The buoy was leaning hard over
with water piled high around its base. When we
drew into the river, of course, the peace and sense of
arrival was the more intense because of the stresses
of the previous half-hour.

As you follow the Grand Chenal, the rocks close in
on either side, not in a threatening way but taking
station as natural breakwaters which give
increasing shelter as you enter the estuary. Bréhat is
left close to port and the cross-tide cuts off as you
drop south of Pointe du Paon. Further upriver,
beyond La Croix lighthouse, the peaceful wooded
banks could easily remind you of the West Country,
except that the waterside houses have shutters and
pitched roofs which are as uniquely Breton as *gâteau
de beurre* or a field of artichokes. If you are ghosting
up under sail, some unmistakable Gallic clues may
drift across to set the scene; the buzzing of a moped,
probably ridden by an *ouvrier* in faded blue
overalls; or a couple of fishermen in an open boat,
volubly setting the world to rights above the chug
of the engine.

Given the right weather, this delightful estuary is
readily accessible during a summer cruise in the
Channel Islands area. It lies some 40 miles SSW of St
Peter Port and a similar distance from St Helier or St
Malo. If you are working east along the Brittany
coast, the Trieux is an easy day's sail round Les
Héaux from Tréguier or Perros. Most yachts go up to
Lézardrieux first, five miles upstream from Bréhat,
where the restful marinas will settle an agreeable
lethargy upon the hardiest of skippers. From this
sheltered base, it is easy to drop down to one of
Bréhat's anchorages for an afternoon, or to venture
further inland when the tide serves, to sample some
of rural Brittany at its best.

APPROACHES AND ENTRY

There are basically four routes into the Lézardrieux
estuary, two which approach the north side of
Bréhat and two the south side:

● The Grand Chenal, from the north-east, is the
main 'big-ship' approach to the river and the
natural route if you are coming from Guernsey or,
depending on weather and visibility, from Jersey.

Chapter 4

Perdrix green beacon tower, on the west side of the Lézardrieux River, is the last mark before you reach the marinas

- The Moisie Passage, from the NNW, joins the Grand Chenal off the NW tip of Bréhat. The Moisie is useful in fair weather and reasonable visibility if you are bound to or from Tréguier or further west along the coast. It can only be taken by day and is easier when leaving the estuary than when arriving.
- The Ferlas Channel, running east-west between Bréhat and the mainland, can be used at night with care. This is the obvious route when arriving from St Malo, and an alternative to the Grand Chenal in moderate weather when coming from Jersey.
- Chenal de la Trinité, which joins the Ferlas Channel at its eastern end, provides a short cut between Bréhat and the Anse de Paimpol by day only.

The Grand Chenal: This long approach to the Lézardrieux River is not difficult, but there are dangers several miles from the low-lying coast and you need to be on your guard against the powerful cross-tides which sweep round this corner between Les Héaux and La Horaine. These streams can exceed the rates given in the tidal atlases, especially during the middle hours of the flood.

Coming from Guernsey, either west or east-about Roches Douvres, it's useful to make for a waypoint about a mile NW of Nord Horaine N-cardinal buoy.

This buoy, left to port on the way in, itself lies just under a mile N of La Horaine lighthouse, which stands near the end of the rocky dangers extending three miles NE from Bréhat. As you approach the Nord Horaine waypoint from the north, Les Héaux lighthouse will be nearly 6 miles away on the west side of the estuary, so you may not see it if the visibility is hazy.

If you arrive off the estuary during the early flood, which is quite likely if you have worked the tides from either Guernsey or Jersey to best advantage,

the stream will be running strongly ESE. Allow generously for this set on the approach, to avoid being carried east of La Horaine. GPS is invaluable here in poor visibility.

From the outer waypoint, the Grand Chenal leads 225°T into the river and it's about four miles until you are abreast the north tip of Bréhat. Leave Les Echaudés red can buoy half a mile to port, Les Sirlots green conical buoy two cables to starboard and Basse de Pen-Azen red can buoy ¼ mile to port. You'll need to allow for cross-tide until you are south of Pointe du Paon, so try to pick up the Grand Chenal leading marks – La Croix lighthouse in line with Bodic tower. La Croix is white with a red castellated top and stands well back into the river. Bodic is high on the hillside, two miles behind La Croix on the west bank, and looks rather like a space rocket poking up through the trees.

If you can identify the marks, the leading line is useful in the outer reaches of the estuary, while you are trying to line yourself up and allow for the tide. Once you draw level with Bréhat, you can stray from the transit on either hand. One red and three green beacon towers mark the edges of the safe water, and the rocks on both sides are steep-to. This makes it fairly easy to work in or out under sail. As you near

La Croix, come to starboard to pass between the lighthouse and Moguedhier green beacon. Continue south-westwards to enter the river proper, leaving Le Vincre red beacon tower and Vieille de Loguivy W-cardinal buoy to port.

The river is straightforward south of this point. There are one or two beacon towers, but otherwise simply carry on upstream between the steep wooded banks. The small town of Lézardrieux lies three miles above Loguivy, just beyond where the river narrows at Perdrix. Leave Perdrix green tower 70–80 metres to starboard and then Roc'h Minguy red beacon and Donan Rocks (prominent above water) to port. You will see the Yacht Club de Trieux pontoons on the west shore just past the quay. Visitors berth at the outer end of the downstream pontoon, or at a vacant finger as directed. There are also some visitors' mooring trots opposite the marina.

At night: In some respects, so long as you have reasonable visibility, the Grand Chenal can be easier to enter by night than by day. The two outer lighthouses, La Horaine (*Fl(3)12s*) and Les Héaux (*Oc(3)WRG.12s*), guard the east and west sides of the estuary respectively, while La Croix (*DirOc.4s19M*) and Bodic (*Dir Q.22M*) are usually visible from

The entrance to Lézardrieux inner marina

Just above Lézardrieux, red and green beacon towers mark a double bend below the suspension bridge before the river widens out

several miles seaward of Nord Horaine. Back-bearings of Roches Douvres lighthouse (*Fl.5s*) or Barnouic tower (*VQ(3)5s*) can be useful in the outer approaches until the Grand Chenal leading lights have been identified and lined up.

Leaving the Trieux estuary at night via the Grand Chenal is relatively easy so long as you can pick up both leading lights at 10 miles range. In more murky conditions, you have to be very careful to allow for cross-tide once you draw north of Bréhat.

The Moisie Passage: This rather narrow channel leads into the Trieux from the NNW, skirting the edge of the reefs which extend north-east from Sillon de Talber, and keeping to the west of several shoal areas, including Plateau des Sirlots, which lurk in the outer reaches of the estuary. The Moisie Passage is useful if you are approaching Lézardrieux from round Les Héaux, or if you are leaving the river bound west along the coast. It needs moderate visibility and is best taken above half-tide, otherwise the safe corridor becomes very narrow in the northern part, especially between Noguejou Bihan and La Traverse. In fresh onshore winds, it is preferable to use the Grand Chenal.

Coming from seaward, you join the Moisie Passage 1¾ miles due E of Les Héaux lighthouse, preferably

well into the flood. From here, the leading marks on Ile de Bréhat will be 3½ miles away and difficult to make out, but steer to make good 160ºT and aim to leave Moisie E-cardinal beacon tower 100m to starboard. From the Moisie tower, continue on the same line to leave Noguejou Bihan E-cardinal beacon close to starboard. You will pass just west of three drying rocks – Ar Mesclek, Pierre Rouge and La Traverse. Now try to pick up the leading line through the glasses – Rosédo white pyramid, at the NW tip of Bréhat, in line with St Michel chapel on the hill behind it, bearing 160ºT.

Don't worry too much if you can't identify the transit, but continue making good 160ºT, checking your progress with back bearings of Noguejou Bihan or Moisie – these two in transit astern bearing 335ºT lead safely towards Bréhat slightly east of the St Michel line. About ½ mile from Bréhat, leave Vieille du Tréou green beacon tower close to starboard. Continue towards Rosédo pyramid if you are bound for La Corderie anchorage on the west side of Bréhat, or turn south-west to follow the Grand Chenal and enter the river.

The Moisie Passage is easier to use when leaving the estuary, because you can pick up the leading marks easily near Vieille du Tréou and then set off towards Moisie beacon tower with Rosédo and St

Michel chapel in transit astern bearing 160°T. In hazy weather the marks may become difficult to see after a while, but it's only 1½ miles from Vieille du Tréou to Noguejou Bihan and then another ½ mile to Moisie beacon tower. If you have left Lézardrieux at local HW and carried the first of the ebb downstream, there should be plenty of depth over the various dangers which lie close to the east of the St Michel leading line.

The Ferlas Channel: This route to and from the Lézardrieux river leads east-west between Ile de Bréhat and the mainland. It is well marked and can be used at any state of tide, although the outer approaches need some care if visibility is less than about three miles. Coming west along the coast from St Malo, you will probably pass a couple of miles N of Grand Léjon and then make for a position somewhere near Cain Ar Monse N-cardinal buoy, two miles east of Bréhat roadstead. You needn't pass north of Cain Ar Monse, except perhaps near low springs, and a useful landfall waypoint is 1½ miles ESE of the buoy. You can use the same waypoint coming up from Portrieux or Binic, having passed east of Basse St Brieuc and Les Calemarguiers E-

cardinal buoys and a good mile east of Les Charpentiers E-cardinal beacon tower, which marks the seaward end of the rocks bordering the north side of the Anse de Paimpol.

From this waypoint, make good 277°T to leave Cain Ar Monse buoy not quite ½ mile to the north, Men Gam E-cardinal tower 3 cables to the south, and pass midway between Lel ar Serive S-cardinal and Cadenenou N-cardinal buoys. If you can identify the transit of La Croix lighthouse (several miles distant in the Lézardrieux estuary) open just south of Ile Raguénes (off the SW corner of Bréhat) bearing 277°T, this line leads in from the landfall waypoint to a position nicely in the middle of Bréhat Roadstead.

When lining up for the Ferlas Channel, you need to allow for the strong tidal streams in the offing, which set NNW on the ebb and SSE on the flood. Rates here can reach 4–5 knots at springs, a tricky cross-tide if the visibility is poor. Once into the Ferlas, between Bréhat and the mainland, the streams more or less follow the channel, setting west on the ebb and east on the flood at up to 4 knots. Directions and rates vary locally near the entrances to secondary channels such as the Chenal de la Trinité and the Kerpont Passage.

The visitors' trots in the Lézardrieux River opposite the marinas

From Bréhat Roadstead,
the Ferlas leads a shade
south of west and it's
usually easiest to keep
over to the north side and
follow the S-cardinal
beacons along to the
narrows opposite Roc'h
Rouray. Pass rather
closer to Roc'h Rouray
than to Trebeyou S-
cardinal tower, and then
about 75 metres either
side of Rompa red and
black tower. Continue
west by south into the
Lézardrieux River,
leaving the fishing boat
moorings off Loguivy
close to port. Roc'h
Tranquet and Vieille de
Loguivy W-cardinal
buoy are left to starboard.
Note that this buoy has
recently replaced Vieille
de Loguivy beacon tower
and is moored a little way
SW of where the tower
once stood.

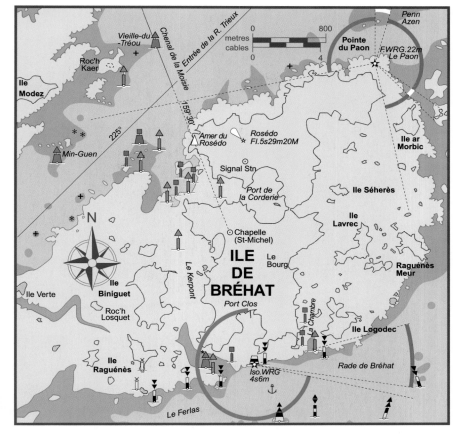

At night: The Ferlas leading lights bring you in from
the ESE on a similar line to that described above. The
offshore waypoint lies near the north edge of the
white sector of Men Joliguet (*Iso.WRG.4s*) and about
3¼ miles from it.

From the waypoint, keep this white sector bearing
279–283°T until you are just over half a mile from
Men Joliguet, and then follow:

- The narrow white sector of Roche Quinonec
  (*DirQ.WRG*) bearing 257–258°T, to a position
  some 120 metres south of Rompa (unlit).
- The white sector of Kermouster light
  (*DirFl.WRG.2s*) bearing 270–272°T, for a mile from
  Rompa.
- Turn SW into the Lézardrieux River to follow
  Coatmer leading lights (*F.RG*) and then the white
  sector of Perdrix (*Fl(2)WG.6s*).

ANCHORAGES AROUND BRÉHAT

La Corderie: La Corderie is the long inlet on the
west side of Bréhat between the two 'halves' of the
island. In the days of sail this bay was an active
haven for fishing boats and small coasters, probably
because of its ease of access from the Grand Chenal.
First make a position 200–250 metres west of Rosédo
white pyramid daymark and then head due south
for ¼ mile, between Men-Robin green spar beacon

and Kervarec Rock. Once past Kervarec, which is the
prominent islet on the north side of the entrance to
La Corderie, turn ESE between two red port-hand
spar beacons and a green starboard hand. At springs
you need to fetch up just inside these outer spars, but
at neaps you can sound in further, towards or just
beyond the next green. Don't confuse La Corderie
entrance beacons with a pair of beacons a little
further south, which mark the narrow mouth of the
Kerpont Passage.

La Corderie is the most secluded of the Bréhat
anchorages. Protected by land on three sides and
with the natural breakwater of the estuary reefs not
far to the west and north-west, it offers good shelter
under most conditions, except in very strong winds
from between N and W. In these conditions it's the
swell which makes the anchorage difficult,
especially on the flood. Bilge-keelers or yachts with
legs can find peace and quiet by edging well into the
inlet and drying out.

At the head of La Corderie is Pont ar Prat, the
narrow causeway connecting the two parts of
Bréhat. Walking south from here, it is not far to the
village of Le Bourg. If you head north, the terrain
becomes more rugged and the trees more scarce. The
track forks left to Rosédo lighthouse and the
semaphore station, and right to the craggy
promontory of Pointe du Paon.

La Chambre anchorage, tucked into the south-east corner of Ile de Bréhat

Port Clos: Despite being Bréhat's principal link with the mainland, Port Clos is not particularly convenient for yachts, except for a short stay or unless you can take the ground and tuck right into the north-west corner. One of the drawbacks when anchoring off is that the local vedettes are continually coming and going with day tourists from Arcouest.

The outer anchorage will be subject to eddies from the strong streams which run along the south coast of the island between Le Ferlas and the Kerpont Passage, so someone really ought to stay aboard the yacht all the time.

Port Clos has various landing slips – there's a low-water causeway out on Grereva Point, a half-tide landing on the west side of the harbour, and a stone jetty at the head of the harbour. Just above the jetty, conspicuous from the Ferlas Channel, the Hôtel Bellevue is a good bet for lunch. From here it is only a short stroll into Le Bourg.

La Chambre: Bréhat's most popular anchorage lies just east of Port Clos, between the SE tip of the island and Ile Logodec. La Chambre is best near neaps, when you can tuck well in and stay afloat. Entry is straightforward, heading north into the inlet from

the Ferlas Channel. La Chambre S-cardinal beacon marks a drying rock a cable SE of the mouth. A little way east of this beacon, you will often see a long line of yellow fishing floats.

Leave the outer red spar beacon to port, the green spar to starboard, and watch the echo-sounder as you approach the inner red beacons. The further in you can anchor the better, but do the sums carefully because the tide starts falling quickly a couple of hours after HW. Bilge-keelers or yachts with legs can edge towards the local moorings and take the ground on the sandy bottom. At springs, you may have to fetch up 50 metres or so WSW of the green entrance beacon to stay afloat – this spot catches the tidal stream in the Ferlas Channel and some of the wash from the vedettes.

La Chambre fills up with yachts at weekends in high season, but is comfortable for an overnight stay mid-week in moderate weather. It is sheltered from the west, north and north-east, and easy to leave at night if the weather changes. The landing slip is on the west side of La Chambre. From here, a narrow, sandy path winds northwards along the coast between well kept houses and quiet, secluded gardens to Le Bourg.

Lézardrieux Port Guide

Harbour Masters: Thierry Calliot and Olivier Paranthoen, Port de Plaisance, Lézardrieux (Tel +33 296 20 14 22). VHF Ch 9 from 0700-2200 during the season.

Weather forecasts: Posted at the Bureau du Port during the season, but ask at the office if, early in the morning, it hasn't yet been pinned up. The Jersey Radio forecast is useful for this area (VHF Ch 25 or 82 at 0645, 0745 and 0845 British local time, and then 1245, 1845, 2245 GMT). CROSS Corsen forecasts go out in clear French on VHF Ch 79 from Cap Fréhel at 0545, 0803, 1203, 1603 and 2003 French local time. Météo France recorded forecast on 08.36.68.08.22.

Fuel: Diesel and petrol from the marina fuelling berth 0830–1030 and 1500–1630 local time.

Water and electricity: At the pontoons

Yacht Club: The YC de Trieux has a convivial bar and visitors are welcome to drop in for a drink or a morning café-croissant. Open 0900 to 0200 during the summer.

Showers: At the two marina facilities blocks and at the Yacht Club de Trieux.

Gas: Camping Gaz from Trieux Marine, opposite the inner marina basin.

Repairs and engineers: Three good yards, on the concourse opposite the inner marina basin, can between them sort out any repairs: Trieux Marine (Tel: 02 96 20 14 71); Ets. Ruffloc'h (Tel: 02 96 22 10 36); Ateliers du Trieux (Tel: 02 96 20 17 76).

Sail repairs: Voile Performance, on the marina concourse (Tel: 02.96.20.10.62).

Rigging repairs: Technique Gréement, 73 Rue du Port (Tel: 02.96.22.10.94)

Shopping: Butcher, baker and good supermarket up in town.

Banks: Two small banks up in the town square – Crédit Agricole and Crédit Mutuel.

Buses/trains: Two buses a day from Lézardrieux (outside Auberge du Trieux) to Lannion, where (after a long wait) you can catch another to Morlaix, then a taxi to the Roscoff ferry. Nearest station at Paimpol, 6km by bus or taxi from Lézardrieux. Trains from Paimpol via Pontrieux to Guingamp and thence east to St Malo via Rennes or west to Morlaix and Roscoff.

Restaurants

Up in town, I usually make for the **Auberge du Trieux** – turn left at the far end of the square and it's about 150 yards along on the left at Impasse du Four Neuf (Tel 02 96 20 10 70). The new proprietors, Dominique and Maudez Le Corre, have devised some interesting menus, although I think their wine list needs developing. You'll certainly enjoy an excellent evening and be well looked after.

Down near the marinas, the convivial '**La Marina' Hôtel-Bar-Restaurant du Port** is a good bet for coffee, lunch, dinner or just for a drink (Tel 02 96 20 10 31). Hervé and Claudine Guegou are most genial hosts.

My favourite crêperie, **Moulin de la Galette**, is on the right as you start to climb the hill up to town (Tel 02 96 20 18 36). Further up the hill, on the right just before the church, the **Avel-Mor** crêperie is also excellent (Tel 02 96 22 21 38).

BERTHING AT LÉZARDRIEUX

Most yachts stay at this quiet and friendly town for at least one night during a visit to the Trieux estuary. The pilotage upriver to Lézardrieux is straightforward and the two sheltered marinas are situated on the west shore, about 3½ miles above La Croix lighthouse. The river narrows just before you reach Lézardrieux – leave Perdrix green beacon tower 80 metres to starboard and then leave Roc'h Minguy red beacon and the islet of Roche Donan to port. You'll see the outer marina just beyond the town quay on the starboard hand.

Outer marina: This is the first marina you come to, to starboard just past the quay where the local sand-barges unload. If there's room, moor alongside the outer pontoon of the downstream line (marked

Visiteurs), or in one of the downstream facing fingers nearest to it. If in doubt, try calling 'Port de Lézardrieux' on VHF Channel 9, or moor at any pontoon and ask at the *Bureau du Port* at the head of the downstream line.

The tide can set strongly through the pontoons, so take care when choosing and approaching a berth. Visiting yachts moor at the outer end of the downstream pontoon if there's room, but you can use a vacant finger as directed. There are visitors' moorings in the river opposite the marina, and a long waiting pontoon where you can wait for the inner marina to open or wait for slack water to berth at the outer marina.

Inner marina: The newer inner marina lies just upstream from the original marina. You enter between a red and a green spar beacon across an

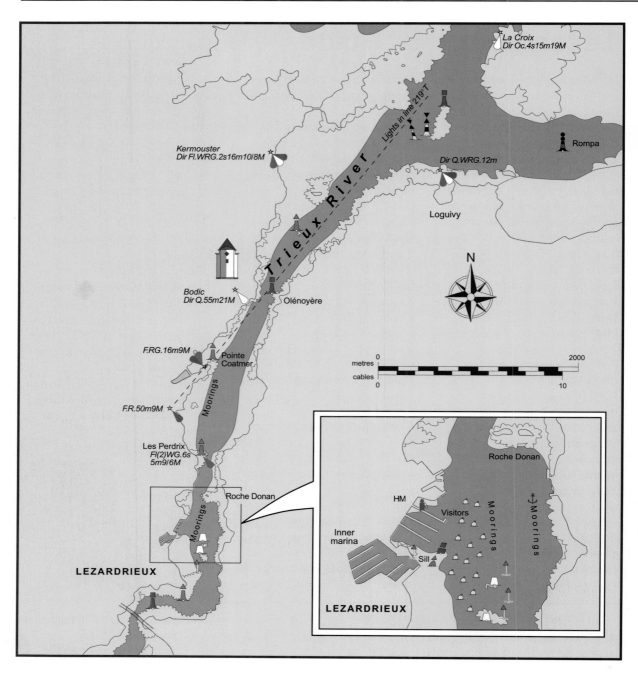

Map labels:

- La Croix / Dir Oc.4s15m19M
- Lights in line 219°T
- Rompa
- Kermouster / Dir Fl.WRG.2s16m10/8M
- Dir Q.WRG.12m
- Trieux River
- Loguivy
- Bodic / Dir Q.55m21M
- Olénoyère
- N
- F.RG.16m9M
- Pointe Coatmer
- metres / cables
- 0 ... 2000
- 0 ... 10
- F.R.50m9M
- Moorings
- Les Perdrix / Fl(2)WG.6s / 5m9/6M
- Roche Donan
- Moorings
- LEZARDRIEUX

Inset (LEZARDRIEUX):

- Roche Donan
- HM
- Visitors
- Moorings
- Moorings
- Inner marina
- Sill
- LEZARDRIEUX

automatic sill, which is open for about three hours each side of high water. Visitors can be allocated a berth in this marina, but ask at the *Bureau du Port* first.

These inner pontoons are more sheltered than the river marina and are out of the fast-running tide. However, the river marina has the advantage that you can leave at any time, and it's also cooler in high summer, when the new marina can be very hot in the middle of the day.

River moorings: Visitors can use the trot moorings just opposite the marinas, which some yachtsmen prefer to the more gregarious pontoons. There are also some attractive moorings in the bight just

below Perdrix green beacon tower, off the west shore. Charges for the moorings are a little under two-thirds of the marina rates. Be careful when coming ashore in the dinghy because the tide runs strongly in the river near springs. Those who value peace and quiet above convenience can sometimes find a vacant trot over on the east side of the river.

ASHORE AT LÉZARDRIEUX

On the concourse between the two marinas, the Yacht Club de Trieux has a pleasant spacious bar and a welcoming atmosphere. The small town of

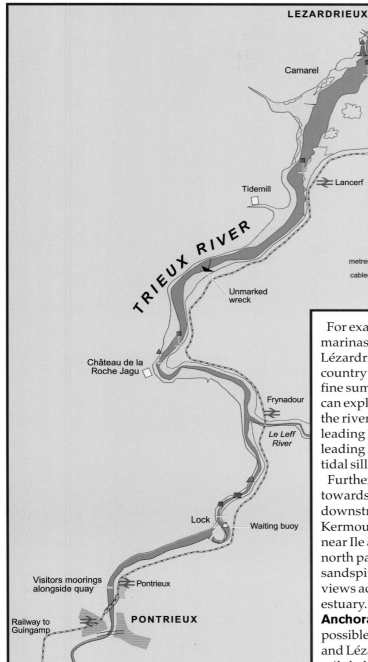

Chapter 4

For example, if you set off north from the marinas, following the D20 downstream out of Lézardrieux, you come out into restful farming country which shimmers in lazy French heat on a fine summer day. Depending on your energy, you can explore various lanes that lead down towards the river – one takes you to the Coatmer rear leading light, the next down to Coatmer front leading light and the local *parc à huitres* behind its tidal sill.

Further down the D20, you can follow a track towards Bodic leading light. Press on another mile downstream to reach the peaceful hamlet of Kermouster and the picturesque estuary shores near Ile à Bois. Energetic walkers might carry on north past Pommelin and Lanmodez to the long sandspit of Sillon de Talber and its fascinating views across the reefs and islets of the outer estuary.

Anchorages in the river: There are various possible anchorages in the river between Loguivy and Lézardrieux, but the best spot is in the half mile below Perdrix, off the west shore and clear of the local moorings. Don't anchor out in the fairway, because the local sand barges often navigate at night.

THE RIVER ABOVE LÉZARDRIEUX

Just above the Lézardrieux marinas, the river narrows and makes a sinuous double bend before the suspension bridge, which has about 17m clearance at MHWS. Rocky ledges extend well out from either bank, marked by large red and green beacon towers. The tide can be strong and the wind

Lézardrieux is ten minutes walk up the hill, with a good butcher and baker in the square, a useful supermarket, a couple of small banks and a post office. The supermarket is 100 metres past the post office on the left.

The peace and quiet of Lézardrieux has changed little since we used to anchor off the quay long before even the first marina was built. Time passes amiably between leisurely meals, and there are some excellent country and coastal walks to help you work up an appetite for the next menu.

Dried out at La Corderie, on the west side of Bréhat

The snug pontoons in the Lézardrieux inner marina

fluky in this stretch, so you need to be vigilant when going through under sail.

  Above the bridge you dog-leg past a pair of beacon towers and then the river widens considerably for almost a mile. The channel is not marked across this expanse and lies roughly a quarter of the width off the west shore. Before the river narrows again, there's an anchorage off the west bank near some small boat moorings and then a plateau of rocks stretches well out from the east shore, marked by a red beacon tower. Leave this tower to port and thereafter follow the line of the river, keeping to the outside of the bends. The upper reaches dry at springs, but by choosing your spot carefully you can lie afloat at neaps as far up as the tight bend at La Roche-Jagu, 3 miles above Lézardrieux. This peaceful anchorage beneath the wooded banks is overlooked by an impressive 16th century chateau, which is well worth the climb to visit if you have an afternoon to spare.

PONTRIEUX

This unassuming country town lies not quite five miles above Lézardrieux. You lock into a canal basin and carry on past the tall buildings of a dairy and the sand dredgers' quays, before arriving at the attractive yacht berths on the port hand. There are showers nearby and the town centre is only ten minutes walk away. The basin has between 2–4 metres depth at mean tides. The locals always welcome visiting yachts and the trip up to Pontrieux is ideal if you appreciate the gentle pace of rural

Lézardrieux inner marina is a heat-trap in high summer

Brittany and like a change from harsh sea air.

Leave Lézardrieux at around half-flood, so as to reach La Roche-Jagu no earlier than 2½ hrs before high water. Above the chateau, keep close to whichever side of the river is flanked by cliffs and stay wide of the shelving meadow banks. In the straight stretch before Pontrieux lock, leave a green buoy to starboard and then a red buoy to port by at least 5m. You'll see the lock on the starboard hand as the river curves to port.

There's a waiting buoy just upstream from the lock entrance, but leave a red post beacon well to

Pontrieux Port Guide

Harbour Master: Yves Fertier. Bureau du Port at 64 Rue du Port, Pontrieux (Tel: 02 96 95 34 87).
VHF: Call Port de Pontrieux on Ch 12.
Weather forecasts: Pontrieux tends to be rather out of touch with the weather at sea. Météo France recorded forecast on 08.36.68.08.22.
Fuel: Petrol or diesel by jerrycan from the town garage, 15 minutes walk from the quay. The Harbourmaster has a hand-trolley you can borrow.
Water: At the quay. Your own hose will be useful.
Showers: At the shower block on the quay.

Gas: From a small shop in town near La Place de la Liberté
Repairs: Not easy. The nearest boatbuilders and engineers are at Paimpol, a 25 minute train ride from the station near the harbour. 'Services et Loisirs' in town may be able to help with minor engine problems.
Shopping: Pontrieux town centre has a wide selection of shops, 10 minutes walk from the harbour.
Banks: There are two banks in Place Yves le Trocquer.
Launderette: A dry-cleaners in the Rue St Yves will do laundry.
Bus/train connections: From Pontrieux station, close to the harbour, there are five trains a day both to Paimpol and Guingamp, with good connections to Paris, Rennes, St Malo, Morlaix (and thence by bus or taxi to Roscoff) and Brest. The town garage can arrange hire-cars from Paimpol. Local taxi at the Bar des Pompiers, just off the town square

Restaurants
Good value lunch near the harbour at the **Café de l'Abbatoir** (Mon-Fri) or in town at the **Restaurant de la Vallée** (Mon-Sat). Dinner at **Restaurant Le Bail** (during the season) near the Mairie. There's an interesting restaurant at the **Château de la Roche-Jagu** (best arrange for a taxi at the Bar des Pompiers).

The rocky channels off the west coast of Ile de Bréhat

port as you approach it. Smaller boats can lie alongside the short quay immediately east of the gates, although it's not safe to dry out here and you should return downstream if, for any reason, you don't enter the basin. You can call the lock-keeper on VHF Ch 12 or 16 and the lock can be worked from 1½ hrs before to 1 hr after high water. When leaving Pontrieux, it is best to lock out as near high water as possible.

DAY TRIPS AROUND THE TRIEUX

Lézardrieux makes a perfect base for family cruising as there are various diversions within easy reach of the marinas. A day trip to Ile de Bréhat is a must if the weather is fine. I would make for Port de la Corderie rather than La Chambre, because the latter tends to become more crowded. La Corderie has a pleasant beach on its south side and there's also plenty of scope for exploring in the dinghy. If the children are off on their own though, keep an eye on the potentially strong tidal stream out near the entrance to the Kerpont Passage. You can land at the jetty on the north side of the anchorage and walk round the island, either heading south to Le Bourg or north towards Pointe du Paon.

A trip up the Trieux River is another possibility. You needn't aim to lock in at Pontrieux, but you might cruise up as far as the lock on the tide and then drop back downstream before the ebb starts in earnest. There are various tranquil spots in the lower reaches where you can anchor for lunch and a siesta. If the tides are not convenient and you have an outboard, you could always leave the boat at one of the Lézardrieux marinas and make a dinghy expedition up-river.

For those who have bikes aboard or who are keen on walking, there is some attractive country to explore around Lézardrieux. Try setting off northwards from the marina, meandering the lanes and tracks which more or less follow the west bank of the river downstream.

If you are staying at Pontrieux for a day or two, the train ride to Paimpol can make a pleasant outing, taking in a leisurely lunch at the popular and bustling Restaurant du Port, or perhaps at the more elegant Repaire de Kerroc'h.

PASSAGES BRITTANY I

PASSAGES ROUND LES HÉAUX

Sillon de Talber and the tail of rocks straggling seawards to Les Héaux, seem to form a natural and psychological divide between two mini cruising areas which each have a distinctive atmosphere. To the east of Les Héaux is the Channel Islands area, bordered by the Cherbourg Peninsula and that part

of the Brittany coast which encloses the Gulf of St Malo between Mont St Michel and Bréhat. The main French harbours are mostly an easy day sail from one or other of the Channel Islands – Granville and St Malo from Jersey, Paimpol and Lézardrieux from Guernsey or Jersey – and once you have reached France, the Islands never seem far away. But west of Les Héaux feels more foreign somehow, and you might be said to have reached the real nub of North Brittany, those 30 plus miles

of rocky coastline between the Tréguier River and Roscoff.

Rounding Les Héaux is not difficult, but you have to keep your wits about you and time the tides with care. The streams are powerful off this corner, especially across the Lézardrieux estuary between Les Héaux and La Horaine. The area is known for its sinister patches of overfalls, which swirl uneasily in calm weather and break heavily in a fresh wind over the tide. Because the dangers extend several miles

Les Héaux lighthouse from northward

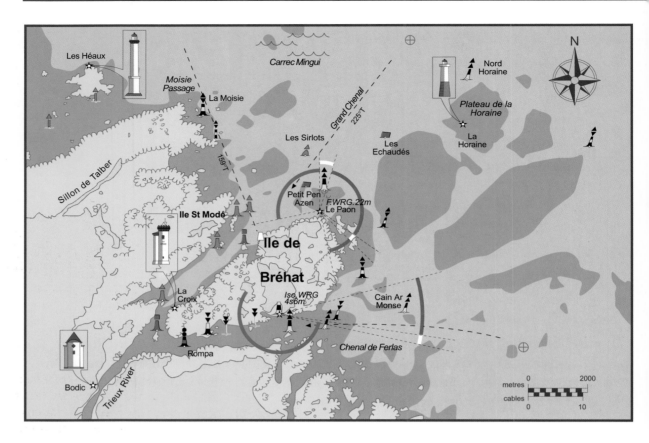

offshore, you can find yourself short of landmarks in hazy visibility. The good news is that, by working the tides to advantage, you can be accelerated round Les Héaux faster than the navigator can keep up with the plotting.

WESTWARDS ROUND LES HÉAUX

If you are bound from Lézardrieux round Les Héaux, it's best to leave Lézardrieux marina near local high water, taking the first of the ebb down-river and aiming to pick up the west-going stream offshore. When you reach Ile de Bréhat, you have to decide whether to take the Moisie Passage out of the estuary, or to stay with the Grand Chenal and go right out and round the various shoals which the Moisie cuts inside. The Moisie Passage is much to be preferred, because it saves a good four miles and adds a bit more pilotage interest to the trip, but the Grand Chenal is safer in fresh onshore winds and when visibility is less than about two miles.

The Moisie Passage leading marks are easy to pick up when you are leaving the estuary – Rosédo white pyramid at the NW tip of Bréhat in transit astern with St Michel chapel bearing 160°T. This line passes close inside various drying shoals and leaves the following marks close to port – La Vieille du Tréou green beacon tower, Noguejou Bihan E-

cardinal beacon, and Moisie E-cardinal beacon tower. Even though, near high water, you should have plenty of depth over the unmarked dangers to starboard, it's wise not to stray from the transit. The marks on Bréhat often become difficult to make out as you approach Noguejou Bihan and Moisie, but leaving these two close to port and making good 340°T will take you out into the clear water north-east of Les Héaux.

If you opt for the 'big ship' route via the Grand Chenal, bear in mind that the westerly set will increase as you draw north of Bréhat. From Les Sirlots green conical buoy, aim to make good NNE for three miles, until you are clear of the Roch ar Bel and Carrec Mingui overfalls, before turning west to round Les Héaux. You can check your set by back-bearings of Pointe du Paon or Rosédo on Bréhat, and your seaward progress by crossing these with bearings of Les Héaux or La Horaine lighthouses. GPS is invaluable in this area of strong cross-tides, enabling you to make good an efficient track without going too far out of your way.

Les Héaux is steep-to immediately on its seaward side. You need not stay more than about $\frac{3}{4}$ mile north of the outer rocks (Men Lem and Les Trois Branches) as you go round, and it's safe to tack in a bit closer than this if you are working against the wind. However, there are extensive drying rocks up to two miles west and west-north-west of Les Héaux, marked at their extremity by La Jument N-cardinal buoy. Keep an eye on your westerly set and be sure to pass north of La Jument before altering course for Basse Crublent red buoy, the outer mark for the Tréguier River, just over two miles to the WSW.

EASTWARDS ROUND LES HÉAUX

La Jument buoy is the key distance-off mark when you are rounding Les Héaux from west to east. From La Jument, make good ENE to clear the outer rocks by ¾ mile. If you are heading for the Lézardrieux estuary via the Moisie Passage, alter to the ESE as soon as Les Héaux lighthouse is abeam, but otherwise continue ENE to pass seaward of Roch ar Bel and Carrec Mingui overfalls. For the Moisie Passage, follow the directions given in the Lézardrieux chapter. If you are taking the Grand Chenal into Lézardrieux, make good due south true once you have passed Roch ar Bel, allowing for the cross-tide to join the main La Croix leading line not quite ½ mile ENE of Les Sirlots green conical buoy. Thereafter follow the directions for Lézardrieux.

Moisie E-cardinal beacon tower is left about 100 m to the west when you are using the Moisie Passage

PASSE DE LA GAÎNE

The Passe de la Gaîne is the narrow passage which leads inside Les Héaux, between the lighthouse and Le Sillon de Talber. In suitable conditions above half-tide it offers a useful daytime short cut between Lézardrieux and Tréguier, but the pilotage needs care as there is not much room to stray from the leading line.

Chapter 5

The picture-book chapel of St Michel, the back leading mark for the Moisie Passage

The white Rosédo pyramid on the west coast of Ile de Bréhat, seen here almost in transit with the St. Michel chapel

PASSE DE LA GAÎNE WESTWARDS

If conditions are suitable for Passe de la Gaîne, you will have taken the Moisie Passage out of the Lézardrieux estuary, following the directions given above in 'Westwards round Les Héaux'. Once Moisie beacon tower is ½ mile astern and before Les Héaux lighthouse bears due west true, come to port to make good west true and bring the lighthouse fine on the starboard bow.

About ¼ mile SE of Les Héaux lighthouse is an outlying above-water rock two metres high – Roc'h ar Hanap. You enter Passe de la Gaîne by making good 241°T and leaving Roc'h ar Hanap 1½–2 cables to starboard. Thereafter leave the first green beacon a cable to starboard and steer to leave the second green beacon only 150 metres to starboard. The leading marks for the Passe de la Gaîne will be 4–6 miles distant in the Tréguier estuary, about a finger to the right of Plougrescant church spire – Men Noblance black and white beacon on the south tip of Ile d'Er in line with a similar beacon on the mainland behind it, bearing 241°T. If you can make out these marks, all well and good, but otherwise take the beacons as your points of reference until the transit comes into view.

Not quite ¾ mile beyond the second green beacon, you pass between a red and a green beacon which form a gateway through the Pont de la Gaîne. This gate lies 4 cables south-east of Les Duono, a prominent group of above-water rocks 7 metres high, and the green beacon of the pair stands close east of Le Colombier, a hump-backed above-water rock which appears, at a distance, to be well isolated from Les Duono. Once past Pont de la Gaîne, keep on the leading marks to pass close south of Petit Pen ar Guezec green conical buoy and thereafter follow the directions for the Tréguier River.

Fresh onshore winds can cause a swell in the Passe de la Gaîne, especially near high water, which will make it more difficult to pick out the leading marks as well as creating a rather malevolent atmosphere. Visibility and height of tide are critical – you should be able to see at least three miles and you need a good five metres rise above datum. The shallowest part of the passage dries two metres, midway between the two green beacons, and it's best to edge very slightly north of the leading line in this stretch.

PASSE DE LA GAÎNE EASTWARDS

When heading east through the Passe de la Gaîne, from Tréguier towards Lézardrieux, you have the advantage of being able to identify and line up the leading marks at close range. Reverse the directions given in 'Passe de la Gaîne westwards' above. Aim to pass the Pont de la Gaîne beacons just before half flood, which will give you plenty of rise in the Passe de la Gaîne and the Moisie Passage, as well as a fair tide into the Lézardrieux estuary.

CÔTE DE GRANIT ROSE

TRÉGUIER RIVER

Similar in some ways to the Trieux, the delightful Tréguier River narrows more quickly and is even quieter and more rural as you wind inland. The approach is often easier than the Trieux because the cross-tides are not so savage and the entrance is more compact. The old town of Tréguier lies 6 miles upstream and the marina is handy for shops and restaurants. You can anchor in a pool ¾ mile below the marina, or nearer the mouth at Roche Jaune.

Tréguier is a Brittany jewel, uncut but quite exquisite, an ancient market town commanding the confluence of two peaceful rivers – the Guindy and the Jaudy. Although Tréguier is the largest port-of-call along the magical Côte de Granit Rose, the town itself is invisible from offshore and stays well hidden until the last bend in the river. As you first approach the outer estuary from seaward, there hardly seems a penetrable gap in the coast, let alone an idyllic sheltered valley winding inland through placid Brittany farmland.

To the east, an impressive dragon's tail of reefs straggles offshore from the low sandspit of Sillon de Talber, ending in an isolated outcrop and the tall lighthouse of Les Héaux. This impressive tower is 48 metres high, a welcome yet forbidding sight in uneasy weather. To the west, a strangely anonymous rocky shore falls away towards Anse de Perros and its cordon of islands. Ahead you sense an inlet of sorts, but the way in doesn't reveal itself until the last moment, when you spot Basse Crublent, the crucial outer buoy.

La Corne lighthouse

Basse Crublent lies about four miles west of Les Héaux lighthouse, and the Grande Passe leads south-east from this buoy before turning south-west into the river. The outer estuary is littered with rocks, like the Trieux, but is not so wide as the latter, the cross-tides are not so powerful and the marks are closer together. Approaching from seaward, you can somehow sense a promise of shelter not far away, whereas the Trieux usually remains enigmatic and reserves its welcome until your arrival is well advanced.

The Grande Passe leaves a low-lying island – Ile d'Er – and its off-lying rocks to starboard, and the various drying dangers of Basses du Corbeau and Basses de Roc'h Hir to port. A mile and a half after the dog-leg to the south-west, the prominent white lighthouse of La Corne guards the entrance to the river proper. Above La Corne the channel narrows considerably but is well marked right up to Tréguier by buoys and beacons. You need to follow the marks carefully because the mudbanks shelve steeply outside the fairway. Most yachts can reach Tréguier at any state of tide, although those with deeper draught may have to wait for an hour or two after a low water spring. So long as you trickle up gently with the flood, there is no great problem about nudging aground in the soft mud.

TIDES

HW Tréguier is at HW St Helier −0055 approx
Heights above datum: 9.7m MHWS, 0.9m MLWS,
7.4m MHWN, 3.3m MLWN.
Streams may reach 3-4 knots at springs in the offing
near Basse Crublent buoy, and you can experience
faster rates in the river, especially through the marina
during the middle hours of the ebb.

CHARTS

Use Admiralty Charts 2668 and 2669 for passage
planning, 3670 for the coastal approaches to
Tréguier and 3672 for the Tréguier River. The French
SHOM chart 7126 is useful if you have a taste for the
more intricate local channels and off-beat
anchorages.

HAZARDS

There are numerous drying rocks between Les
Héaux and Tréguier entrance. Coming from
eastward, it's important to stay north of La Jument N-
cardinal buoy and then find Basse Crublent red
buoy. Allow for any cross-set between Basse
Crublent and the first pair of buoys in the Grande
Passe – Le Corbeau red can and Pierre à l'Anglais
green conical. A powerful current runs through
Tréguier marina and it is preferable to arrive or leave
near slack water.

WAYPOINTS

P1 $1\frac{1}{4}$ miles due N of Les Héaux lighthouse –
48°55.82'N, 03°05.09'W
P2 $2\frac{1}{2}$ miles due N of Les Héaux lighthouse –
48°57.07'N, 03°05.09'W
P3 $\frac{1}{4}$ mile due N of La Jument N-cardinal buoy
– 48°55.66'N, 03°07.94'W
P4   3 cables 287°T from Basse Crublent buoy
– 48°54.44'N, 03°11.51'W
P5   1 cable E of Petit Pen ar Guézec green buoy
– 48°52.58'N, 03°09.17'W
P6   1 cable N of La Corne lighthouse
– 48°51.50'N, 03°10.53'W

smells hold a tempting promise of shellfish and you
reach the charming village of Roche Jaune on the
starboard hand. Here are the distinctive Breton
houses with their high-pitched roofs, traditional
shutters and spacious rambling gardens. Fishermen
sit expectantly on the quay, small open boats potter
about, the sun feels warm and you realise why you
came to North Brittany.

Further upstream you pass a fish-farm to port,

where caged young specimens thrash about to the
annoyance of passing gulls. Then, round a curve in
the valley, you see the soaring pierced spire of
Tréguier cathedral, which has been watching over
the river for centuries.

The marina provides a snug berth and Monsieur
David Beron, the Maître de Port, will make you feel
at home. Because the tides can be strong through the
marina pontoons, you should time your arrival (and
departure) for as near slack water as possible. Safely
moored and fendered, you can relax, pour a well-
earned drink and savour your arrival in this
splendid historic town.

There are many sides to Tréguier's character, as a
couple of lazy days here soon reveal. The old quarter
is a treasure-trove of medieval timbered buildings,
which lean together overhead as you wander the
ancient cobbled streets and alleys. The famous St
Tugdual cathedral dominates the main square and
the magnificent open-work spire is a unique
emblem for the town and surrounding country.

Tréguier was a busy trading port in the days of sail,
as you might guess from the fine stone quays just
below the marina. On a still summer morning, as
you linger over coffee at the Café du Port, it's easy to
imagine the harbour packed with cod-fishing
schooners, coasting luggers and the outlandish
bisquines that were once a common sight on the
Côte de Granit Rose. North Brittany has the sea in
her veins and the gentle ghosts of past mariners flit
along the quayside at Tréguier, probably on their
way for a *petit rouge* at the smoky inner bar just
behind you.

As the tide slips past and the sonorous Catholic toll
of the great cathedral bell drifts across the river, it
seems as if time has hardly touched Tréguier. On
market days, old rural habits continue. The town is a
lively spectacle of colour and bonhomie when the
main cathedral square and Place du Général de
Gaulle are packed with stalls. You can buy almost
anything here, but the local Breton vegetables are
usually the best bet. Here you know that onions are
onions and potatoes taste like they used to. Real
fleshy tomatoes cry out for olive oil and basil,
reminding you that lunch is not far away. The
buxom farmers wives who run the stalls add up
three bills at once, slip you an extra tomato for luck
and twirl their paper bags with panache.

Towards midday, the market crowds thin out as
tantalising smells waft from kitchen windows and
you start to hear the convivial clatter of cutlery. As
the cathedral chimes strike twelve, the square seems
suddenly empty. It is time, across the whole of
France, for lunch.

The English are apt to fret around noon, when shops
and banks close, harbourmasters vanish and even the

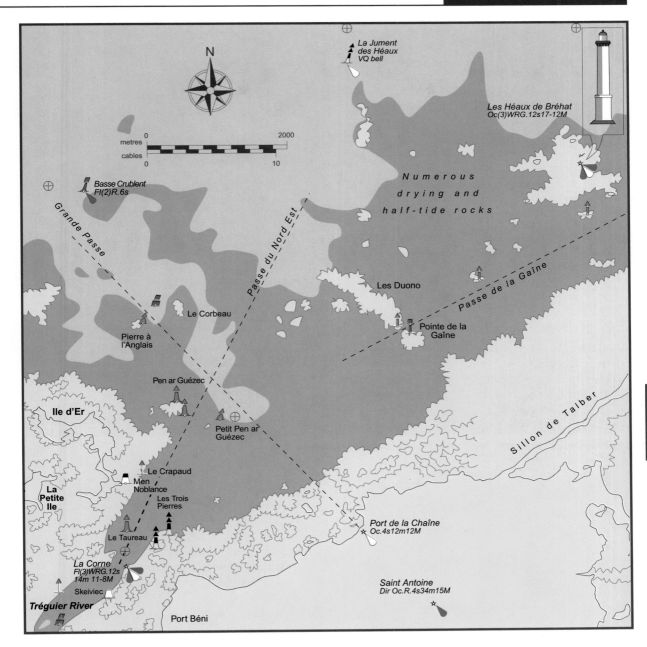

La Jument
des Héaux
VQ bell

Les Héaux de Bréhat
Oc(3)WRG.12s17-12M

N u m e r o u s
d r y i n g   a n d
h a l f - t i d e   r o c k s

Basse Crublent
Fl(2)R.6s

Grande Passe

Passe du Nord Est

Les Duono

Passe de la Gaîne

Le Corbeau

Pierre à
l'Anglais

Pointe de la
Gaîne

Pen ar Guézec

Sillon de Talber

Ile d'Er

Petit Pen ar
Guézec

Le Crapaud
Men
Noblance

La
Petite
Ile

Les Trois
Pierres

Le Taureau

Port de la Chaîne
Oc.4s12m12M

La Corne
Fl(3)WRG.12s
14m 11-8M

Skeiviec

Saint Antoine
Dir Oc.R.4s34m15M

Tréguier River

Port Béni

metres 0 ... 2000
cables 0 ... 10

most dedicated marine engineers pack up their tools. But this is a country where people still have time for lunch, look forward to lunch, enjoy their lunch. Here is a true hallmark of civilisation, and long may it continue. Munching a snatched sandwich is a meagre occupation for the middle of the day.

So in Tréguier you should start browsing the menus well before the magic hour. Then simply choose a comfortable table, empty your mind of schedules and plans, sit back and relax. The perfect lunch will unfold in the next two hours, in just the right order at just the right pace. The Auberge du Trégor is a good choice, just off the cathedral square.

After lunch, meandering back towards the river,

you might visit the Musée Renan, a little way down Rue Renan on the corner of Rue Stanco. Here is the old timbered house where Ernest Renan was born, a 19th century philosopher and the most famous son of Tréguier. Rue Renan was once the main street linking the port and town centre – the river used to lap the bottom of Rue Renan before the present quays were built.

If you are cruising early in the season, your visit may coincide with the famous Pardon of Saint Yves, patron saint of lawyers, a spectacular gathering held each year on the Sunday nearest to 19th May. A mass at the cathedral is followed by a long procession of dignitaries and visiting lawyers, which winds

Most yachts can get up the river to Tréguier marina at any state of tide

through the town and out to the neighbouring village of Minihy-Tréguier.

Before leaving Tréguier, you must certainly visit that most revered of French chandlers, 'Co-Per Marine', on the east side of the bridge just above the marina. Here at Trédarzec, an elegant old tide mill discreetly houses, on three storeys, an Aladdin's cave of real chandlery, some traditional and some elegantly modern. As you open the door, forgotten smells of canvas, natural rope, tarred marlin and linseed oil make you catch a nostalgic breath. From far inside comes the low murmur of French voices, discussing shackles and breaking strains with serious intent. Naval bronze rubs shoulders with gleaming stainless steel. Don't miss it.

APPROACH AND ENTRY

There are three possible routes into the Tréguier estuary:

- The Grande Passe, from the NW, is the main, most often used approach. It can be taken by day or night at any state of tide.
- The Passe du Nord-Est, from the direction of La Jument buoy, is a bit tricky and tends to be used mostly by locals. It needs good visibility and can only be taken by day, preferably above half-tide.

- The Passe de la Gaîne, between Les Héaux lighthouse and Sillon de Talber, provides a short cut to or from the Lézardrieux estuary by day only. To navigate this passage safely, you ought to have 3 miles visibility and a good 5 metres above datum.

The Grande Passe: The outer mark is Basse Crublent red whistle buoy, about 4 miles west of Les Héaux lighthouse and 2½ miles north-east of Pointe du Chateau. Coming from the east round Les Héaux you will probably have picked up La Jument N-cardinal buoy first, from which Basse Crublent bears 242°T not quite 2½ miles. Coming from the west, say from Perros or Port Blanc, stay a good 2 miles offshore to avoid various coastal dangers, before edging inshore again for Basse Crublent. Coming from seaward, Pointe du Château can be identified from a distance by Plougrescant church spire, the most prominent landmark along this stretch of coast apart from Les Héaux. A useful landfall waypoint is a position 3 cables WNW of Basse Crublent.

From this waypoint, make good 142°T to pass between Pierre à l'Anglais green conical buoy and Le Corbeau red can, allowing carefully for cross-tide and keeping slightly nearer Le Corbeau if anything. These two buoys lie just over a mile from Basse Crublent, so they are usually not too difficult to find

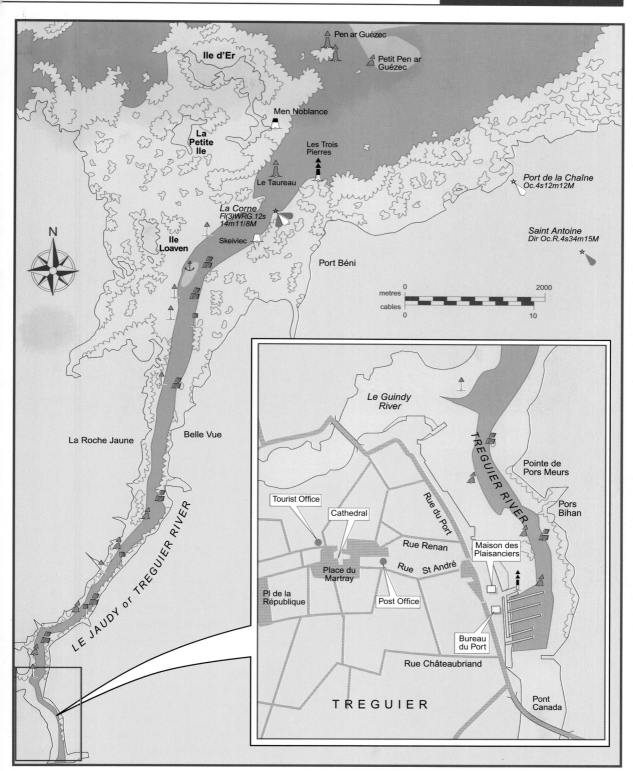

even in murky visibility. Note, however, that the charted leading marks for the Grande Passe – Port de la Chaîne white house in line with St Antoine lighthouse bearing 137°T – are not at all easy to identify by day, so it is best simply to shape a course between the buoys.

From the gateway formed by Pierre a l'Anglais and Le Corbeau, make good 137°T for a mile to leave Petit Pen ar Guézec green conical buoy close to starboard. This track leaves the two Pen ar Guezec green beacon towers a good 3 cables to starboard, although above half-tide you can short

Looking downstream from Pont Canada towards Tréguier marina

The lively Tréguier market in Place du Martray

cut the green conical buoy and leave the beacon towers just a cable to starboard, following round to the south and then the SSW to pass inside Petit Pen ar Guézec rock and join the Passe du Nord-Est. A useful transit for this route is the large water tower on with Pleubian church spire bearing 154°T. This line leads directly from Basse Crublent buoy through the red and green gateway to a point a cable east of the Pen ar Guézec beacon towers.

Near low water, after passing Basse Crublent buoy, be sure to keep safely west of Basse Crublent rock, which has only 1.3m over it at LAT.

From Petit Pen ar Guézec buoy head SW towards La Corne, not quite 1½ miles away, keeping an eye out for the numerous small crab-pot floats in this part of the estuary. The transit for this leg is Skeiviec white pyramid beacon kept just to the right of La Corne lighthouse bearing 215°T. This line leaves two green spar beacons each ¼ mile to starboard and Les Trois Pierres N-cardinal beacon tower 150 metres to port. Once abreast Les Trois Pierres, come to starboard to pass midway between La Corne and Le Petit Taureau green beacon tower, but then steer to leave Banc du Taureau green conical buoy close to starboard. Turn to starboard round this green buoy and steer 235°T until you have picked up the first red fairway buoy opposite Ile Loaven. Thereafter simply follow the buoys and spar beacons up-river.

Tréguier marina and the famous pierced spire of the cathedral church

At night: The leading lights are straightforward in reasonable visibility. Stay seaward of Basse Crublent (*Fl(2)R.6s*) until you pick up the transit of Port de la Chaîne (*Oc,4s*) and St-Antoine (*DirOc.R.4s*) bearing 137ºT. This line leads between Le Corbeau and Pierre à l'Anglais (both unlit) and just E of Petit Pen ar Guézec (unlit), where you pick up the white sector of La Corne (*Fl(3)WRG.12s*). Passing the lighthouse needs a little care, because neither Le Petit Taureau tower nor Banc du Taureau buoy are lit. Once round Le Taureau buoy, the SW white sector of La Corne leads to the first port-hand fairway buoy (*Fl.R*), after which all the river buoys are lit.

Passe du Nord-Est: This daytime-only passage is not very often used by visiting yachts, but it saves a couple of miles between La Jument N-cardinal buoy and the Tréguier estuary. It needs good visibility, a quiet sea, and should be taken above half-tide. From close alongside La Jument buoy, bring Tréguier cathedral spire between the two Pen ar Guézec beacon towers bearing 205ºT and follow this transit for about a mile. When Les Duono rocks (just over a mile away to port) definitely bear less than 160ºT, alter course towards Les Duono until Tréguier spire comes into line with Skeiviec white pyramid beacon bearing 207ºT. Follow this transit carefully, leaving Roc'h Hir (only just showing at high water) not quite ¼ mile to port.

Once into the estuary, you can either continue along this transit to La Corne, leaving the nearest green beacon tower a cable to starboard, or you can veer to the south to leave Petit Pen ar Guézec buoy to starboard and pick up Skeiviec beacon in line with La Corne bearing 215ºT. The Passe du Nord-Est is usually more straightforward when you are leaving the estuary, because it is easier to pick up the marks. If in doubt about the visibility or swell, it is safer to stick with the Grande Passe just for the sake of two miles.

Passe de la Gaîne: This short-cut passage from Lézardrieux is described in 'Passages round Les Héaux'.

BERTHING AT TRÉGUIER

Tréguier marina is very friendly and agreeable, whether you are there just for a night and a good meal or lingering a few days to get to know the town and the surrounding country. The facilities are comprehensive and the Maître de Port, David Beron, is most helpful. The tide in the river runs strongly through the marina pontoons, especially on the ebb, and you should always plan to approach or leave Tréguier marina within an hour of slack water. Once alongside, make sure you are well secured with double springs and plenty of fenders.

The visitors' berths are at the end of the two downstream pontoons and are clearly marked as you arrive through the approach channel. These outside berths are the easiest to approach and leave, although when they are full you may be directed to a pontoon further in.

Most yachts can get up to Tréguier Marina at almost any state of tide, although towards low springs the last half mile is touch and go. If you wait downstream for the tide, aim to arrive at the marina just half-an-hour before high water. It's feasible to come up or leave at night, providing you take it slowly, follow the buoyed channel carefully and watch out for the occasional sand-barge moving around at odd hours.

Anchorages in the river

There are various anchorages in the river below Tréguier, although you have to choose your spot with care. Always show a riding light at night.

Château de Kestellic: The most popular anchorage is a mile downstream from the marina, a cable below No 10 red buoy that marks the edge of Banc de Ven. Anchor under the west shore in 6–7 metres, opposite Château de Kestellic.

Mouillage de Palamos: Further downstream, you can anchor off the west side of the river up to a cable upstream or downstream from No 6 red buoy. Use Admiralty Chart 3672, but don't anchor much outside the buoyed channel – drying mud extends well out from the shore.

La Roche Jaune: You can still find room to anchor a little way downstream from Roche Jaune village, clear of the moorings, or you may find a vacant mooring. Use Admiralty 3672 to find the best spot. The small village centre, half a mile up the hill from the riverside, has a few basic shops and a

---

Tréguier Port Guide

(Telephoning Tréguier from the UK dial 00 33 296 etc)
Harbourmaster: David Beron at the *Maison des Plaisanciers*, Tréguier Marina, VHF Ch 9 (Tel: 02.96.92.42.37).
Fuel: Diesel alongside the marina fuelling berth.
Weather: Local forecast posted daily at the *Maison des Plaisanciers*. The Jersey Radio Channel Islands forecasts are useful for this area if you can receive them up the river (chances are better near HW). Jersey Radio forecasts are on VHF Ch 25 or 82 at 0645, 0745 and 0845 local time, and then 1245, 1845 and 2245 GMT. CROSS Corsen forecasts in clear French on VHF Ch 79 from Cap Fréhel at 0545, 0803, 1203, 1633 and 2003 French local time and from Ile de Batz at 0515, 0733, 1133, 1603 and 1933 French local time. Météo France recorded forecast on 08.36.68.08.22.
Water and electricity: At the

marina pontoons.
Showers: At the *Maison des Plaisanciers*
Laundrette: La Lavandière at 22 Rue Saint-André, the hill that leads from the Hôtel de l'Estuaire to the cathedral square (open 0900-1200, 1400-1800). Also a laundrette at the north end of Rue Marcellin Berthelot, opposite the Restaurant St Bernard.
Yacht Club: Club Nautique du Trégor (02.96.92.37.49).
Gas: Camping Gaz from 'Marina Sports' on Les Quais near the *Maisons des Plaisanciers* (Tel: 02.96.92.47.60).
Chandler: Co-Per Marine, Pont Canada, 22220 Trédarzec, Tréguier (Tel: 02.96.92.35.72). Also 'Marina Sports' near the *Maison des Plaisanciers* (Tel: 02.96.92.47.60).
Repairs: Chantier Naval du Jaudy are based about a kilometre from the marina at Plouguiel (Tel: 02.96.92.15.15) and do all kinds of repairs. Chantier

Nautique Gelgon (Tel: 02.96.92.67.00) are based five kilometres north-west of Tréguier at Penvénan. Both yards work regularly at the marina.
Engineers: Chantier Naval du Jaudy and Nautique Gelgon, as above.
Banks with cashpoints: In and around Place du Martray.
Shopping: Full range of shops up the hill in Tréguier. Useful '8 à Huit' min-market behind the cathedral in Boulevard Anatole Le Braz. Nearest large supermarket is a mile out of town on the D786 to Lannion.
Tourist office: At the Mairie in Place du Général Leclerc (behind the cathedral).
Changing crews
There are buses west to Lannion or east to Paimpol. A local train runs between Lannion and Plouaret, on the Brest-Morlaix-St Brieuc line, with connections east to Rennes and St Malo, or west to Morlaix and the Plymouth-Roscoff ferry. From Paimpol you join this main line via Pontrieux and Guingamp.

The winding Guindy River just behind Tréguier town

cafe which are quite adequate for simple day-to-day provisions. There is a water tap at the quay.

Pen Paluc'h: Just over half a mile downstream from Roche Jaune village, you can anchor off the west bank near the promontory of Pen Paluc'h, between No 1 green buoy and the green beacon marking Roc Don.

UPSTREAM FROM TRÉGUIER

At around half-flood, taking care with the current through the marina, it's intriguing to venture above Pont Canada in the dinghy, when the mudbanks are starting to cover and oyster-catchers are getting their feet wet. The east shore is marshy, with a few ancient slips where locals sit for long peaceful hours at the end of a fishing line. The river divides a kilometre above the bridge, a shallow creek opening towards Pouldouran and the Jaudy turning south-west past remote corners of rural Brittany that few visitors see.

You pass the tiny commune of Sainte Anne, where chickens wander on the bank. Then a muddy inlet branches south to Kergomart, little more than a farm and a couple of cottages. You pass a landing place on each bank, once the site of a rustic ferry, where passengers pulled across the river using a rope. Then the Jaudy turns a double bend and you see the bridge at La Roche Derrien, a diminutive market town with several imposing church spires. Tréguier feels far from the sea, but Roche Derrien is more rural still. Few of its inhabitants probably visit the coast from one year to the next.

HISTORIC TRÉGUIER

Centrepiece of Tréguier is the famous cathedral church of Saint Tugdual. The oldest parts of the cathedral were built towards the end of the 13th century and the soaring open-work spire dominates the town and the surrounding country. Saint Tugdual originally came to Brittany from

Tréguier Restaurants

Tréguier has an excellent choice of restaurants, bars and bistros, so you will eat well almost anywhere in this charming market town.

Just behind the marina is the

Restaurant Les Trois Rivières in the Aigue Marine Hôtel, the most convenient but also one of the best choices in Tréguier (Tel 02.96.92.97.00). The hotel looks slightly garish from the outside, but you will eat extremely well and be well looked after. The cuisine is modern and imaginative, making good use of local produce and seafood.

The **Hôtel de l'Estuaire** is also handy for the marina, just downstream on Place du Général de Gaulle. We've always dined well in the comfortable restaurant overlooking the river (Tel: 02.96.92.30.25). **L'Estuaire** is run by the Geffroy family and has a reliably traditional style.

Auberge du Trégor at 3 Rue St Yves is very pleasant (Tel: 02.96.92.32.34) – follow Rue St Yves out of the cathedral square and it's a little way along on the left.

La Canotier is another good bet (especially for lunch) at 5 Rue Ernest Renan (Tel: 02.96.92.41.70).

For something light and tasty at lunchtime, try the **Crêperie des Halles** at 16 Rue Ernest Renan (Tel: 02.96.92.39.15). To reach Rue Renan from the marina, follow the quay road downstream from the Maison des Plaisanciers until you reach the **Hôtel de l'Estuaire**. Rue Ernest Renan leads inland just beyond the hotel and the convivial **Café du Port**, an attractive route up to the town centre even if you are not looking for a bite to eat.

Cornwall, although how he found his way safely into the river before the Basse Crublent buoy marked the entrance remains a mystery. Tugdual is said to have been related to King Arthur, another strand in the complex historic and cultural links between Cornwall and Brittany.

'Monsieur Saint Yves', Tréguier's other notable Breton saint, was a popular working lawyer during the 13th century. He was also chaplain to the Bishop of Rennes. St Yves was a stalwart upholder of justice for the poor and one of the earliest architects of free legal aid. In due course he became the patron saint of lawyers and advocates. The Pardon of St Yves takes place each year on the Sunday nearest 19th May and is attended by lawyers from all over Europe. This annual pilgrimage is also known as the Pardon of the Poor, a reference to St Yves rigorous spirit of justice rather than to any patronly professional support of the prosperous lawyers who gather to take part in the mass and the colourful procession through the town.

The history of the port of Tréguier can be glimpsed in old pictures and engravings in restaurants and cafés around the town. The substantial town quays were once packed with sailing coasters and fishing luggers, which had to work the tides carefully to get up and down the river. During the long Napoleonic Wars, the Tréguier River was an important staging post for French coastal traffic, which was forced by the powerful British Channel Fleet to creep with great circumspection close inshore.

You can see one important reason for this from a quick study of Admiralty Chart 3670. Using the delicate Passe de la Gaîne inside Les Héaux, it was possible for small ships and barges to sail between Tréguier and Paimpol inside a protecting barrier of reefs which the much larger British ships dared not penetrate.

Up in town, you should find time to spend a couple of hours browsing round the cathedral, the chapter house and the cloisters. If you have a taste for small local museums, Ernest Renan's house is also worth a visit and provides some fascinating insights into the traditional values and culture of small-town Brittany.

DAY TRIPS FROM TRÉGUIER

Tréguier doesn't have quite the same scope as Lézardrieux for day trips. The marina represents the head of navigation for most boats because the bridge only has about three metres clearance at high water, although you can explore the 3 miles up to Roche Derrien by dinghy on the tide. If conditions are rough at sea, or even if they aren't, you can drop down-river for a day to one of the anchorages near Roche Jaune, perhaps staying overnight before moving on round the coast the next morning.

Biking or hiking: If you carry bicycles on board or decide to hire, there is plenty to explore in the country lanes each side of the Tréguier River. On the west side, take the road through Plouguiel and follow the D8 north past Plougrescant towards Pointe du Château and Le Gouffre. A maze of fascinating tracks skirts the north end of the peninsula, giving glimpses of the estuary to the east and open sea to the north and west. Out on the coast at Le Gouffre you come across a miniature stone cottage built between two large rocks. This tiny retreat has become a famous and much photographed logo for North Brittany.

The east side of the river is equally rewarding. Crossing Pont Canada, you can meander through Trédarzec hamlet and follow the D20 north towards Kerbors and Pleubian, diverting down narrow lanes to see the river from unusual vantage points.

By car to Guingamp: If you hire a car, it's only about 15 miles south from Tréguier to the magnificent old walled town of Guingamp, which is the local centre for all aspects of the Breton culture. Here all the street signs are in both French and Breton, and the courses at Guingamp University are all bilingual. You can visit La Basilique church, the splendid 15th century Château de Pierre II, and stroll around the ancient ramparts of the town.

If you are in Guingamp for lunch or dinner, you must eat at Le Relais du Roy in the main square (42 Place du Centre, Tel: 02.96.43.76.62). Monsieur and Madame Mallegols will look after you extremely well.

Cycle hire: Cycles L. Gégou, on the quay road (Tel: 02.96.92.31.22)
Local taxi: Tel: 02.96.92.23.95
Car hire: At the Station Service Elf just opposite the marina (Tel: 02.96.92.30.52)

The visitors' berths are at the end of the two downstream pontoons and are clearly marked

PORT BLANC

Port Blanc is a small natural harbour protected by off-lying rocks and islets about six miles west of the Tréguier estuary. The anchorage is ruggedly attractive and secure in most weathers, although winds from between NW and NE send in a rolling swell which becomes heavy and dangerous

in the entrance if conditions freshen, especially near HW. The approach is from NNW and the gap in the rocks can be difficult to make out until you get close. The village has a hôtel-restaurant, a boulangerie, and a general store.

Port Blanc never seems to change. Midway between Tréguier entrance and Perros-Guirec, it is often passed unnoticed by yachts on passage between these two. The harbour is really a natural

bay, partly sheltered from seaward by a pink granite cordon of rocks and islets and the small wooded island of St Gildas. Quite a few local fishing boats and yachts moor off the seafront and there are a dozen or so white visitors' buoys in the main part of the harbour. The nearest landing from these buoys is the slip in the SW corner of the harbour. A swell always seems to find its way into Port Blanc when the wind is anywhere onshore,

Gabriel of Dart leaving Port Blanc under sail. Les Sept Iles are in the background

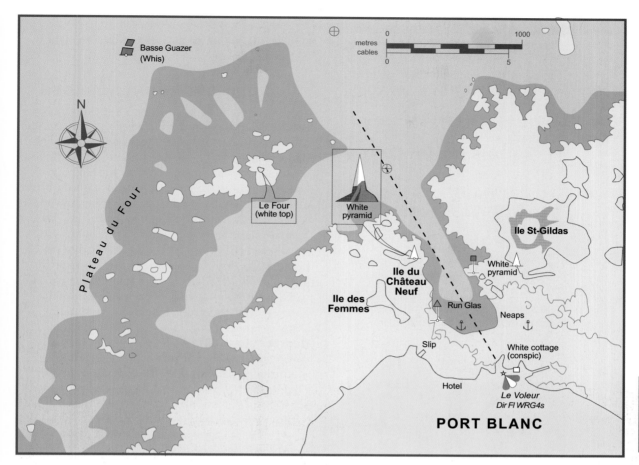

Basse Guazer
(Whis)

metres
cables

0   1000

0   5

N

P l a t e a u   d u   F o u r

Le Four
(white top)

White
pyramid

Ile St-Gildas

Ile du
Château
Neuf

White
pyramid

Ile des
Femmes

Run Glas

Neaps

Slip

White cottage
(conspic)

Hotel

Le Voleur
Dir Fl WRG4s

PORT BLANC

although you can usually avoid the worst of the roll by a careful choice of anchorage. In fresh weather from between NW and NE, the sea starts breaking heavily in the entrance and it can become dangerous to enter or leave.

In the SE corner of the bay, which dries at LAT, some more local moorings are clustered off a small stone pier and slip. At neaps you can stay afloat just outside these moorings or, with moderate draught, you can tuck close under the S side of Ile St Gildas. Port Blanc village is delightfully low-key. You will find a small bureau de port on the seafront, but no showers or other facilities. The Grand Hôtel is a good bet for lunch or dinner. There's a useful café-alimentation and a boulangerie about 10 minutes walk inland from the bureau de port.

APPROACH AND ENTRY

The approach is from NNW, leaving to starboard the various rocky dangers of Plateau du Four which lurk up to a mile ESE of Basse Guazer red whistle-buoy, and then leaving Ile St Gildas to port. Coming from the W, either from Perros or from further along the coast, pass well N of Basse Guazer buoy before making for the first waypoint, not quite a mile ENE

of the buoy. A bearing of Ile Rouzic, easternmost of Les Sept Iles, can be useful for lining yourself up. Coming from the E, either from Tréguier or round Les Héaux, stay a good 2–2½ miles offshore once W of Basse Crublent buoy and only turn in towards the first Port Blanc waypoint when Plougrescant church spire bears less than 135°T.

Since the charted leading marks are almost impossible to make out, it's best to identify the prominent white pyramid on Ile du Chateau Neuf (16m high) which is left close to starboard as you go through the narrow entrance. There is a less obvious white pyramid on the SW corner of Ile St Gildas. Also try to pick out a conspicuous white cottage standing on its own at the back of the harbour, very close NE of where Le Voleur lighthouse is shown on the chart, at the head of the nearby stone pier. This cottage bearing 329°T leads in safely on a similar track to the official leading line, but use it with caution until the entrance becomes clear, in case you've latched onto the wrong white cottage!

Allow carefully for any cross-tide until you are well inshore, to avoid being set towards either Plateau du Four or the ½ mile expanse of drying rocks N of Ile St Gildas. Having left Château Neuf white pyramid to

TIDES

HW Port Blanc is at HW St Helier –0105 approx.
Heights above datum: 9.6m MHWS, 1.3m MLWS,
7.4m MHWN, 3.5m MLWN.
Streams are moderate, setting W by S across the
entrance on the ebb and E by N on the flood. Rates
reach $2\frac{1}{2}$–3 kts at springs but only about $1\frac{1}{2}$ kts at
neaps.

CHARTS

Admiralty: 3670, 3672   French SHOM: 7125

WAYPOINTS

Approach WP, a mile NNW of Port Blanc entrance
and 9 cables ENE of Basse Guazer red whistle buoy
– 48°52.07'N, 03°19.70'W
Inner WP, just off Port Blanc entrance on the leading
line and 6 cables due E of Le Four Rock
– 48°51.13'N, 03°19.20'W

HAZARDS

A plateau of drying and awash rocks stretches more
than half a mile E and nearly a mile ESE of Basse
Guazer buoy, so don't come S of this buoy unless it is
$\frac{3}{4}$ mile west of you. Drying rocks extend up to $1\frac{1}{2}$ miles
offshore between Tréguier entrance and Port Blanc,
so make a safe offing when coming from this
direction, well outside the direct line between Basse
Crublent and Basse Guazer buoys.

starboard, leave Roc'h Huz red beacon 100 metres to
port and then look out ahead and slightly to
starboard for a vacant mooring buoy or a spot to
anchor. It can be dangerous to approach Port Blanc
in fresh onshore winds, partly because the sea is
liable to break in the entrance but also because a
heavy swell makes it even more difficult to pick out
the marks and the gap in the rocks.

At night: The approach to Port Blanc is
straightforward at night in quiet conditions and
reasonable visibility, using the white sector of Le
Voleur (*Fl.WRG.4s*). It's important to pick up this
light at least $1\frac{1}{2}$ miles from the entrance, because
Basse Guazer buoy is unlit. Coming from the W
outside Ile Tomé, you can use Ile aux Moines light
(*Fl(3)15s*) and the white sector of Pointe de Mean
Ruz (*Oc.WR.4s*) until you see the green and then
the white sector of Le Voleur. From Perros, simply
stay on the Kerprigent-Le Colombier leading line
until you pick up Le Voleur. Coming from the E,
you can use bearings of Les Héaux
(*Oc(3)WRG.12s*) and then Ile aux Moines (*Fl(3).15s*)

as clearing lines until the red and then the white
sectors of Le Voleur come into view.

MOORINGS AND ANCHORAGES

You have a greater choice of anchorages if you visit
Port Blanc at neaps, when it's possible to find shelter
from practically any wind direction.

Visitors' moorings: There are about a dozen white
visitors' buoys in the main part of the harbour.
These moorings are secure in most weathers, but an
uneasy swell rolls into the harbour when the wind
is anywhere onshore. It is best to make for Perros or
Tréguier if the forecast suggests freshening winds
from between NW and NE, when the surge in Port
Blanc will create unpleasant conditions aboard.
The most sheltered anchorage at springs is usually
well inside the moorings in the south part of the
harbour off the seafront, landing at the small
slipway there.

Near the stone pier: At neaps, you can anchor in
the SE corner of the harbour, just outside the local
moorings which are laid to the N of the stone pier.
Bilge-keelers or moderate-draught keel yachts with
legs can anchor and dry out in the small inner
harbour behind the pier, although you should
reconnoitre the bottom at LW before deciding where
to fetch up. Having chosen your spot, enter as near
HW as possible. It's not advisable to lie against the
quay at the back of the inner harbour, because this is
used by the local fishermen.

Off Ile St Gildas: At dead neaps, you can edge into
the shallow water just S of Ile St Gildas, with the
white pyramid on the SW tip of the island bearing
due N true and Roc'h Louet bearing W or a little N of
W. This position has a sandy bottom and is well
protected from onshore swell; it has about 6ft
minimum depth when the height of LW at St Helier
is 4m. Watch out for the strings of small crab-pot
markers in this corner of the harbour.

FACILITIES

Port Blanc is only a small seaside village and the
harbour is used mainly by local yachts and fishing
boats. It has no special facilities except the visitors'
moorings. There are two landing places – a slip at the
west end of the seafront and the slip and stone pier in
the SE corner of the harbour. The latter has a water
tap behind the hut on the fishermen's quay. The only
nearby shops are a boulangerie and a combined cafe
and general store about 10 minutes walk inland
from the seafront. You can get a good meal at the
Grand Hôtel.

PERROS-GUIREC

Perros-Guirec is an established resort, parts of which are still rather elegant in the old tradition of fashionable seaside towns. The harbour lies at the head of the shallow Anse de Perros, a wide sandy bay partly sheltered from seaward by Ile Tomé. The avant-port, which dries, is protected by a breakwater

and used by local fishing boats. The inner basin – known as the Bassin à Flot du Linkin – is retained by a long sill and entered through a small lock-gate near HW. You can reckon on about 2.5m average depth at the pontoon berths, which are perfectly sheltered and handy for shops and restaurants.

When you first arrive at Perros-Guirec, it can seem unexpectedly sophisticated after the sleepy square at Lézardrieux or the quaint timbered streets of Tréguier. As you come into the Anse de Perros, the prosperous well-spaced villas set among the pines and mimosa up on Pointe du Chateau create the elegant facade of a traditional seaside resort, rather like a latter-day Torquay or Bournemouth with shutters.

Other impressions begin to compete as you approach the harbour. A few fishing boats will

probably be rafted inside the breakwater, with all the usual comings and goings around the paraphernalia stacked on the quay. Beyond the sill across the inner basin, the apartment blocks on the waterfront contrast oddly with the more ornate architecture of uptown Perros. The rows of yachts moored at the pontoons take the harsh edge off this concrete esplanade, but you can't help wondering if you are still in Brittany.

As you edge towards the narrow lock next to the breakwater, a small crowd of locals will almost certainly be gathered to watch the new arrivals and pass the time of day. Your attention will be divided between giving them a cheery wave, trying to catch the lock-keeper's berthing instructions, and aiming for the middle of what appears to be a deliberately miserly gap, constructed for the express purpose of

Chapter 6

You enter the marina near high water through a single (and rather narrow) lock-gate

TIDES

HW Perros is at HW St Helier –0105 approx.
Heights above datum: 9.3m MHWS, 0.9m MLWS,
7.2m MHWN, 3.4m MLWN.
The streams well inside Anse de Perros are
moderate. In the west channel between Ile Tomé and
the shore, the SE-going and NW-going streams may
reach 2½–3 kts at springs. In the east channel, the
NE-going stream can reach 4½ kts and the SW-going
stream 4 kts.

CHARTS

Admiralty: 3670, 3672
French SHOM: 7125

HAZARDS

The approaches are well marked, except for several
drying rocks which extend for over ½ mile off the NE
tip of Ile Tomé. Avoid being set towards these
dangers when using the east channel.

WAYPOINTS

East channel approach, close NW of Basse Guazer
red whistle buoy – 48° 51.69'N, 03° 20.98'W
West Channel approach, ¾M W of Les Couillons de
Tomé W-cardinal buoy – 48° 50.92'N, 03° 26.73'W
Inner WP in the Anse de Perros, ¼M SSW of Pierre du
Chenal beacon tower – 48° 49.14'N, 03° 24.76'W

providing entertainment for the onlookers.

Once through the lock, you turn hard to port and
make for the visitors' berths near the town end of the
sill. There are usually plenty of vacant spaces, but
the finger pontoons are quite short and bounce up
and down alarmingly as you jump ashore. The
curious thing about Perros, though, is how soon you
feel part of your surroundings having made fast. An
hour or so after arriving, it somehow seems as if
you've been there for days. The place absorbs
visitors quite naturally, without any comment or
fuss. The town is friendly and comfortably well-
used, with a good selection of shops and restaurants
close to hand. The showers and bureau de port are
just over the road and right a bit from the pontoons,
in what looks like an ordinary detached house in a
small row.

Because Perros seems to provide everything you
need in such a relaxed and unassuming way, you
can find time slipping by more quickly than in some
of the more obviously Breton ports of call on this
coast. Still, what's wrong with that? The only point
to bear in mind is that you can only leave near high
water and this constraint has a bearing on your

future passage-making as the lock times move on
each day. There are also occasions, at dead neaps,
when the tide doesn't quite manage to struggle up to
the level inside the sill. The gate may then stay
closed for a couple of days and you will be forced to
sample some of the restaurants or menus that you
haven't yet tried.

APPROACH AND ENTRY

The two possible approaches to the shallow Anse
de Perros are either east or west of Ile Tomé, a small
but prominent island which lies a mile offshore
from the bay and partially protects it from seaward.
Both approaches are navigable by day or night at
most states of tide as far as the outer anchorage
under Pointe du Château, but the depths start
becoming very thin near LW springs once you drop
south of Ile Tomé. The last mile from the anchorage
to Perros harbour can only be negotiated within 2-3
hrs of HW.

Passe de l'Est: First reach a position close NW of
Basse Guazer red whistle buoy, which guards the
NW corner of Plateau du Four. Note how the tide is
setting as you pass the buoy and then steer to make
good 224°T for 3 miles to fetch Pierre à Jean Rouzic
green conical buoy, just off the SE tip of Ile Tome. As
you draw inshore, the stream will begin to follow the
line of the channel. Don't stray too near the various
unmarked rocks which straggle more than ½ mile
ENE of the N end of Tomé, or the drying ledges
which extend up to a mile offshore on your port
hand. It can be useful to take back-bearings of Basse
Guazer buoy, keeping it at 046°T until you can
identify the green conical. Leave the latter close to
starboard and continue on the same line to leave
Pierre du Chenal isolated danger beacon tower a
good 100 metres to starboard and Cribineyer red can
buoy a similar distance to port.

The lock into Perros marina is open for about 1½ hrs
each side of HW at springs and perhaps for only half
an hour *before* HW at dead neaps, with gradual
variations in between. If you are early for the gate, or
have missed it altogether, you can anchor and stay
afloat in the Anse de Perros 2-3 cables E of Pointe du
Château, or a bit further SW into the bay if the depth
allows. The spring tide anchorage is just over to
starboard once you have passed Cribineyer buoy
and before you reach Roc'h Hu de Perros red beacon
tower. This spot is reasonably protected from
between WNW through S to E, although a gentle
scend usually rolls in with the late flood. Several
heavy-duty visitors' moorings are laid in the deepest
part of the anchorage during the season.

When you have enough rise of tide to approach
Perros harbour, set off towards Gommonenou red

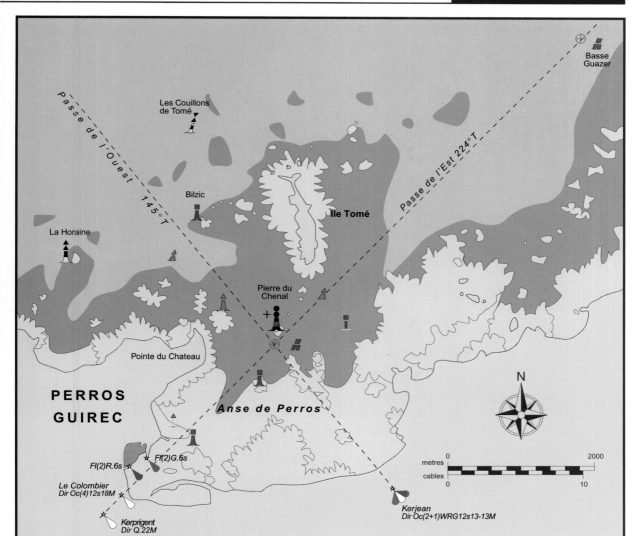

Les Couillons
de Tomé

Bilzic

Ile Tomé

La Horaine

Pierre du
Chenal

Pointe du Chateau

**PERROS
GUIREC**

Anse de Perros

Fl(2)R.6s   Fl(2)G.6s

Le Colombier
Dir Oc(4)12s18M

Kerprigent
Dir Q.22M

Kerjean
Dir Oc(2+1)WRG12s13-13M

Basse
Guazer

Passe de l'Ouest 145°T

Passe de l'Est 224°T

N

metres   0   2000

cables   0   10

beacon tower, conspicuous to the left of the breakwater at the head of the bay. As you get closer, steer to leave the local moorings and Lost ar C'hraou green spar beacon to starboard and Gommonenou 150 metres to port. Round the breakwater head fairly close to, keeping an eye open for fishing boats or other yachts coming out and leaving a small red buoy to port. The sill is marked by a line of red-and-white posts. Follow the breakwater north towards the lock, which looks alarmingly narrow from a distance (it doesn't get much wider, either). If the gate is not open, you can lie alongside the quay temporarily.

At night: The Passe de l'Est leading lights are Le Colombier (*DirOc(4)12s*) in line with Kerprigent (*DirQ*) bearing 224ºT, and these two can be seen from well NE of Basse Guazer buoy in good visibility. When approaching from the E along the coast, you can use Les Héaux (*Oc(3)WRG.12s*) and Ile aux Moines (*Fl(3)15s*) as clearing lines for the off-lying

dangers between Tréguier entrance and Basse Guazer. Note that Basse Guazer buoy, Pierre à Jean Rouzic buoy and the various beacon towers in the Anse de Perros are unlit. Perros breakwater head is lit (*Fl(2)G.6s*), as is the small red buoy (*Fl.R*) just inside the breakwater.

Passe de l'Ouest: This channel approaches the Anse de Perros W of Ile Tomé and can be taken by day or night at almost any state of tide – the least depth is 1 metre at LAT. Coming from Trégastel or Ploumanac'h, you will normally round Pointe de Mean Ruz fairly close-to and then enter Passe de l'Ouest by leaving La Horaine N-cardinal beacon tower 3-4 cables to starboard and La Fronde green conical buoy a cable to starboard. Coming from seaward or from further W along the coast, it is convenient, having arrived between Ile au Moines and the mainland, to make for a waypoint about ¾ mile due W of Les Couillons de Tomé W-cardinal buoy. From here, make good 143ºT to pass midway

The lock-gate, control tower and signal lights at Perros-Guirec

between Bilzic red beacon tower and La Fronde green conical buoy, and then steer to leave Roche Bernard green beacon tower 200-250 metres to starboard.

You need to have checked the height of tide carefully before continuing any further SE, because the shallowest part of this passage – 1 metre LAT over hard rock – lies just beyond a line joining Roche Bernard and Pierre du Chenal beacon towers. With sufficient rise, say within 4 hrs of HW at springs so long as there's no swell, you can turn to starboard into the Pointe du Château anchorage once you are between the two towers.

At night: The Passe de l'Ouest leading light is the narrow white sector of Kerjean (*Oc(2+1)WRG.12s*), which stands over on the SE side of the Anse de Perros. The green sector comes into view from about midway between Ile aux Moines and Pointe de Mean Ruz in good visibility. You will pick up the white sector at the outer waypoint (which is ¾ mile W of Les Couillons de Tomé W-cardinal buoy – unlit) soon after the white of Mean Ruz has turned back to red. Simply follow Kerjean, bearing 143°–144°T, until you are ½ mile due E of Pointe du Château and the Chenal de l'Est leading lights come into transit – Le Colombier (*DirOc(4)12s*) on with Kerprigent (*DirQ*) bearing 224°T. This second line leads right up to Perros breakwater head (*Fl(2)G*) in principle, although Kerprigent dips behind Le Colombier as you get close inshore. Watch out for moored boats and Lost ar C'hraou unlit green beacon as you come within ½ mile of the harbour. Round the breakwater fairly close-to, leaving the small red buoy (*Fl.R*) to port.

How you feel your way into the outer anchorage at night depends largely on visibility. If conditions are clear and moonlit, you can usually see enough to turn to the S once you are safely past Roche Bernard, fetching up when the main bulk of Pointe du Château is nicely abeam to starboard. If the night is

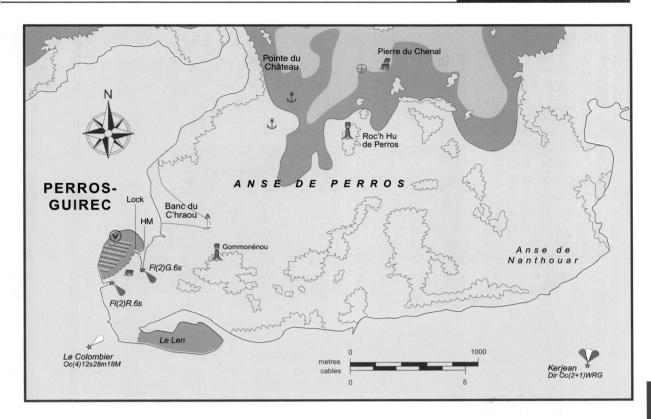

black and seemingly impenetrable, carefully follow Kerjean white sector to where Colombier and Kerprigent come into transit; from this precisely charted position (which I have included as an inner 'homing' waypoint for this chapter) you can edge gently due W true for a couple of cables before anchoring.

MOORINGS AND ANCHORAGES

Outer anchorage E of Pointe du Château: Much of the Anse de Perros dries at LAT and you can only approach the harbour within 2-3 hrs of HW. While waiting for the tide, or if you simply want to stay overnight without locking into the *port de plaisance*, you can anchor and stay afloat 2-3 cables due E of Pointe du Château, in 2-2½ metres LAT if you find the deepest part of the pool. This spot is reasonably sheltered from between WNW through S to E, although it is feasible to wait here safely in quite brisk onshore winds, albeit in some discomfort. At neaps, you can edge further SW into the bay and stay afloat, obtaining better shelter under the land in a north-westerly or even a northerly.

Perros avant-port: You can lie alongside the breakwater quay if you arrive at the harbour before the lock is open or if, having just left the inner basin, you want to wait for an hour or two before setting off on passage. The quay is used by fishing boats, so

don't leave a yacht unattended. It is safe to take the ground alongside if, for example, you need to clear rope or weed from your prop, but ask the lock-keeper first, because he should know which stretch of quay is most likely to be free. The short jetty on the W side of the avant-port is used exclusively by fishing boats.

Perros marina (Bassin à Flot du Linkin): The marina pontoons are ranged along the waterfront on the W side of the inner basin and visitors normally berth at one of the two lines of pontoons nearest the sill. The lock-gate opening times are scheduled a month in advance and are posted at the lock and at the head of the pontoons. As a rough guide, the gate should open for about 1½ hrs each side of HW at springs and for only half an hour *before* HW at dead neaps, with gradual variations in between. At night you should aim to arrive or leave in the half-hour before HW, because the opening period is likely to be curtailed.

You can reckon on about 2.5m average depth at the pontoon berths, which are perfectly sheltered and handy for shops and restaurants.

FACILITIES

Water and power are laid on at the pontoons and you'll find a laundrette on the quay. The showers and WCs are at the Capitainerie (which looks like an ordinary detached house) just over the road opposite the most northerly pontoon. The yacht club fuel berth in the NE corner of the basin supplies diesel or petrol.

For most engine problems or other repairs, it's best to contact Le Locat Marine, who are based on the industrial estate three kilometres from the harbour out on the Lannion road (Tel 02.96.23.05.08). The Harbour Master will phone for you if your French is a bit rusty. Ship Marine have a chandlery just south of the marina in Rue Ernest Renan (Tel 02.96.91.11.88).

The harbour area has a fair choice of shops and restaurants, and the centre of Perros-Guirec is a kilometre up the hill. You will find a good boulangerie along to your left as you face the waterfront, just beyond Le Suroit restaurant on the same side of Rue Ernest Renan. Le Suroit is friendly, good value and very handy for the marina. If you walk a bit further south along Rue Ernest Renan, you come to a roundabout with the Hôtel les Sternes on the far side. The hôtel-restaurant, La Cervoise, is worth this extra stroll if you like eating in more pampered surroundings. See the Port Guide for notes on some other Perros restaurants.

DAY TRIPS FROM PERROS

Since you'll be locked into the inner basin, it's not usually convenient to make day trips in the boat from Perros unless high water happens to fall at about 7 or 8 in the morning and evening. If this is the case, you could plan an excursion out to the Sept Iles anchorage between Ile aux Moines and Ile Bono, returning either to Perros in the evening (you might want to try another of the restaurants) or perhaps going into Ploumanac'h for a change of scene. You would have the advantages of a safe rise of tide for approaching the anchorage, plus the increased shelter of low water while you were there. See the next chapter for pilotage details. If you are cruising with the family, why not leave the boat safely at the marina and walk through Perros-Guirec to one of the beaches for the day – either the wide silver sands of the Plage de Trestraou, or the more secluded Plage de Trestrignel just north of Pointe du Château.

The marina basin at Perros is retained by a long sill which covers before high water and is marked by red-and-white posts

Perros-Guirec Port Guide

Harbour Master: Louis Morvan, Capitainerie, 17 Rue Anatole-le-Braz (Tel: 02.96.49.80.50), just opposite the St Paul pontoon. Lock office (Tel: 02.96.23.19.03).
VHF: Call 'Port de Perros', Ch 9 or 16
Weather forecasts: Posted when available at the Capitainerie and lock office. CROSS Corsen forecasts go out in clear French on VHF Ch 79 from Ile de Batz at 0515, 0733, 1133, 1603 and 1933 French local time. Météo France recorded forecast on 08.36.68.08.22.
Fuel: Pontoon with diesel and petrol at the Société des Régates Perrosienne, 100 metres north of the lock in the NE corner of the inner basin.
Water: At the marina pontoons
Showers: At the bureau de port, opposite the northernmost pontoon
Gas: At the small general store near the post office, a bit further north along the road from the bureau de port.
Chandlery: Ship Marine, near the marina at 91 rue Ernest Renan (Tel: 02.96.91.11.88
Repairs: Le Locat Marine, ZA St Quay-Perros (Tel: 02.96.23.05.08). Ouest Nautic (Yvon Keraudren), near the marina at 65 Rue Ernest Renan (Tel: 02 96 23 38 49). Chantier Naval Philippe Le Treize, ZA St Méen, Perros-Guirec (Tel: 02 96 23 15 28).

Engineers: Le Locat Marine (as above). Plaisance Service, Route de Perros, St Quay-Perros (Tel: 02.96.23.05.89).
Electronics: Le Locat Marine or Ship Marine, as above.
Sails and rigging: Voiles Erton, Route de Perros, Perros-Guirec (Tel: 02.96.91.05.04).
Shopping: You will find a reasonable selection of small shops in the harbour area, with a

greater choice about a kilometre up the hill in the centre of Perros-Guirec.
Banks: The banks are up the hill in the main part of town.
Laundrette: Laverie du Port at 7 Rue Anatole Le Braz.
Bus/train connections: Perros has no railway station, but there are buses to Lannion, from which a local rail service connects with the main east-west line via Plouaret.
Car hire: Avis office at 127 Boulevard de la Corniche (Tel: 02 96 91 46 23).
Bike hire: Perros Cycles at 12-14 Boulevard Aristide Briand (Tel: 02 96 23 13 08).

Restaurants

There are restaurants to suit all tastes at Perros, and the consolation of bad weather is that you can spend a pleasant few days sampling a wide range of menus. I have included here those restaurants I have tried and enjoyed.

Near the harbour; The hotel **Au Bon Accueil** is practically opposite the marina in Rue de Landerval, just behind the quay – their restaurant is on the opposite side of the road from the main building and is well recommended (Tel 02.96.23.24.11). Handy for the marina is **Le Relais du Port** at 45 Rue Anatole Le Braz (Tel: 02 96 91 28 30). For an inexpensive evening out, **Le Suroît** is reliable, good value and handy for the marina, opposite the fisherman's jetty just south of the pontoons (Tel 02.96.23.23.83). Continuing a bit further south from Le Suroît along Rue Ernest Renan, you come to a roundabout with the **Hotel les Sternes** on the far side. I have had some good meals at the comfortable hotel restaurant, **La Cervoise.**

Up in Perros-Guirec: My favourite Perros bistro is the **Restaurant la Gremaillère**, up in the Place de l'Eglise near the town centre. This is a good 20 minutes walk up the hill from the harbour, but the distance is just about right for sharpening your appetite before dinner and settling the digestion afterwards.

LES SEPT ILES

This string of small islands and reefs lies just off the Brittany coast to the north of Perros and Ploumanac'h. The two largest islands, Ile aux Moines and Ile Bono, are close together on the south-west corner of the plateau. Being fairly clean on their south sides, they form a natural anchorage which is open to the south

and east but reasonably sheltered in moderate northerlies or north-westerlies.

The powerful lighthouse on Ile aux Moines (*Fl(3)15s*) is a key mark if you are approaching the coast at night anywhere between Lézardrieux and Roscoff. Unlit dangers extend 1¾ miles N, nearly 3½ miles ENE, and just over a mile W of the lighthouse. Les Dervinis, an isolated rock drying 3.2m not quite a mile SE of Ile Bono, is marked on its south side by an unlit S-cardinal buoy.

There is a clear passage between Les Sept Iles and the mainland (i.e. between Les Dervinis buoy and Les Couillons de Tomé W-cardinal buoy, and between Ile aux Moines and Pointe de Mean Ruz) but you often get uneasy overfalls over Basse Meur and Basse du Chenal, especially on a weather-going tide. Allow carefully for the strong tides when navigating anywhere near Sept Iles at night or in poor visibility. The streams can set athwart your intended track at up to 4 knots and it's easy to find yourself being carried towards danger without realising it.

The anchorage between Ile aux Moines and Ile Bono makes a pleasant lunchtime stopover in quiet summer weather. You can stay overnight if conditions look settled, or move into Perros or Ploumanac'h at the end of the day. Should you decide to stay, the anchorage is easy to leave at night if the wind shifts, using Ile aux Moines lighthouse and the white sector of Kerjean light. The latter will take you safely into the Anse de Perros by the Passe de l'Ouest, and you can then wait in the Pointe du Château anchorage until the tide is high enough to enter the harbour.

The whole area of reefs and islets north and east of Ile aux Moines is protected as a bird sanctuary. You can anchor off Moines and land on the island, but don't disturb the nesting birds by exploring beyond its shores.

APPROACH AND ENTRY

The approach is from between S and SE, preferably above half-tide and ideally near HW. Apart from Les Dervinis, which is marked by its S-cardinal

Les Sept Iles from westward. The powerful light on Ile aux Moines is a key mark if you are approaching this coast at night

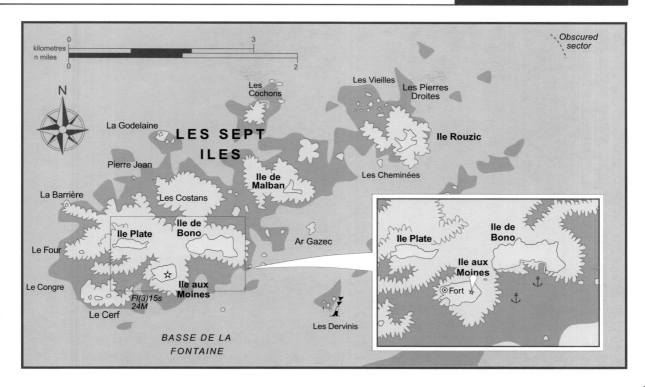

Chapter 6

buoy, there are four other dangers south of Ile aux Moines and Ile Bono which become significant near LW springs:

- A rock drying 1.3m, 3 cables SSE of the SE tip of Ile Bono.
- A rock awash, $\frac{1}{2}$ mile due S of the highest part of Ile Bono.
- A rock with 0.3m over it, about $\frac{1}{4}$ mile due S of the highest part of Ile Bono.
- A rock with 0.6m over it, close E of the islet which lies just S of Ile aux Moines.

These shoals are safely covered above half-tide and are clearly marked on Admiralty 3670, which is the best chart to use for navigating near Sept Iles.

With sufficient rise of tide over these dangers, you can simply approach the bay formed by Ile aux Moines and Ile Bono from the SSE, allowing for any cross-tide and leaving Les Dervinis W-cardinal buoy not quite $\frac{3}{4}$ mile to starboard. Near low water though, the easiest steering line is to keep the west edge of Ile Bono bearing due north true until you are $\frac{1}{4}$ mile from the islet which lies just south of Ile aux Moines.

Then make a positive curve to starboard to leave the islet 2 cables to the west and so avoid the 0.6m sounding. This last approach line has Mean Ruz lighthouse bearing due south true astern until Ile aux Moines lighthouse bears due west true. Fetch up close to the east of Ile aux Moines, or off Ile Bono as the wind dictates.

At night: Although most strangers would avoid entering Sept Iles anchorage at night, this is quite straightforward in good visibility, quiet conditions and above half-tide. From a position a good mile SSE of Ile aux Moines light, come onto the boundary between the white and green sectors of Kerjean (the leading light for Perros Passe de l'Ouest) and keep this bearing 143°T astern until Ile aux Moines light bears due west true. Then edge west just until Kerjean shows green and anchor. Leaving Sept Iles at night, simply reverse these directions if you can see Kerjean, or else come out with Ile aux Moines light bearing 317°T astern until you pick up Kerjean or reach the Passe de l'Ouest waypoint.

PLOUMANAC'H

The coast immediately opposite Ile aux Moines is an intricate jumble of pink granite rocks and islets, behind which lie the picturesque anchorage and harbour of Ploumanac'h. The entrance, close west of Pointe de Mean Ruz, seems little more than a gap in the rocks as you approach, but a narrow channel leads SSW between red and green spar beacons, leaving to starboard a prominent *château* on a small private island. There are two visitors' buoys in the outer anchorage, opposite the *château* slip. Within about 2 hrs of HW, you can follow the beacons into the sheltered inner harbour, where a sill retains an average depth of about 1.8m. The moorings here are handy for shops and restaurants. It is not recommended to enter or leave at night, or in fresh winds from between NW through N to ENE.

Just a few miles west of Perros-Guirec, tucked in behind Pointe de Mean Ruz, the outer pool at Ploumanac'h is one of the most enchanting anchorages in North Brittany. You lie in a narrow lagoon, surrounded by pink granite which has been sculpted into strange unworldly shapes by the elements. Between you and the sea is a picture-book château on its own miniature island, and a maze of rocks and islets which provide good shelter except from the north and north-east. A couple of miles offshore are the friendly humps of Les Sept Iles, which act as partial breakwaters for this stretch of coast. Opposite the anchorage is a small sun-trapped beach of white sand. The water is clear and there's not much of it under the keel at low tide. On a warm summer day, you can swim across to the beach if the tide is not too strong, or perhaps take the dinghy for a foray among the shallow rocky channels in search of

shellfish. If the forecast looks dubious, there is the option of retreating further into the lagoon near high water, crossing a sill to enter a land-locked inner harbour. Although it is usually rather crowded in here, you can secure to a visitors' mooring and stay afloat at all states of tide. There are good landing places with shops and restaurants nearby. Ploumanac'h should not be missed if you have cruised as far as Perros, even if you only have time to nose into the entrance for a quick look see.

APPROACH

The narrow entrance to Ploumanac'h lies 2 cables W of Pointe de Mean Ruz, which is the long rocky promontory you see a couple of miles away on the port bow as you leave the Anse de Perros by the Passe de l'Ouest. Mean Ruz has a distinctive lighthouse on its northern tip, built four-square in the local granite and, with its castellated top, looking like a small castle turret. It is fairly easy to identify from eastward, but tends to merge with the background when viewed at a distance from the NW or from seaward near Ile aux Moines. You should only approach Ploumanac'h by day and in reasonably quiet conditions.

From eastward: Coming from Perros via the Passe de l'Ouest, make good 286°T from midway between La Fronde green conical buoy and Bilzic red beacon tower. This track leads $\frac{1}{4}$ mile N of Mean Ruz promontory and you should round the lighthouse by 2 cables in

The Ploumanac'h entrance channel lies close to the south-east of Château Costaérès

order to approach the outer green entrance beacon from a little east of north. Coming along the coast north of Ile Tomé, perhaps direct from Les Héaux or Tréguier, it may be useful to make for the Perros Passe de l'Ouest outer waypoint before homing onto the Ploumanac'h waypoint two cables NW of Mean Ruz lighthouse. Be sure to stay clear of the various drying rocks which extend ½ mile NE from the north end of Ile Tomé, and aim to leave Les Couillons de Tomé W-cardinal buoy at least two cables to the south.

From westward: Coming up from Morlaix or round from Lannion or Trébeurden, it's important to give a wide berth to the various dangers forming the plateau which extends 2 miles N of Ile Grande and 2½ miles W of Trégastel. The W-cardinal buoy just west of Bar all Gall shoal is well south of the NW corner of the plateau and should be left at least a mile to the south before you make easting towards Ploumanac'h. Alternatively, do not let Ile aux Moines lighthouse bear less than 060ºT until Pointe de Mean Ruz bears at least 105ºT. Once the entrance beacons for Trégastel are abeam, it's safe to close the

coast within ¼ mile until you can identify Mean Ruz lighthouse and Ploumanac'h entrance. Make the final approach to the outer green spar beacon from a little east of north.

ENTRY

Leave the outer green beacon close to starboard and then follow the port-hand red spar beacons and another green at about 214ºT. This line leaves the prominent Château Costaérès to starboard and you will have reached the outer anchorage when the ornate entrance gate which leads into the *château* grounds is abeam and the 4th red beacon is close to port. Immediately beyond this beacon are two heavy-duty moorings, at which most yachts should just stay afloat around neaps.

If the moorings are in use, you can anchor on the west side of the channel, preferably fore-and-aft to avoid swinging into the fairway. It's not feasible to edge much further south and remain afloat near low water springs, but at neaps you can fetch up in the shallow bay on the west side of the channel, more or less opposite the stone landing slip on the east side.

MOORINGS AND ANCHORAGES

Outer anchorages: The narrow channel into Ploumanac'h dries at LAT to the south of the *château*, and the two mooring buoys just beyond the 4th red spar beacon are only just afloat at MLWS. Between springs and neaps, especially if the tides are taking off, you can edge further in and anchor in the shallow bay on the west side of the channel, opposite or just south of the stone landing slip on the east side.

To avoid swinging into the fairway, it's useful to moor fore-and-aft using the kedge, because there is usually quite a procession of local boats to and from the inner harbour. These outer anchorages are well sheltered in winds from between NW through S to SE, not too bad in due easterlies, but vulnerable to swell in fresh onshore winds from between NW through N to ENE.

Inner harbour: Ploumanac'h inner harbour is a natural land-locked bay which used to dry until a sill was built across the narrow entrance. You lie afloat at all states of tide in perfect shelter, with access about 2 hrs either side of HW for most keel boats and more like 3 hrs either side of HW if you draw a metre or less. The average depth in the pool is about 1.8m. The harbour becomes quite crowded during the season, but the trot moorings are well packed and there is usually room to squeeze in. There are good landing places with shops and restaurants nearby.

TIDES

HW Ploumanac'h is at HW St Helier –0115 approx.
Heights above datum: 9.0m MHWS, 1.1m MLWS, 7.1m MHWN, 3.4m MLWN.
Streams reach 4 kts at springs between the mainland and Les Sept Iles, but are quite moderate inshore off Ploumanac'h entrance.

CHARTS

Admiralty: 3670
French SHOM: 7125

HAZARDS

Be sure to leave Mean Ruz lighthouse 2 cables to port as you come in from seaward, because drying ledges extend NW from the point for some distance. Keep an eye out for small crab-pot floats in the immediate approaches. The entrance is tricky in swell and dangerous in strong north-easterlies.

WAYPOINTS

Off Ploumanac'h entrance, 2 cables NW of Pointe de Mean Ruz lighthouse – 48°50.44'N, 03°29.16'W.

Within about 2 hrs of HW, you can continue SSW and then turn SE into the sheltered inner harbour, passing over the sill across the narrows opposite Quai de Padel.

The Ploumanac'h entrance seems little more than a gap in the rocks, but is well marked by red and green spar beacons. It is one of the most enchanting anchorages in North Brittany.

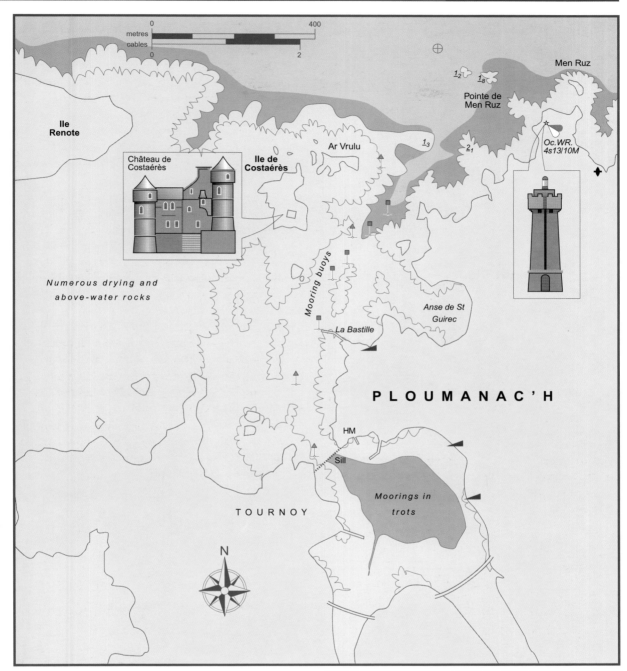

FACILITIES

There are WCs and a fresh water tap at the small
Capitainerie building near the landing on the east
side of the narrows (Tel: 02 96 91 44 31). I have had
some good meals at the Hôtel des Rochers, just along
the quay from the Capitainerie. There are basic
shops and more restaurants about five minutes walk
from the landing, in and near the Place du Centre
(follow Rue du Centre from the NE corner of the
harbour). If you are anchored outside, you can either
take the dinghy into the harbour or else land at the
stone slip on the east side of the anchorage and then
walk ½km due east towards the Place du Centre.

The distinctive stone lighthouse on Pointe de Mean Ruz

TRÉGASTEL

About 1½ miles west of Ploumanac'h, Trégastel is a natural harbour and anchorage which, although it seems fairly open, is partly protected by off-lying rocks and islets. Plenty of heavy-duty moorings are laid there during the season and, since you can enter or leave at any state of tide (by day only),

Trégastel can be a useful passage haven between Perros and Morlaix. The entrance lies just west of a small islet – Ile Dhu – with a red spar beacon on its west side. About ¼ mile WNW of Ile Dhu, Le Taureau green beacon stands on a rock drying 4.5m. To enter Trégastel, approach from seaward steering between Ile Dhu beacon and Le Taureau.

There are two more red beacons south of Ile Dhu and a green beacon close NW of the third red. It's simplest to follow the red beacons south, entering the harbour area between the third red and its opposite green. At neaps you can tuck behind Ile Ronde and stay afloat in the shallow bay known as

Coz Porz. Near springs you have to stay just inside the inner pair of beacons. Trégastel is open to the N and NW, but in moderate weather you'll be secure at the buoys whatever the wind direction.

The approach to Trégastel is fairly straightforward from eastward, because you can follow the comparatively steep-to coast round from Pointe de Mean Ruz until you reach Ile Dhu. Coming from the west though, you have to avoid the various dangers extending 2 miles north of Ile Grande and a similar distance west of Trégastel entrance. Bar all Gall W-cardinal buoy is well south of the NW corner of this plateau and should be left at least a mile to the south

before you make easting towards Ile Dhu. Alternatively, as with the approach to Ploumanac'h from the west, don't let Ile aux Moines lighthouse bear less than 060ºT until Pointe de Mean Ruz bears at least 105ºT.

Coming in from seaward, between Les Sept Iles and Plateau des Triagoz, it's useful to identify the conspicuous white radome about 3 miles inland from Trégastel; the radome bearing a shade east of south true leads safely clear of the western rocks of

Sept Iles towards Le Taureau beacon tower. Trégastel is not lit and is not safe for strangers to enter at night.

Trégastel is a beach resort with a selection of hotels and restaurants on the seafront, but no shops conveniently close to the anchorage. I have had some good *fruits de mer* lunches at the Hôtel Armoric. There are WCs and a fresh water tap near the Poste de Sauvage on the beach at Coz Porz. Good swimming in clear water over silver sand.

Chapter 6

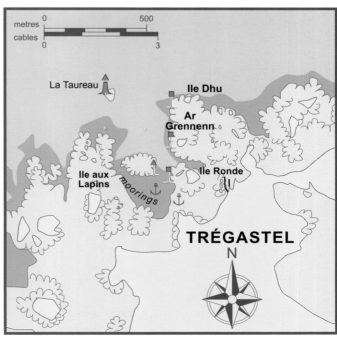

ILE GRANDE

A little over three miles SW of Trégastel, the small island of Ile Grande is joined to the mainland by a causeway and surrounded by rocks and islets in practically every direction. With careful pilotage, Ile Grande has two interesting fair-weather anchorages: one close off its NE tip, to the south of Ile Morville, and another off its SW side, in a narrow channel SE of Ile Losquet.

Neither anchorage is safe to leave after dark, so you should only stay overnight in settled weather.

Ile Morville anchorage: Referring to Admiralty Chart No 3669, approach from a position close west of Bar all Gall W-cardinal buoy, preferably near a neap high water when the stream is slack. You will need to make good south-east for a mile towards Le Corbeau, the 17m high turret-shaped rock 3 cables NW of the NE tip of Ile Grande. Close NW of Le Corbeau is a much lower rock – Men Haer (sometimes called Mean Gaez) – with a drying tail extending about a cable on its W side. From Bar all Gall buoy, keep the prominent white radome (two miles inland behind Ile Grande) bearing 129°T just left of Men Haer and Le Corbeau; this transit avoids the various rocks on the port hand. As you come within a cable of Men Haer, steer to leave it and Le Corbeau close to starboard, and continue south-east between Ile Grande and Ile Morville to enter the shallow pool opposite the stone landing jetty off Ile Grande.

This spot is fairly well protected in any moderate winds from between NW through S to NE, but rather vulnerable to onshore swell from between NW and NE. At MLWS there's about 2 metres depth in the narrows midway between Ile Grande and Ile Morville. If you can take the ground safely, there are plenty of good places to dry out on sand to the east and south of the pool.

Ile Losquet anchorage: The simplest approach is from due west, leaving Le Crapaud W-cardinal buoy a mile to the south and then bringing the versatile white radome to bear 095°T. Close the coast on this bearing, which should keep the highest point

The long stone jetty at the south-west tip of Ile Grande

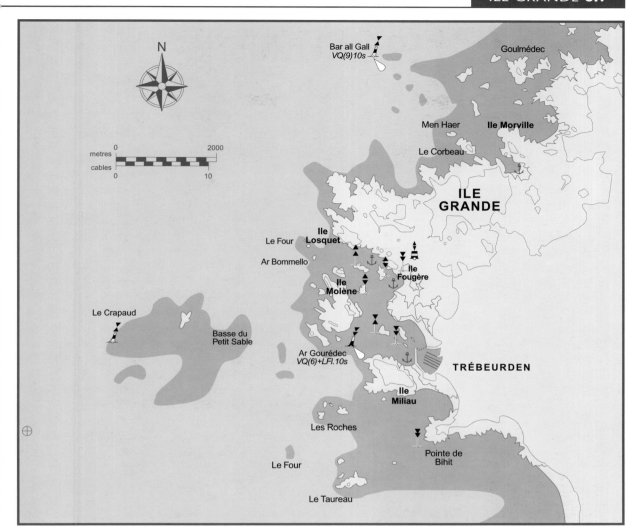

of the low-lying Ile Fougère in transit with the radome. This line leads between Le Four rock (dries 3.6m) and Ar Bommello (dries 3.9m), and then close north of Morguen N-cardinal beacon. Depending on the wind direction, you can either fetch up between Morguen beacon and Ile Losquet, or else continue on the transit towards Ile Fougère and anchor close off its west side.

Above half-tide, you can round Ile Fougère to the south, leave Karreg Jentil S-cardinal beacon close to port and then edge NNE towards Karreg ar Meg E-cardinal beacon tower. At dead neaps, most yachts will just stay afloat slightly NW of a line between Karreg Jentil beacon and Karreg ar Meg tower. This anchorage is reasonably well sheltered except in a south-westerly.

About ½ mile north-east of Karreg ar Meg is the long stone landing jetty at the SW tip of Ile Grande. Lifting keel boats or bilge-keelers of modest draught can find a snug and peaceful berth by approaching the jetty near high water, anchoring near the local boats, and drying out on the wide area of firm sand off the end of the jetty. There's a small village on the island, about a kilometre along the lane from the landing.

Chapter 6

TRÉBEURDEN

The seaside resort of Trébeurden lies on the attractive west-facing stretch of coast between Ile Grande and the Lannion River. This area has a number of interesting anchorages, but the most straightforward haven to enter is the attractive bay just north of Ile Milliau, a fairly sheltered spot except in due westerlies. A spacious marina lies in the crook of the bay between Ile Milliau and the mainland, accessible via a sill for 4-5 hrs either side of HW. This well-equipped *port de plaisance* is snug in all weathers and provides a useful base for day sailing in the Bay of Lannion.

Trébeurden lies halfway along the North Brittany coast, just round the corner from Ploumanac'h and a comfortable tide west from Lézardrieux or Tréguier. The well-equipped marina is tucked into the crook of the splendid sandy bay behind Ile Milliau and is sheltered from seaward by a string of low islands.

Inside the islands, a summer paradise of shallow channels meanders north for a couple of miles towards Ile Grande, marked here and there by beacons. For anyone with shoal draught or a lifting keel, here is the secret Brittany to which few visitors venture. At neaps in quiet weather, deserted hideaways abound for anyone armed with the French Chart 7124.

Trébeurden has a rather nostalgic atmosphere of holidays by the sea. Anchored out in the bay, perhaps off Ile Molène's golden beach, you can't help thinking of snorkels and shrimping nets, mysterious rocky pools left by the tide, pottering in the dinghy and sand between your toes. The area is popular with scuba divers, so watch out for rubber dinghies flying flag 'A'.

The mainland coast looks like the French seaside, an amiable mix of family hotels, comfortable villas and summer cottages dotted among the pines. There are cafés and bars near the marina, but the small town is a ten minute stroll up the hill which winds inland past the Hotel Ker an Nod.

Trébeurden is an ideal base for family cruising, with enough happening in the evenings to keep the

The marina at Trébeurden

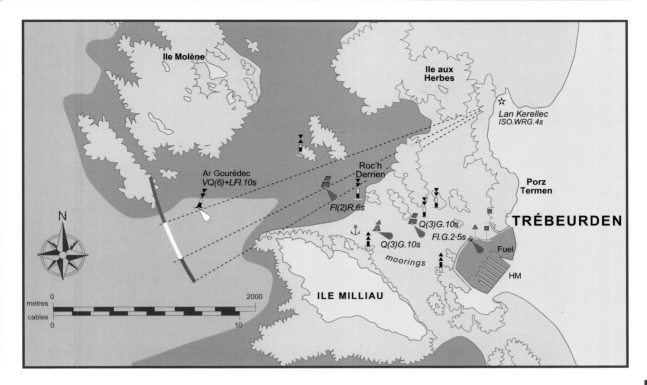

Chapter 6

crew amused. South of the marina, the silver sands of Trez Meur sweep round towards Pointe de Bihit and the Lannion River, a calm retreat where you can anchor in the pool off Le Yaudet.

In the evening, seen from the vantage of Trébeurden marina, the sun sets over Ile Molène, sharpening the whole chain of islands in dramatic silhouette. You might see a sail creeping round the tip of Milliau, or a tiny vedette bearing home one of Brittany's countless optimistic fishermen. All seems well with the world.

APPROACH AND ENTRY

From the north and east: Coming round the coast from the east, say from Perros or Ploumanac'h, the 'big-ship' route to Trébeurden gives a wide berth to the extensive dangers north of Ile Grande and then approaches Le Crapaud W-cardinal buoy from northward. Leave the buoy close to the east and continue south for not quite 1½ miles until you are clear to make for the NW tip of Ile Milliau. A convenient turning waypoint is a position half a mile SW of Le Crapaud buoy (see sketch chart on p 203).

In quiet conditions and good visibility, you can save about 6 miles by cutting inside Le Crapaud as follows: From Bar all Gall west-cardinal buoy, continue west-south-west until Ile Losquet bears about 135°T. Then turn to make good due south, steering to leave Ile Losquet and Ile Molène a mile to the east. This line would cross Basse du Petit Sable

and the eastern edge of the dangers surrounding Le Crapaud – no real problem above half-tide, but nearer low water you'll need to edge inshore into deeper water before coming abreast of Ile Molène.

The simplest way of avoiding Basse du Petit Sable is to bring the highest part of Pointe de Bihit just open to the south of the south-west edge of Ile Milliau, bearing about 128°T. Then keep a little way seaward of this transit by making good SSE for just over a mile and leaving the flat profile of Ar Vesleg rock (12m high) about 3 cables to port. Turn to port towards Ile Milliau and Trébeurden entrance once Ar Gourédec south-cardinal buoy bears less than 070°T.

From the west: If approaching Trébeurden from the west, say from Roscoff or Morlaix, you can make directly for the north-west tip of Ile Milliau, having passed midway between Plateau de la Méloine and Les Chaises de Primel.

Final approach: Approach Trébeurden from the WSW, between Ar Gourédec S-cardinal buoy and the NW tip of Ile Milliau.

From Ar Gourédec, follow the north coast of Ile Milliau round to pick up the red and green channel buoys for the final approach to the marina. If early or late on the tide, lie to one of the yellow waiting buoys just north of Milliau.

At night: Lan Kerellec sector light leads you in from the WSW, Ar Gourédec S-cardinal buoy is lit and you can then pick up the red and green lit buoys leading to the marina entrance.

TIDES

HW Trébeurden is at HW Brest +0105 approx.
Heights above datum: 9.1m MHWS; 1.3m MLWS;
7.2m MHWN; 3.5m MLWN.
Streams can reach 3-4 knots at springs locally
between Plateau des Triagoz and the mainland, but
are more moderate in the Bay of Lannion and the
immediate approaches to Trébeurden.

CHARTS

Admiralty: 3669
French SHOM: 7124

HAZARDS

Coming from the east between Les Sept Iles and the
mainland, give a wide berth to the plateau of dangers
extending 2 miles N of Ile Grande and a similar
distance W of Trégastel. Avoid Le Crapaud and its
surrounding rocky shoals, which lie 1-2½ miles W of
Ile Molène and are marked only on their west edge by
Le Crapaud buoy.

WAYPOINTS

P1 ½ mile SW of Le Crapaud W-cardinal buoy
    48°46.30'N 03°40.92'W
P2 6 cables 236°T from Ar Veskleg rock
    48°46.21'N 03°37.57'W
P3 150m south of Ar Gourédec S-cardinal buoy
    48°46.40'N 03°36.49'W

MOORINGS AND ANCHORAGES
TRÉBEURDEN MARINA

The marina is entered across an automatic sill
which has a wide window of access. At springs the
sill opens for at least 3½ hours each side of high
water and at neaps there is often 24 hour access or
only a short spell when the gate closes. As soon
as the gate opens you have 1.60 metres depth over
the sill.

The port signal lights are on the main breakwater
and are visible as you make the final approach from
the west. The main lights to watch for are:
- 2 vert greens and one white = OK to enter or leave
- 3 vert reds = No entry or exit.

If in doubt call 'Port de Trébeurden' on VHF Ch 9.
For boats arriving early or late on the tide, there are
ten yellow waiting buoys out in deep water north of
Ile Milliau, marked 'Port Trébeurden'.

As you come in through the marina sill, the visitors'
berths are on pontoon 'F', which is the second on
your port hand.

OUTER MOORINGS

In quiet weather you can stay quite snugly
overnight on one of the waiting moorings north of
Ile Milliau. Sometimes you can find a local mooring
free further in off the north-east side of the island,
where most boats will stay afloat between springs
and neaps. Take careful soundings though, and
work out the low water depth before settling down
to dinner.

The north end of Ile Milliau, which shelters the Trébeurden marina from the west

The marina is entered across an automatic sill which has a wide window of access

ANCHORAGES

North of Ile Milliau: There is room to anchor between Ile Milliau and the marina, especially towards neaps, but you should keep south of the buoyed approach channel and work out the low water depth carefully. Even in calm weather, a slight scend rolls in near the top of the tide, but it's easy to enter the marina from here if necessary, or to clear out to sea. The best shelter is from the south and east, although Milliau provides some lee in south-westerlies. Ile Molène and its surrounding islands give reasonable protection in light to moderate north-westerlies, but any significant swell from the west or north-west soon finds its way in.

Off Ile Molène: One of my favourite anchorages is off the beach some 200 metres south-east of Ile Molène. You can edge closer inshore at neaps, fetching up about 50 metres east of Roc'h C'hwenou (14 metres high). Work out the low water depth carefully and don't swing on too wide a scope.

Between Ile Milliau and Ile Grande: For a couple of hours each side of high water, you can follow the beacons north from Ile Milliau, inside Ile Molène, to reach various shoal-water or drying anchorages that few visiting yachts explore. Fairly quiet weather is needed for such nosing about, although this area is sheltered in strong easterlies or south-easterlies. The French SHOM chart 7151 is recommended.

Working north from near Ar Gourédec S-cardinal buoy, make good about 028°T towards the east edge of Ile Fougère. This track leaves An Erviniou W-cardinal beacon and Karreg Wenn Vras rocks each about a cable to starboard, and Les Trois Frères E-cardinal beacon a good two cables to port.

At dead neaps, most yachts will just stay afloat slightly north-west of a line between Karreg Jentil beacon and Karreg ar Meg tower. This anchorage is reasonably sheltered in westerlies and north-westerlies.

About a quarter of a mile north-east of Karreg ar Meg is the long stone landing jetty at the south-west tip of Ile Grande, a wild but fascinating spot distinctly off the beaten track. Boats that can take the ground safely can approach the jetty near high water, anchor near the local boats and dry out on the wide area of firm sand off the end of the jetty. You'll have few neighbours and nobody will bother you for harbour dues.

ASHORE

The small town of Trébeurden has everything you might need in the way of shops, albeit a short hike up the hill. There are some fine coastal walks, both south and north from the marina, and much of the shoreline and most of the islands around Trébeurden are now protected by the Conservatoire du Littoral.

Heading south from the marina, you can take the Grande Randonée cliff path past Trez Meur towards Pointe de Bihit, then round to Beg Léguer and the mouth of the Lannion River. Energetic walkers can follow the north bank of the river to Lannion town, returning to Trébeurden by bus or taxi. The best return bus leaves from near Lannion post office (ligne 15), arriving opposite Trébeurden post office.

North of Trébeurden, the Grande Randonée path winds along the coast past Lan Kerellec and Goas Treiz, and thence through the Marais du Quellen to the causeway road leading out to Ile Grande. This is a fascinating walk with some fine views over the rocky channels between Ile Molène and Ile Grande. The Ornithological Centre on Ile Grande is well worth a visit (but closed in the mornings on Saturday and Sunday).

Those who prefer exploring on two wheels can hire bikes or small motor scooters from Le P'tit Garage in Trébeurden, just up from the post office on the right-hand side (Tel 02 96 23 52 61).

Lannion is the nearest large town to Trébeurden, a fine old provincial capital with some intriguing back-streets, meandering alleys and unexpected squares. There is a large colourful market on Thursdays. The morning bus from Trébeurden post office (ligne 15) gets you to Lannion in plenty of time for a stroll round the town and lunch at one of the numerous restaurants.

I rather like Le Tire-Bouchon for lunch, just south-east of Place du Général Leclerc in Rue de Keriavily (Tel 02 96 46 71 88). To return to Trébeurden, catch a ligne 15 bus from Lannion Post Office.

DAY TRIPS FROM TRÉBEURDEN

Trébeurden marina provides an ideal base for local pottering in and around the attractive Bay of Lannion. Just north of Trébeurden is a maze of fascinating shallow channels between Ile Molène and Ile Grande, which you can have great fun exploring in the dinghy.

The peaceful Lannion River lies only a few miles south-east of Trébeurden and is well worth a visit, either as a day trip from the marina if the tide serves, or staying overnight in the pool opposite Le Yaudet village. Enter the river on the last two hours of flood, leaving two green beacon towers on the south side of the estuary each 100 metres to starboard and following the curve of the south shore gradually round to port towards the narrow inner mouth. Sound carefully to find the best spot off Le Yaudet. From the landing on the south bank, it's only 10 minutes puffing and wheezing up the steep path to Le Yaudet, where you can eat at the Ar Vro Hôtel, Les Genets d'Or, or at the Crêperie du Yaudet (at the top of the hill opposite a stone calvary). The Lannion River is one of the most charming backwaters of the North Brittany coast. Few visiting yachts seem to call here, although the river is not difficult to enter in any reasonable weather with sufficient rise of tide. A spring high water makes the approach simpler, but neaps give you more scope in the anchorage. About five miles SSW of Trébeurden is the picturesque sandy bay and small drying harbour at Locquirec, which makes an ideal destination for a family expedition on a quiet summer day.

Moorings and anchorages off Ile Milliau

Trébeurden Port Guide

Bureau du Port: Mme Dominique Bernabé runs the marina and you'll meet her in the office (Tel 02.96.23.64.00, Fax 02.96.15.40.87). The marina listens on VHF Ch 9 from 0600-midnight during the season.

Fuel: Diesel and petrol from the inner end of 'G' pontoon. Opening hours: 1000-1200, 1600-1800, although in season fuel is usually obtainable whenever the marina gate is open.

Weather forecasts: The local forecast is posted at the harbour office from 0800 each morning. CROSS Corsen broadcasts forecasts in French on VHF Ch 79 from Ile de Batz (at 0515, 0733, 1133, 1603 and 1933 French local time). Météo France recorded forecast on 08 36 68 08 22.

Water and electricity: At the marina pontoons

Showers: At the marina facilities building (10Fr *jeton* from the Bureau du Port)

Laundry: At the marina facilities building.

Yacht Club: Yacht Club de Trébeurden (Tel: 02.96.15.45.97)

Chandler: Cap Marine (Tel: 02.96.15.49.49) is a well-stocked chandler based in the marina facilities building.

Camping Gaz: At Cap Marine

Charts: At Cap Marine

Repairs: The nearby Chantier du Toëno work at the marina and can handle most repairs (Tel: 02.96.23.63.55 or mobile 06.09.98.65.14). The marina now run their own *Services du Port* and are able to crane boats out.

Banks: Nearest cash machine in the *Intermarché* supermarket car park, on the left off the road up to Le Bourg. Also the Crédit Agricole bank in Le Bourg.

Shopping: In the marina facilities building you'll find a baker and small grocers. Up in town,

10-15 minutes walk from the marina, there's a useful *Super Jodi* mini-market near the *Office de Tourisme* in Place de Crec'h-Héry. Baker just opposite, at the top of Rue de Trozoul, and fresh fish from the *poissonerie*. Good butcher a little further up past the *Super Jodi* on the left. Larger *Intermarché* supermarket beyond butcher and well up Rue des Plages on the left.

Tourist office: Place de Crec'h-Héry (Tel: 02.96.23.51.64).

Bike hire: Le P'tit Garage (Tel: 02.96.23.52.61).

Local taxi: Tel 06.08.61.15.91

Changing crews: Buses to Lannion, where you can catch a local train connecting with the main Brest-St Brieuc line at Plouaret. From Lannion you can catch a bus to Morlaix and then another bus or taxi to Roscoff and the Brittany Ferries terminal for Plymouth.

Restaurants

The **Hôtel Ker an Nod** (Tel 02 96 23 50 21) has a relaxed family restaurant, just north of the marina at the head of the slip road that leads down to the harbour. The two modern hotels on the marina concourse – **La Tourelle** and **La Potinière** – can serve a turn if you don't want to walk far.

Crêperie des Iles, overlooking the marina, can be pleasant if you can sit out on the terrace. My favourite lunchtime crêperie – **Le Goëland** – is up at 14 Rue de Trozoul (leave the Hôtel Ker an Nod to port, walk up the hill under the bridge and it's on the left).

For a comfortable evening out, stroll up to the **Manoir de Lan Kerellec** (Tel: 02.96.15.47.47), which overlooks the sea towards Ile Molène. Follow Rue de Pors-Termen north past the Hôtel Ker an Nod and take the third left into Allée Centrale de Lan Kerellec. A first-class dining room and impeccable wine list.

One of my favourites for lunch or dinner is the **Hôtel Ti Al Lannec** (Tel: 02.96.15.01.01), only a short stroll from Place de Crec'h-Héry. From the tourist office head SE along Allée Mézo Guen. Ti Al Lannec stands in spacious grounds overlooking Plage de Tresmeur.

CHAPTER 7

PASSAGES BRITTANY II

TRÉGUIER TO MORLAIX

Many yachts on a leisurely summer cruise will take this fascinating stretch of coast in several short hops, given the tempting possibilities of calling at Port Blanc, Perros-Guirec, Ploumanac'h, Les Sept Iles, Trégastel, Trébeurden or the Lannion River on the way. But anyone making the passage

in one hop can reckon on about 30 miles from Basse Crublent buoy, off Tréguier entrance, to Stolvezen buoy, the outer mark for the Grand Chenal de Morlaix. Most boats under sail will cover this distance easily on a single tide if the wind is fairish, although ideally you ought to leave Tréguier marina about 1½ hours before local high water and push the last of the flood down-river, in order to

catch the first trickle of west-going stream off Basse Crublent.

The shortest and most interesting route westwards is inside Les Sept Iles, keeping 1-1½ miles off the north tip of Ile Tomé, rather than standing well offshore outside the islands. From the Tréguier entrance waypoint, 3 cables WNW of Basse Crublent buoy, make for a position a couple

The white pyramid on Ile du Château Neuf, just off Port Blanc, can be a useful mark when you are coasting westwards from Tréguier

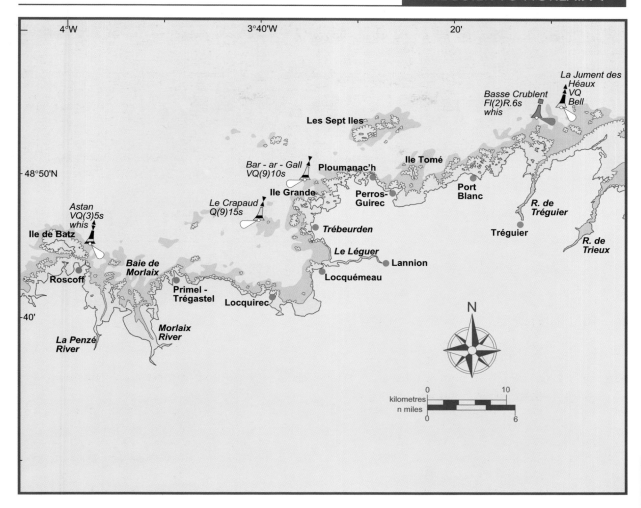

of miles south-east of Ile aux Moines, the only island of the Sept Iles group which has a lighthouse. A useful waypoint (48°51.68'N, 03°26.44'W) is midway between Les Dervinis S-cardinal buoy and Les Couillons de Tomé W-cardinal buoy. Don't stray south of track when coasting towards this waypoint, because drying dangers extend up to two miles offshore between Basse Crublent and the Basse Guazer red buoy.

The tide will be gathering strength as you reach Sept Iles, and it accelerates in any case between the islands and the mainland. You can expect to cross various patches of turbulent water along this stretch, especially near springs with a westerly wind. Keep a close check on your position, because it's easy to be set closer towards Sept Iles than intended. Once west of Ile aux Moines, there is a slightly tricky corner to negotiate, avoiding the various drying dangers which extend for just over two miles west of Trégastel entrance. Bar all Gall W-cardinal buoy marks the western edge of these dangers, but is moored well south of their

Gateway to the Morlaix River - picturesque Ile Louet and the gaunt 16th-century fortifications on Ile Taureau

northern limit. Because you can't use the buoy simply as a corner mark, you have to be sure to stay north of the unmarked dangers until it's safe to turn to the south-west.

Without GPS, you can use clearing lines provided by bearings of Ile aux Moines lighthouse, Pointe de Mean Ruz on the mainland opposite, or the short stubby tower on Plateau des Triagoz, off on the starboard bow. One strategy is to have Pointe de Mean Ruz bearing no less than 110°T until Ile aux Moines lighthouse bears 060°T, and then steer WSW with Ile aux Moines bearing no less than 060°T until you have passed west of Bar all Gall

buoy. For the next leg, you have the option of passing outside or inside Plateau de la Méloine; inside is usually better, avoiding the risk of being caught offshore when the tide turns foul.

From a position three cables or so NW of Bar all Gall buoy, a track of 235°T takes you nicely down for 11 miles towards Pointe de Primel, leaving the main group of Méloine rocks a mile to starboard and Les Chaises de Primel about ¾ mile to port. Pointe de Primel has a distinctive shape, looking rather like a giant snail from this direction. If you have carried a full period of ebb round from Tréguier, most of the Chaises de Primel will be

Pointe de Primel is a distinctive headland on the east side of the Morlaix estuary

Basse Crublent buoy off the mouth of the Tréguier River

Chapter 7

exposed as you pass, although there's a patch on the north side which dries only 1.6 metres. Off Pointe de Primel, you can decide whether to tuck into Primel harbour and wait for sufficient rise of tide to take the Chenal de Tréguier into the Morlaix estuary, or to carry on across to Stolvezen buoy and enter the estuary via the Grand Chenal or Chenal Ouest de Ricard.

Yachts bound for the anchorage over at Port Bloscon may find it easier, especially in thick weather, to stay outside Plateau de la Méloine and Plateau des Duons, finally approaching the Roscoff peninsula from the north-east. Entering the Morlaix estuary in murky conditions isn't much fun, even with GPS and radar, but the Chenal de

Tréguier about an hour before high water is the best bet, so long as you find La Pierre Noire green beacon and then follow an accurate compass course towards a position midway between Grand Aremen and Petit Aremen beacon towers.

If you leave Tréguier late on the tide for Morlaix, or a headwind makes the going slow, Ploumanac'h is worth keeping in mind as a staging-post. The outer anchorage is accessible (by day only) at any state of tide, except in fresh onshore weather. Ploumanac'h doesn't involve much of a diversion, as you'd be passing Pointe de Mean Ruz fairly close in any case; you can therefore decide to tuck in almost on the spur of the moment if Morlaix looks like being a bit of a slog.

BAY OF MORLAIX

LANNION RIVER

The peaceful and unspoilt Lannion River, also known as Le Léguer River, flows through a narrow wooded valley into the east side of the Bay of Lannion. The entrance lies 2½ miles SSE along the coast from Trébeurden and some 5 miles SE of Le Crapaud W-cardinal buoy. Most of the river dries at LAT,

right to the outer mouth between Pointe du Dourven and Pointe Servel, but most boats can just stay afloat in the sheltered pool off Le Yaudet even near low springs. The estuary is open to the north-west and can be dangerous in fresh winds or swell from this direction, although there is usually no problem in light to moderate westerlies or north-westerlies. Strangers should only enter or leave in

Anchor just north of the moorings off Le Yaudet

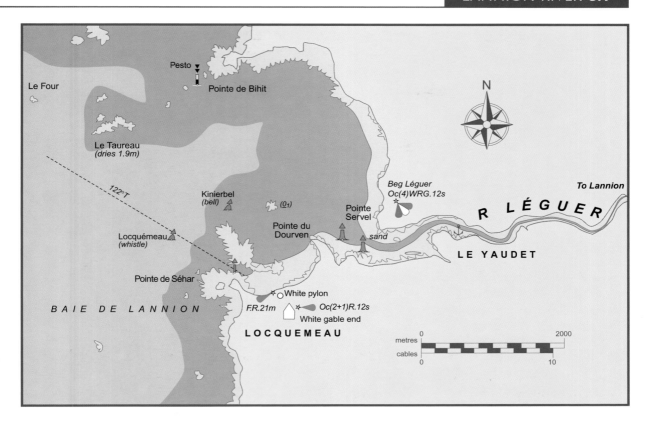

daylight, despite the fact that the local sand-dredgers come in and out at night using the white sector of Beg Léguer light.

APPROACH AND ENTRY

Approach from due west above half-flood, leaving Le Taureau rock (1.9m high) about $\frac{1}{2}$ mile to the north, Locquémeau green conical buoy (unlit with a whistle) $\frac{1}{2}$ mile to the south, and Kinierbel green conical buoy (unlit with a bell) 2 cables to the south. Coming down from Le Crapaud buoy, make good about 140ºT for just under 3 miles before turning east towards the estuary. Coming from Trébeurden, it's safest to pass west of Les Roches (which dry 6.7m) and the outlier Le Four (dries 3.5m) before turning south and then south-east to leave Le Taureau to the north.

Having passed Le Taureau and the Kinierbel buoy, carry on due east towards Beg Léguer lighthouse for another $\frac{1}{2}$ mile until the inner of the two green beacon towers off the south shore of the estuary is just open to the east of the outer, bearing

about 130ºT. Turn to the south-east to follow this transit into the river, leaving the two beacon towers each 100 metres to starboard and following the curve of the south shore gradually round to port. This wide sweep avoids the sand-bank which extends well out into midstream from the north shore – you will see a low rocky islet on the west edge of this bank.

As you pass the islet, the narrow 'inner mouth' of the river is over on the port bow. There are some moorings off the north bank of the narrows, immediately opposite a prominent stone cottage

Looking downstream past the narrow 'inner mouth' of the Lannion River

and landing slip. A scrub-covered promontory juts out from the south shore. Once the islet is just abaft your port beam, steer to enter the narrows between the landing and the promontory at about 050°T, leaving the moorings to port. Once through this neck, you'll see some more moorings to starboard, in a quiet bay off the south bank. You can anchor just clear of these moorings, in about 2½ metres at MLWS and sheltered from all quarters. From the landing it's only 15 minutes walk up the hill to Le Yaudet village, where you'll find a small shop and two hôtel-restaurants – the Ar Vro (Tel: 02.96.35.24.21) and Les Genets d'Or (Tel: 02. 96.35.24.17). The Crêperie du Yaudet is at the top of the hill opposite a stone calvary.

There are few more restful spots to linger for a day or two than this anchorage at Le Yaudet. The restaurants are worth trying and it's interesting to take the dinghy the three miles up to Lannion on the tide. You'll find some good walks ashore, especially by following the lanes which lead downstream on the south side of the river towards Pointe du Dourven and Locquémeau. There's also a good walk along the north shore of the river to Lannion town – land at the slip on the north side of the river entrance and follow the Grande Randonée signs along the riverside paths. If you feel energetic, you can follow this path in the opposite direction, heading broadly north-west towards Trébeurden.

LOCQUÉMEAU

Locquémeau is a small fishing harbour just to the east of low-lying Pointe de Séhar, on the south side of the approach to the Lannion River. Pointe de Séhar lies a little over ½ mile south of Kinierbel green conical buoy (unlit, with a bell) and is easily identified by its rather austere cluster of white houses.

The Kinierbel buoy marks the extremity of a long plateau of drying rocks which extends north from Pointe de Séhar and partly protects Locquémeau from swell. Most of the harbour dries at LAT, but you can reach the end of the landing slip at MLWS and stay afloat in the outer part of the harbour at neaps.

Approach from the north-west, leaving Locquémeau green conical whistle buoy close to starboard and making good 122°T towards the end of the landing slip – the leading marks are a white pylon on the shore in transit with a white lighthouse cottage behind it bearing 122°T. With drying rocks close either side of this track, there's something to be said for entering Locquémeau near low water, when most of the rocks are visible and you can judge how far to edge into the harbour area. There are no real facilities at Locquémeau, but it can be interesting to visit in quiet weather, perhaps if you are day cruising from Trébeurden marina. However, you shouldn't approach Locquémeau if the wind is more than about force 3 from anywhere between west and north.

LOCQUIREC

Locquirec is a small drying harbour tucked under the east side of Pointe de Locquirec, about 5 miles SSW of Trébeurden on the south coast of the Bay of Lannion. Pointe de Locquirec forms the west arm of a picturesque sandy bay, which dries right out at springs and is bordered

on the east side by Pointe de Plestin. Locquirec has no marina or any other special facilities for yachts, but there are a few shops and restaurants and it's well worth visiting in settled weather for its simple charm and peace and quiet. There's a good crêperie – *Les Algues* – just up behind the harbour. This is Brittany off the beaten track.

If you take the ground easily, you can sound carefully into the harbour an hour or so before high water and position yourself to dry out on the firm sandy bottom. At neaps, keel boats can anchor about a cable east of the harbour breakwater, where you

should just stay afloat at dead neap low water with 1.5 metres draught. At springs you can anchor about 3 cables east of the north tip of Pointe de Locquirec, in the area known locally as the Mouillage de la Palud.

During the summer, the local *Mairie* lays moorings in the approaches to Locquirec, just outside the five metre contour to the north-west of Pointe de Plestin. Five of these moorings are usually reserved for visitors and it's quite snug to stay here overnight with the wind offshore from between south-west through south to south-east.

Locquirec harbour has a firm sandy bottom and is worth a visit if you can take the ground

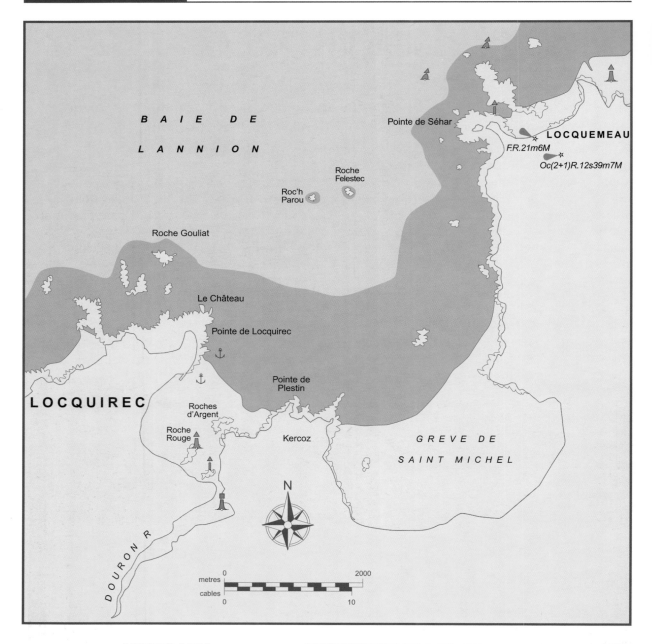

B A I E   D E
L A N N I O N

Pointe de Séhar

LOCQUEMEAU
F.R.21m6M
Oc(2+1)R.12s39m7M

Roche
Felestec

Roc'h
Parou

Roche Gouliat

Le Château

Pointe de Locquirec

Pointe de
Plestin

LOCQUIREC

Roches
d'Argent

Roche
Rouge

Kercoz

G R E V E   D E
S A I N T   M I C H E L

N

D O U R O N   R

metres   0   2000
cables   0   10

APPROACH

Aim to approach Pointe de Locquirec from just east of north, so as to pass between the various dangers NNW of the headland (the outer being Roche Gouliat, dries 4.9m) and the two isolated rocks which lie 1½ miles to the north-east (Roc'h Parou dries 1.6m and Roche Felestec dries 1.3m), although the latter pair will be safely covered above half-tide. A useful steering mark is to keep Roche du Château, a 17 metre islet 2 cables north of Pointe de Locquirec, in line with the highest part of the headland bearing about 200ºT. When about ½ mile from Le Château, come to port to leave it and Pointe de Locquirec a good ½ mile to the west.

PRIMEL

This often bustling, rather functional fishing harbour lies a couple of miles east of the entrance to the Morlaix River. Although it has limited room to anchor and no real facilities for yachts, Primel is at least accessible at most states of tide except in onshore swell. It can be a useful

port-of-call for an hour or two if, having carried the west-going stream down from Perros, Ploumanac'h or Trébeurden, you find yourself off the Morlaix estuary near low water, which is too early to start the nine-mile trip up to Morlaix lock. Primel's narrow entrance leads between rocks to a natural inlet protected by a breakwater.

Pointe de Primel, the east arm of the entrance, has a distinctive profile and is usually easy to identify from any direction. Coming from the east inside Plateau de la Méloine, pass midway between Grande Roche de Méloine and Les Chaises de

Primel and then make good WSW for a position $\frac{1}{2}$ mile NW of Pointe de Primel. Coming from seaward, outside Plateau de la Méloine, pass west of Méloine W-cardinal buoy and Les Trepieds rocks (dry 3.4m) before heading SSE to keep Pointe de Primel fine on the port bow.

Coming from Roscoff, Bloscon or Ile de Batz, pass close south of Plateau des Duons before heading due east to keep Pointe de Primel fine on the starboard bow. Coming from the Morlaix River, either via the Grand Chenal or Chenal de Tréguier, turn to starboard and steer for Pointe de Primel

Primel is a handy bolt-hole in which to wait for enough tide to enter the Morlaix estuary

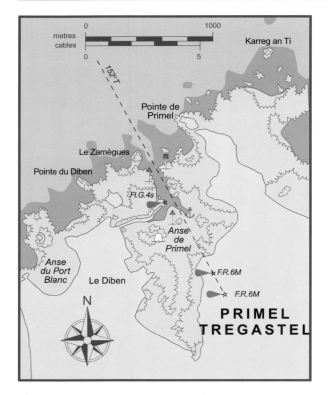

This position lies on the Primel leading line 8 cables out from the breakwater head. Don't venture any closer inshore until you have identified the leading marks on the hill behind the harbour breakwater – white beacons with red vertical stripes. Keep these exactly in transit bearing 152°T, leaving Le Zamègues rock (above-water with a white and green painted mark) close to starboard before passing between Roche Raoul green spar and Roche Camm red spar beacons.

Dangers lurk close either side of the line, so stay dead on the marks as far as the breakwater and then edge to port a little, aiming to fetch up about a cable ESE of the breakwater head and 100 metres NNE of Roche an Trez Braz green spar beacon. Entry at night is not difficult provided you stay at least ½ mile offshore until you pick up the leading lights – 2 fixed reds in transit bearing 152°T. The breakwater head has a light (Fl.G.4s) but Pointe de Primel is unlit.

If the tide serves, you can sometimes lie alongside a fishing boat for a while, on the inside of the breakwater, but the frequent comings and goings make it easier to stay at anchor. There are no useful shops close to the harbour and the nearest restaurant is the Hôtel L'Abbesse, towards the head of Anse de Primel on the west side. Bilge or lifting-keelers can edge further into the inlet and dry out near the local moorings.

when its seaward tip bears due east true.

Whatever the direction of approach, it's convenient to make for an entrance waypoint (48°43.56′N, 03°49.93′W) ½ mile north-west of Pointe de Primel.

Looking out through Primel entrance. When coming in, Le Zamègues rock and Roche Raoul green beacon are left to starboard

MORLAIX

The Bay of Morlaix is three miles wide between Primel and the Plateau des Duons. Two main entrance channels – the Grand Chenal and Chenal de Tréguier – lead south through a cordon of rocks and islets into the sheltered but mostly shallow lower reaches of the Morlaix River.

Although you can enter the estuary by the Grand Chenal at any state of tide, by day or night, to anchor or pick up a mooring east of Pen Lann point, the river practically dries at low springs only two miles further upstream. Above half-flood, however, you can make the six mile passage inland from Pen Lann up to Morlaix, locking into a wet basin close to the old town.

Whenever I approach the Morlaix estuary and contemplate the ragged skyline of rocks, islets and beacon towers which seem to form an almost impenetrable barrier to the river beyond, I am struck by a sense of scale and history. The estuary feels large as river entrances go, and it's certainly a good five miles across the outer part of the mouth between the low profile of Roscoff to the west and Pointe de Primel to the east. The whole bay is also well filled with navigational interest, since many of the off-lying rocks are large enough to qualify as small islands.

The historical associations are perhaps less tangible. Away to starboard though, the ornate silhouettes of the various spires at Roscoff and St-Pol-de-Léon seem old even from a distance. The prominent Kreisker Chapel at St-Pol has indeed been a feature of this Brittany landscape for 600 years. Up ahead, at the end of the rocky corridor of the Grand Chenal, the gaunt 16th century fort on Ile du Taureau forms, with Ile Louet just opposite, the final gateway into the estuary. As you get closer to the fort, it is easy to drift back in time and imagine the thunder of cannon as the local garrison raked the narrows which would provide the only way in for a ship-of-war. Once past the fort, the lower reaches of the river open out to a width of nearly two miles and there's little sign of civilisation to jolt you into the

TIDES

HW off Pen Lann is at HW Brest +0100 approx.
Heights above datum: 9.0m MHWS, 1.3m MLWS,
7.0m MHWN, 3.5m MLWN.
Spring streams in the Bay of Morlaix can reach 2–3
knots locally, but are unpredictable in direction,
especially near Plateau des Duons. The maximum
rate in the Morlaix river is about 2 knots.

CHARTS

Admiralty: 2745 (3669 for outer approaches)
French SHOM: 7095

HAZARDS

You need to fix your position accurately in the Bay of
Morlaix and pick up the outer marks for the Chenal de
Tréguier or the Grand Chenal before closing the
estuary. Poor visibility is the worst hazard, because
the various rocks and beacon towers can easily be
confused. Approaching the Grand Chenal from
Roscoff or Bloscon, avoid the dangers on the SW
edge of Plateau des Duons and up to 3 cables E of
Le Menk W-cardinal beacon tower.

WAYPOINTS

Chenal de Tréguier entrance, $\frac{1}{2}$ mile NNE of La Pierre
Noire green beacon – 48°43.06'N, 03°51.69'W
Grand Chenal entrance, just $\frac{1}{4}$ mile north-west of
Stolvezen red buoy – 48°42.90'N, 03°53.45'W

---

present. The gradual transition between open sea,
rocky channels, estuary and peaceful river is a
striking feature of a visit to Morlaix. Try to arrive
under sail if you can. A chugging diesel seems
strangely at odds with the slow pulse of this ancient
seascape.

To starboard, just south of Ile Louet's picture-book
cottage and lighthouse, the wooded promontory of
Pen Lann shelters the visitors' moorings and
anchorage close off its south-east corner. Except in
fresh southerlies or south-easterlies, this is a snug
spot to lie overnight, whether or not you are
planning to carry on upstream. If you are bound for
Morlaix, a good time to leave the anchorage is about
$2\frac{1}{2}$ hours before high water. The Rade de Morlaix
trends SSE from Pen Lann, the buoyed channel
flanked on either hand with broad mud-flats and
oyster-beds marked by withies. You might see a flat-
bottomed barge working these beds to harvest that
vital ingredient for your evening fruits de mer.

After a couple of miles the river narrows at
Dourduff and the buoys become more frequent as

the fairway curves to starboard and winds through
the local moorings off Locquénolé. Thereafter, the
banks close in for the last two miles up to Morlaix
lock. The channel is well marked, but don't cut any
corners. For the last mile, pairs of leading marks
ashore take over from buoys and beacons, and a
fairly busy road follows the west side of the river.
The final stretch is partly industrial, with several
small factories and the sand-dredgers' quays to
starboard. Just before the lock you pass under a road
bridge, with 33 metres clearance. The lock is on the
west bank and you can wait at the quay just outside
it if the gates aren't open.

The sleepy locked basin has that timeless solidity of
old Breton trading ports, while the spectacular stone
viaduct has looked down on the town since 1864.
Opposite the yacht club, on Quai de Leon, barges
still unload locally dredged sand for building.

The berthing is pleasantly low-key with a slightly
dusty atmosphere, rather like Morlaix itself.
Although some of the pontoons have short fingers
and feel a bit rickety, the basin is perfectly sheltered
and yachts are snug here in any weather. A short
stroll along Quai de Tréguier takes you into the
charming old town, which has some of the best
preserved timbered buildings in Brittany.

APPROACHES AND ENTRY

There are three channels into the Morlaix River:
Chenal de Tréguier, the Grand Chenal and the
Chenal Ouest de Ricard. The Chenal de Tréguier, on
the east side of the estuary, is relatively shallow and
should only be taken above half-flood, but provides
the shortest way in if you are coming round from
Primel, or if you are approaching Morlaix from the
east inside Plateau de la Méloine. It can be used at
night with care. The Grand Chenal is deep for most
of its length and can be taken by most yachts at any
state of tide, by day or night, although the fairway is
narrow between Ricard beacon tower and Les
Cahers rock near low water. Chenal Ouest de Ricard,
just west of the Grand Chenal, carries the deepest
water of all three, but is only feasible in daylight.

Trying to enter the Morlaix estuary in poor
visibility can be somewhat nerve-racking. Without
GPS, the easiest approach is from the direction of
Pointe de Primel, where the coastal dangers are
comparatively steep-to. The Chenal de Tréguier
about an hour before high water is usually the safest
way in, so long as you can find La Pierre Noire green
beacon and then follow an accurate compass course
towards a position midway between Grand Aremen
and Petit Aremen beacon towers.

Chenal de Tréguier: If you are coasting towards
Morlaix from the east, inside Plateau de la Méloine,
leave Les Chaises de Primel and Pointe de Primel

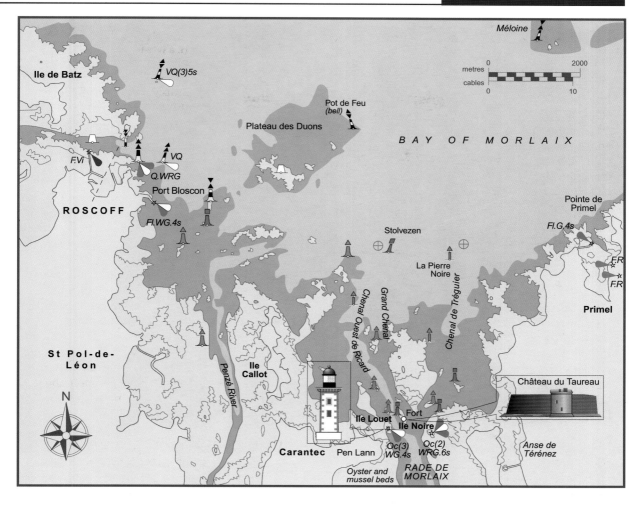

each about ¾ mile to the south before making for a waypoint ½ mile NNE of La Pierre Noire green beacon. Coming out of Primel, turn to port and head for this waypoint when the seaward tip of Pointe de Primel bears more than due east true. If you are approaching directly from seaward, leave Méloine W-cardinal whistle buoy (unlit) 3 cables to the east and make good 190ºT towards the same waypoint.

Make 190ºT from this entrance waypoint, leaving La Pierre Noire beacon 300 metres to starboard and heading towards a pair of beacon towers two miles into the estuary – Grand Aremen green and Petit Aremen red. This track leaves Jaune du Large rock (with a red-and-white painted mark) ¼ mile to port and Tourghi beacon two cables to starboard. Pass midway between Grand and Petit Aremen, leave La Chambre green beacon tower 100 metres to starboard, and then come to starboard to enter the river, steering something like 212ºT to leave Ile Noire 250 metres to port and making for La Barre de Flot green conical buoy. The moorings off Pen Lann are about ¼ mile WSW of this buoy, which you can pass either side above half-tide. If bound upstream for

Morlaix, turn SSE for No 2 red buoy when you are about a cable from La Barre de Flot.

Grand Chenal: The Grand Chenal is entered just over a mile west of the Chenal de Tréguier, from an outer waypoint about ¼ mile north-west of Stolvezen red buoy. From here make good just east of south to pass close to the east of Ile Ricard, steering to leave Ricard green beacon tower 50 metres to starboard, Gouesles rock (6 metres high with a red-and-white painted mark) a good cable to port and Le Beclem islet (20 metres high) 2 cables to port. Continue at 176ºT to leave La Morlouine green beacon 50 metres to starboard and Les Cahers (a small tooth-shaped rock with a red-and-white painted mark) 150 metres to port.

Continue on the same line towards Le Corbeau green beacon tower, leaving Calhic green beacon tower 250 metres to starboard, before edging to port to pass midway between Le Corbeau and Le Taureau towers and thence between Ile Louet and Château du Taureau. If bound upstream for Morlaix, steer to leave La Barre de Flot green conical buoy close to starboard before picking up the buoyed channel SSE into the river. If making for the Pen

The picture-book island of Ile Louet, which is left close to starboard as you enter the Morlaix River by the Grand Chenal

Lann anchorage or moorings, you can cut to starboard between Le Pichet red beacon and La Barre de Flot except near low water.

Chenal Ouest de Ricard: This channel starts near the Grand Chenal waypoint, passes west of Ile Ricard, and rejoins the Grand Chenal east of Calhic green beacon tower. It carries more depth than the Grand Chenal and is useful for larger yachts entering the estuary near low tide, but can only be taken by day. Enter midway between La Vieille green beacon tower and Stolvezen red buoy, making good 189°T to leave two green beacons – La Fourche and La Noire – each 150 metres to starboard. Petit Ricard rocks, opposite La Noire beacon, are left a cable to port. Once past La Noire, come to the SSE on about 160ºT to leave Ile Ricard a cable to port, Morlouine green beacon – one of the Grand Chenal marks – two cables to port, but Bizinennou green beacon only 100 metres to starboard. Then alter a bit further to port to leave Calhic green beacon tower at least a cable to starboard and so join the Grand Chenal.

At night: None of the buoys, beacons or beacon towers in the Morlaix estuary is lit. Apart from the leading lights for the Grand Chenal and Chenal de Tréguier, the only useful lights when approaching the estuary are:

To the west – Ile de Batz main lighthouse (*Fl(4)25s23M*); Ar Chaden beacon tower (*Q(6)+LFl.WR*), ¼ mile north of Pointe de Bloscon; and Port Bloscon breakwater light (*Fl.WG.4s*).

To the north-east – in clear visibility, you can see Les Sept Iles (*Fl(3)15s24M*) and the much lower light on Plateau des Triagoz (*Oc(2)WR.6s14M*).

In clear visibility, especially with GPS, you can use bearings of Les Sept Iles, Triagoz and Ile de Batz to approach the Morlaix estuary from the east inside Plateau de la Méloine. Bear in mind though, that Méloine and Les Chaises de Primel are unlit. If in doubt, stay seaward of Méloine until you pick up the Chenal de Tréguier leading lights. Approaching the Morlaix estuary from offshore, pick up either the Grand Chenal or Chenal de Tréguier leading lights in order to come in safely between Pot de Fer E-cardinal buoy (unlit with a bell) and Méloine W-cardinal buoy (unlit with a whistle). Coming from Roscoff or Bloscon in fair weather, you can use the white sector of Ar Chaden light (*Q(6)+LFl*) to pass between Plateau des Duons and Les Bisayers before picking up the Grand Chenal leading lights.

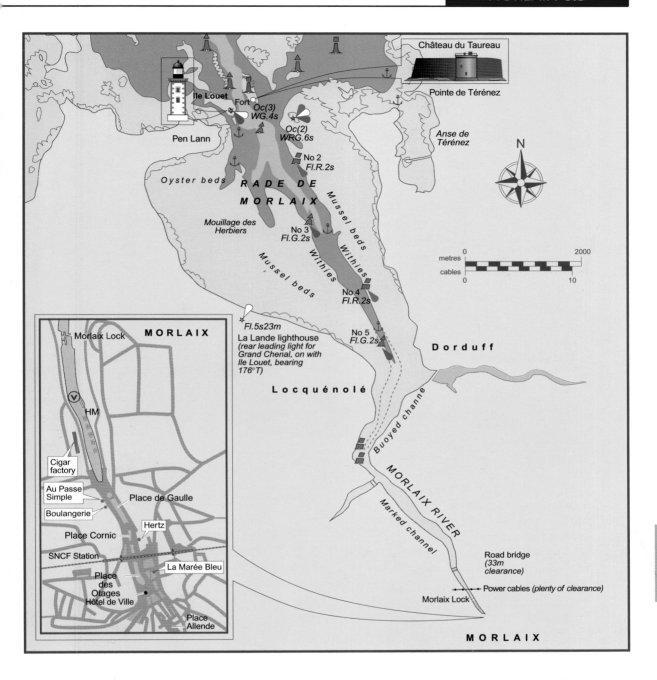

Château du Taureau

Pointe de Térénez

Ile Louet

Fort

*Oc(3)
WG.4s*

*Oc(2)
WRG.6s*

Pen Lann

Anse de
Térénez

No 2
Fl.R.2s

Oyster beds

RADE DE
MORLAIX

Mussel beds

Mouillage des
Herbiers

Withies

No 3
Fl.G.2s

Mussel beds

Withies

No 4
Fl.R.2s

N

metres   0   2000
cables   0   10

Fl.5s23m
La Lande lighthouse
(rear leading light for
Grand Chenal, on with
Ile Louet, bearing
176°T)

No 5
Fl.G.2s

Dorduff

Locquénolé

Buoyed channel

MORLAIX RIVER

Marked channel

Road bridge
(33m
clearance)

Power cables (plenty of clearance)

Morlaix Lock

MORLAIX

Inset map (lower left):

Morlaix Lock

MORLAIX

HM

Cigar
factory

Au Passe
Simple

Boulangerie

Place de Gaulle

Hertz

Place Cornic

SNCF Station

La Marée Bleu

Place
des
Otages
Hôtel de Ville

Place
Allende

Chapter 8

La Lande (*Fl.5s*), standing well up on the hillside at the back of the estuary, serves as the rear leading light for both the Grand Chenal and the Chenal de Tréguier. You can see La Lande from well offshore in good visibility, although it dips behind the land as you close the coast on either side of the entrance. For the Grand Chenal, bring Ile Louet light (*Oc(3)WG.12s*) in line with La Lande behind it bearing 176°T. For the Chenal de Tréguier, bring Ile Noire light (*Oc(2)WRG.6s*) in line with La Lande bearing 190°T.

The Grand Chenal leaves you slightly in the lurch with lights for the last half mile between Calhic beacon tower and Ile Louet, because you have to hold a compass course while trying to spot a pair of unlit beacon towers and leave Château du Taureau safely to port. You should avoid using this channel in a rising onshore wind, deteriorating visibility, or any conditions which would make it difficult to pick your way through this inner part of the narrows.

Although the Chenal de Tréguier should only be used above half-tide, the lights do at least take you right into the lower part of the estuary; depth permitting, therefore, it is usually the safer route at night. Whichever entrance you choose, it's a sound precaution to double-check the characteristics and bearing of the leading lights while you are still out in safe water.

Grand Chenal at night: Bring the white sector of Ile Louet light (*Oc(3)WG.12s*) in line with La Lande (*Fl.5s23M*) behind it bearing 176°T and stay dead on this transit as you approach Ricard beacon tower (unlit) and negotiate the narrows just east of Ile Ricard. Identify Ile Noire light (*Oc(2)WRG.6s*), whose red sector you should see over on the port bow. As soon as Ile Noire changes from red to green (bearing 135°T), come to port a shade to steer 161°T, with Ile Louet light now fine on your starboard bow. This track leads between Le Corbeau and Le Taureau beacon towers (both unlit) and then between Château du Taureau and Ile Louet.

You need to hold an accurate course for this stretch, using a searchlight to pick out the unlit beacon towers. Ile Louet light will change from white to green as it comes abeam. The easiest way to reach the Pen Lann anchorage is to continue on 161°T until Ile Louet changes back to white and then steer 215–220°T towards the south-east shore of Pen Lann. Use the searchlight again to spot the white mooring buoys, and to avoid La Barre de Flot green buoy (unlit) which should be fine ahead to port just before you turn for Pen Lann. In fresh southerlies or south-easterlies, and depending on the tides, you'll find better shelter by following the lit buoys upstream for another mile or two, anchoring between No 3 green (*Fl.G.2s*) and No 4 red (*Fl.R.2s*) at springs, or between No 4 red (*Fl.R.2s*) and No 5 green (*Fl.G.2s*) at neaps.

Chenal de Tréguier at night: Given sufficient rise of tide (preferably above half-flood), bring the red sector of Ile Noire light (*Oc(2)WRG.6s*) in line with La Lande (*Fl.5s*) bearing 190°T. Follow this transit accurately until Ile Louet light, over on the starboard bow, changes from white to green (when bearing 244°T) and then steer 220–225°T towards the Pen Lann anchorage. Ile Noire will change from red to green as it draws abeam to port and Ile Louet changes back to white as you near the anchorage. A

Morlaix marina basin, looking north towards the lock

searchlight is useful for picking out the various unlit beacon towers, La Barre de Flot green conical buoy, and the white mooring buoys off Pen Lann. If you are continuing upstream for a mile or two, perhaps to find better shelter in fresh southerlies or south-easterlies, turn to the SSE and head for No 2 red buoy (*Fl.R.2s*) when Ile Noire green sector bears due east true.

The river above Pen Lann: For the first two miles above Pen Lann, the channel leads SSE between broad mud-flats and the patches of rather emaciated withies marking oyster beds. Two red and two green buoys, well spaced, take you up to where the river starts to narrow, just below Dourduff village on the east bank and Locquénolé, on the west. This is the limit of navigation either at night or near low water; you can anchor opposite Dourduff at neaps, but depths shoal quickly thereafter. The channel buoys are now smaller but more frequent and the fairway curves across towards the west bank through the local moorings off Locquénolé.

If you are planning to catch the first lock into Morlaix basin, which is 1½ hours before high water, you should really be passing Locquénolé no later than 2¼ hours before high water. Although the banks are close together between Locquénolé and Morlaix, you still have to follow the marks carefully. For the last mile or so, the buoys and spar beacons give way to pairs of leading marks (mostly red-and-white X's) on either side of the river, and a fairly busy road runs close alongside to starboard.

The final stretch leads through the light-industrial outskirts of Morlaix, under a road bridge with 33 metres clearance, and so to the lock on the west bank. A little way above the bridge, watch out for a silting mudbank that tends to build off the west bank.

Just outside the gates is a quay where you can moor safely within two hours of high water, but this is not a good place to dry out if you happen to miss the last lock – better to return downstream to an anchorage below Dourduff.

Lock times: The lock is operated three times in each direction on each tide, during daylight hours only.

- 1st lock – 1½ hours before HW
- 2nd lock – At HW
- 3rd lock – 1 hour after HW

Locking is sometimes more frequent at busy summer periods. Coming upstream, you need to be passing Pen Lann just before half-flood to catch the first inward lock.

Note that the river is not lit above Dourduff and night navigation is forbidden. You can telephone the lock-keeper's office on 02.98.88.54.92.

MORLAIX BASIN

This sleepy, unassuming locked basin is close to the centre of Morlaix and perfectly sheltered. There are pontoon berths on the east side, where the Yacht Club de Morlaix are always very welcoming, or you can lie alongside the rather dusty quays on the west side. The basin can be very hot and airless in high summer, when some crews may find the Gallic whiff of drains a bit too unassuming. For myself, I have always enjoyed Morlaix's workaday, unyachtified atmosphere. The town bustles in the morning and late afternoon, but an agreeable torpor settles over the port area for two or three hours after midday. Morlaix is a good place to change crews, and you can safely leave a boat here for a few weeks by arrangement with the Yacht Club.

MOORINGS AND ANCHORAGES

Bloscon: There were some local moorings to the south of Bloscon ferry port, just round the corner from Roscoff on the north-west side of the Bay of Morlaix, although there is work in progress to extend the commercial quays here. If you can find an empty mooring or anchor south of the quays, this is a useful billet if you arrive off the estuary at an inconvenient time for going up to Morlaix basin, at night perhaps, or having carried the flood from L'Abervrac'h.

Bloscon is sheltered in westerly weather, not too bad in southerlies, but exposed in anything from the east. Keep clear of the ferries and the Ro-Ro terminal and avoid Ar Pourven shoal, which extends well south of Ar Pourven N-cardinal buoy.

Pen Lann: The anchorage off the south-east side of Pen Lann is about 3–4 cables south of Ile Louet and accessible at any state of tide by day or night. Having reached this spot, you are well protected from the full weight of the sea and can lie safely in most weathers, either overnight or while waiting for the tide up to Morlaix. There are several heavy-duty moorings in the deepest part of the anchorage.

In strong northerlies, you can edge a bit further west under the lee of Pen Lann except at extreme springs. In strong southerlies or south-easterlies, there'll be a brisk chop coming down the river, although the fetch is not very great. In strong north-

Chapter 8

easterlies, a swell rolls in between Ile Noire and Château du Taureau, especially on the flood. If the anchorage becomes uncomfortable in any of these conditions, you can easily move further upstream towards Dourduff to find better shelter.

Térénez: This tranquil drying inlet on the east side of the Morlaix estuary is reached via the Chenal de Tréguier, above half-tide in daylight only. It offers a pleasant anchorage in quiet weather and is sheltered in strong winds from between south through east to north-east. Follow the directions for the outer part of Chenal de Tréguier, but alter to the south-east when Tourghi green beacon is two cables abeam to starboard, steering for Annomer green beacon $\frac{1}{2}$ mile away. Leave Annomer 100m to starboard and then head SSE towards Pointe de Térénez, a low promontory with a few houses at its tip.

At neaps, moderate draft boats can anchor and stay afloat close south of Pointe de Térénez, clear of the local moorings. This spot is protected from all winds except fresh north-westerlies and there are a couple of landing slips at the end of the point. Bilge-keelers may edge further into the inlet and take the ground on a mostly sandy bottom (but refer to Admiralty Chart No 2745). At springs, most keel boats will stay afloat just outside the mouth of the inlet, 2–3 cables NW of Pointe de Térénez – don't anchor too close to Pointe de Térénez, because drying rocks extend for about a cable off to the NW. In north-easterlies, fetch up a bit closer under the lee of Pointe St Samson, which is the next headland to the north.

Carantec: There is an attractive fair-weather anchorage on the NW side of Pen Lann in Kélenn bay, half a mile or so to the NE of Carantec at springs but closer inshore at neaps. You can reach or leave this bay at practically any state of tide, although only in daylight. Coming from seaward, follow the directions for the Chenal Ouest de Ricard but continue to make good just west of south when La Noire green beacon is abeam to starboard. Leave Le Courgik green beacon a cable to starboard and Bizinennou green beacon $1\frac{1}{2}$ cables to port, bringing two white leading marks ahead of you into line at 188°T – the white-painted above-water rock Pierre de Carantec (which looks like a well used pair of bottom teeth), and Kergrist white pyramid on the shore behind it. At springs, follow this transit accurately almost as far as you can, but edge to port a little before reaching Pierre de Carantec and fetch up a cable NNE of it, so that Grand Cochon beacon tower is a good 2 cables to the east and Basse Plate rock (dries 6.8m) just over a cable to the east. This spot has about $\frac{1}{2}$ metre at LAT, so can be used by moderate draft yachts even at MLWS in quiet conditions. The anchorage is open from between NW through N to E, but is reasonable in westerlies and well sheltered in any winds from the south. At neaps, steer south-west when Pierre de Carantec is a cable off, leaving it to port and fetching up in Kélenn bay off the landing slip as depths allow.

Above half-tide, following Admiralty 2745 or the French 5827, there's a useful daylight short cut between Kélenn bay and the Morlaix river via the narrow channel, marked by beacons, between Pen Lann and Ile Louet. This route is often more straightforward nearer half-tide than at high water, because the various outcrops of rock (such as Basse Plate) are then easier to identify.

Mouillage des Herbiers: A tongue of deepish water extends upstream for $\frac{1}{2}$-$\frac{3}{4}$ mile from the Pen Lann anchorage, more or less parallel with the main river channel but a bit to the west of it. The upper part of this cul-de-sac offers better shelter than Pen Lann in fresh southerlies or south-easterlies, being closer to a weather shore and partly sheltered by mud-banks, especially near low tide. Fetch up well clear of any oyster beds, which are marked by patches of withies. You should show a good riding light at night, because this anchorage is sometimes used by sand-dredgers and oyster boats.

The Morlaix River opposite Dourduff and Locquénolé, where the buoyed channel winds through the local moorings

Upper Rade de Morlaix: The river channel carries water at any tide as far as No 4 red buoy, just over 1½ miles above Pen Lann. You can anchor and stay afloat between No 3 green and No 4 red at springs, or between No 4 red and Dourduff at neaps, either stretch being more sheltered than Pen Lann in fresh southerlies or south-easterlies. Fetch up well to one side of the fairway and show a riding light at night.

Dourduff: You can anchor opposite Dourduff at neaps, between No 5 green buoy and the end of Dourduff promontory, but the depths shoal quickly above the next green buoy. No 5 is the last lit buoy, so you can just reach this anchorage at night with care.

FACILITIES

The locked basin at Morlaix offers sheltered pontoon berths just a short stroll from the town centre, which has a useful selection of shops and restaurants. Although the overall set-up of this *port de plaisance* is rather more low-key than you'll find in some marinas, you have showers and WCs close to hand, water points at most of the pontoons, and power can be laid on by arrangement with the Yacht Club. You'll find various boatyards and marine engineers about half a mile downstream from the lock, on the west side of the river. Morlaix is a handy place to change crews, with good rail connections and the Roscoff ferry not far away.

ASHORE IN MORLAIX

A short stroll from Morlaix basin takes you towards the viaduct and town centre. Morlaix is famous for its splendidly preserved timbered buildings dating back to the 15th and 16th centuries. Many are ornately decorated with carved statues of saints and particularly colourful examples can be seen around Place Allende des Halles, a couple of blocks south-east of the Hôtel de Ville.

Place Allende des Halles is a partly raised square, with steps leading off to intriguing back-streets. You can pass a pleasant day wandering the old quarters of Morlaix, pausing now and again at tempting

Chapter 8

Morlaix Port Guide

(Telephoning Morlaix numbers from the UK dial 00 33 298 etc)

Harbourmaster: Monsieur Didier Pignolet at the Bureau du Port, Quai de Tréguier (Tel or Fax: +33 298 62 13 14). VHF Ch 9.

Lockmaster: Écluse de Morlaix, Route de Carantec, Tel 02.98.88.54.92

Fuel: Diesel berth opposite Bureau du Port during office hours (0800-1200, 1330-1700).

Water: At the pontoons.

Weather forecasts: Posted daily at the Bureau du Port. Météo France recorded forecasts on 08 36 68 08 08 or 08 36 68 08 29.

Gas: Camping Gaz and Butane from Loisirs Nautiques at Allée St François along Route de Carantec, on the west side of the river downstream from the lock (Tel 02 98 88 27 30, Fax 02 98 88 82 36).

Chandler: Also at Loisirs Nautiques.

Yacht Clubs: Yacht Club de Morlaix (YCM) on Quai de Tréguier (Clubhouse Tel 02 98 88 38 00).

Showers: At the Yacht Club next to the Bureau du Port.

Banks: Several banks with cashpoints in town.

Shops: Good food shopping in the town centre and at the covered market at Place Allende des Halles. Monoprix supermarket in Rue de l'Auditoire. Good baker near the port on west side of Place Charles de Gaulle.

Repairs: At Loisirs Nautiques (see Chandler above).

Engine repairs: Mecamar Mechanique Marine (Tel 02 98 88 12 25),also at Allée St François along Route de Carantec, near Loisirs Nautiques).

Travel: Brittany Ferries Roscoff-Plymouth Ro-Ro service (Roscoff office Tel 02 98 29 28 00, UK reservations office Tel +44 (0)990 360360). SNCF train enquiries Tel 08 36 35 35 35 or Morlaix station Tel 02 98 63 56 18 (Morlaix is on the main line between Brest and Rennes). Morlaix airport, a short taxi ride from the port, has regular connections to London via Brest-Guipavas airport (Brit Air reservations Tel: 02 98 62 77 77). Hertz car hire on east side of Place Cornic just north of viaduct. Local buses to Roscoff and Lannion.

Restaurants

Morlaix has plenty of restaurants and bistros to suit all tastes and budgets, but three of my favourites are:

La Marée Bleue at 3 Rampe St Melaine (Tel 02 98 63 24 21), just south of the viaduct off the east side of Place des Otages.

Restaurant de la Reine Anne at 45 Rue du Mur (Tel 02 98 88 08 29), just off the SW corner of Place Allende des Halles.

Au Passe Simple at 21 Place Charles de Gaulle (Tel 02 98 63 81 39), near the head of the basin.

cafés. The helpful tourist office near the viaduct will give you a map showing showing various town walks, of which the 'Circuit des Trois Collines' is particularly fascinating.

Down on the west side of the basin, the elegant façade of the Morlaix cigar factory could slip your notice as a going concern, but this amazing old building houses one of the principal cigar makers in Europe. In the prosperous era of colonial trading, tobacco was shipped direct to the quayside. The factory runs occasional guided tours, but you need to enquire in advance.

Morlaix station is at the top of town – follow the old steps (Venelle de la Roche) on the west side of Place Cornic just north of the viaduct. The station connects west to Brest and east towards St Brieuc, Rennes and Paris. Local SNCF coaches run to Roscoff from Morlaix station and TDF coaches from the viaduct.

DAY TRIPS FROM MORLAIX

The Morlaix estuary provides some interesting scope for gentle summer pottering, although Morlaix itself is a bit of a haul upstream to serve as a convenient daily base. Given a reasonably settled spell, you might spend a pleasant couple of days sampling some of the estuary anchorages – from Térénez on the east side to the Penzé River west of Carantec – knowing that you can always retreat to Pen Lann or Morlaix if conditions deteriorate.

Even if you have ear-marked Morlaix as the westernmost port-of-call in your cruise, it's well worth trying to stretch a point to visit Ile de Batz for a day, anchoring or picking up a mooring in the Canal de l'Ile de Batz off Portz Kernoc'h and landing with the dinghy for a stroll round the island. Batz takes you back in time in the most beguiling way.

THE PENZÉ RIVER

The Penzé River opens into the west side of the Bay of Morlaix, between Ile de Callot and the mainland coast that trends south from Roscoff and Port Bloscon. Although the outer estuary is over a mile wide, there is only a narrow channel which doesn't dry, flanked by mud-flats and oyster beds, and navigable only by day for about four miles as far as St Yves. The main hazards are right at the entrance, within a mile east and south-east of Bloscon, where the various shoals and drying rocks are tricky near low water. The best time to approach Penzé is about half-flood, when you have sufficient rise of tide over the unmarked dangers.

The Penzé River is quiet and unassuming, and somewhat off the usual beaten track for visiting yachts. There are various possible anchorages between the lower reaches west of Ile de Callot and the narrows off St Yves, just downstream from Pont de la Corde. Above this high road bridge, which has about 11 metres clearance, the river dries at LAT, although most boats will stay afloat in the first half-mile at neaps. On the late flood near high water, boats that can pass under Pont de la Corde can venture above St Yves for nearly three miles as far as the small village of Penzé.

Just upstream from the bridge is a wide quay, beyond which the moorings peter out. Then a straight reach lies ahead, with woods on either bank and a distant railway bridge. The channel is well

The attractive and sheltered upper reaches of the Penzé River at St Yves

Chapter 8

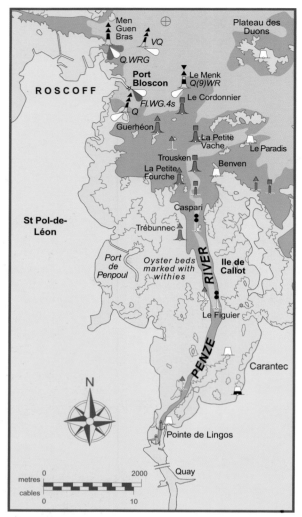

Map labels:
Men Guen Bras · VQ · Q.WRG · Plateau des Duons · ROSCOFF · Port Bloscon · Le Menk Q(9)WR · Le Cordonnier · Fl.WG.4s · Q · Guerhéon · La Petite Vache · Le Paradis · Trousken · Benven · La Petite Fourche · Caspari · St Pol-de-Léon · Trébunnec · Port de Penpoul · Oyster beds marked with withies · Ile de Callot · PENZE RIVER · Le Figuier · Carantec · N · Pointe de Lingos · Quay · metres 0 2000 · cables 0 10

marked by buoys. Once past the railway bridge, the river winds through peaceful farmland, with few signs of habitation until you reach the outskirts of Penzé. The last part of the channel is very narrow before you finally reach a cul-de-sac, with stone quays on either hand and the old arched bridge barring further progress.

This is definitely the head of navigation, a forgotten river port three miles above St Yves, once used by sailing barges for landing building sand dredged from the Chenal de Batz. There are no barges now, but the quays are sound. The best spot for yachts to dry out is alongside the higher part of the east quay, between two piles and just downstream from a ladder. Here, you lie next to a neatly kept garden area with wooden seats and picnic tables. Next to the bridge is the village loo, with a water tap outside.

APPROACH AND ENTRY

You can only enter or leave the Penzé River in daylight, preferably above half-tide with a safe depth over the various unmarked dangers near the mouth.

From Bloscon: The easiest approach is from Port Bloscon at around half-flood. Head south-east from Ar Pourven N-cardinal buoy, which lies just east of the Bloscon moorings, steering to leave Guerhéon green beacon tower 100 metres to starboard. Continue a shade south of south-east towards Trousken red beacon tower, turning south before you reach Trousken to pass between it and La Petite Fourche green beacon tower. Thereafter follow the beacons south by east for $1\frac{3}{4}$ miles towards Carantec, leaving an area of oyster bed withies off the drying harbour of Penpoul to starboard.

When abreast the north end of the Carantec peninsula, turn SSW at Le Figuier isolated danger beacon to follow the upper river towards Pointe de Lingos, leaving Ile Toull Houarn a good cable to starboard and Ile Penzornou a bit closer to port. After Ile Penzornou, leave a green beacon close to starboard and edge towards the west side of the river before curving to port as the white beacon on Pointe de Lingos comes abreast. There are quite a few moorings in this last stretch before the bridge, with long landing slips on either side of the river at St Yves.

From due north: Coming straight in from seaward or from the east end of the Canal de l'Ile de Batz (again, at or above half-flood), leave Le Menk W-cardinal beacon tower and Le Cordonnier red beacon tower each a couple of cables to port before leaving Guerhéon green beacon tower to starboard and proceeding as above. Basse du Cordonnier, a rock drying one metre midway between Cordonnier and Guerhéon beacon towers, is safe to pass over at half-tide.

From the east: Coming from the Morlaix estuary or from the direction of Pointe de Primel, there are several approaches to the Penzé River using the large-scale Admiralty Chart 2745. How you avoid the various dangers depends on the state of the tide, but the easiest route at or above half-flood is to pass midway between Plateau des Duons and Les Bisayers rocks before turning WSW to leave Le Cordonnier red beacon tower a cable to starboard. When abreast of Le Cordonnier, turn south to leave La Vache red beacon tower well to port and pass between Trousken red beacon tower and La Petite Fourche green beacon tower, continuing thereafter as above.

ANCHORAGES

Once south of the chapel spire on Ile de Callot, you can use Admiralty 2745 to anchor wherever convenient. You'll find progressively better

The Penzé River at Pont de la Corde. The bridge has 11m clearance at MHW

shelter the further upstream you go, but in quiet weather, if you don't want to venture right up to St Yves, there's a good spot just east of the channel opposite the south part of Ile de Callot, with good holding in mud. Another possibility is opposite Carantec, about 1½-2 cables ENE of Ile Toull Houarn. In the upper reaches, near St Yves, you can fetch up near the two landing slips, clear of the local moorings.

Yachts of modest draught that take the ground safely can edge into Port de Penpoul near high water, the shallow drying harbour on the west side of the estuary opposite St Pol de Léon. Penpoul is sheltered by a long breakwater and you approach the entrance on a south-westerly course from a position about a cable east of Trébunnec green beacon tower. You can either dry out alongside the breakwater quay, or sit on legs or bilge-keels in the middle of the wide harbour area.

Penpoul is 20 minutes stroll from St Pol de Léon, a charming market town with a good range of shops and one or two congenial restaurants. You can visit the old cathedral and the Kreisker Chapel, whose spires are so prominent from seaward as you approach the estuary.

Stormalong dried out alongside the Penzé quay

PORT BLOSCON

Bloscon is the deep-water ferry port in the north-west corner of the Morlaix estuary, close east of Roscoff. The ferry terminal and commercial port area are sheltered from seaward by a substantial breakwater stretching south-east from the Brittany Ferries Ro-Ro ramp. Although Bloscon doesn't really cater for yachts, it remains a useful overnight staging post in suitable conditions if, for example, you are coasting between Tréguier and L'Abervrac'h in either direction.

So long as you keep well clear to the south of all the ferry and harbour operations, you can tuck fairly close inshore and either anchor just over a cable WSW of Ar Pourven N-cardinal buoy, or use one of the local moorings if vacant. This spot is sheltered from between SW through W to NNW and has the advantage of being accessible at any state of tide, by day or night. You can usually land by dinghy at the southernmost quay at Bloscon (not the ferry quay), although the ladders are not particularly easy and you shouldn't leave a dinghy there for long. There's also a small landing slip in the crook of the small bay about 100 metres south of the commercial quays. Once ashore, you have access to the facilities in the ferry terminal and Roscoff town is only about 15 minutes walk.

Bloscon is the deep water ferry port just round the corner from Roscoff

ROSCOFF

Well known as a car-ferry port, Roscoff lies at the north tip of the low peninsula that forms the west arm of the wide Morlaix and Penzé estuaries. The town and harbour face north across the east end of the narrow Canal de l'Ile de Batz, from where you approach the harbour. The deep-water

Brittany Ferries terminal is half-a-mile east of Roscoff, just round the corner at Bloscon.

Because Roscoff harbour starts to dry soon after half-ebb, it's not all that popular with visiting yachts, although the inner quays offer peaceful and sheltered berths if you can take the ground safely, except when strong north-easterlies send in a swell. Most yachts can enter or leave for about $2\frac{1}{2}$ hours either side of HW.

For non-sailing tourists, 'Roscoff' usually conjures up either the memories or the prospect of long summer holidays in Brittany. This is partly an association with cross-Channel ferries, but there is also something about the word itself which conveys the essence of Gallic foreignness. It doesn't sound quite French, but it does have an authentic rasp of Breton. In a different era, Roscoff was famous for its 'Onion Johnnies', those inimitable onion sellers on bicycles who provided, for many English

housewives, their first experience of a real live Frenchman.

Although most yachtsmen know Roscoff as one of the larger ports on the North Brittany coast, few of them ever call there. Because the harbour dries, it's not particularly convenient for visiting yachts, and there seem to be less cruising crews each year who value the seclusion which a little inconvenience can bring. Staying overnight in Roscoff means either settling on legs or bilge-keels in the middle of the inner harbour, or else leaning against one of the quays, scrambling up a slippery ladder to get ashore, and rubbing shoulders with fishing boats which arrive and leave at all hours.

I must say that I find the salty ambience of drying out rather attractive. Time slows right down when reckoned by your rise and fall against a solid stone quay. Roscoff is one of the few North Brittany harbours with no pontoon berths for yachts and I for

Roscoff dries, although there are still proposals to convert the inner harbour into a small sill marina

TIDES

HW Roscoff is at HW Brest +0100 approx.
Heights above datum: 8.9m MHWS, 1.3m MLWS,
7.0m MHWN, 3.4m MLWN.
The streams in the Canal de l'Ile de Batz can reach
4 knots at springs, the east-going stream starting at
about HW Brest −0435 and the west-going stream
at HW Brest +0110.

CHARTS

Admiralty: 2745
French SHOM: 7095

HAZARDS

Approaching Roscoff from the west, there are the
various marked dangers of the Canal de l'Ile de Batz.
From the east, avoid the unlit Plateau des Duons, two
miles E of Roscoff entrance. Coming from seaward,
give a wide berth to the extensive drying rocks off the
north and east coasts of Ile de Batz.

WAYPOINTS

Eastern approach to the Canal de l'Ile de Batz, $\frac{3}{4}$ mile
due E of Ar Chaden light beacon
– 48°43.98'N, 03°57.03'W
Entrance waypoint for Roscoff harbour, a cable
WSW of Ar Chaden light beacon
– 48°43.95'N, 03°58.28'W

one like to escape from organised facilities once in
a while.

Roscoff town, despite an invasion of English cars in
high season, somehow manages to
assert its individuality and maintain a
friendly small-scale atmosphere. It's a
good place to shop, there are several
banks, and you can usually find a
restaurant to suit the mood. To avoid
crowds for an hour or two, you can
always take a taxi south for a few miles
to the old cathedral town of St Pol de
Léon, with its imposing central square
and quaint narrow streets.

The coast around Roscoff is quite
distinctive. If you were set down
blindfold on the jetty and had your
mask taken away, it would only take a
moment to recognise where you were.
There are several ornate church spires on the
skyline, which are often a great help on a hazy day as
you approach from the north-east. The long low-
water landing for the Ile de Batz vedettes is an
unmistakable feature, supported on tall stilts like a
bridge for a good quarter of a mile and marked at its

north tip by a curious horn-shaped beacon.
Clustered around this landing are the numerous
cardinal beacons and towers which lead through the
narrow eastern end of the Canal de l'Ile de Batz.
Over to the north-west, the low profile of Batz seems
almost part of the mainland, its south-east corner
only half a mile from the end of the low-water
landing. The tall lighthouse at the west end of the
island can be glimpsed from many fascinating
angles as you wander round Roscoff.

APPROACHES AND ENTRY

The entrance to Roscoff lies on the south side of the
east end of the Canal de l'Ile de Batz. Most yachts can
reckon the harbour as being safely accessible for
about 2½ hours either side of HW, although strangers
should enter on the flood if possible. This normally
fits in when arriving from the west – from
L'Abervrac'h for example – but yachts coming from
the east will usually be arriving off Roscoff near low
water. In this case you can anchor or moor south of
Port Bloscon before moving round to Roscoff just
before high water. The harbour approaches are
reasonably well protected in most conditions except
strong winds from between north and east.

From the west: Follow the directions for the Canal
de l'Ile de Batz (see the Ile de Batz chapter) to a
position midway between Roc'h Zu N-cardinal
beacon and Ar Chaden S-cardinal tower before
turning SSE towards Roscoff west breakwater head.
Allowing for whatever tide is setting across the
entrance, make good 210°T with the white mark on
the breakwater head in transit with an elegant four-
square lighthouse tower at the back of the harbour.

This line leaves Roc'h Zu beacon just
over a cable to starboard and Roc'h
Rannic N-cardinal tower a similar
distance to port. Once abreast the east
breakwater head, you can quit the
transit to enter the harbour.

From the east: Enter the Canal de
l'Ile de Batz close south of Ar Chaden
S-cardinal tower and then pick up the
marks as above. When coming round
from Bloscon near high water you can
pass south of Basse de Bloscon N-
cardinal buoy, but don't turn towards
Men Guen Bras N-cardinal beacon
tower until you are midway between
Basse de Bloscon buoy and Bloscon breakwater
head.

At night: The approach from the east is
straightforward at night in reasonable visibility,
using Ile de Batz lighthouse (*Fl(4)25s.23M*), the
white sectors of Men Guen Bras and Ar Chaden, and

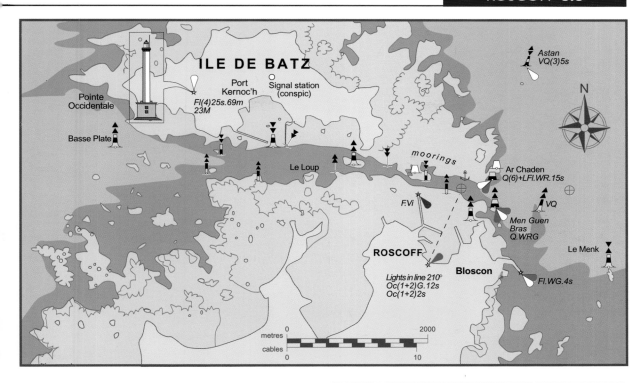

then picking up the Roscoff leading lights – the west breakwater head (*Oc.G(2+1)12s*) in line with the harbour lighthouse (*Oc(2+1)12s*) bearing 210ºT.

The Canal de l'Ile de Batz is unlit to the west of Roscoff entrance, so it's not feasible to approach from the west at night by this route; you would have to round Batz at a safe distance to the north and east and come in from the east as above.

MOORINGS AND ANCHORAGES

Roscoff harbour: Visitors should make for the Vieux Port, turning to starboard beyond the inner mole. Bilge or lifting-keelers, or yachts with legs, can sometimes use a vacant mooring. For keel boats, the best quay for drying out is the inner side of the inner mole. The harbour is sheltered in most conditions, although you can get a nasty swell rolling in during strong north-easterlies.

Outside the harbour: In quiet weather, while waiting for the tide to enter Roscoff, you can anchor off the harbour in about 2-3 metres on a direct line between Roc'h Zu beacon and Ar Chaden tower, or use one of the moorings to the west of Ile Pighet.

Ile de Batz: There are various anchorages off Ile de Batz (see next chapter) where you can wait for sufficient rise of tide to enter Roscoff.

FACILITIES

Facilities for yachts are limited at Roscoff, although every so often the local Mairie revives the continuing debate about proposals to build a sill across part of the Vieux Port to form a wet basin

The very Breton harbour lighthouse at Roscoff

You can dry out against the south side of the mole in Roscoff's inner harbour

with pontoon berths. These plans have been on the stocks for a long time – the case continues.

At present, fresh water and electricity are available at the quay on the south-west side of the Vieux Port, with toilets and wash-basins close by. There is no alongside fuelling berth for yachts, but you can obtain diesel or petrol by jerrycan from the service station in town.

DAY TRIPS FROM ROSCOFF

Roscoff is not an easy harbour for coming and going for day trips in the boat, or for leaving her unattended if you fancy anything more than just a quick expedition ashore. However, if the tides happen to suit, say with high water at about eight in the morning and evening, you can have a full day's excursion over on Ile de Batz. Taking your own boat, you can leave after breakfast and make for one of the anchorages off Port Kernoc'h, only about $1\frac{1}{2}$ miles away. You might even edge into Kernoc'h itself and dry out if you get over there in good time.

If, on the other hand, you decide to leave the boat in Roscoff, there will be time to see her safely dried out before taking one of the vedettes over to Batz. Mid-week is best, to miss the worst of the crowds. There are some attractive walks on the island, and you can usually find a sheltered sandy beach. If the lighthouse is open to visitors, the spectacular views from the top are well worth the 200ft climb.

Roscoff Port Guide

Harbour Master: At the Bureau du Port on Quai du Général de Gaulle, near the root of the inner mole (Tel: 02.98.69.76.37).

VHF: Ch 09 during office hours.

Weather forecasts: Posted at the Bureau du Port during the season. Recorded Météo France forecast on 08.36.68.08.29.

The most useful forecasts are from CROSS Corsen on VHF Ch 79. Times vary according to which transmitter you pick up, but Ile Batz broadcasts at: 0515, 0733, 1133, 1603, 1933 (French local time). Bulletins are in French and repeated slowly, providing the most reliable weather information for this part of North Brittany. If necessary, call CROSS Corsen in English on Ch 16 and they'll give you the forecast in English.

Fuel: Alongside the harbour quay near high water by arrangement with Co-operative Maritime (see 'chandler' below). Otherwise, the nearest service station is at the Champion supermarket, about 3km inland from the harbour.

Water: At the quay on the south-west side of the Vieux Port

Showers: On Quai du Général de Gaulle, near the Sainte Anne Chapel and the Tourist Office. You need to buy jetons from the Tourist Office or Bureau du Port.

Laundrette: Ferry Laverie at 23 Rue Jules Ferry, about 10 mins walk from the Vieux Port (Tel: 02.98.69.74.08).

Camping Gaz: At Co-operative Maritime (see 'chandler' below). Also at the Champion supermarket, about 3km inland from the harbour.

Calor Gas: At the Champion supermarket.

Chandler: Co-operative Maritime, just behind the Vieux Port at 5 Rue Amiral Courbet (Tel: 02.98.69.70.47).

Repairs: Roscoff Service Plaisance, ZAD de Bloscon (Tel: 02.98.61.29.29), near the ferry port. Also Chantier Naval Yvin, ZAD de Bloscon (Tel: 02.98.61.27.97).

Marine engineers: As for 'repairs' above.

Shopping: Roscoff town centre has a good selection of shops, with a Wednesday market on the quay, just in front of the main lighthouse. There's a good Champion supermarket about 3km inland from the harbour.

Banks: Several with cashpoints in town centre.

Bus/train connections: Local buses and occasional trains to Morlaix, with main line rail connections westward to Brest or east via Rennes. Brittany Ferries services to Plymouth and Cork from the Bloscon terminal.

Taxis: At the Bloscon ferry terminal or call Armor Taxi on 02.98.69.70.67.

Car hire: Garage Renault – Roscoff Automobile at 69 Rue Albert de Mun (Tel: 02.98.69.72.09), about $1\frac{1}{2}$ km from the harbour.

Bike hire: Cycles Desbordes at 13 Rue Brizeux (Tel: 02.98.69.72.44), about a kilometre from the harbour.

Restaurants

Roscoff has a wide selection of restaurants and hôtel-restaurants to suit most tastes and pockets, although some are rather geared up for British tourists. I would choose from the following: **Les Chardons Bleus**, 4 Rue Amiral Réveillère (Tel 02.98.69.72.03) – walk west a little from the harbour area and it's on the left just before La Place Lacaze Duthiers; **Bistro Le Surcouf** at 14 Rue Amiral Réveillère (Tel: 02.98.69.71.89) has good value menus and retains the feel of a traditional French restaurant even though it is now frequented by many visitors to Roscoff.

A reliable choice is the **Restaurant An Avel Mor** in the Hotel Regina, at 1 Rue Ropartz Morvan (Tel: 02.98.61.23.55), just outside the station, about 10 minutes walk south from the Vieux Port. One of my favourites, especially for lunch, is **La Bellevue** on Boulevard Sainte Barbe (Tel: 02.98.61.15.67) – follow the harbour eastwards right round towards Chapelle Sainte Barbe and **La Bellevue** is on the corner opposite the east mole.

Another good bet is **L'Écume des Jours** on Quai d'Auxerre (Tel: 02.98.61.22.83) – the front entrance is just east of the main lighthouse and there's a back door on Rue Amiral Courbet.

ILE DE BATZ

This picturesque, rather windswept island lies close north-west of Roscoff, separated from the mainland by a narrow channel known as the Canal de l'Ile de Batz – sometimes called the Chenal de Batz. Only two miles long and barely more than half a mile wide, Ile de Batz is low-lying and has a permanent population of about 800. Its only harbour, Port Kernoc'h, occupies a sheltered bay half-way along the south coast and has a small village clustered behind it. Port Kernoc'h dries at low springs to firm sand and is an attractive spot for yachts that can take the ground safely.

The north and east coasts of Ile de Batz are bordered by extensive drying rocks which reach nearly three quarters of a mile offshore in places. The most westerly headland, Pointe Occidentale, has a spur of drying rocks stretching about half a mile due west, with two outliers a couple of cables further off – Mean Audi (dries 0.1m) and Toull al Leac'h (dries 1.0m). These dangers have to be avoided when approaching the west entrance of the Canal de l'Ile de Batz.

The most prominent landmark on the island is the 200 ft main lighthouse, which stands about midway between Pointe Occidentale and Port Kernoc'h. Also conspicuous is the Ile de Batz signal station, a little way inland to the north of Port Kernoc'h.

Malvoch S-cardinal beacon in front of Port Kernoc'h

CANAL DE L'ILE DE BATZ AND APPROACHES TO PORT KERNOC'H

This narrow channel between Ile de Batz and the mainland is well marked by beacons and can be taken by most yachts by day only, in reasonable visibility and preferably above half-tide. The rise of tide is necessary because the east end of the channel almost dries at LAT, although you can get through with care at low water neaps. In practice the tide is rarely a problem, because yachts heading west from Morlaix, the Penzé River, Bloscon or Roscoff would normally leave near high water in order to carry a full period of west-going stream. Similarly, yachts arriving from the west – say from L'Abervrac'h – would aim to carry a full spell of east-going stream and be arriving off the west entrance of the Canal de l'Ile de Batz on the last of the flood.

From the east: Using the latest edition of Admiralty chart 2745, enter the Canal de l'Ile de Batz between Ar Chaden S-cardinal tower and Men Guen Bras N-cardinal tower, staying much closer – about 70 metres – to Ar Chaden. Continue westwards to leave Roc'h Zu N-cardinal beacon a similar distance to port and then steer between the distinctive horn-shaped beacon, which marks the north end of the Roscoff low-water landing, and the S-cardinal beacon close SSE of Duslen white tower.

Now alter to the north-west towards Pen ar Cleguer, the south-east tip of Ile de Batz, steering to leave An Oan south beacon 70 metres to starboard and passing midway between Pen ar Cleguer and Per Roch N-cardinal tower. When skirting Per Roch, bear in mind that drying rocks extend for nearly 200 metres WNW and ESE of the beacon tower itself.

Once you are safely clear of Per Roch and its dangers, steer west again for a position close south of Malvoch beacon tower, which stands on the west side of the entrance to Port Kernoc'h, the only harbour on Batz. On the east side, just opposite Malvoch, a S-cardinal spar beacon marks the end of a long low-water landing slip. Near high water, you can enter Port Kernoc'h between these two marks.

If you are continuing right through the Canal de l'Ile de Batz, now make good a little south of west to pass between La Croix south beacon and l'Oignon north beacon, keeping much closer to

The landing slip on the north side of Ile aux Moutons

l'Oignon and the south side of the channel. Once abreast l'Oignon beacon, steer towards Basse Plate N-cardinal tower on a line to leave it about 100 metres to port. When leaving Basse Plate to head westwards along the coast, steer just south of true west for a couple of miles, until you are clear of the rocky ledges that extend well out from Ile de Batz on the north side, and the extensive rocky shoals stretching well seaward of Ile de Siec on the south side.

From the west: Use the latest edition of Admiralty chart 2745. When approaching the Canal de l'Ile de Batz from the west, keep the main lighthouse at about 080°T until you come within a couple of miles of the island with Basse Plate N-cardinal tower bearing just over 095°T. Then steer towards Basse Plate on a line to leave it about 100 metres to starboard. From Basse Plate, head ESE to pass between La Croix south beacon and l'Oignon north beacon, keeping much closer to l'Oignon and the south side of the channel. Once abreast l'Oignon beacon, steer a shade north of east for a position close south of Malvoch beacon tower and the entrance to Port Kernoc'h.

If you are continuing right through the Canal de l'Ile de Batz, make good more or less due east true for half a mile, heading towards the south-eastern point of Ile de Batz – Pen ar Cleguer. Then gradually turn south-eastwards to pass between Pen ar Cleguer and Per Roch N-cardinal tower, bearing in mind that drying rocks extend for nearly 200 metres WNW and ESE of the beacon tower itself. Leave An Oan south-cardinal beacon 70 metres to port and steer to pass between the S-cardinal beacon close SSE of Duslen white tower and the distinctive horn-shaped beacon that marks the north end of the Roscoff low-water landing.

Once you are south of Duslen, make good a little south of east to leave Roc'h Zu N-cardinal beacon about 70 metres to starboard and then exit the Canal de l'Ile de Batz between Ar Chaden S-cardinal tower and Men Guen Bras N-cardinal tower, staying much closer – again about 70 metres – to Ar Chaden.

PORT KERNOC'H

This attractive drying harbour is protected from the west by the natural curve of the bay and by a long breakwater which stretches ESE from the lifeboat house towards Malvoch tower. On the east side of the harbour, the low-water landing slip for the

The popular beach on the north side of Port Kernoc'h

tourist vedettes runs due south from Ile aux
Moutons. Most of the slip covers at high tide and its
outer end is marked by a S-cardinal spar beacon.
Enter the harbour between this beacon and Malvoch
tower, making sure you don't stray over the slip. At
neaps, moderate draught yachts can stay afloat a
little way into the harbour, but you should take
careful soundings while there's still time to retreat.
At springs, you have to anchor just outside the
harbour to stay afloat, 1–2 cables due east of the
slipway beacon.

Port Kernoc'h has a firm sandy bottom for drying
out, although there are various rocky patches which
need to be avoided. You can usually see these clearly
when the water is calm, although the position of the
local moorings gives some guidance on where the
bottom is clean. You can land with a dinghy at the
slip if the tide is well out, but the easiest landing
place above half-tide is the quay behind Ile aux
Moutons. Near high water you can take the dinghy
into the small inner harbour area in the NW corner
of Port Kernoc'h, which is closer to the village than
the Ile aux Moutons landing.

ANCHORAGES AND MOORINGS IN THE CANAL DE L'ILE DE BATZ

There are some moorings and several possible
anchorages in the Canal de l'Ile de Batz, which are
reasonably sheltered either by the island or the
mainland unless the wind is fresh from between
west and south-west or east and south-east.
However, whether you are on a buoy or at anchor,
you should only stay overnight if the weather looks
definitely settled; only the extreme eastern end of
the Canal de l'Ile de Batz is safe to negotiate at night
and you would be unpleasantly trapped if
conditions changed for the worse.

Working from the east, the first spot is between Ile
Pighet and Duslen white beacon towers, but closer
to Ile Pighet than to Duslen. One of the moorings is
preferable to anchoring here, because of the
narrowness of the channel and the strong stream at
springs. At neaps, you can tuck in further north to
miss the worst of the tide. This location is a useful
temporary anchorage if you are waiting for
sufficient rise to enter Roscoff.

A mile further into the sound, you can fetch up
1–2 cables east of the south beacon which marks
the end of the Port Kernoc'h low water landing
slip. Near neaps it's possible to edge inshore to
find quieter water, but make sure that the landing
slip beacon bears no less than about 265°M as
there are ledges of drying rocks north of this
clearing line.

On the west side of Port Kernoc'h entrance, you can
fetch up a cable or so WSW of Malvoch beacon tower,
but avoid swinging too close to Basse Malvoch rock
(nearly awash at LAT) near low springs.

PASSAGES BRITTANY III

Morlaix to L'abervrac'h

Making a passage via the Chenal de Batz, you can reckon on just under 35 miles from the outer marks of the Morlaix estuary to Le Libenter W-cardinal buoy off L'Abervrac'h entrance. This is a full tide for those under sail, and rather more if the wind is contrary. Ideally, therefore, a yacht working

westwards from Morlaix should aim to be somewhere off Stolvezen red buoy at or a shade before slack water high, just as the stream is thinking of starting to trickle west. This means leaving Morlaix basin on the first lock of the tide, 1½ hours before high water, and then pushing the last of the flood downstream.

I always think that a gentle hour of motoring down a river and out into a partly sheltered estuary is an ideal way to start a passage, especially early in the

morning. There is time to ease yourself fully awake and gradually come to terms with the day with a mug of whatever you need to get into gear. There's also an opportunity to assess the weather as you approach the sea by stages, and perhaps hear various forecasts on the way. By the time your bow lifts to the first salt-water wave, you often feel reasonably prepared and as much in control of things as the sea ever lets you be.

In most circumstances, it's both quicker and more

Duslen white beacon, just opposite the low water landing in the Chenal de Batz

interesting to take the Chenal de Batz past Roscoff, rather than work offshore and skirt round the dangers to the east and north of the island. Sometimes a thick morning mist in the estuary makes the navigator think about heading straight out to sea into clear water. Yet at slack water high on a calm morning, it's not difficult to pick your way from the Stolvezen buoy to the east entrance of the Chenal de Batz, even without GPS assistance. From a starting position about 300 metres due west of Stolvezen, a track of 293°T for just over three miles leads across to Roscoff and the Chenal de Batz. This line leaves the following dangers and marks as follows:

- La Vieille green beacon tower 1½ cables to the south.
- Les Cochons Noirs rocks (usually not quite covered on most high waters) 1½ cables to the south.
- Les Bisayers above-water rocks a quarter of a mile to the south.
- Plateau des Duons white tower about half a mile to the north, but the south-west tip of the plateau (well-covered near high water) only a cable to the north.
- Le Menk W-cardinal beacon tower two cables to the south, but the north-east tip of the Basse du Menk plateau (well-covered near high water) less than a cable to the south.

As you approach the Chenal de Batz, leave Basse de Bloscon N-cardinal buoy close to the south. The entrance leads between Ar Chaden south tower and Men Guen Bras north tower, but it's best to stay on line towards Ar Chaden and keep close to this tower before edging to port towards the curious horn-shaped beacon which marks the outer end of the Roscoff low-water landing jetty, unmistakable on its long line of stilts. Thereafter, follow the directions in the Chenal de Batz chapter.

Emerging at the west end of the Chenal de Batz, close north of Basse Plate N-cardinal beacon tower, it's a good idea to head more or less due west for a mile or so, to clear the dangers lurking off the west tip of Ile de Batz to starboard and off the mainland to port. The low-lying rocky coastline ahead will probably look hard and rather austere after the attractive passage inside Batz. You can feel a bit isolated and exposed along this stretch of North Brittany, especially if the wind is in the west and you pick up the first stirrings of an Atlantic swell. However, it's only about 16 miles along to the next passage waypoint – Aman ar Ross N-cardinal whistle buoy – and then 10 miles beyond that to L'Abervrac'h entrance.

The coast is rather enigmatic between Ile de Batz and the tall Ile Vierge lighthouse off L'Abervrac'h. There are plenty of water-towers – too many for navigation in fact, because you can't usually tell which is which – but back-bearings of Ile de Batz lighthouse are the most useful for keeping a safe distance out from the various off-lying rocks. I prefer to stay outside a direct line drawn on the chart between Batz lighthouse and Aman ar Ross buoy.

The Ile de Batz low water landing on the north side of the Chenal de Batz

The stark stone lighthouse towards the west end of Ile de Batz, a key mark for the passage between Batz and L'Abervrac'h

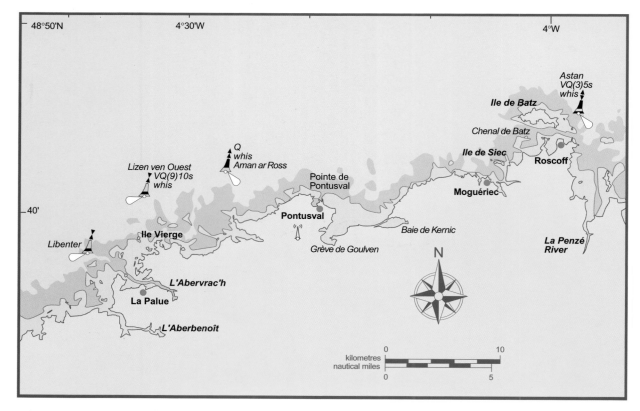

The tall radio mast a couple of miles inland from Pointe de Beg-Pol helps you to gauge your progress as you cross the shallow bay formed by Anse de Kernic and La Grève de Goulven.

Just over a mile before the radio mast bears due south, you come abreast the small natural harbour of Pontusval, which appears from seaward to be almost completely hemmed in by rocks. You'll see a red beacon tower in the entrance and an E-cardinal buoy not quite a mile north of it. You would normally leave this buoy about 1½ miles to the south by staying just outside the Batz to Aman ar Ross clearing line.

From Aman ar Ross buoy, make good 252°T for 4½ miles to pass just outside Lizen Ven W-cardinal whistle buoy, which guards the north-west corner of the Lizen Ven plateau. At this point, the 250ft high Ile Vierge lighthouse is only a couple of miles to the south.

The last leg down to Le Libenter W-cardinal buoy can be a bit tricky, because you need to make the final approach from just west of north. A direct line from Lizen Ven to Le Libenter would take you perilously close to the Libenter shoal, with the added complication that the tide might now be starting to set eastward again, onto the dangers that you are trying to skirt. So the best strategy from Lizen Ven buoy is to make good 240°T for about four miles, until Le Libenter is bearing a shade east of south and just over a mile distant. Then you can

turn south and approach the buoy on this line. In poor visibility, err on the side of standing on too far past Le Libenter, rather than turning inshore too soon. The buoy's whistle can be useful even in a summer haze.

The unusual mauve and white beacon at the end of Roscoff's low water landing is a useful mark in the Chenal de Batz

CÔTE DES ABERS

ILE DE SIEC AND MOGUÉRIEC

Ile de Siec lies close to the mainland coast of North Brittany, about four miles WSW of Roscoff and a little over two miles SSW of the west entrance to the Chenal de Batz. Numerous drying rocks extend up to $1\frac{1}{2}$ miles offshore between Roscoff and Ile de Siec, but there's an interesting and secluded anchorage about a cable south-west of the west tip of the island, sheltered in moderate weather from between north-east through east to south. About a mile south by west from Ile de Siec, at the mouth of the narrow Rivière du Guillec, is the small fishing village of Moguériec. A stone pier protects its local moorings from the north. Near neaps, in quiet or offshore weather, you can anchor

and stay afloat about two cables NNE of Moguériec pierhead.

Arriving at Ile de Siec or Moguériec is not difficult in reasonable visibility, especially if you've just come out of the west end of the Canal de Batz. Approach from the NNW within two hours of high water, from a position 2¼ miles due west of Basse Plate north beacon tower. You should make good 162ºT from this outer waypoint towards Moguériec pierhead (about three miles away), steering to pass a quarter of a mile west of Golchedec islet, close off the west tip of Ile de Siec. There are various dangers to the west of this line, of which the most significant is Méan Névez rock (dries 3.3 metres).

Once the west tip of Ile de Siec bears just north of east, come to port and fetch up in the small bay formed by Golchedec, Ile de Siec and Querelevran rock. At neaps, in quiet weather, you can edge further east between Ile de Siec and Querelevran, but be sure to anchor clear of the rocky ledges on either hand. There is a small pier harbour opposite Querelevran, at the south-west corner of Ile de Siec, where a few local open boats are moored. You can land here with the dinghy and walk round the island, which is only half a mile long and joined to the mainland by a wide sand spit at low tide. There

are one or two ruined cottages on Ile de Siec, the relics of some nasty incidents during the 1939-45 war. These ruins give the anchorage a rather wild and haunted atmosphere. If you need to leave the anchorage at night you can go out on the white

Looking north-eastward out past Moguériec entrance

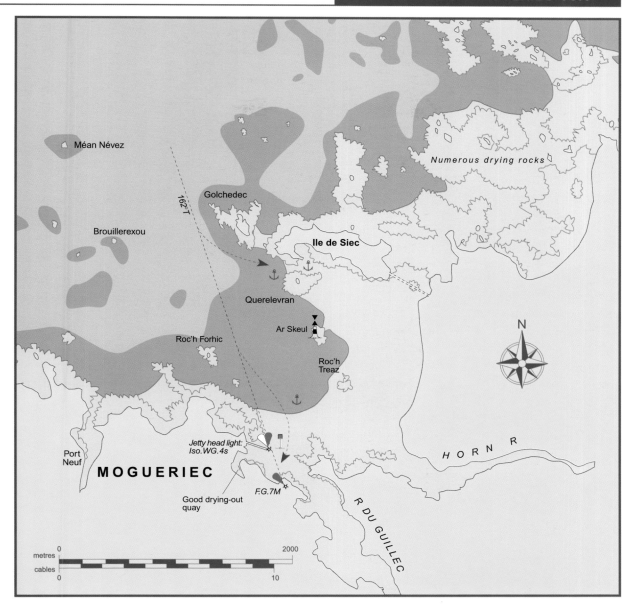

Méan Névez

162ºT

Golchedec

Brouillerexou

Ile de Siec

Numerous drying rocks

Querelevran

Roc'h Forhic

Ar Skeul

Roc'h
Treaz

N

Port
Neuf

MOGUERIEC

Jetty head light:
Iso.WG.4s

Good drying-out
quay

F.G.7M

H O R N   R

R DU GUILLEC

metres | 0 | | | | | 2000
cables | 0 | | | | | 10

sector of Moguériec pierhead light, which leads
safely to the west of Golchedec at 342ºT.

Moguériec is a peaceful village, with the Hôtel la
Marine (Tel: 02.98.29.99.52) at the head of the jetty.
Across a small lane behind the hotel is the Bar-
Crêperie à l'Ancre, where you can enjoy a drink or a
light lunch. About ten minutes walk from the
harbour you'll find a couple of small shops,
including an *Alimentation Générale*. The harbour has
a good quay on its south side, where a keel boat can
dry out in settled weather. But the most sheltered
spot for drying out is well into the harbour inlet,
after you have turned to port beyond the first quay.
There's a good drying quay here on the east side, if
you can find room among the fishing boats.

Chapter 10

PONTUSVAL

This rather exposed natural harbour, which always seems hemmed in by rocks, lies 12 miles WSW along the coast from Ile de Batz and about 10 miles ENE from Ile Vierge lighthouse. Not many yachts call at Pontusval, perhaps because the coastline on either side often looks so inhospitable. Yet the approach is actually quite straightforward in quiet weather and reasonable visibility – by day only though, and preferably above half-tide. The most useful landmarks are Pointe de Beg-Pol lighthouse, a mile west of the entrance; a tall radio mast a couple of miles inland from the lighthouse; and a signal station on a low promontory between Beg-Pol and

Bilge-keelers can find perfect shelter on a sandy bottom in the inner part of the harbour

Pontusval. You'll find a surfeit of water towers, so be careful about using these for establishing your position. The easiest strategy is to reach Pontusval E-cardinal buoy first and then make good 178°T towards the entrance (less than a mile away from the buoy) allowing carefully for any cross-tide.

Going in, leave Pecher green buoy to starboard, An Neudenn red beacon tower to port, and three white-painted rocks to starboard. At springs, keel boats should fetch up opposite the second white rock; at neaps you can venture past the third white rock, anchoring in mid-channel between this and Kinloc'h du Dédans spar beacon. Bilge-keelers

The signal station between Beg-Pol and Pontusval

You enter Pontusval between the red beacon tower and the three white-painted rocks

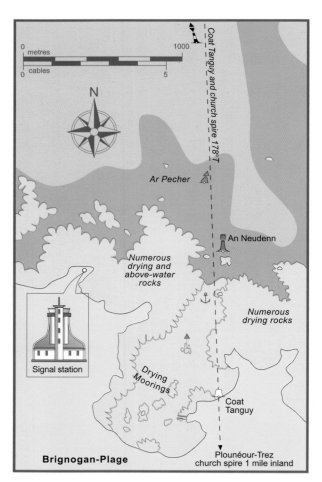

can edge right into the inner harbour area and take the ground near any of the local moorings.

Pontusval can be useful in quiet or southerly weather if you run out of fair tide on passage between L'Abervrac'h and the Ile de Batz. It can sometimes happen that you are hurrying back from South Brittany at the end of a cruise and, having come up the Chenal du Four in good time, you find yourself with enough fair stream to carry on past L'Abervrac'h but not get as far as Batz.

ASHORE

In the seaside village of Brignogan-Plage, you'll find a 'Proxi' supermarket in Rue Naot Hir and a poissonerie in Rue de l'Église. In the main street, Avenue du Général de Gaulle, are a good boulangerie, a boucherie-charcuterie, two banks, a post office and several cafés, You can also hire a bike from Fily Cycles (Tel 02.98.83.09.67) on Rue Naot Hir, just along from the Proxi.

You can get an excellent meal at the comfortable Hôtel Le Castel Regis (Tel 02.98.83.40.22), set in its own grounds on a small peninsula at the head of the slip on the east side of the inner harbour. The restaurant here has splendid views across the bay. Another option is the Hôtel Ar Reder Mor (Tel 02.98.83.40.09), in the main street about 400 yards from the beach.

L'ABERVRAC'H

The L'Abervrac'h estuary is the most westerly port-of-call along the North Brittany coast that can be entered at any state of tide by day or night. It provides a natural cruising cross-roads for yachts bound in either direction through the Chenal du Four between the English Channel and L'Iroise.

The land on either side of the estuary is flat and windswept and some yachtsmen find L'Abervrac'h rather bleak, but it's secure and conveniently placed for passage-making. The Yacht Club des Abers have a small marina and some visitors' moorings at La Palue, or you can anchor further upstream between Pointe Cameuleut and Paluden. Although the entrance is fringed with plenty of rocks, the Grand Chenal is well marked and generally easy of access except in poor visibility. The shopping and boatyard facilities at L'Abervrac'h are limited.

Chapter 10

L'ABERVRAC'H INFORMATION

TIDES

HW L'Abervrac'h is at HW Brest +0020 approx. Heights above datum: 8.0m MHWS, 1.1m MLWS, 6.1m MHWN, 2.9m MLWN.
The streams set ENE and WSW across the entrance near Le Libenter buoy, reaching $2\frac{1}{2}$–3 knots at springs. The eastgoing stream starts at HW Brest −0415 off Le Libenter and the westgoing at HW Brest +0130. In the estuary south of Bréac'h Verr green beacon tower, the tide follows the line of the channel, reaching $2\frac{1}{2}$ knots at springs.

CHARTS

Admiralty: 1432, 3668
French SHOM: 7094

HAZARDS

Drying rocks extend two miles offshore on either side of L'Abervrac'h entrance and even further off to the east of Ile Vierge. Coming from the east, it's important to stay outside Aman ar Ross N-cardinal and Lizen Ven W-cardinal buoys as you round Ile Vierge. On the final approach, you must avoid Le Libenter rocks, which border the north side of the Grand Chenal. Le Libenter buoy should be approached from just west of north when arriving from the east, preferably from the outer waypoint a mile north of the buoy.

WAYPOINTS

Outer waypoint, just over a mile N by W of Le Libenter W-cardinal buoy
– 48°38.75'N, 04° 38.39'W
Grand Chenal entrance waypoint 2 cables SW of Le Libenter buoy on leading line
– 48°37.44'N, 04°38.54'W

The L'Abervrac'h estuary, right at the north-west corner of Finistère, has a very distinctive atmosphere. The coast on either side is low-lying with a good many offshore rocks, and the tall lighthouse on Ile Vierge tends to accentuate the rather austere impression you get from seaward. A long Atlantic swell often rolls in to add to the general sense of unease you can feel when navigating hereabouts. A few miles west of the estuary are the reefs where the ill-fated tanker Amoco Cadiz ran aground and parts of her rusting hull can still be seen at low water not far north-east of the stubby Corn Carhai light-tower.

Despite these forbidding aspects of the landfall,

L'Abervrac'h itself usually seems welcoming once you have found the Libenter buoy and lined up the marks for the Grand Chenal. It's only $1\frac{1}{2}$ miles from here to the Pot de Beurre beacon towers, where you turn south-east to enter the river proper. If you've come in from a boisterous sea, things quieten down appreciably as you draw south of Iles de la Croix on the starboard hand. In a fresh westerly, you can look forward to a splendid sail for the last couple of miles up to La Palue. The wind may seem harder and more gusty as it filters across the outer skerries and Presqu'ile Ste Marguerite, but the increasingly calm water allows you to enjoy the changing vistas of small

islands and intriguing channels while reaching upriver at a cracking pace.

You pass close east of Ile Cézon, with its old fort and large white painted disc, and then to the west of Enez Terc'h island, which has an obelisk on its south-east side. L'Abervrac'h is dead ahead, with the prominent white building of the merchant navy apprentices college up on the hill and the lifeboat house and slip down off La Palue. The Yacht Club des Abers pontoons are just beyond the lifeboat slip and there are plenty of visitors moorings out in the river immediately opposite. If you prefer to carry on upstream to anchor, the channel heads east for a while past the moorings to leave some oyster bed withies and a green conical buoy to starboard before turning back to the south-east past Pointe Cameuleut.

Ashore at La Palue, you walk across a wide concourse past the yacht club building and a crêperie before reaching a small road running parallel with the shore. You will find only a small épicerie, a couple of cafés and a restaurant along this road. The nearest real village is at Landéda, about two kilometres inland to the south-west – take the road which leads away from the river opposite the head of the landing slip. There is a fuelling quay (diesel only) at the head of the pontoons, and the showers and bar at the yacht club are always very

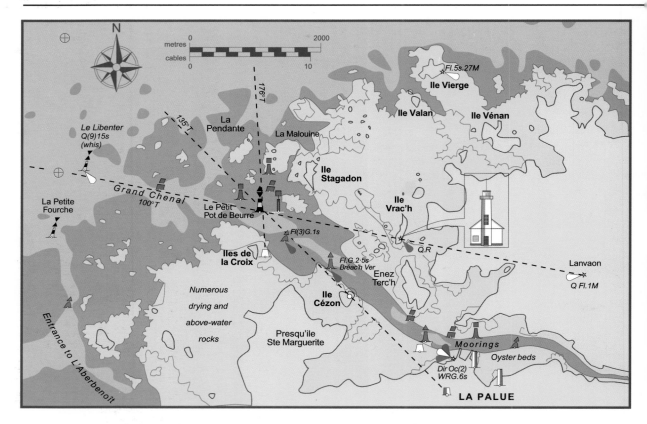

pleasant. During the season, a travelling baker arrives most mornings near the yacht club.

APPROACHES AND ENTRY

When arriving from the west, perhaps having just come up the Chenal du Four, the approach to L'Abervrac'h is fairly straightforward. It is five miles at 082ºT from Grande Basse de Portsall buoy (the 'corner-mark' for the Chenal du Four) and the L'Abervrac'h entrance waypoint two cables south-west of Le Libenter buoy. In reasonable visibility, Ile Vierge provides an unmistakable steering mark until you pick up Le Libenter.

Coming along the coast from the east, follow the directions given in the previous 'passages' section. The important point is to make the final approach to Le Libenter buoy from west of north, to be sure of clearing the Libenter shoal. Make for the approach waypoint just over a mile north of Le Libenter buoy before turning in towards the entrance. Allow carefully for any east-going stream, checking the bearing of Le Libenter to make sure you are heading inshore on a safe line.

There are three entrance channels into L'Abervrac'h: the Grand Chenal, the Chenal de la Pendante, and the Chenal de la Malouine. The Grand Chenal can be taken by day or night, at any state of tide and in most weathers. La Pendante and

La Malouine should only be used by day, in calm conditions and preferably above half-tide. La Malouine can be handy if you are bound eastward along the coast from L'Abervrac'h.

The Grand Chenal: From two cables south-west of Le Libenter W-cardinal whistle buoy, pick up the Grand Chenal leading marks – the lighthouse at the south tip of Ile Vrac'h in transit with Lanvaon lighthouse behind it bearing 100ºT. Ile Vrac'h lighthouse is low down, a white tower with a red top at the end of a small white house, and Lanvaon is up on the hill with a steep gabled roof. If you can't quite identify these marks, simply make good 100ºT to leave Le Trépied red buoy close to port and continue on the same line to leave Grand Pot de Beurre red beacon a cable to port and Petit Pot de Beurre E-cardinal tower 100 metres to port. Bear in mind that the flood sets ENE across the outer part of the Grand Chenal towards the Libenter reef, but don't over-compensate for this and stray too far south of the leading line, because a long tail of drying rocks extends WNW from Iles de la Croix. Any swell breaks heavily on these rocks, especially near low water.

Off Petit Pot de Beurre, come to starboard to leave Basse de la Croix green buoy 100 metres to starboard and then head south-east up the estuary to leave Bréac'h Verr green tower 100 metres to starboard and Ile Cézon with its white painted disc on the side of the old fort a cable to starboard. The leading marks for this stretch – La Palue lighthouse in transit with two red and white beacons behind it bearing 128°T – can be difficult to make out and it's usually easier just to steer upstream between Ile Cézon and Enez Terc'h island until you pick up the green tower and red buoys that take you round into the mooring area off La Palue.

Chenal de la Pendante: This channel leads in from the north-west to skirt the north-east side of the Libenter reef, but can only be used by day and above half-tide. While out in safe water, clear of the northern rocks of Le Libenter, bring Petit Pot de Beurre E-cardinal tower (which shows up mostly black at a distance) just open to the west of Ile de Cézon white disc behind it, with the white disc bearing 136°T. The official leading line is Ile Cézon white disc in transit at 136°T with Amer de la Pendante black beacon, up on the hillside some way to the right of the long white building of the merchant navy apprentices college. However, Amer de la Pendante can be difficult to spot and Petit Pot de Beurre is usually a better bet. The channel then leaves La Pendante isolated above-water rock a cable to port and Petit Pot de Beurre close to starboard to join the main part of the estuary.

In my view the Pendante channel is best avoided. It doesn't save much distance over the Grand Chenal when coming round the coast from the east, and

The slightly rickety pontoons at La Palue, just south of the lifeboat slip

Le Libenter W-cardinal buoy is the crucial outer mark for entering L'Abervrac'h

you often have to get rather too close to the Libenter reef before the marks become clear.

Chenal de la Malouine: This narrow channel leads in from the north towards Petit Pot de Beurre E-cardinal tower, between La Malouine rock (17 metres high) and the drying ledges to the north-east of La Pendante rock. It involves about three miles saving in distance if you are approaching L'Abervrac'h along the coast from the east, but can only be used by day in calm conditions and with at least 3–4 miles visibility.

From Lizen Venn W-cardinal buoy, make good 219°T for just under three miles for a position 1½ miles due west of Ile Vierge lighthouse. La Malouine rock will then be three quarters of a mile a shade east of south, and Petit Pot de Beurre tower should be visible in the estuary just to the right of Malouine. Bring Petit Pot de Beurre to bear 176°T exactly on with Petite Ile de la Croix white pyramid beacon a little way behind it and approach the shore on this transit. The line first leaves the distinctive group of three rocks, Tri Men, about 3½ cables to port, before you enter the narrows to leave an above-water rock at the north end of La Pendante ledges a cable to starboard, La Malouine rock 120m to port and Carrec Bazil red beacon tower close to port. Once past Carrec Bazil, you can edge a little to

The L'Abervrac'h estuary opposite La Palue

Visitors' moorings at L'Abervrac'h, just upstream from La Palue

the east of the transit to leave two red buoys close to port and so enter the estuary.

In principle, you can use the Chenal de la Malouine at any state of tide, but it's wise to have a good three metres above datum. La Malouine is easiest to use on the way out of L'Abervrac'h, and the three mile bonus when you are bound east can be very welcome.

In poor visibility: Mist and haze are common along this coast, and I can recall various occasions when we've been either trapped in L'Abervrac'h by a real fog, or had to abandon calling there and come straight home across the Channel after picking our way up the Chenal du Four. Finding the entrance safely in even moderately poor visibility can be a daunting prospect, but it's not too difficult if you use GPS carefully and strategically. The key lies in

approaching Le Libenter buoy from a safe direction and being prepared to pull out to sea again rather than over-run your distance.

From the west: Coming from the Chenal du Four in murky conditions, it makes sense to find Basse de Portsall whistle buoy before turning east for L'Abervrac'h. This gives you a five-mile run to Le Libenter in clear water with the stream only slightly athwart your track. It is worth going right up to Basse de Portsall before taking a departure on this leg; as well as this reducing the navigation error, you can also note how the tide is setting past the buoy.

Even using GPS, it's important to have worked out what your log reading should be when you are due to reach Le Libenter. In very calm conditions, when the buoy's whistle may be little more than an

L'Abervrac'h Port Guide

Harbour control: Monsieur Jean Troadec, Maître de Port, Capitainerie, Port de L'Abervrac'h, 29870 Landéda (Tel: 02.98.04.91.62, Fax: 02.98.04.85.54).

Yacht Club: Yacht Club des Abers (Tel 02.98.04.92.60)

VHF: Ch 16/9 (from 0700–2230 during the season).

Weather forecasts: Posted at the Capitainerie twice a day during the season. Recorded Météo France forecast Tel: 08.68.08.29. The most useful VHF forecasts are from CROSS Corsen on VHF Ch 79. Times vary according to which transmitter you pick up, but Le Stiff on Ushant broadcasts at: 0503, 0715, 1115, 1545, 1915 (French local time). Bulletins are in French and repeated slowly, providing the most reliable weather information for this corner of Brittany. If necessary, call CROSS Corsen in English on Ch 16 and they'll give you the forecast in English. Ushant Traffic Control transmits French shipping forecasts on Ch 79 at 0950 French local time during the summer, then every three hours thereafter (at 1250, 1550 etc).

Fuel: Diesel from quay at the head of the Yacht Club des Abers pontoons. Opening hours are variable – contact the Capitainerie.

Water: At the pontoons or quay

Showers: At the Yacht Club

Chandlery: Coopérative Maritime (Tel: 02.98.04.90.16)

Repairs: Chantier Naval de L'Abervrac'h (Louis Georgelin), Saint-Antoine, L'Abervrac'h (Tel: 02.98.04.99.36).

Marine engineers: Jean-Louis Laot, ZAC de Bel-Air, 29870 Landéda (Tel: 02.98.04.93.73).

Shopping: Small épicerie and travelling shop at La Palue near the port, otherwise at Landéda village, two kilometres inland to the south-west. The nearest major shopping is at Lannilis where there is a Leclerc supermarket and good individual shops.

Banks: Nearest banks are at Lannilis.

Bus/train connections: Infrequent buses via Lannilis to Brest, where you have good rail connections to anywhere else in France and an airport with UK flights.

Restaurants

L'Abervrac'h: L'Escale Café-Restaurant (Tel 02.98.04.90.11) is just opposite the UPCA sailing school at La Palue – good value and friendly. **Olez eo Bet** is near the yacht club, with a convivial crêperie next door.

The **Hôtel La Baie des Anges** (Tel 02.98.04.90.04), is just round the corner past the lifeboat slip – a good choice in the evening. One of my favourites for a light lunch is the **Crêperie Avel Mor**, just across the road from the yacht club.

Paluden: Le Relais de l'Aber is always a sound bet for lunch or dinner, next to the D113, just south of the old road bridge (Tel 02.98.04.01.21).

---

intermittent grunt, there is always the risk of passing close without realising it and then blundering on towards the Libenter reef. You can afford only a quarter of a mile of over-run before turning due west into safe water and deciding what to do next.

From seaward: Arriving off this corner in poor visibility from across the Channel, I tend to make for Basse de Portsall buoy rather than Le Libenter, as this keeps you out in the relatively clear water between L'Abervrac'h entrance and the north end of the Chenal du Four. By aiming to close the coast in this vicinity, you at least ought to be fairly confident that you are safely west of Ile Vierge, and not to the east in amongst the Lizen Ven or Aman ar Ross rocks. When you spot Basse de Portsall, you can either make for L'Abervrac'h as above, or carry on down through the Four if the tide happens to serve.

From the east: Approaching L'Abervrac'h from the east in murky visibility can be tricky, but you can usually pick your way as far as Lizen Ven without collecting too many grey hairs. Then it's a question of keeping well north of the Libenter shoal until Le Libenter buoy is bearing just east of south and you can head down towards it.

In any of these strategies for poor visibility, it's a good idea to steer right up to Le Libenter buoy once you've found it and then make two hops into the Grand Chenal – just over half a mile at 109°T for Le Trépied red buoy and then just under a mile at 101°T for Petit Pot de Beurre E-cardinal beacon tower. Once into the estuary, it's not difficult to pick your way up to La Palue.

At night: Only the Grand Chenal is navigable at night, and the first set of leading lights – Ile Vrac'h (*Q.R.6M*) in transit with Lanvaon (*Q.10M*) bearing 100°T – takes you close south-east of Petit Pot de Beurre. Then pick up La Palue directional light (*DirOc(2)WRG.6s13/11M*) whose white sector leads into the river at 128°T. On the final approach to La Palue, a searchlight is useful to pick your way through the moorings.

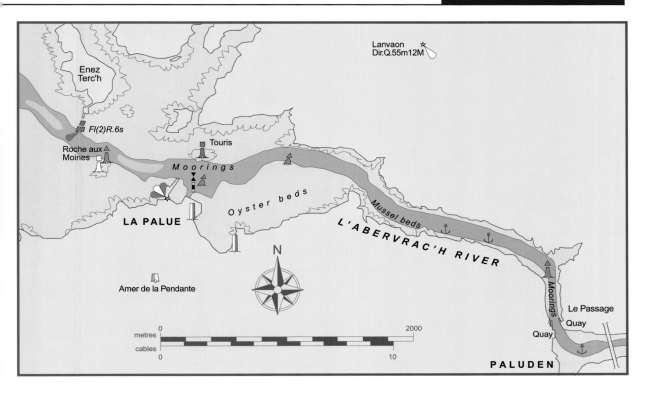

MOORINGS AND ANCHORAGES

Yacht Club des Abers pontoons: Visiting yachts are welcome at the pontoon berths off the main quay a little way south-east of the lifeboat slip. The yacht club bar and showers are close to hand, as are the small shop and cafés in the village. Because the pontoon fingers are rather short, larger yachts are more secure on one of the visitors' moorings. Near low water, watch out for the small drying patch, marked by a green buoy and a W-cardinal spar beacon, just upstream from the outer end of the pontoons.

Visitors' moorings: The Yacht Club has plenty of visitors' moorings opposite the marina off La Palue. They are the same price as the pontoon berths, but the dues include a launch service during the season. The moorings are a better bet for larger yachts, especially in strong winds when the pontoons tend to be a bit rickety. Upstream of the lifeboat slip, you are not allowed to anchor off La Palue.

Upstream at Paluden: Above La Palue, the river curves ENE and then south-east again to skirt a broad area of mud-flats and oyster beds marked by withies. Past Pointe Cameuleut there are oyster beds on both sides of the river, but the withies extend well out from the north side. You can anchor off the south bank in the straight stretch for half a mile above Pointe Cameuleut, or sometimes pick up a vacant mooring. Beyond Beg ar Toul green beacon tower,

the river turns south for a quarter of a mile, past some mooring trots on the west side and then between Le Passage and Paluden quays. A small pool opens up above the quays and a low road bridge bars further progress upstream. This pool provides an attractive and perfectly sheltered anchorage.

Paluden is a restful spot, whether you lie in the pool or moor fore-and-aft at one of the trots just downstream from the quay. The Relais de l'Aber restaurant is handy on the south side of the pool and it's about two kilometres walk south into the small town of Lannilis, where there are banks and good shops.

FACILITIES

L'Abervrac'h is a useful passage port, provided you are fully stored and everything is well on board. There is a choice of moorings or pontoon berths, you can get diesel at the quay, and the Yacht Club des Abers have good showers and a bar. However, L'Abervrac'h is not a good place for shopping expeditions, whether for food or chandlery, and it's a bit out on a limb for coping with breakdowns and repairs. The Yacht Club des Abers have a slip and a 12 ton travelift, but spare parts usually have to be tracked down by taking a taxi into Brest. There is an engineer at Segalen Garage, 5 kilometres inland at Lannilis.

Chapter 10

A local fishing boat at L'Abervrac'h. The land around the estuary is low-lying

The sheltered visitors' moorings up at Paluden

A DAY AWAY

Having reached L'Abervrac'h, most yachts seem to be 'in transit' and are either on their way home against a deadline or keen to catch the next tide south through the Chenal du Four. With a day to spare though, you could meander upstream to the sheltered pool at Paluden and have a meal in the evening at Le Relais de l'Aber. There are also some good walks around the L'Abervrac'h estuary. If you are moored down at La Palue, it's pleasant to stroll west round the coast from the harbour area and out to the beaches and dunes around Presqu'ile Ste-Marguerite. By making a day of it, you can look forward to a leisurely lunch of *fruits de mer* at the Hotel des Dunes (02.98.04.90.92).

L'ABERBENOIT

Although this peaceful unspoilt estuary lies only a couple of miles south of the entrance to L'Abervrac'h, most navigators, having successfully located Le Libenter buoy, seem to press on up the Grand Chenal to La Palue rather than become involved in the slightly more intricate pilotage

required to get into L'Aberbenoît. Yet the attractive anchorages are worth a bit of effort with the binoculars to pick out the various rather small buoys and beacons leading south and then south-east from near the same entrance waypoint you'd use for lining up for L'Abervrac'h. However, you need to pay more attention to the sea conditions and rise of tide when entering L'Aberbenoît. The approaches and river mouth are relatively shallow and more susceptible than L'Abervrac'h to the effects of onshore swell; they should be avoided in fresh winds from between north and west. In principle, entry is possible at any state of tide, except

near low water springs, but it's preferable to go in above half-flood if possible. You cannot approach or leave L'Aberbenoît at night.

APPROACH AND ENTRY

From the L'Abervrac'h entrance waypoint, two cables south-west of Le Libenter W-cardinal whistle buoy, make about 195°T for just under half a mile to leave La Petite Fourche W-cardinal buoy close to port. Then come round to 172°T to leave Ruzven Est green buoy, not quite three quarters of a mile away, close to starboard.

Carry on at 172°T towards Basse du Chenal green

Although not much visited by yachts on passage, L'Aberbenoît is very attractive and perfectly sheltered

Local moorings in the sleepy estuary of L'Aberbenoît

buoy, leaving La Jument rock, off the west side of Ile Guénioc, about 300 metres to port. When La Jument is abeam, you have a choice of routes:

Main channel: The main channel is to the south-east, leaving the red spar beacon off the south end of Ile Guénioc 100 metres to port, Carrec ar Poul Doun red spar beacon 150 metres to port, and Men Renéad green buoy 80-90 metres to starboard. From Men Renéad buoy steer about 158ºT to leave La Jument de Garo red spar beacon not quite 100 metres to port before coming back to the south-east to leave Ar Gazel green buoy close to starboard and Le Chien black-red-black beacon tower to port. Leave Kervigorn green buoy well to starboard and several withies off the east headland to port as you enter the river.

West channel: When La Jument de Guénioc and Ile Guénioc are abeam, you can continue at 172ºT to leave Basse du Chenal green buoy close to starboard and then come to port a shade to leave Poul Orvil small W-cardinal buoy close to port. Carry on past

Poul Orvil buoy for a good cable to clear Poul Orvil rocks before heading south-east to leave La Jument de Garo red spar beacon not quite 100 metres to port and Ar Gazel green buoy close to starboard, thereby joining the main channel as above.

MOORINGS AND ANCHORAGES

In quiet or offshore weather, you can anchor off the sandy beach a little way inside the entrance on the west side, outside the line of local moorings. Otherwise, carry on upstream for another half a mile to Le Passage, fetching up in midstream clear of the moorings either just below or just above Pointe du Passage and its landing slip. At springs, only bilge-keelers should venture for more than a quarter of a mile above Le Passage, where the river starts to shoal quite quickly. Near neaps though, moderate draught yachts can anchor in the wide upper reaches of the river below St Pabu quay. You may be able to use a vacant mooring, but make sure you choose one that's sturdy enough for your

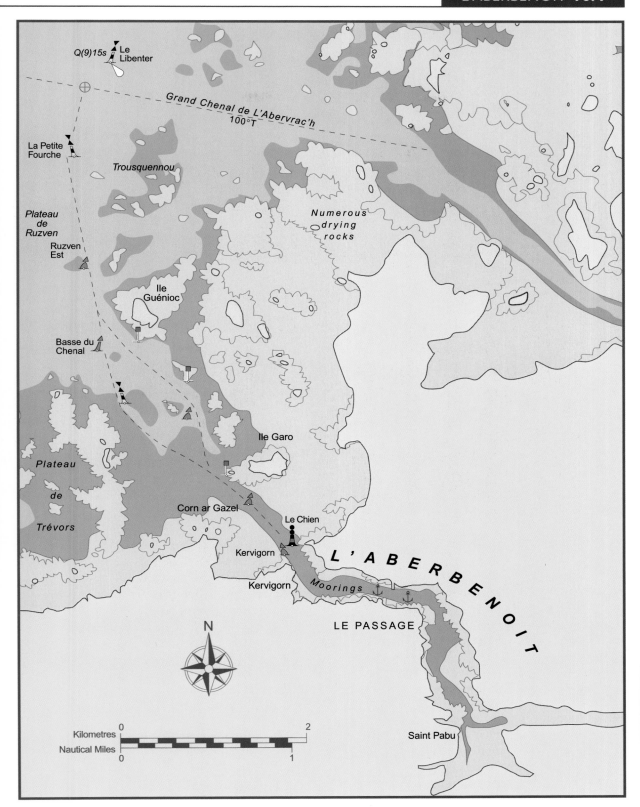

tonnage. It's wise to set a riding light at night, because you can find large sand-dredgers or the local seaweed-gathering boats moving about at odd hours.

FACILITIES

L'Aberbenoît is rather off the beaten track and the lower part of the estuary is some distance from a village. The best landing place is Le Passage, at the

Local sand-barges at L'Aberbenoît help keep the entrance channel clear of silt

small stone slip on the west bank, and you'll find a water tap behind the hut at the head of this slip. There are a couple of small shops including a pharmacy and a hairdresser about 15 minutes walk up the hill at Kervasdou. A fair sized general store is just under a mile from the quay by a road junction and slightly further on there is a garage, or you can hike a bit further south-east into St Pabu village. There's a boatyard at St Pabu – the Chantier Naval des Abers (Tel: 02.98.89.86.55).

If you take the dinghy upriver a little way, you can land at a quay on the north shore and select fresh shell-fish for supper at the Vivier de Prat-ar-Coum. At certain times of year they have good local ormers, which are becoming increasingly rare. We always enjoy choosing a meaty crab or lobster, although the chances are you'll have to cook it yourself on board.

If you prefer to be waited on, there's a charming crêperie Pors ar Vilin in an old Breton house close to the south bank of the river (Tel 02.98.89.86.26).

PASSAGES
BRITTANY IV

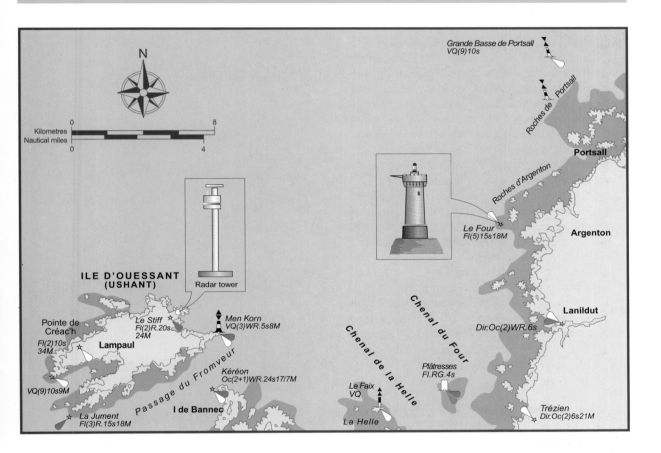

L'Abervrac'h to the
Chenal du Four

The Chenal du Four is a well marked and often used passage between the west coast of the Brest peninsula and the off-lying islands of Ushant, Molène, Quéménès and Béniguet. It provides the most common route for yachts bound between the English Channel and the Bay of Biscay. The Chenal du Four is wider than it appears on a small-scale chart and is quite straightforward in reasonable visibility, by day or night, so long as you carry the stream in your favour. You often meet a somewhat forbidding

Atlantic swell in the northern approaches between L'Abervrac'h and Le Four lighthouse, but further south the islands give some shelter and the swell usually dies down. However, this southern part of the channel, between Pointe de Corsen and Pointe de St Mathieu, can be choppy in a fresh wind against tide.

The north-south streams in the Four are about $2\frac{1}{2}$ hours out of phase with the east-west streams on the north coast. This works to your advantage when returning north towards the Channel, but shortens the tidal window for cruising south from L'Abervrac'h.

I usually leave L'Abervrac'h for the Four an hour before HW Brest, with the tide still foul on the north coast as far as Grande Basse de Portsall buoy. Much depends on your cruising speed and how readily you are prepared to motor. The real deadline is to reach the south end of the Chenal du Four before LW Brest, when the flood starts coming back. From L'Abervrac'h entrance to St Mathieu is about 23 miles.

From Le Libenter W-cardinal buoy off L'Abervrac'h entrance, make good 260ºT for five miles towards Grande Basse de Portsall W-cardinal buoy, the corner-mark for this stretch of coast. You'll be stemming the last of the flood on this leg, but should be well placed to catch most of the fair stream in the Four. The ebb starts running south near Le Four lighthouse about half an hour after HW Brest. You needn't actually round Basse de Portsall buoy, but it's wise to come within $\frac{1}{2}$ mile of it before turning SSW to pass outside the much smaller W-cardinal buoy guarding the Brividic shoal, which lies $1\frac{1}{2}$ miles south of Grande Basse de Portsall.

From the Brividic buoy, make good 205ºT for four miles to pass a good half mile west of Le Four lighthouse, a gaunt stone tower which stands about a mile off the mainland coast. Don't cut this tower any closer because there's a plateau of dangers not far to the north-east. Once past Le Four, make good 190ºT to leave Les Liniou, a distinctive string of above-water rocks, about three quarters of a mile to port. Staying on this course for three miles beyond Les Liniou, you come to the gateway for the southern part of the Chenal du Four – La Valbelle red pillar buoy left close to port and Les Plâtresses white tower to starboard.

The leading marks for this part of the Four Channel are the two lighthouses of Kermorvan and Pointe de St Mathieu in transit bearing 158ºT. This line is useful at night, but I have never found it either necessary or easy to pick out during the day, when it's simpler to follow the buoys SSE and then south along the fairway. When working down against the wind, you can tack outside the buoys to

gain ground so long as you refer carefully to Admiralty Chart No 3345. When under sail though, keep a close eye on time and tide. You should try to reach Pointe de St Mathieu before the new flood starts coming back because the streams are strong in the shallow southern part of the Chenal du Four.

The fishing harbour of Le Conquet lies a couple of miles from the southern end of the Chenal du Four, easily identified by the square white lighthouse on Kermorvan Point. Many yachtsmen remember Le Conquet as a handy bolt-hole if you ran out of fair tide in the Four, but the port has become more focused on fishing and yachts are no longer allowed to anchor in the outer harbour. If you can take the ground safely, there's usually plenty of room in the drying area beyond the inner mole.

The Chenal du Four is not simply a short cut to the south, but an attractive cruising area in its own right. L'Aberildut is one of the most delightful ports of call in Brittany and Ushant is much easier to approach than it seems, provided you are careful with the tides.

Opposite the southern part of the Four, the much smaller islands of Molène, Quéménès and Béniguet are tantalising silhouettes as you pass. Molène has a small harbour and a surprisingly large population. Quéménès has a secret anchorage when the weather is right. Béniguet is nearest to the mainland, with a golden beach that switches your mood into holiday gear. The rocky north feels safely astern and the languid south is not far ahead.

Entering L'Iroise off Pointe de St Mathieu, you can feel the ghosts of a colourful maritime history all around. Up on the headland by the lighthouse, the ancient abbey is a spectacular reminder of Brittany's long attraction as a refuge for wandering saints. To the east, through the Goulet de Brest, you catch a glimpse of France's most renowned naval harbour. Further round are the untamed cliffs near Camaret and Toulinguet, with the islets of Les Tas de Pois stretching away towards Cap de la Chèvre. Far to the south, on a clear day, the long straight edge of Pointe du Raz reaches out towards the low-lying Ile de Sein. **At night**: Ile Vierge (*Fl.5s.27M*) is a good powerful light for the stretch between L'Abervrac'h and the north end of the Chenal du Four. Grande Basse de Portsall buoy is lit (*VQ(9)10s4M*) and can be crossed with Corn Carhai light-tower (*Fl(3)12s9M*) as you

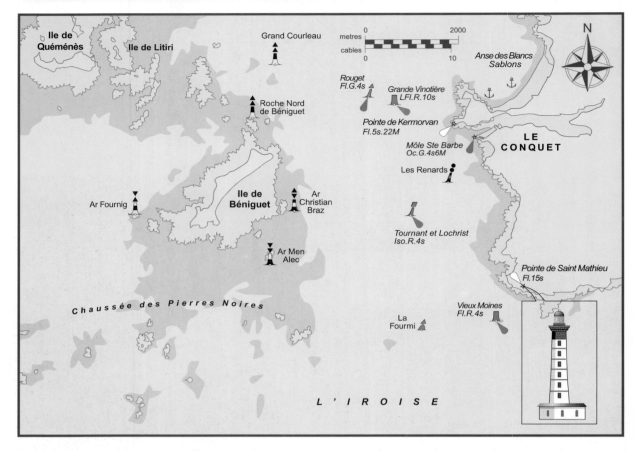

Le Four lighthouse is left about half a mile to the east in the Chenal du Four

work down towards Le Four (*Fl(5)15s21M*). Away to the south-west is the brilliant white of Créac'h lighthouse on Ushant (*Fl(2)10s34M*). Keep a good mile off Le Four at night and then head towards Les Plâtresses tower in its green sector (*Fl.RG.4s6M*). The Chenal du Four north leading lights should line up when you are about a mile N by E of Plâtresses – Kermorvan lighthouse (*Fl.5s22M*) in transit at 158ºT with Pointe de St-Mathieu (*Fl.15s29M*, but intense fixed white when dead on line). This transit leaves La Valbelle buoy (*Fl(2)R6s5M*) 1½ cables to the east and St Paul buoy (*Oc(2)R.9s4M*) not quite a cable to the east.

Just over a mile from Kermorvan you pick up the white sector of Pointe de Corsen lighthouse (*DirQ.WRG.12-8M*) which, kept astern at 012º-015ºT, leads down past Le Conquet between La Grande Vinotière tower (*LFl.R.10s5M*) and Rouget green buoy (*Fl.G,4s*). Once south of Grande Vinotière, shape a course to the SSE passing close either side of Tournant et Lochrist buoy (*IsoR.4s2M*). If you are bound south across L'Iroise, line up the last set of leading lights – Trézien (*DirOc(2)6s20M*) in transit with Kermorvan (*Fl.5s22M*) astern bearing 007ºT, which takes you clear of the Chenal du Four into open water. If you are heading for Brest or Camaret, steer to leave Les Vieux Moines tower (*Fl.R.4s5M*) off Pointe de St Mathieu about four cables to port.

HARBOURS NEAR THE CHENAL DU FOUR

This west end of Brittany is littered with off-lying rocks and exposed to the full force of the Atlantic

USHANT

Ile d'Ouessant, plain Ushant in English, is one of the most famous navigation marks in the world and yet few mariners think of it as a real island with over 3,000 inhabitants. Créac'h light is the most powerful in Europe, but those who see it are usually more concerned with giving it a wide berth than wondering about the community living under the constant sweep of its arc. Yet the island seems surprisingly heavily populated and what strikes you first when wandering ashore is the considerable number of houses. It's difficult to work out quite what everybody does and how the economy is sustained. But many of the houses on Ushant are

The inner harbour at Lampaul, where shoal draught boats can take the ground

holiday homes and only occupied during the season.

Agriculture is carried out at near subsistence level. Sheep are the main commodity and the Ushant lamb *pré-salé* still has a certain reputation among gourmets. There is some fishing, but tourism now represents the largest source of income. Regular ferries run out from Brest and Le Conquet, bringing boatloads of day visitors in July and August. There are some fine walks around the island, with

spectacular coastal views out across Ushant's rocky tide-swept approaches.

APPROACHES

For yachts coming from England or North Brittany, Ushant is most easily reached either from L'Abervrac'h or L'Aberildut, both relatively short hops which allow you to time your approach according to weather and tides. Admiralty chart 2694 makes it all look fairly clear. For a first visit to

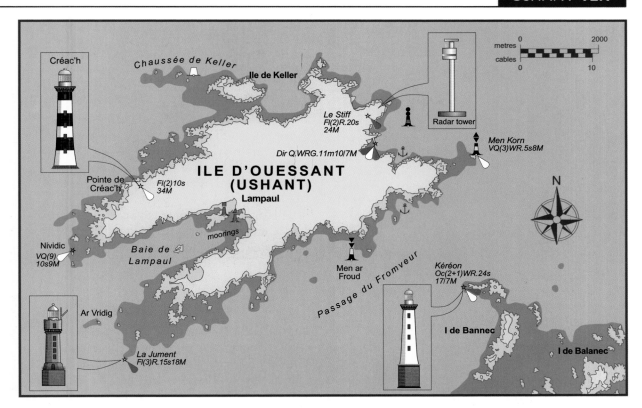

Ushant, a force 3-4 is as much as you want, at as near dead neaps as possible. Aim to approach the island near slack water – good times to leave L'Aberildut entrance are either one and a half hours before HW Brest or four and a half hours after.

A good time to leave L'Abervrac'h is slightly earlier than if you were bound south through the Chenal du Four, say a couple of hours before local high water. You have to push the last of the east-going stream along to Basse de Portsall buoy, but the tide will then be fairly slack for the crossing to Ushant. You also have the option of carrying on down the Chenal du Four if the weather or swell looks unsuitable in the offing.

From Basse de Portsall buoy, it's usually convenient to set a course for Men Corn E-cardinal tower off the south arm of the Baie du Stiff. Approaching Ushant, you then have the choice of making for one of the anchorages in the Baie du Stiff or edging south and continuing down the Passage du Fromveur and round into Lampaul.

Baie du Stiff is easy to identify by the high, rather unearthly radar control tower on its north headland. Le Stiff lighthouse, not far south-west of the tower, seems almost miniature by comparison. The bay itself is gaunt and somewhat forbidding, but provides several reasonable anchorages in moderate westerly weather. The landing jetty for the ferries is on the north side of Porz Liboudou, the middle inlet

in the Baie du Stiff. There are some visitor's moorings to the south of the ferry landing. The nearest shops are two miles away at Lampaul.

If conditions permit, it's better to try and get round to Lampaul, which is most attractive and worth the effort. Although the Baie de Lampaul is open to the south-west, it's nearly a mile and a half long and moderate winds from as far south as west cause no great problems at the visitors' moorings at the head of the bay.

There are three clusters of moorings off Lampaul, to the south-east of Men-ar-Groas green beacon tower, which marks the west end of a long drying ledge extending well out from the south side of the entrance to Lampaul's small drying harbour. In any easterly weather, these moorings are perfectly

the outlying dangers north-west of the beacon tower. Therefore make good 295°T for about a mile until Le Stiff radar control tower is open to the north of Le Corce rock (34 metres high in the middle of the Baie de Lampaul) and bearing 055°T. Then enter the bay on this line, altering to starboard when safely abreast the south headland to pass close south of Le Corce and a good cable south of Le Grand Truc. At the head of the bay, make for the visitors' moorings in the shallow bight south-east of Men-ar-Groas green beacon tower.

The entrance to Lampaul's small drying harbour lies 150 metres north-east of Men-ar-Groas. In settled weather, yachts of moderate draught can edge into near high water and dry out alongside one of the quays.

ANCHORAGES

Baie du Stiff: The east-facing Baie du Stiff offers reasonable shelter in westerlies and makes a fairly straightforward landfall from the north end of the Chenal du Four. There are three smaller inlets within the wider bay – Portz Liboudou, Portz Aheac'h and Baie Poull Ifern. Portz Liboudou, where the ferries land, is now well taken up with moorings. For anchoring in peace and quiet, make for Portz Aheac'h or Poull Ifern.

Portz Darland: This anchorage in the south-east corner of the island is protected in north-westerlies and not far from the Baie du Stiff. Approach from the SSE, preferably near low water when the tide is slack and the various drying rocks on either hand are well exposed. From at least half a mile offshore, identify the stone jetty on the west side of Portz Darland and the sandy beach just east of the jetty. Bring Le Stiff lighthouse into line with the east end of the beach bearing 340°T and close the shore on this transit leaving Men Darland rock (drying 7.5m) and Fret Kas rocks (drying 5.8m) each a cable to port. Anchor off the jetty, as close to the beach as your draught allows.

Penn ar Roc'h: About 1½ miles WSW of Portz Darland is the Baie de Pen ar Roc'h, which has anchorages on its west side about a cable north of Roc'h Nel (10m high) or further north in the Anse de Boug an Dour. Approach from the south-east near slack water, leaving Roc'h Nel a cable to port and referring to the French SHOM Chart No 7123.

Lampaul: There is still room to anchor off Lampaul, a little way south-west of the landing pontoon that extends beyond the lifeboat slip. There are also various possible anchorages further out in the Baie de Lampaul depending on wind direction.

sheltered. Even at low water, you can land with the dinghy at the pontoon just west of the lifeboat slip, which is on the north side of the harbour approach. The village has all the basic shops, a post office and a couple of hotels where you can eat well.

Passage du Fromveur: One of the most notorious stretches of water off the Brittany coast, the Passage du Fromveur is not to be trifled with. The streams can reach eight or nine knots at springs and steep overfalls are quickly set up in even a gentle wind against the tide. However, around neaps in quiet weather, Fromveur can be quite docile, giving you a quick passage round the south coast of Ushant.

When sailing south-westwards through the Passage du Fromveur towards Lampaul, try to follow a line leading about half a mile outside all the charted coastal dangers. It's then fairly easy to keep track of your position and you are near enough to the shore to avoid the risk of being carried past the entrance to Lampaul in the mainstream of Fromveur. As you clear Penn ar Roc'h though, beware of the tide setting slightly west over the dangers between La Jument beacon tower and Ushant.

Approaching Lampaul: Having rounded La Jument by a quarter of a mile, it's important to clear

PORTSALL

Having reached this far corner of north-west Brittany, most yachts are keen to hurry past with a fair tide, bound either south for the warmer waters of Biscay, or making for home at the end of a cruise. However, if you have quiet weather and some time to spare, the anchorage off Portsall

is easy enough to enter from the north end of the Chenal du Four. It can also provide a useful bolt-hole if you miss the tide in either direction. Coming from the north or round from L'Abervrac'h or L'Aberbenoît, make good due south true for just over 1½ miles from Brividic W-cardinal buoy, keeping at least half a mile west of Men Glaz rock (4.9 metres high) and the outer dangers at the south-west tip of the Roches de Portsall. When Men ar Pic green beacon tower bears due east true, head towards it on this bearing. Coming from the south

round Le Four lighthouse, be sure to stay well outside Roches d'Argenton, a long string of drying dangers extending 2½ miles north-east of Le Four, before approaching Men ar Pic green tower from more or less due west.

Enter Portsall outer anchorage using Admiralty Chart 1432, heading a shade north of east to leave Bosven Aval rock (4.9m high) to port, Men ar Pic green beacon tower to starboard, and Ile Verte south rock (4.9m high) to port. Near LW avoid Basse Idic (awash at LAT two cables east by north from Men ar

Looking WNW at sunset from the Portsall anchorage

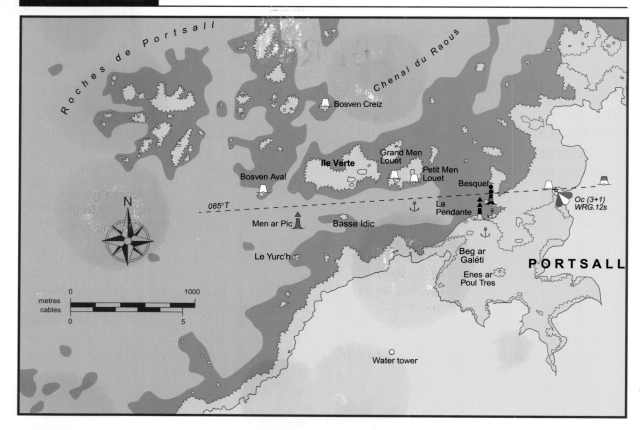

Pic) and fetch up $1-1\frac{1}{2}$ cables south of Grand Men Louet islet (11m high). This outer anchorage is easy to leave at night, using the white sector of Portsall light (*Oc(3+1)12s16M*). With sufficient rise of tide you can continue just beyond Basse Karrat (0.1m at LAT) to anchor 100 metres west of Besquel black-red-black beacon or 60 metres south-east of La Pendante N-cardinal tower.

Near neaps you will find better shelter from swell by edging closer to Portsall harbour and anchoring 100 metres south of La Pendante. Towards high water in quiet weather, bilge-keelers can edge due south and then east into Portsall harbour, taking care to avoid Enes ar Poul Tres rocks on the way. You can dry out on a firm sandy bottom near the moorings, and the inner harbour area is fairly well sheltered, even from moderate north-westerlies.

Portsall is a pleasant little seaside town with a few small shops and a couple of cafés. You'll find a small supermarket in the Rue de Croas-ar-Rheun. There's a fresh water tap behind the small fuelling hut on the fishermen's quay on the north side of the inner part of the harbour. The Restaurant Beg-ar-Mor and the Hôtel de Bretagne are about 15 minutes walk from the harbour, at the junction with the main road to Ploudalmezeau.

Grande Basse de Portsall W-cardinal buoy leaning to a steady run of tide

L'ABERILDUT

The entrance to L'Aberildut lies three miles south of Le Four lighthouse. Some older charts show the whole inlet as drying, but the dogleg gap in the coast actually carries a good eight feet depth, even at low springs, and there's plenty of water inside for just under half a mile. You moor fore-and-aft to trots,

opposite the sleepy village on the north shore, with its long landing slip and picturesque waterfront of cottage gardens. The south shore is low farmland, with cattle grazing and skylarks rising on drowsy summer days.

You feel comfortably landlocked in L'Aberildut, although the Chenal du Four is easy to reach again at any state of tide. Local fishing boats come and go at their pontoon near the entrance. You can get water here, usually by mooring alongside a fishing boat and passing the hose across. Diesel is available near high tide, alongside the quay just downstream from the pontoon.

On the quayside is Lanildut Marine, a useful local boatyard. There's also a good chandler, Aber Accastillage, up behind the yard (Tel 02.98.04.40.72).

Opposite the chandler is the pleasantly low-key Bureau du Port. The harbourmaster, Monsieur Jean Cahaignon, keeps L'Aberildut ticking over with a light touch.

At low water, the banks of the inlet dry well out, especially off the village where the sand is fairly firm and traditional wooden yachts sit upright on legs. The moored boats stay afloat in a narrow gully and the open sea feels even further away.

Landing at the slip, you turn east along the tiny main street, where the shops and a couple of restaurants are clustered together. We usually make for Le Neptune (Tel 02.98.04.30.03) overlooking the river, but Le Gulf Stream is also a sound choice.

To reach the post office, continue a little further

The sleepy waterfront and shallow bay opposite the snug moorings in L'Aberildut

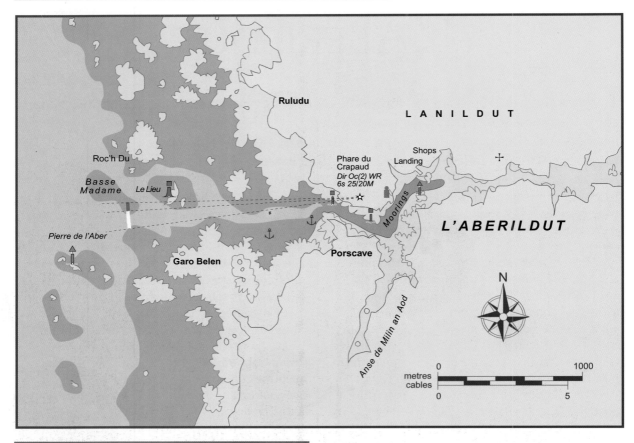

Le Lieu red beacon tower, the conspicuous port-hand mark
close off the entrance to L'Aberildut

upstream, skirting the drying beach and following
the curve of the road towards the church. The post
office is opposite the church on the north side of the
road. Next to the church is a tourist Information
office, open during the summer. Beyond the church,
you can cut back towards the waterside and join a
peaceful path that follows the ria inland for over a
mile towards the neighbouring village of Brélès. If
you continue along the road past the church, there's
a garage further along on the left.

APPROACH AND ENTRY

Admiralty Chart 2694 gives you the whole picture
and Admiralty 3345 is best for approaching
L'Aberildut.

Arriving from the north, pass just over half a mile
west of Le Four lighthouse and then skirt the
prominent Les Liniou rocks a similar distance off.
From Les Liniou, make good due south for 1½ miles
and try to spot Le Lieu red beacon tower inshore, off
the entrance to L'Aberildut. Le Lieu is usually easy
to identify since there are no other red beacon
towers off this section of coast south of Les Liniou.

Continue south until Le Lieu bears just north of
east magnetic. If arriving from the south, reach a
similar approach position by heading north from La

Moor fore-and-aft to trots opposite the village on the north shore

Valbelle red buoy for about 1¼ miles, until Le Lieu bears just north of east magnetic. From this approach position, turn inshore to keep Le Lieu fine on the port bow at just north of east magnetic.

Before you reach Le Lieu, Pierre de Laber green spar beacon is left about 250 metres to starboard. Then steer to leave Le Lieu a little over 100 metres to port and the above water rocks just opposite Le Lieu about 100 metres to starboard. Steer towards the small lighthouse on the north side of L'Aberildut entrance.

Although L'Aberildut is shown on many charts as drying, you can enter at any tide and stay afloat on the trots inside. The narrow dogleg entrance has a drying spur off the south point, so keep over towards the first red post on the north side of the narrows. The shallowest part of the entrance has about eight feet depth at ordinary low springs.

Once you are well into the channel, start edging over towards the south side so as to leave the inner red post beacon well to port. Then curve north-east to follow the lines of trots into the inlet.

OUTSIDE ANCHORAGE

In quiet or easterly weather, you can anchor off a sandy beach just outside the south arm of the entrance. This is a useful passage anchorage because you can leave safely at night using the white sector of L'Aberildut lighthouse (*DirOc(2)WR.6s25/20M*).

LE CONQUET

The fishing harbour of Le Conquet lies a couple of miles from the southern end of the Chenal du Four, easily identified by the square white lighthouse on Kermorvan Point. Many yachtsmen remember Le Conquet as a handy bolt-hole if you ran out of fair tide in the Four, but the port has become much more focused on fishing and yachts are no longer allowed to anchor in the outer harbour. If you can take the ground safely, there's usually plenty of room in the drying area beyond the inner mole. You'll find a water tap at the small quay on the east side of this mole.

The entrance to Le Conquet is straightforward, immediately south of Pointe de Kermorvan and its distinctive four-square lighthouse. Approach at about ENE to steer between La Louve red beacon tower and the breakwater head. At night, you need to keep fairly close to the breakwater head because La Louve is unlit.

The town itself is friendly and rather pleasant, with a good selection of shops and a colourful market in Place de la Poste on Thursday mornings. Above the outer breakwater, overlooking the Chenal du Four and the off-lying islands, the comfortable dining room at the Hôtel de la Pointe de Sainte-Barbe offers spectacular views and excellent fish and *fruits de mer*

The main breakwater at Le Conquet, which is used regularly by the Ushant ferries

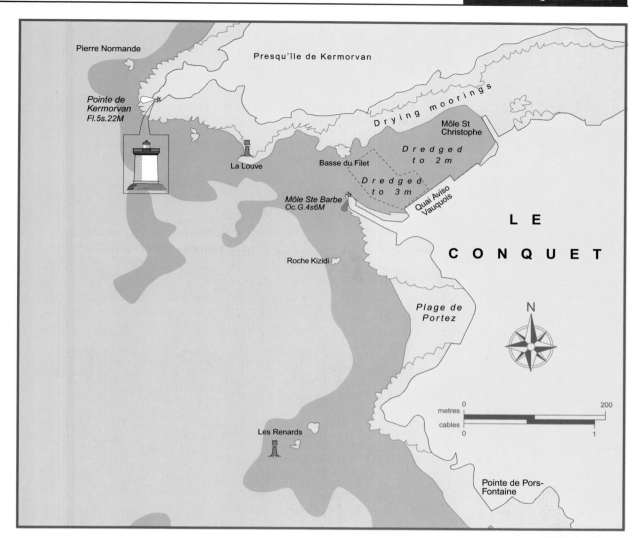

on its *menu gastronomique* (Tel 02.98.89.00.26). La Taverne du Port, at 18 Rue Saint-Christophe, has a convivial terrace with a view across the harbour and is a particularly good bet for lunch (Tel 02.98.89.10.90). The Relais du Vieux Port, on Quai du Drellac'h, also has a waterside terrace and a good selection of fish and shellfish (Tel 02.98.89.15.91).

Up in the town there are several good crêperies. Les Boucaniers occupies a splendid 16th century building in Rue Poncelin (Tel 02.98.89.06.25). La Goël is just opposite the town church (Tel 02.98.89.12.08) and Morskoul is in Rue Troadec (Tel 02.98.89.11.95). Le Conquet has no fuelling berth for yachts and the nearest service station is a fair hike from the landing place, about a kilometre to the east out of town.

There's a useful chandler – Co-operative Maritime – in Rue Lieutenant Jourden. You can get Camping Gaz at the Co-operative Maritime, or at Galeries d'Armor in Place de Llandeilo.

Pointe de Kermorvan and its distinctive four-square lighthouse

INDEX